THE INTERFACE BETWEEN EU AND INTERNATIONAL LAW

Despite their many obvious interconnections, EU and international law are all too often studied and practised in different spheres. While it is natural for each to insist on its own unique characteristics, and in particular for the EU to emphasise its *sui generis* nature, important insights might be lost because of this exclusionary approach. This book aims to break through some of those barriers and to show how more interaction between the two spheres might be encouraged. In so doing, it offers a constitutional dimension but also a substantive one, examining policy areas where EU and international law and their respective actors work alongside each other. Offering a 360-degree view on both EU and international institutional and substantive law, this collection presents a refreshing perspective on a long-standing issue.

Volume 89 in the Series Modern Studies in European Law

Modern Studies in European Law

Recent titles in this series:

Human Rights Between Law and Politics:
The Margin of Appreciation in Post-National Contexts
Edited by Petr Agha

The European Union and Social Security Law
Jaan Paju

The Rule of Law in the European Union: The Internal Dimension
Theodore Konstadinides

The Division of Competences between the EU and the Member States:
Reflections on the Past, the Present and the Future
Edited by Sacha Garben and Inge Govaere

Unity in Adversity: EU Citizenship, Social Justice and the Cautionary
Tale of the UK
Charlotte O'Brien

The Use of Force and Article 2 of the ECHR in Light of European Conflicts
Hannah Russell

Environmental Crime in Europe
Edited by Andrew Farmer, Michael Faure and Grazia Maria Vagliasindi

Questioning EU Citizenship: Judges and the Limits of Free Movement
and Solidarity in the EU
Edited by Daniel Thym

The European Union under Transnational Law: A Pluralist Appraisal
Matej Avbelj

Illegally Staying in the EU: An Analysis of Illegality in EU Migration Law
Benedita Menezes Queiroz

Social Legitimacy in the Internal Market: A Dialogue of Mutual Responsiveness
Jotte Mulder

The EU Better Regulation Agenda: A Critical Assessment
Edited by Sacha Garben and Inge Govaere

Administrative Regulation Beyond the Non-Delegation Doctrine:
A Study on EU Agencies
Marta Simoncini

For the complete list of titles in this series, see
'Modern Studies in European Law' link at
www.bloomsburyprofessional.com/uk/series/modern-studies-in-european-law

The Interface Between EU and International Law

Contemporary Reflections

Edited by
Inge Govaere
and
Sacha Garben

•HART•
OXFORD • LONDON • NEW YORK • NEW DELHI • SYDNEY

HART PUBLISHING

Bloomsbury Publishing Plc

Kemp House, Chawley Park, Cumnor Hill, Oxford, OX2 9PH, UK

HART PUBLISHING, the Hart/Stag logo, BLOOMSBURY and the Diana logo are trademarks of Bloomsbury Publishing Plc

First published in Great Britain 2019

A catalogue record for this book is available from the British Library.

Library of Congress Cataloging-in-Publication data

Names: Govaere, Inge, editor. | Garben, Sacha, 1982-, editor.

Title: The interface between EU and international law : contemporary reflections / edited by Inge Govaere, Sacha Garben.

Description: Chicago : Hart Publishing, 2019. | Series: Modern studies in European law | Includes bibliographical references and index.

Identifiers: LCCN 2018054818 (print) | LCCN 2018055183 (ebook) | ISBN 9781509923397 (EPub) | ISBN 9781509923380 (hardback)

Subjects: LCSH: International law—European Union countries. | International and municipal law—European Union countries. | Law—European Union countries. | European Union. | BISAC: LAW / International. | LAW / Comparative.

Classification: LCC KJE5057 (ebook) | LCC KJE5057 .I58 2019 (print) | DDC 341.242/2—dc23

LC record available at https://lccn.loc.gov/2018054818

ISBN: HB: 978-1-50992-338-0
ePDF: 978-1-50992-340-3
ePub: 978-1-50992-339-7

Typeset by Compuscript Ltd, Shannon

CONTENTS

PART III
THE EU AND 'THIRD' COUNTRIES

PART IV
A VIEW FROM PRACTICE: COMMENTS ON CURRENT DEVELOPMENTS IN THE INTERFACE BETWEEN EU AND INTERNATIONAL LAW

LIST OF CONTRIBUTORS

Laurens Ankersmit, Assistant Professor, Amsterdam Centre for European Law and Governance, University of Amsterdam.

Kieran Bradley, Special Adviser at the Court of Justice of European Union.

Jenö Czuczai, Legal Adviser, Legal Service of the Council of the EU (currently temporarily seconded to the Office of the Head of the GIP/Cabinet of the Council) and Visiting Professor, College of Europe, Bruges.

Ricardo da Silva Passos, Judge at the General Court of the EU.

Vincent Delhomme, Academic Assistant in the European Legal Studies Department at the College of Europe.

Christina Eckes, Professor of European Law at the University of Amsterdam, Amsterdam Centre for European Law and Governance (ACELG).

Sacha Garben, Professor, European Legal Studies Department, College of Europe, Bruges.

Inge Govaere, Jean Monnet Chair in EU Legal Studies and Director of the Ghent European Law Institute (GELI) at Ghent University and Director of the European Legal Studies Department, College of Europe, Bruges.

Michael Hahn, Professor, Institute of European and International Economic Law & World Trade Institute, University of Bern.

Christophe Hillion, Professor of Institutional Law in the EU at Leiden University.

Violeta Moreno-Lax, Senior Lecturer at Queen Mary University of London and Visiting Professor at the College of Europe.

Nicola Notaro, Head of the Nature Protection Unit at the European Commission, Directorate General for the Environment and Visiting Professor at the College of Europe in Bruges.

Mario Pagano, PhD candidate at the European University Institute in Florence.

Pierre Thielbörger, Professor for German Public Law and Public International Law at Ruhr University Bochum and Executive Director of the Institute for the International Law of Peace and Armed Conflict (IFHC) at Ruhr University Bochum.

Guillaume Van der Loo, Postdoctoral FWO researcher at the Ghent European Law Institute (GELI) at Ghent University and researcher Centre for European Policy Studies (CEPS), Brussels.

Ramses Wessel, Professor of International and European Law and Governance at the University of Twente in the Netherlands.

Introduction: The Interface between EU and International Law

INGE GOVAERE AND SACHA GARBEN*

Over 60 years of EU legal integration leads to the paradoxical finding that the Court of Justice of the European Union's (CJEU) self-proclaimed 'new and autonomous EU legal order'[1] is increasingly taken for granted, whilst at the same time being subject to more and more persistent pressure and critique. The recent *Achmea*[2] case, the pending Advisory Opinion 1/17 on the compatibility of the Investor-State-Dispute-Settlement (ISDS) provisions with the autonomy of the EU legal order,[3] the earlier *Kadi*[4] saga and CJEU Opinion 2/13 on the EU accession to the ECHR,[5] are all most symptomatic but by no means unique cases in this respect. The underlying factors are not only external, such as globalisation and internationalisation of the law.[6] Internal EU law dynamics, in particular the ever-increasing expansion of EU competence,[7] EU territorial enlargement,[8]

* Sacha Garben is currently on leave from the European Commission. The views expressed in this paper do not in any way represent those of the European Commission.

[1] A '*new legal order of international law*' was created by the Member States of the European Economic Community, according to the Court of Justice in Case 26/62 *NV Algemene Transport- en Expeditie Onderneming van Gend & Loos tegen Nederlandse administratie der belastingen* [1963] ECR 1. In Case 6/64 *Flaminio Costa v ENEL* [1964] ECR 585, the Court indicated that this order was to be understood as autonomous as it considered the Treaties '*an independent source of law*', which in the original French version was referred to as '*une source autonome*'.

[2] Case C-284/16 *Slowakische Republik v Achmea BV* Judgment of the Court (Grand Chamber) of 6 March 2018 ECLI:EU:C:2018:158.

[3] Advisory Opinion 1/17, CETA ISDS, request introduced by Belgium. For an analysis of the compatibility of ISDS with the autonomous EU legal order, see I Govaere, 'TTIP and Dispute Settlement: Potential Consequences for the Autonomous EU Legal Order' in Bándi, Barak, Debisso (eds), *Speeches and Presentations from the XXVII FIDE Congress, Congress Proceedings* Vol 4, 2016, 123–44.

[4] Case C-584/10 P *Commission v Kadi* ECLI:EU:C:2013:518.

[5] Opinion 2/13 *EU Accession to ECHR* ECLI:EU:C:2014:2454.

[6] M Hiscock and W van Caenegem (eds), *The Internationalisation of Law: Legislation, Decision-Making, Practice and Education* (Edward Elgar Publishing, 2010).

[7] I Govaere, 'To Give or to Grab: The Principle of Full, Crippled and Split Conferral of Powers Post-Lisbon' in M Cremona (ed), *Structural Principles in EU External Relations Law* (Hart Publishing, 2018) 71–91; S Garben and I. Govaere (eds), *The Division of Competences between the European Union and its Member States: Reflections on the Past, Present and Future* (Hart Publishing, 2017).

[8] See in particular the contributions in Part VI of I Govaere, P Van Elsuwege, A Stanislas and E Lannon (eds), *The European Union in the World, Essays in Honour of Marc Maresceau* (Martinus Nijhoff Publishers, 2014).

as well as the 'maturing' of the EU into a forceful and visible international actor culminating in the Lisbon Treaty, are at the crux of the paradox.

The focus of the debate has also radically shifted in recent years. In the aftermath of the *van Gend & Loos* case, the main issue was how to distinguish EU law from international law, in a clear 'move away' from international law. Currently, the key question has rather become how the EU legal order should integrate and interact with international law, thus presenting a radically opposite 'move towards' international law.

I. Part I: A Horizontal, Holistic Approach

Before turning to a 'vertical' and topical assessment, the first three contributions, contained in the first part of this book, offer complementary approaches to come to terms with this dynamic process of interacting legal systems from a 'horizontal' and holistic perspective.

It is submitted that although topical differences can be pinpointed, also a holistic and horizontally applicable approach to the relationship between EU and international law can be discerned in the Treaties and in the case law of the CJEU. The EU as a whole has legal personality pursuant to Article 47 of the Treaty on European Union (TEU). It is also the EU, as a subject of international law, that may contract international rights and obligations, set up other international organisations and participate in international dispute settlement mechanisms.[9] In so doing, the CJEU has since the *International Fruit Company* case[10] consistently held that the EU is necessarily bound to respect 'international law'. The latter concept is not limited to agreements which the EU itself has concluded (or where the principle of substitution for the Member States applies such as for the General Agreement on Tariffs and Trade (GATT)). The CJEU clarified that the EU is also bound to respect principles of customary international law, even if those are codified in agreements to which the EU is not a party.[11] As a subject of international law, the EU should furthermore be able to participate in setting up other international organisations, as well as international dispute settlement mechanisms. Already in Opinion 1/76, the CJEU accepted, as a matter of principle, that decisions taken by such bodies will be binding on the EU and its institutions including the CJEU itself.[12] The difficulty lies in the condition, namely that this may not affect the 'autonomy' of the specific EU legal order with its characteristics of primacy, direct effect and uniform interpretation. This raises

[9] Opinion 1/76 *Draft Agreement establishing a European laying-up fund for inland waterway vessels* ECLI:EU:C:1977:63.

[10] Joined Cases 21/72 to 24/72 *International Fruit Company* ECLI:EU:C:1972:115.

[11] Case C-162/96 *Racke* ECLI:EU:C:1998:293 and Case C-366/10 *Air Transport Association of America (ATAA)* ECLI:EU:C:2011:864.

[12] Opinion 1/76 (n 9).

the complex question of how to find mechanisms allowing the smooth interconnection of the increasingly interdependent EU and international legal orders, whilst nonetheless firmly safeguarding the distinctive features of the specific EU legal order.

The contribution by Inge Govaere suggests that the establishment of the autonomous EU legal order and its interaction with international law, as perceived and developed by the CJEU, can best be captured by reference to an inflating 'balloon'. Through referring to an 'inflating balloon dynamic' the chapter proposes an imagery of this interactive transformation process over time, thereby critically analysing shifting causes, effects and remedies. It is a deliberate choice not to zoom in on one specific case study or topic, such as the interconnection with the United Nations (UN) or the European Convention on Human Rights (ECHR) or the highly topical investment treaties. Instead, a holistic approach is adopted to pinpoint the complex 'process' of interconnecting legal systems specifically from the perspective of the EU. In search of distinctive elements of structural pressure on the autonomous EU legal order, a distinction is made between factors internal and external to the European integration process. It is further considered and assessed what mechanisms may serve to foster a positive interaction, rather than conflict, with international law. The chapter suggests that

> the capacity for the EU to maintain an enduring structural autonomy necessarily goes hand in hand with continuously and proactively fostering a relationship of symbiosis rather than clash with international law.

It deploys the imagery of the balloon with a membrane which should necessarily be hermetically closed but at the same time also sufficiently resilient to withstand some pressure without puncturing. Against this backdrop it is assessed whether the Lisbon Treaty sufficiently addressed those challenges and offers elements to forecast whether the EU balloon is meant to continue fly or rather deflate.

The paper by Violeta Moreno-Lax critically examines the development of the concept of the autonomous EU legal order by the Court of Justice over time. She traces its evolution from its initial use, for largely internal purposes, to describe the distinctiveness of EU law as the consequence of integration, to subsequently become the normative cause of the European project. She sets out how 'autonomy has transformed from being a key tool to preserve "the specific characteristics of the EU and EU law", to denoting the (normative aspiration of) closeness and self-sufficiency of the regime in its entirety', going from being

> a (privileged) means securing the (formal) emancipation of EU law from its international roots, to becoming a (rootless) end in itself, detached from any identifiable value base – whether in the Rule of Law or in fundamental rights – despite Article 2 TEU.

Her approach is critical indeed; she argues that 'in the post Opinion 2/13 isolationist era, a point of axiological vacuum has been reached, in which "autonomy" per se has become a (new, if not the ultimate) value of the EU legal order'. This objectivisation, and veneration, of autonomy has not only substantively detached

EU law from international law and its principles, but she argues has uprooted the EU system as a whole, disconnecting it from its own founding values, 'posing grave problems of legitimacy and self-justification'.

In the third and final chapter of Part I, Ramses Wessel explores the interface between EU and international law as academic disciplines, offering context to the differences and commonalities between the two levels as perceived by those who study, work with and build them. Several areas of joint interest are identified, where constructive mutual engagement by these two (mostly) separate disciplines holds the potential for learning and insight: the nature of the legal system; (transnational) constitutionalism; the position of the individual (the citizen, the national); democracy and legitimacy; autonomy and responsibility; territoriality; instruments; and the hierarchy of norms. These links are to serve as 'bridges' between the 'different legal systems' and not to undermine the 'specialness' and autonomy of EU law. The point made by the chapter is a fundamental one. Indeed, it would seem that if the EU is to (continue to) successfully mediate potential conflict with the international level through the 'integration' of international law into the EU legal framework, and move beyond the current 'isolationist trend' described by Moreno-Lax, it is imperative that EU law as a discipline features a sufficient knowledge base, and a similar integration, of international law in its study and scholarship. Furthermore, the identification of such conceptual bridges may allow scholars to transcend the competing claims and interpretations of the different levels, which will necessarily have a different point of departure and as such may be inherently irreconcilable, to resolve theoretical conflicts and point to practical implementation thereof.

II. Part II: The Interaction between EU and International Law in Selected Areas

The first part of the book, having offered a range of analytical tools to understand and bridge the various, at times seemingly disparate, instances of interaction and friction between EU and international law, it is in the second part of the book that these tools can be put to use. Each chapter focuses on a specific area or topic where interaction between EU and international law has proven particularly important and/or problematic. Perhaps the most obvious choice in this respect is the issue of fundamental rights, as already became clear in Violeta Moreno-Lax' chapter two. The issue is examined in more detail by Cristina Eckes in chapter four and, as far as fundamental social rights are concerned, by Sacha Garben in chapter five. As Christina Eckes says, '[h]uman rights are a special case when it comes to the interaction of different legal spheres', going as far as claiming that 'fundamental rights constitute the most difficult area when pondering questions of resilience, autonomy and porosity of one legal sphere vis-à-vis another'. Sacha Garben agrees that '[f]undamental rights have been, and continue to be, pivotal in defining the relationship between the international, EU and national legal orders', noting that it is on this issue that national constitutional courts, the CJEU as well as the European Court of Human Rights (ECtHR)

> all claim a certain measure of final authority, which may theoretically be reconcilable as 'constitutional pluralism' but nevertheless leads to an uncomfortable state of affairs both from the perspective of the international rule of law and from a more practical point of view.

Eckes' chapter proposes to think differently about these questions by shifting the focus to theories of rights rather than judicial practices. In line with Wessel's contribution, this allows us to build a conceptual bridge between the different interpretations of the relationship between the legal regimes protecting fundamental rights in Europe by the various courts, which all consider this question 'from the perspective of their own legal order', making their claims inherently irreconcilable. The bridge proposed by Eckes, on the basis of a theoretical examination, is 'a reflexive right to justification as the origin of all rights', which means that the appropriate level and forum for human rights protection needs to be established in light of 'the ability of the political structures to make reflexive justification possible'. According to Eckes, this is only 'rudimentary in the international context'. While the national context of modern democracies in principle would allow this, it risks ignoring the interests of those affected by the externalities of national political decisions in a globalised world. Perhaps to some surprise, it is thus the EU that emerges with the most credible claim as the appropriate level for the deliberation of fundamental rights standards, as it not only possesses the necessary political structures but is also sufficiently inclusive. That finding supports her argument that EU accession to the ECHR would be undesirable. Moreover, accession would upset the delicate balance between the various irreconcilable claims to sovereignty and autonomy by national courts and the CJEU, by allowing 'national courts to challenge the core relationship between national, international and EU law from within the logic of EU law', undermining the CJEU's monopoly on the interpretation of EU law by relying on ECtHR judgments as part of the EU legal order. This precarious internal balance, already under mounting pressure due to challenges from national constitutional courts such as in Poland, the Czech Republic and Denmark, would be fundamentally and irrevocably disturbed by EU accession to the ECHR under the terms that had been proposed; it would have punctured the EU balloon. This goes to show how complex and multifaceted the interaction is between internal and external structural pressures on the EU, and indeed, as Inge Govaere has posited, that when the EU balloon is inflated to near maximum capacity this renders its membrane all the more vulnerable to puncturing from the outside.

For similar reasons, Sacha Garben in chapter five opposes the EU's accession to the European Social Charter (ESC) of the Council of Europe. ESC accession has been mooted in light of a number of sensitive conflicts that have arisen between national, EU and international law in the area of social rights, particularly in relation to the CJEU's case law on the right to strike and take collective action in the context of the internal market in *Viking* and *Laval*,[13] and the EU's Euro-crisis governance. Garben maps these frictions, examining the extent and degree of incompatibility, revealing that the instances of 'hard conflict' may be fewer than assumed, even if they are fundamental. She furthermore analyses the underlying dynamics giving rise to these frictions in light of Inge Govaere's 'balloon theory'. The cause is indeed found to be the (over)inflation of the balloon of European integration. However, it is not so much the EU's own development of social rights, but instead the 2004 Eastern Enlargement and the EU's expanded economic governance powers since the 2008 economic crisis that have led to this problematic over-inflation. Garben considers that

> [at] the heart of both developments is the structural internal pressure of profound socio-economic divergence and the EU's attempts (legally, politically) to increase convergence in response. This, in turn, leads to external pressures, in the form of frictions with international social norms and actors.

While a solution should be found to these cases of substantive conflict, Garben argues that EU accession to the ESC would be ineffective and potentially incompatible with the autonomy of the EU legal order if it were to make the CJEU subject to the 'jurisdiction' of the European Committee of Social Rights. Much less intrusive options are available, namely to improve the integration of external social norms in the EU legal order. The ESC already has a special constitutional status, not unlike the ECHR. The CJEU and the Commission should re-calibrate their weighing of economic and social values and rights in light of these external sources (and pressures), and thereby resolve the substantive conflict. Such 'elasticity' would make fundamental institutional changes unnecessary.

Perhaps one of the key messages of chapters four and five is that substantive conflict between national, international and EU norms may occur, and these need to be taken seriously, but that resolving them should not have to lead to fundamental institutional changes to the EU legal order, especially not where they could jeopardise the autonomy thereof. What complicates matters, however, is that substantive and institutional questions are not always separable, as chapter seven on the interplay between international and EU environmental law shows. Nicola Notaro and Mario Pagano discuss the 'on-going and recently escalating conflict' between EU and international law in the context of the Aarhus Convention on access to information, public participation and access to justice in the environmental field. At the heart of the controversy is the CJEU's restrictive *Plaumann* case law[14] on locus standi under Article 263(4) of the Treaty on the Functioning of the European Union (TFEU), which makes it virtually impossible for environmental non-governmental organisations (NGOs) to challenge EU legislation

[13] Case C-438/05 *International Transport Workers' Federation and Finnish Seamen's Union v Viking Line ABP and OÜ Viking Line Eesti* [2007] ECR I–10779 and Case C-341/05 *Laval un Partneri Ltd v Svenska Byggnadsarbetareförbundet, Svenska Byggnadsarbetareförbundets avdelning 1, Byggettan and Svenska Elektrikerförbundet* [2007] ECR I–11767.

[14] Case 25/62 *Plaumann & Co v Commission of the European Economic Community* ECLI:EU:C:1963:17.

directly before the CJEU. The EU being party to the Convention, it is directly subject to the obligations contained therein, as interpreted by the Aarhus Convention Compliance Committee. This Committee has found the EU in breach of Article 9(3) on access to justice for members of the public. As Notaro and Pagano note, while the nature of the Committee is 'non-confrontational, non-judicial and consultative', its findings 'recommended amendments of constitutional relevance in the EU legal order and its system of judicial protection, and provided an alternative interpretation – even if not definitive – of EU law provisions'. As it turns out, the EU's reservation upon joining the Convention that the EU institutions will apply the Convention within the framework of their existing and future rules in an attempt to 'preserve [the EU's] *sui generis* character and its constitutional autonomy' have not been able to prevent a certain challenge to that autonomy. Admittedly, the non-binding nature of the Committee's recommendations may mean that 'its findings are no real threat for the constitutional autonomy of the EU legal system' in a legalistic sense, but as Notaro and Pagano stress, it presents a political challenge – which may equally threaten the integrity of the EU balloon.

From a substantive perspective, it is not always intuitive to support the EU's position in the specific conflicts reported in chapters two, four, five and six. A certain impression lingers that compared to the international level, its standard of human rights, social rights and environmental rights protection tends to be lower. This needs to be put into perspective. First of all, in the vast majority of cases in all these areas, EU and international law are fully in line with each other. As Notaro and Pagano note in relation to environmental law, the interaction 'has most often been based on mutual supportiveness, enrichment and cross-fertilisation'. All three chapters show that in fact, the EU and its legal measures are often a catalyst for the international protection of the interests at stake, and for the international measures that protect them. The so-called 'Brussels-effect',[15] according to which the EU successfully exports its high regulatory standards to the rest of the world in a range of areas due to legal, economic and political dynamics, can also clearly be detected in the environmental, social and human rights areas. In the rare instances where this is not the case, and where the EU sets the standard at a lower level than the international norm, this can often be explained by the fact that the EU has to weigh these interests against others, such as economic rights and the effectiveness and integrity of EU law. While controversial, as critically examined by Violeta Moreno-Lax in chapter two, this is nevertheless an important deliberation that underlines the fundamental difference between EU and international law: where the latter is fragmented and subject-specific, the former is coherent, consisting of a 'thick' and interconnected web of substantive norms of all kinds, embedded in a polity and adopted, as well as mediated, following inclusive political decision-making. It is the difference between a governance level and a legal order.

[15] A Bradford, 'The Brussels Effect' (2012) 107(1) *Northwestern University Law Review* 1.

Eckes' argument in relation to human rights may thus be applied to social and environmental rights as well: arguably the EU is the most appropriate level to make decisions in areas where the global nature of the issues make the national level ineffective, but where the international level does not provide sufficiently holistic, coherent and democratic rule. That is not to say that there is no scope for improvement on the EU's engagement with the international level, as argued by Moreno-Lax in chapter two, or on its 'deliberative credentials' and actual substantive output; there indisputably is.[16] The EU still has a penchant for economic integration, which is understandable in light of its origins but can no longer stand in view of what the EU has become: the very autonomous legal order that the CJEU proclaimed it to be, *avant la lettre*, all those years ago. In this sense, it could be argued that the EU needs to take itself seriously as such, and dare claim its mandate and step up to its responsibility to be a fully-fledged polity instead of merely a market, to integrate trade with other interests in a balanced way, and to do so, as much as possible, through its most 'deliberative' and (thus) legitimate mode of governance: the legislative process.[17] Such an approach stands in sharp contrast to the one pertaining that the EU should move closer to international law by subjecting itself directly to external norms and bodies interpreting the compatibility of EU law with those norms.

The final chapter of this second part – 'Implementing International Norms through EU Procedure? The Case of Business and Human Rights' by Pierre Thielbörger – underscores both the insight that the EU's specific features as compared to the international level should be celebrated as its strength and that there is great potential for positive interaction and synergy between the EU and international levels, moving beyond a focus on their rivalry and incompatibility. Thielbörger sets out the global governance approach behind the United Nations Guiding Principles on Business and Human Rights and discusses their current domestic implementation in the EU, and the shortcoming thereof. In a proposal that seeks to deploy 'the strength of the one [level] to make up for the weakness of the other', he suggests that an Open Method of Coordination process should be launched by the EU to improve the implementation of the Principles. This would allow the EU to incorporate the crucially important topic of business and human rights into its activities, and it would allow the UN to benefit from the EU's effective policy- and enforcement apparatus. The fact that 'understanding the issue of business and human rights in Europe as a joint project between the UN and the EU – with both institutions holding distinct roles – is […] the most promising way forward to achieve real policy change' has indeed been recognised by the EU Fundamental Rights Agency, which has proposed to proceed precisely along these lines. This final chapter thus concludes the book's part on specific areas of

[16] See S Garben, 'The Constitutional (Im)balance between "the Market" and "the Social" in the European Union' (2017) 13(1) *European Constitutional Law Review* 23.
[17] ibid.

interaction between EU and international law on a happy note, with a concrete example for synergetic future cooperation in practice.

III. Part III: The EU and 'Third' Countries

In analysing the interface between EU and international law from an EU perspective, as is the subject of this book, an obvious distinction to make is the one between 'the internal' and 'the external'. But as we have also seen in the book's first two parts, internal and external factors, pressures and dynamics are often interlinked and interdependent, rendering the analysis more complex (and all the more interesting). For one, any internal EU policy may, in principle, have an external dimension. The CJEU has long since recognised this in its case law on implied powers, but it risks being overlooked in the general study of EU law, thus re-emphasising Ramses Wessel's point in chapter three. Furthermore, even in entirely 'internal' decision-making, Member States regularly deploy international elements through the use of 'parallel' measures outside the EU legal and institutional framework *stricto sensu*. Important examples of this practice are located in the areas of economic governance and migration, such as the EU-Turkey statement discussed by Ricardo Da Silva Passos in chapter 12. While this phenomenon has a long tradition in the European integration process, especially in areas where the EU's competence is (considered to be) limited, such as education,[18] the recent use of this 'mixed method' in high-profile crisis situations leads to a significant degree of inter-governmentalisation of EU decision-making. The CJEU may have validated this practice in *Pringle* for those instances where a 'specific' EU competence is lacking,[19] it has nevertheless been pointed out that this mixed method poses a range of legitimacy problems.[20] It also dilutes the EU's specific features, putting internal structural pressure on the hermetically closed EU law system,[21] similar to that of the intergovernmentalism of the Common Foreign and Security Policy (CFSP) as discussed by Inge Govaere in chapter one.

The difficulty of separating 'the internal' from 'the external' is even more pronounced in the case of the EU's 'external relations', where these dimensions are inherently mixed. The third part of the book delves into this matter, taking a broad view of the EU's relationship to third counties to encompass not only the

[18] See S Garben, *EU Higher Education Law: The Bologna Process and Harmonization by Stealth* (Kluwer Law International, 2011).

[19] Case C-370/12 *Thomas Pringle v Government of Ireland and Others* ECLI:EU:C:2012:756.

[20] C Timmermans, 'The Competence Divide of the Lisbon Treaty Six Years After' in S Garben and I Govaere (eds), *The Division of Competences between the European Union and its Member States: Reflections on the Past, Present and Future* (Hart Publishing, 2017).

[21] As this issue has been discussed in a previous publication, it will not be repeated in the present volume. See S Garben and I Govaere (eds), *The Division of Competences between the European Union and its Member States: Reflections on the Past, Present and Future* (Hart Publishing, 2017).

EU's trade and association agreements, but also the issue of (potential) accession, where the external becomes the internal, and on the other hand the issue of secession, where the internal becomes the external. As the various contributions in this part show, these subject matters have the interplay between EU and international law at their very core, and as such they make up the lion's share of the interface between EU and international law. The analyses in chapters eight to 11 confirm the findings in the previous two parts that overall, EU and international law interact in a non-conflictual and often even synergetic manner. EU involvement in international relations tends to counteract the traditional 'softness' of international law, mitigates raw political power-play, promotes multilateralism and internationalism generally, and at the same time enhances the EU's global profile – which may in turn strengthen its hand internally, thereby showing another way in which 'the external' and 'the internal' interact. Although all chapters deal with topics of high political sensitivity, actual tensions between EU and international law are limited, even if the EU is sometimes accused of engaging with, and relying on, international law in a 'selfish manner' as Guillaume Van der Loo puts it in chapter 10. This aligns with the findings of the previous two parts that notwithstanding the EU's commitment to the respect for, and development of, international law, it will always seek to safeguard its own autonomy, integrity and prosperity.

If the chapters of Part II looked at various conflicts, Part III instead reveals a number of interesting 'inconsistencies' and 'inadequacies'. Kieran Bradley in chapter eight points out 'the inadequacy of Article 50 TEU as a whole in light of the relevant provisions of the [Vienna Convention on the Law of Treaties]', Christophe Hillion and Vincent Delhomme in chapter nine criticise 'the recurring inconsistencies between the pre-accession conditions and [EU] membership obligations', Guillaume Van der Loo in chapter 10 discusses 'the inconsistency in the case law [relating] to the CJEU's selective usage of international treaty law' and 'the Union's trade policies towards disputed territories [which] can hardly be described as consistent'. In chapter 11, Michael Hahn delves into a different kind of conflict, not between EU and international law, but instead between the EU and the US based on international law. His account once again underlines the EU's general commitment to the international rule of law, as well as the deep interconnection between the internal and the external, pointing out that

> in a world that seems to move to less rules-based approaches, one of the original functions of the Union becomes more evident than ever: to protect the many small and medium-sized European countries from becoming an afterthought for the world's old and new superpowers: *l'unité fait la force*.

That very idea of 'stronger together' was recently rejected in the UK. Kieran Bradley discusses Brexit in chapter eight in light of the relationship between EU and international law. He observes: '[i]f ever there was an agreement which was situated on the cusp of European Union and public international law, it is the withdrawal agreement foreseen by Article 50(2) TEU'. The interests and political stakes are so high in the volatile Brexit process, beset by insecurity, that it is logical that the various parties scramble for any available legal argument to suit their particular agenda. The chapter shows how the ambiguous nature of this unprecedented situation, that necessarily integrates both internal and external elements, invites arguments about potentially applicable international law provisions. Some argue that the answer to crucial issues, such as the UK's financial obligations upon leaving and the (ir)revocability of the notification of the intention to withdraw, turns on whether they are examined under the EU Treaties or instead under the Vienna Convention. From the perspective of the EU as an autonomous legal order, the answer would seem to be that leaving the EU would have to be determined on the basis of its own terms, ie the EU Treaties. This actually seems to be the position of the Vienna Convention as well: if a Treaty provides for a withdrawal procedure, then that procedure should be followed. EU and international law thus seem largely in line. While, as Bradley points out, a possible future interpretation of Article 50 TEU would invite the CJEU 'to revisit the role of international law in the Union's legal order and indeed, for the greater good of the wider community, interpret certain provisions of international law, including the Vienna Convention', any such interpretation is unlikely to fundamentally alter the relationship between EU and international law in a *Kadi*-like way. It is the relationship between the EU and the UK, and the UK's relationship to EU and international law, that is fundamentally altered by Brexit. Neither does the existence of Article 50 TEU *in abstracto*, or Brexit in particular, seem to provide any conclusive 'evidence' on the EU's 'international' as opposed to '*sui generis*' or 'federal' nature: while it is indeed rare for constitutional orders to allow secession, there are some exceptions, of which – to some irony – the UK itself is one.[22]

Chapter nine turns to the opposite situation, of accession to the Union. Christophe Hillion and Vincent Delhomme examine the extra-territorial application of the EU acquis in this context, demonstrating how the EU's accession policy potentially helps the promotion of, and compliance with, international norms and more generally contributes to 'hardening international law'. It can be a win-win situation: '[w]hile the EU has borrowed and instrumentalised international norms for its own purposes, it has also strengthened their normative effect'. As such, EU enlargement policy has a positive effect on international law. At the same time, as we have seen in previous contributions, enlargement adds to internal structural pressures that in turn may complicate the EU's relationship with the international level. While the accession process is in principle specifically designed to limit the legal and structural divergence that might result from the integration of a new member into the EU fold, it would appear that it has not been able to fully meet its mark in this regard. As Sacha Garben discussed in

[22] N Skoutaris, 'Never Letting Go: Why Scotland is at Constitutional Stalemate over Brexit' (LSE British Politics and Society, 2016) http://blogs.lse.ac.uk/politicsandpolicy/never-letting-go-why-scotland-is-at-constitutional-stalemate-over-brexit/.

chapter five, persisting socio-economic divergence resulting from enlargement is likely to have played a role in a number of key internal and external controversies in the area of social rights. As Hillion and Delhomme show in chapter nine, the accession process remains wanting for the 'value-convergence' that it should ensure. A striking mismatch between EU internal and external competences on human rights is at the heart of this problem:

> [t]he disconnection between the EU acquis as applicable to the Member States and the accession acquis is [...] problematic [...] because of the well-established double standard critic that undermines the effectiveness of the whole projection of EU norms [and] because backsliding does happen.

According to Hillion and Delhomme, the EU needs to strive for a more harmonious interaction between the internal and the external: as 'the extra-territorial application of EU norms serves its purposes only insofar as substantive and institutional coherence between the internal and the external is secured'.

Incoherence in EU law and policy in an external context is also at the core of Guillaume Van der Loo's contribution. In chapter 10, he considers the EU's approach to the politically thorny question of 'disputed territories'. This issue rears its head in the EU's trade policy, where it has to be decided how an international agreement is to apply to these territories over which the trading partner does not exercise effective control or which has not been recognised by the EU. While recognising the pronounced differences in the various situations that are examined, which include the application of the EU-Israel Association Agreement to the occupied territories of the West Bank and the Gaza Strip, the EU-Morocco Association Agreement to the Western Sahara and the EU-Ukraine Agreement to Crimea and Sebastopol, Van der Loo's comparative assessment nevertheless reveals a certain selectivity in the CJEU's usage of international treaty law. He argues that this is not so much to safeguard the autonomy of the EU legal order, but instead for more pragmatic reasons: to dodge sensitive political issues. Often the CJEU is being put in that situation by the other EU institutions, which are equally inconsistent in their approach to these sensitive questions for obvious (geo-)political reasons.

Geo-politics similarly take centre-stage in chapter 11, where Michael Hahn examines the EU's reaction to the 'existential crisis of the US-led multilateral trading system', brought about by the Trump administration. The central takeaway is not, according to Hahn, the fact that the current US administration is considering measures potentially incompatible with the World Trade Organization (WTO), as 'many states have done that in the past, and pushing the envelope of legality has a long and distinguished pedigree'. Instead, 'what is disturbing, is that WTO law compatibility seems to not be any longer part of the political calculus'. In reaction to the US position, the EU has engaged in multiple efforts 'to strengthen its rules-based approach to international economic governance', seeking common ground and attempting to build bridges. The US measures concerning steel and aluminum, however, seem to call for a tougher response, but still based on international law rather than in contradiction with it. Indeed, by comparison, the EU can be considered a poster child for the multilateral world order, its sometimes selective or even selfish treatment of international law notwithstanding.

IV. Part IV: A View from Practice: Comments on Current Developments in the Interface between EU and International Law

The Lisbon Treaty has marked an important new phase in the relationship between EU and international law, instigating new and refueling old debates. While many of the themes explored in this book are perennial, the field has indeed seen a number of high-profile and important developments recently. 'PNR' Opinion 1/15, 'Singapore' Opinion 2/15, Rosneft and the pending 'CETA' Opinion 1/17, were all mentioned in the more general discussion in Part I of the book, but deserve some further, focalised attention. The contributors to the final part of the book are particularly well-placed to provide such a specific account of these topical issues, as they are working with them directly in their capacity as judge, EU official, lawyer and civil society activist.

Ricardo Da Silva Passos discusses the CJEU's recent case law on international agreements, identifying some differences in approach between the General Court and the CJEU. The contribution considers the case law concerning the Western Sahara, Opinions 1/15, 2/15 and the pending 1/17. Da Silva Passos notes that 'it is a complex issue to ensure the autonomy of the ECJ [European Court of Justice] with the co-existence, and possible interference, of another international judicial body' and recognises that the Court 'has shown a very rigorous defence of the specific characteristics and of the autonomy of the EU legal order, in particular regarding the conditions of judicial review by another international judicial body'. The analysis reminds us that, for the key question of EU autonomy, the CJEU will look at five central principles: (i) the decisions of the international judicial body shall not bind the EU institutions to a particular interpretation of EU law; (ii) the ECJ has the exclusive competence to interpret EU law in accordance with Article 344 TFEU; (iii) the international judicial body shall not, in any way, interfere with the division of powers between the EU and its Member States; (iv) the international judicial body shall not have jurisdiction to interpret EU law in a manner which could affect the monopoly of the ECJ concerning the preliminary rulings procedure; and (v) it shall not have jurisdiction to appreciate the validity of acts adopted by the EU under the CFSP provisions.

Jenö Czuczai in turn looks at the *Rosneft* judgment, considering it 'a good example for smooth interaction between EU law and international law'.[23] In contrast to some critiques that with this judgment 'the Court went too far in order to defend

[23] Case C-72/15 *PJSC Rosneft Oil Company v Her Majesty's Treasury et al* ECLI:EU:C:2017:236.

the autonomy of the EU legal order', the contribution highlights two aspects of the judgment that prove that 'there is still harmony in the Court's constantly developing jurisprudence' and that the Court seeks to respect international obligations. The Court's interpretation of the EU-Russia Partnership Agreement in the context of the Ukrainian crisis simultaneously protected essential EU security interests as well as international peace and security in accordance with the principles and rules of the UN Charter. As a more general point, the contribution emphasises, in line with the findings in the first part of this book, that the place of international law in the EU legal order has been affected by the Lisbon Treaty, which has given it a firmer grounding in primary law. Czuczai also points out some of the 'examples [of problematic interaction between EU and international law] well-known within the EU legal practitioners' circles', such as the Aarhus non-compliance, dealt with in more detail by Nicola Notaro and Mario Pagano in chapter seven.

Aarhus is also a central element of Laurens Ankersmit's chapter, which looks at international dispute settlement from the Investment Court System to the Aarhus Convention's Compliance Committee. The contribution argues that both external oversight mechanisms may be faced with questions of compatibility within the autonomy of the EU legal order, but that in the compliance mechanism under the Aarhus Convention is far less intrusive than the Investment Court System. The latter, Ankersmit argues, 'is explicitly intended as an alternative to judicial relief to domestic courts and may therefore have more significant effects on the powers granted to the EU judiciary in the Treaties', the rulings are binding, may have financial consequences, and can be effectively enforced in domestic legal orders of states, none of which is provided for in the Aarhus Convention. On that basis, the chapter takes issue with the European Commission's stance on both external oversight mechanisms, in that it is 'vehemently opposing the findings of the [Aarhus Convention Compliance Committee], while at the same time extensively promoting the Investment Court System in its trade agreements'. It considers that 'if the Commission is so opposed to endorsing the findings of the [Aarhus Convention Compliance Committee], it should have been even more alarmed by the prospects of the Investment Court System' thus pinpointing certain inconsistencies in approach.

V. Conclusion

Despite their many obvious interconnections, EU and international law are all too often studied and practised in separate spheres and fora. While it is natural for either to insist on their different characteristics, and particularly for the EU to emphasise its autonomous and *sui generis* nature as a constitutional order of states, important insights may be lost because of this exclusionary approach, and in practical terms there is a risk of double emploi, conflicts and contradictions. The aim of this book is to contribute to breaking through some of these barriers, and to reflect on how to ensure a smooth interaction and synergy between EU and International law both in theory and in practice. This therefore includes a more theoretical, constitutional dimension, but also a range of substantive policy areas where EU law and international law, as well as their respective actors and organisations, work alongside each other and perhaps not always in perfect harmony. Through its various contributions, this book addresses both dimensions of the interface between international and European law: the effect of international law on the EU legal order, and the influence of the EU on the international legal order. In both dimensions, there are many interesting recent developments, in case law and policy, which are highlighted and reflected upon both from an academic and a more practical point of view.

Editorial note:

This book would not have been possible without the invaluable help of Mrs. Valérie Hauspie, who has provided excellent organisational support and editorial assistance.

PART I

A Horizontal, Holistic Approach

1

Interconnecting Legal Systems and the Autonomous EU Legal Order: A Balloon Dynamic

INGE GOVAERE

I. The Balloon Dynamic of the Autonomous EU Legal Order

The concept of the new and autonomous EU legal order, as it emanated from the historic *Van Gend & Loos* judgment of the Court of Justice of the European Union (CJEU),[1] can best be pictured as an empty balloon firmly slid in-between public international law and constitutional law.[2] At first this would sit somewhat uneasily and create some friction, but it would not yet raise any major concerns. More important frictions with international law however started to appear with the rapid expansion of the EU integration process both in terms of substantive coverage and territorial scope, due to the constant transfer of competence towards the EU, coupled with the EU enlargement process to include new Member States. The balloon imagery goes that with every such new EU development, more air is automatically blown into the balloon. Yet strongly inflating the EU balloon has as a direct consequence that also more and more international law (and Member States' constitutional law) is systematically squeezed out. It is this gradual but steady EU integration process which inevitably causes increased friction and possibly even resistance against a further expansion of the autonomous EU legal order. Not surprisingly, the biggest friction is likely to relate to the transfer of areas which for a long time were kept outside the EU law balloon and within the sole realm of international law.

[1] Case 32/84 *Van Gend & Loos* ECLI:EU:C:1985:104.

[2] This 'balloon dynamic' was first presented at the 2016 FIDE congress in Budapest, see I Govaere, 'TTIP and Dispute Settlement: Potential Consequences for the Autonomous EU Legal Order' in G Bándi, P Barak, K Debisso (eds), *Speeches and Presentations from the XXVII FIDE Congress*, Congress Proceedings Vol 4, 2016, 123–44.

Concurrently, the EU legal order, as any balloon, gets more fragile when inflated. The necessity to shield the balloon from 'external puncturing' and its ensuing deflation, for instance in terms of forum shopping for dispute settlement, therefore also becomes all the stronger. It was argued before that this gradual EU integration process most likely explains why the crucial debate on EU law compatibility of Investor-State Dispute Settlement (ISDS) in the new and comprehensive EU free trade agreements, such as EU-USA Transatlantic Trade and Investment Partnership (TTIP), EU-Canada Comprehensive Economic and Trade Agreement (CETA) and EU-Singapore Free Trade Agreement (EUSFTA), has only recently arisen.[3] The underlying trigger is undoubtedly the express inclusion of foreign direct investments in Article 207 of the Treaty on the Functioning of the European Union (TFEU) by the Lisbon Treaty, thus unequivocally conferring exclusive common commercial policy competence in the matter to the EU.[4] In so doing, a field traditionally governed by international law was for the first time brought firmly within the balloon of the autonomous EU legal order. In the much awaited Opinion 1/17, the questions posed by Belgium pertain to the compatibility of the ISDS provisions in CETA with the autonomous EU legal order post-Lisbon.[5] Advisory Opinion 1/00 on the European Common Aviation Area shows, however, that it does not suffice to raise questions in terms of possible incompatibility with the EU autonomous legal order for the CJEU also to conclude in that sense;[6] the assessment is much more refined and complex.

Such a complex balloon dynamic process warrants the following threefold analysis. First of all, it is crucial to remember the very *raison d'être* of the EU law balloon and the mechanisms underlying its inflation, so as to understand why and how the CJEU coined the concept of 'autonomous EU legal order' in *Van Gend & Loos*.[7] Many studies and conferences have already been devoted to the

[3] For opposing views, see for instance E-U Petersmann, 'Transformative Transatlantic Free Trade Agreements without Rights and Remedies of Citizens?' (2015) *Journal of International Economic Law* 579–607; R Quick, 'Why TTIP Should Have an Investment Chapter Including ISDS' (2015) *Journal of World Trade* 199–209.

[4] I Govaere, 'TTIP and Dispute Settlement: Potential Consequences for the Autonomous EU Legal Order' (2016) 1 *College of Europe Research Papers in Law* 5–6.

[5] The questions addressed by Belgium to the CJEU are the following:

> '*Specifically, the Kingdom of Belgium is requesting the CJEU to provide an opinion regarding the compatibility of the ICS with:*
>
> *1) The exclusive competence of the CJEU to provide the definitive interpretation of European Union law*
> *2) The general principle of equality and the "practical effect" requirement of European Union law*
> *3) The right of access to the courts*
> *4) The right to an independent and impartial judiciary*'

see 'CETA: Belgian Request for an Opinion from the European Court of Justice' at https://diplomatie.belgium.be/en/newsroom/news/2017/minister_reynders_submits_request_opinion_ceta (last accessed 11 September 2018).

[6] Opinion 1/00 *ECAA* ECLI:EU:C:2002:231. The CJEU came to the conclusion that 'The system of legal supervision proposed by the Agreement on the establishment of a European Common Aviation Area in Articles 17, 23 and 27 and Protocol IV is compatible with the EC Treaty'.

[7] *Van Gend & Loos* (n 1).

study of *Van Gend & Loos* so this will not be repeated here.[8] Second, in order to avoid puncturing the balloon membrane it is crucial to pinpoint clearly the structural pressures that rest on the autonomous EU legal order. Third, it needs to be considered what the possible degree of resilience or elasticity of the EU balloon membrane can be in terms of offering substantive remedies to avoid conflict. The latter two elements are necessarily and inherently intertwined in any single legal analysis performed by the CJEU. The structural membrane serves to safeguard the 'autonomy' of the EU legal order so that, not surprisingly, the CJEU will strive for a strict division and a 'hermetically closed' EU law system. Yet in order to forge acceptance thereof, the CJEU needs, at the same time, to be seen to strive for 'openness' and 'symbioses' with the other legal systems in terms of substantive resilience/elasticity, in relation to both constitutional law of the Member States and international law (including the UN, European Convention for the Protection of Human Rights and Fundamental Freedoms (ECHR)). This contribution will systematically deconstruct those last two distinct yet stringently interrelated elements before turning to the key question in the current Post-Lisbon setting: will the EU balloon likely continue to fly or deflate?

The Lisbon Treaty now expressly states among the EU objectives in Article 3(5) of the Treaty on European Union (TEU) that the Union '… shall contribute to (…) the development of international law, including respect for the principles of the United Nations Charter'. Upon an isolated reading of this new provision of primary EU law, it could be claimed that this objective should always and necessarily take the upper hand and in every instance be given a full effect. The question still remains if, and if so to what extent, in so-doing concessions can or should be made to safeguard the autonomy of the EU legal order, which also derives its logic from primary EU law. Another possibility is more simply to read a codification of consistent case law of the CJEU into this new provision. As an international actor with legal personality the EU should then in its dealings with third countries and other international organisations comply with and contribute to the international legal order, short of any obligation to turn the EU into a traditional 'state like' subject of international law, let alone yielding core features of EU law to international law. There is no doubt that the insertion of this provision in the Lisbon Treaty contains ample potential to refuel a difficult discussion.

In order to grasp the complexity, dynamics and current challenges facing this interconnecting process, it is crucial that the place of the autonomous EU legal order in the larger international legal setting is subjected to a dynamic reassessment on its own merits and, importantly, free from hindsight reasoning. The focus lies on a one-sided analysis, exclusively from an EU law perspective. Equally crucial and interesting questions emerging from a complementary international law perspective, such as determining the impact of EU law on international law

[8] See, amongst others, CJEU, '50th Anniversary of the Judgment in *Van Gend en Loos*' 1963–2013, Conference proceedings, Luxembourg, 13 May 2013, EU publications.

and the 'accommodation' of the EU by other international organisations, will thus be left aside. By way of additional caveat, as the focus is exclusively put on an EU legal analysis, mainly trying to understand the logic of the CJEU, political and economic issues of interconnecting legal orders will only be considered as contextually important but not form the focus of analysis as such.

II. Structural Pressure on the Balloon Membrane

A lot of attention has traditionally gone on the study of the (intra-balloon) development of EU law, looking at the specificities and subject matters of EU law.[9] This concerns the essential and distinctive characteristics of EU law, namely primacy, direct effect and uniform interpretation by the CJEU,[10] but also transfer of competence to the EU in various and ever increasing fields.[11] The balloon dynamic of interaction between EU law and international law is not, however, limited to the process of inflation of the balloon with its ongoing shift in competence towards the EU. It also, if not foremost, points to the need to maintain intact a balloon membrane surrounding that ever expanding autonomous EU legal order. Seen from this perspective, the role of the CJEU in safeguarding a hermetically closed system of EU law appears to be crucial for the very survival of the authenticity of the autonomous EU legal order. The common feature to be discerned in the CJEU's approach is that it seeks to prevent any 'direct' interference of international law within the EU balloon, unless it has been expressly endorsed as 'integrated' or 'incorporated' into the EU legal order.[12] The challenges here are twofold for the EU legal order as set up by *Van Gend & Loos*. It continues to be subject to both internal and external structural pressures, also following the Lisbon Treaty. First, the CJEU's approach to the structural internal pressure post-Lisbon will be briefly pinpointed and some (wider) lessons drawn, before turning to the highly topical issue of increasing external structure pressure.

A. Structural Internal Pressure and the Rule of 'EU' Law

From within, the structural pressure on the hermetically closed EU law system essentially comes from the intergovernmental elements surviving the abolishment

[9] See, eg, A Rosas, L Armati, *EU Constitutional Law, an Introduction* (Hart Publishing, 2018); R Schütze, *European Union Law* (Cambridge University Press, 2015).

[10] See, eg, KJ Alter, *Establishing the Supremacy of European Law: The Making of an International Rule of Law in Europe* (Oxford University Press, 2010); S Weatherill, *Law and Values in the European Union* (Oxford University Press, 2016).

[11] On this issue, see S Garben and I Govaere (eds), *The Division of Competences between the European Union and its Member States: Reflections on the Past, Present and Future* (Hart Publishing, 2017).

[12] See below.

of the pillar structure by the Lisbon Treaty in CFSP matters. The crux of the autonomous EU legal order consists in preserving the unique position bestowed upon the CJEU by the Treaties. Articles 19 TEU and 344 TFEU combined confer exclusive jurisdiction to the CJEU, thereby as a rule preventing forum shopping and excluding any form of international dispute settlement in relation to the intra-balloon issues of EU law. An important exception thereto is still to be found in the 'horizontal pillar' of CFSP,[13] in principle excluding CJEU jurisdiction for CFSP matters other than Article 40 TEU[14] and restrictive measures against natural or legal persons (Articles 24(1) TEU[15] and 275 TFEU[16]). As such, whereas the political power to act is shifted from the Member States to the EU, the judicial control mechanism continues to remain outside the EU legal order.[17] Judicial control over CFSP measures thus lies primarily with the domestic courts of the Member States as well as international courts, such as the European Court of Human Rights (ECtHR).[18]

[13] See I Govaere, 'Multi-faceted Single Legal Personality and a Hidden Horizontal Pillar: EU External Relations Post-Lisbon' (2010–2011) 13 *Cambridge Yearbook of European Legal Studies* 87–112.

[14] Art 40 TEU: 'The implementation of the common foreign and security policy shall not affect the application of the procedures and the extent of the powers of the institutions laid down by the Treaties for the exercise of the Union competences referred to in Articles 3 to 6 of the Treaty on the Functioning of the European Union.

Similarly, the implementation of the policies listed in those Articles shall not affect the application of the procedures and the extent of the powers of the institutions laid down by the Treaties for the exercise of the Union competences under this Chapter.'

[15] Art 24(1) TEU stipulates: 'The Union's competence in matters of common foreign and security policy shall cover all areas of foreign policy and all questions relating to the Union's security, including the progressive framing of a common defence policy that might lead to a common defence.

The common foreign and security policy is subject to specific rules and procedures. It shall be defined and implemented by the European Council and the Council acting unanimously, except where the Treaties provide otherwise. The adoption of legislative acts shall be excluded. The common foreign and security policy shall be put into effect by the High Representative of the Union for Foreign Affairs and Security Policy and by Member States, in accordance with the Treaties. The specific role of the European Parliament and of the Commission in this area is defined by the Treaties. The Court of Justice of the European Union shall not have jurisdiction with respect to these provisions, with the exception of its jurisdiction to monitor compliance with Article 40 of this Treaty and to review the legality of certain decisions as provided for by the second paragraph of Article 275 of the Treaty on the Functioning of the European Union.'

[16] Art 275 TFEU reads as follows: 'The Court of Justice of the European Union shall not have jurisdiction with respect to the provisions relating to the common foreign and security policy nor with respect to acts adopted on the basis of those provisions.

However, the Court shall have jurisdiction to monitor compliance with Article 40 of the Treaty on European Union and to rule on proceedings, brought in accordance with the conditions laid down in the fourth paragraph of Article 263 of this Treaty, reviewing the legality of decisions providing for restrictive measures against natural or legal persons adopted by the Council on the basis of Chapter 2 of Title V of the Treaty on European Union.'

[17] I have labelled this elsewhere as 'crippled' conferral, see I Govaere, 'To Give or to Grab: The Principle of Full, Crippled and Split Conferral of Powers Post-Lisbon' in M Cremona (ed), *Structural Principles in EU External Relations Law* (Hart Publishing, 2018) 71–91.

[18] See, eg, ECtHR, *MSS v Belgium and Greece*, Application No 30696/09, judgment of 21 January 2011, at para 338: 'The Court notes the reference to the Bosphorus judgment (…). The Court found that the protection of fundamental rights afforded by Community law was equivalent to that provided by the Convention system (ibid, § 165). In reaching that conclusion it attached great importance to

According to the Treaties, the CFSP is thus sort of half in and half out of the EU law balloon. It is to a large extent kept outside judicial control by the CJEU in favour of political control mainly by the Council and the High Representative.[19] Nonetheless, the CJEU uses its general jurisdiction to ensure the rule of law under Article 19 TEU in order to minimise the possible negative impact thereof on the autonomous EU legal system. It does so in two ways, one in relation to CFSP agreements, the other relating to autonomous CFSP decisions.

First of all, the CJEU deftly uses the unitary procedure for the conclusion of agreements as laid down in Article 218 TFEU, 'an autonomous and general provision of constitutional scope',[20] to try to ensure some coherence in terms of the level of judicial and democratic control within the broader EU law balloon.[21] The CJEU thus refutes the arguments of the Council to the effect that it would totally lack jurisdiction as soon as it concerns a CFSP agreement. Instead, it points out that an exception to the rule of general jurisdiction conferred upon the CJEU by Article 19 TEU should necessarily be restrictively interpreted.[22]

In the same vein, the CJEU in the *Rosneft* case[23] firmly claimed jurisdiction to give preliminary rulings on the validity of unilateral decisions adopted in relation to the CFSP prescribing restrictive measures against natural or legal persons, in spite of the express Treaty reference only to Article 263 TFEU procedures in that respect. The reasoning employed is as follows:

> Since the purpose of the procedure that enables the Court to give preliminary rulings is to ensure that in the interpretation and application of the Treaties the law is observed, in accordance with the duty assigned to the Court under Article 19(1) TEU, it would be contrary to the objectives of that provision and to the principle of effective judicial protection to adopt a strict interpretation of the jurisdiction conferred on the Court by the second paragraph of Article 275 TFEU, to which reference is made by Article 24(1) TEU.[24]

the role and powers of the Court of Justice of the European Union (CJEC) – now the CJEU – in the matter, considering in practice that the effectiveness of the substantive guarantees of fundamental rights depended on the mechanisms of control set in place to ensure their observance (ibid, § 160). The Court also took care to limit the scope of the Bosphorus judgment to Community law in the strict sense – at the time the "first pillar" of European Union law (§ 72).'

[19] Art 24(3) TEU.

[20] Case C-425/13 *Commission v Council (Negotiating directives)* ECLI:EU:C:2015:483, para 62.

[21] See Case C-658/11 *EP v Commission (Mauritius Agreement)* ECLI:EU:C:2016:435; Case C-263/14 *EP v Council (Tanzania Agreement)* ECLI:EU:C:2016:435.

[22] *Mauritius Agreement*, ibid, at para 70: 'Nevertheless, the final sentence of the second subparagraph of Article 24(1) TEU and the first paragraph of Article 275 TFEU introduce a derogation from the rule of the general jurisdiction which Article 19 TEU confers on the Court to ensure that in the interpretation and application of the Treaties the law is observed, and they must, therefore, be interpreted narrowly.'

[23] Case C-72/15 *Rosneft* ECLI:EU:C:2017:236. For an analysis, see S Poli, 'The Common Foreign Security Policy after Rosneft: Still Imperfect but Gradually Subject to the Rule of Law' (2017) *Common Market Law Review* 1799–1834.

[24] *Rosneft*, ibid, at para 75.

Two distinct lessons can be drawn from those cases, one specific to CFSP and one more generally applicable to the specificity of EU law as compared to international law.

First, although those two remedies fall short of giving the CJEU full jurisdiction with respect to CFSP, they go a long way towards including CFSP matters in the autonomous EU legal order balloon, thereby somewhat alleviating the structural internal pressure. The exact extent of the CJEU's CFSP interpretation exercise is not yet fully in view.[25] But, as the CJEU may not engage in *contra legem* interpretation of express Treaty provisions, certain CFSP matters are bound to remain outside the EU balloon at least until a further Treaty amendment. This then implies that for those aspects of CFSP, legal control if any will continue to be effected at the sole national and international level, including by the ECtHR.[26] The importance of the CJEU judicial review of Article 40 TEU in terms of qualifying the external action of the EU as CFSP-based or not therefore also remains high post-Lisbon.

Second and perhaps more importantly, the more general lesson to be drawn is that the reasoning employed in both cases relies heavily on the role attributed by Article 19 TEU to the CJEU to safeguard and to enforce respect for the rule of specifically 'EU' law. The CJEU made it amply clear already in Advisory Opinion 2/13 on the accession of the EU to the ECHR that it is not sufficient for the EU, under CFSP, to comply with the rule of law under control of the ECHR, in particular if at the same time compliance with the rule of 'EU' law through the CJEU was not guaranteed.[27] The *Rosneft* case further imposes a combined

[25] See, eg, C Hillion, R Wessel, 'The Good, the Bad and the Ugly: Three Levels of Judicial Control over the CFSP' in S Blockmans and P Koutrakos (eds), *Research Handbook on EU Common Foreign and Security Policy* (Edward Elgar Publishing, forthcoming December 2018); R Wessel, 'Integration and Constitutionalisation in EU Foreign and Security Policy' in R Schülze (ed), *Governance and Globalization* (Cambridge University Press, 2018 339–75; G Butler, 'The Coming of Age of the Court's Jurisdiction in the Common Foreign and Security Policy' (2017) *European Constitutional Law Review* 673–703.

[26] See also ECtHR, *MSS v Belgium and Greece* (n 18).

[27] Opinion 2/13 *EU Accession to the ECHR* ECLI:EU:C:2014:2454 para 254–57:

> '254. Nevertheless, on the basis of accession as provided for by the agreement envisaged, the ECtHR would be empowered to rule on the compatibility with the ECHR of certain acts, actions or omissions performed in the context of the CFSP, and notably of those whose legality the Court of Justice cannot, for want of jurisdiction, review in the light of fundamental rights.
>
> 255. Such a situation would effectively entrust the judicial review of those acts, actions or omissions on the part of the EU exclusively to a non-EU body, albeit that any such review would be limited to compliance with the rights guaranteed by the ECHR.
>
> 256. The Court has already had occasion to find that jurisdiction to carry out a judicial review of acts, actions or omissions on the part of the EU, including in the light of fundamental rights, cannot be conferred exclusively on an international court which is outside the institutional and judicial framework of the EU (see, to that effect, Opinion 1/09, EU:C:2011:123, paragraphs 78, 80 and 89).
>
> 257. Therefore, although that is a consequence of the way in which the Court's powers are structured at present, the fact remains that the agreement envisaged fails to have regard to the specific characteristics of EU law with regard to the judicial review of acts, actions or omissions on the part of the EU in CFSP matters.'

reading under Article 19 TEU of the duty of the CJEU to ensure full respect of EU law with the CJEU's earlier finding, in *Les Verts*,[28] that the EU Treaties set up a 'complete' and coherent system of effective judicial remedies in which also the national judges fulfil a crucial role through the preliminary reference procedure.[29] As both Opinion 1/09[30] and the recent *Achmea*[31] case seem to confirm, any attempt to withdraw jurisdiction from the national courts in relation to areas covered by intra-EU balloon matters is therefore also likely to fall foul of the EU autonomous legal order.[32]

B. Structural External Pressure

The latter finding illustrates that it is mainly the external structural pressure coming from more traditional international law settings that forces the CJEU to define what precisely constitutes the autonomy of the EU legal order which may not be affected by international law. The criticism towards cases such as the *Kadi*[33] saga, Opinion 2/13,[34] as well as the discussions triggered by *Achmea*,[35] has exposed the conceptual difficulty of maintaining a closed EU law balloon which is hermetically shielded from international law. The crucial question appears to be whether one can or should be able to identify situations whereby the possibility of forum shopping between the application of EU law or international law is at all warranted. Should UN law and obligations be singled out as such a special case,

[28] Case 294/83 *Les Verts v European Parliament* EU:C:1986:166.

[29] *Rosneft* (n 23) at para 76: 'In those circumstances, provided that the Court has, under Article 24(1) TEU and the second paragraph of Article 275 TFEU, jurisdiction ex ratione materiae to rule on the validity of European Union acts, that is, in particular, where such acts relate to restrictive measures against natural or legal persons, it would be inconsistent with the system of effective judicial protection established by the Treaties to interpret the latter provision as excluding the possibility that the courts and tribunals of Member States may refer questions to the Court on the validity of Council decisions prescribing the adoption of such measures.'

[30] Opinion 1/09 *European and Community Patents Court* ECLI:EU:C:2011:123.

[31] Case C-284/16 *Achmea* ECLI:EU:C:2018:158.

[32] Unless the alternative dispute settlement method introduced may be fully equated with a domestic court of the Member States for the sake of Art 267 TFEU procedures, including as regards forging compliance with the duty to refer.

[33] For the appeal judgments of the CJEU, see Joined Cases C-402/05 P and C-415/05 P *Kadi I* ECLI:EU:C:2008:461; Joined Cases C-584/10 P, C-593/10 P and C-595/10 P *Kadi II* ECLI:EU:C:2013:518. The *Kadi* saga quickly triggered much doctrine, see, eg, the overview given in S Poli, M Tzanou, 'The Kadi Rulings: A Survey of the Literature' (2009) *Yearbook of European Law* 533–58; A Cuyvers, '"Give Me One Good Reason": The Unified Standard of Review for Sanctions after Kadi II' (2014) *Common Market Law Review* 1759–88; C Gearty, 'In Praise of Awkwardness: Kadi in the CJEU' (2014) *European Constitutional Law Review* 15–27.

[34] See, eg, P Eeckhout, 'Opinion 2/13 on EU Accession to the ECHR and Judicial Dialogue: Autonomy or Autarky' (2015) *Fordham International Law Journal* 995; E Spaventa, 'A Very Fearful Court? The Protection of Fundamental Rights in the European Union after Opinion 2/13' (2015) *Maastricht Journal of European and Comparative Law* 35–56.

[35] *Achmea* (n 31), see the various blog posts which quickly picked up on this judgment, awaiting more thorough scholarly analysis.

in particular in view of the above mentioned reference thereto in Article 3(5) TEU? What about the ECHR as expressly mentioned in Article 6 TEU? Or should, in keeping with the zest of the Lisbon Treaty, the question perhaps be answered positively as soon as other subjects of international law, in particular states, would be willing to engage in such a forum shopping exercise regardless of the subject matter? The reasoning then goes that the maturing of the EU into a forceful international actor as envisaged by the Lisbon Treaty necessarily implies that, within its competence, it may assume all rights and obligations as if it were a state. The key question is, of course, whether in a post-Lisbon setting the EU may really simply be equated with a state, or whether it still has distinct characteristics and special features that need to be reckoned with.

The Lisbon Treaty continues to give a strong argument to the CJEU to counter any such general 'state-like' acceptance of international forum shopping; such an interpretation would be difficult to square with, and potentially even undermine, the exclusive jurisdiction of the CJEU under the above mentioned Article 344 TFEU and Article 19 TEU combined.[36] This express exclusion of international dispute settlement by the Treaties applies in a horizontal manner to all matters brought within the EU law balloon. The distinction to be made then is not so much in relation to the importance, or not, of the international legal setting invoked or whether or not states would engage in certain international practices. It is to the contrary solely determined by the nature of the parties and the disputes in which international law is invoked. As such, the CJEU has acknowledged that dispute settlement mechanisms included in international agreements may be turned to in order to settle disputes between, on the one hand, the EU and/or its Member States and, on the other hand, third countries.[37] Triggering external dispute settlement in such cases is not only indicated but necessary as the CJEU, being the domestic supreme court of the EU, has no international jurisdiction over such disputes. At the same time, the CJEU has unequivocally stated in the *Mox*[38] case that to invoke such external dispute settlement mechanisms in order to solve disputes between Member States, and most likely also between the EU and its Member States, for matters falling within EU competence conflicts with the exclusive jurisdiction conferred on the CJEU by Article 344 TFEU combined with Article 4 TEU, the duty of sincere cooperation. The CJEU clarified that considering the hierarchy of norms, dispute settlement provisions in international agreements even if introducing a specialised forum can never set aside those express Treaty obligations.[39]

[36] Distinct from other international courts set up by agreements, such as the International Court of Justice or the ECtHR.

[37] Opinion 1/76 *Draft Agreement establishing a European laying-up fund for inland waterway vessels* ECLI:EU:C:1977:63 at para 5. This is the case for most international agreements.

[38] C-459/03 *Commission v Ireland (Mox)* ECLI:EU:C:2006:345.

[39] For an analysis, see I Govaere, 'Beware of the Trojan Horse: Dispute Settlement in (Mixed) Agreements and the Autonomy of the EU Legal Order' in C Hillion and P Koutrakos (eds), *Mixed Agreements Revisited: The EU and its Member States in the World* (Hart Publishing, 2010) 187–207.

Yet this alone is not sufficient to hermetically close the EU law balloon. Additionally, the CJEU has indicated that at least the following conditions need to be met to safeguard the autonomy of the EU legal order.[40] First of all, the interpretation of provisions of an international agreement pursuant to external dispute settlement should not be binding on the EU as concerns the interpretation and application of internal EU law.[41] Second, the agreement may not lead to an undermining of the objectives enshrined in Article 19 TEU, which apparently should increasingly be understood as respect for the 'rule of EU law' considered as a whole.[42] More than just guaranteeing the CJEU's exclusive jurisdiction for reviewing the legality of EU, this then also means safeguarding the CJEU's crucial role in ensuring the uniform interpretation of EU law as well as safeguarding the position of Member States' courts.[43] Third, the essential character of the powers of the EU and its institutions 'as conceived in the Treaty should remain unaltered'.[44] This implies that external dispute settlement should not affect the allocation of powers between the EU and the Member States, but also that the function of the different EU institutions remain unaffected, in particular also that the CJEU is by its very nature a court whose decisions are binding. These conditions have been progressively clarified in case law but are not necessarily exhaustive. As new questions emerge, for instance in relation to the potential effect of ISDS on the autonomy of the EU legal order,[45] it is to be expected that new and more refined answers may also be formulated by the CJEU in the future whenever it considers it necessary to shield the internal application and development of EU law from the effect of external and international forms of dispute settlement. One can easily understand why for the CJEU it is crucial that the specific and autonomous EU balloon is to be shielded from puncturing by international law interference, however small, as such would inevitably entail the risk of a more or less rapid deflation.

With the coming into force of the Lisbon Treaty, the question nonetheless emerges more forcefully whether the horizontal scope of the exclusive jurisdiction of the CJEU could and should continue to apply without any exception at all. As mentioned above, the newly stated objectives of the EU now include contributing 'to the development of international law, including respect for the principles of the United Nations Charter' (Article 3(5) TEU).[46] Does compliance with this objective of necessity require a limitation on the scope of application

[40] See also I Govaere, 'TTIP and Dispute Settlement: Potential Consequences for the Autonomous EU Legal Order' (2016) 1 *College of Europe, Research Papers in Law* 6.

[41] Opinion 1/91 *EEA I* ECLI:EU:C:1991:490.

[42] See above at section II. A.

[43] Opinion 1/09 *European Patent Court* (n 30).

[44] Opinion 1/00 *ECAA* (n 6).

[45] See Opinion 1/17 *ISDS Provision in CETA* (pending) (n 5).

[46] See above at section II. B.

of the rule of EU law? A positive answer would imply that such an objective was not already successfully pursued by the EU before the Lisbon Treaty. Although at times there may have been friction, there seem to be no compelling examples of (lasting) conflict between EU and UN law to support such a view. As will be argued below, this objective in most cases can continue to be met by the CJEU, within the framework of its exclusive jurisdiction, provided that sufficient attention is given to the resilience or elasticity of the EU law balloon in order to avoid situations of open conflict with international law in general and UN legal obligations in particular.[47]

It is, however, more difficult to easily reach the same conclusion with respect to the express statement in Article 6(2) TEU that '(t)he Union shall accede to the European Convention for the Protection of Human Rights and Fundamental Freedoms'.[48] This new provision inserted by the Lisbon Treaty necessarily and unequivocally prescribes adherence to the jurisdiction of the ECHR. Only the terms of such accession conditions are left to be negotiated in conformity with the EU Treaties. A crucial and novel issue thereby is to what extent, if any, Article 6 TEU necessarily limits, or provides an exception to, the horizontal scope of the exclusive jurisdiction of the CJEU for all matters of EU law within the EU balloon. In Advisory Opinion 2/13,[49] the CJEU does not really address this fundamental question. Instead, it performs a straightforward and systematic check of the draft accession agreement in terms of its compatibility with the autonomous EU legal order. The reference frame thus seems to be that the EU legal order and the exclusive jurisdiction of the CJEU need to be fully safeguarded at all costs, similarly to the standard approach also adopted in relation to any other international agreement concluded by the EU. Not surprisingly, therefore, the outcome of this assessment was negative and the draft accession agreement was found to be incompatible with the Treaties.

Opinion 2/13 thereby leaves wide open the thorny question of the post-Lisbon interpretation to be given to the core Treaty provisions at stake. Does Article 6(2) TEU have equal force and hierarchical ranking to Articles 19 TEU and 344 TFEU? If so, how do those provisions interrelate? In particular, how could each provision be given an '*effet utile*', possibly even a renewed interpretation, considering that they are on the same footing as norms of primary EU law? It seems that if Opinion 2/13 may be subject to criticism, then it is not so much for the CJEU's repeated and forceful attempts to hermetically keep the EU balloon closed. It is rather for doing so without coming to terms with the legal complexities introduced by the Lisbon Treaty and a lack of reflection about the necessity and possible ways in which to redesign the balloon.

[47] See below at section III.
[48] It continues: 'Such accession shall not affect the Union's competences as defined in the Treaties'.
[49] Opinion 2/13 (n 27).

III. Necessary Resilience/Elasticity of the Balloon

The hermetically closed balloon of EU law can, however, only withstand the structural pressure from international law and be shielded from puncturing if EU law proves sufficiently resilient to accommodate international law concerns. This implies that in its case law the CJEU, as guardian of the autonomous EU legal order, shows sufficient flexibility in addressing issues of international law so as to avoid creating situations of open conflict. In other words, it is submitted that the capacity for the EU to maintain an enduring structural autonomy necessarily goes hand in hand with continuously and proactively fostering a relationship of symbiosis rather than clash with international law. Different from a state, the autonomy of the EU legal order is only conditionally accepted so long as there is no open conflict in substance with fundamental values of constitutional and international law. It is important to note that such appraisal ultimately rests not only with the CJEU. It is subject to scrutiny by external fora, in particular the Member States' constitutional courts[50] and the ECtHR,[51] leading to a kind of 'silent constitutional dialogue'.

The CJEU case law seems to meet such concerns in two distinct ways. The first option for the CJEU is to 'incorporate' or 'integrate' international law elements into the formulation of EU law, so as to render the requirements under both legal systems compatible. The second subsidiary option is to conclude to an incompatibility between EU law and international law obligations but at the same time to provide a pragmatic intermediary solution so as to avoid an immediate clash between the two legal orders at stake. Up until now this two-pronged approach has proved on the whole sufficient to avoid open and long lasting conflicts between legal orders, but it cannot be excluded that in the future a different reflection and possible Treaty changes may be warranted.

For the sake of completion, attention will also briefly be drawn to a last option which is expressly written into the Treaties for the benefit of the sole Member States, not the EU as such. It concerns the possibility to set aside conflicting EU Treaty obligations in favour of complying with prior Treaty obligations or for reasons of security interest. These Treaty provisions may facilitate the finding that a Member State is in breach of its EU law obligations as it allows the balloon to be gently pushed aside without any risk of puncturing.

[50] See, eg, JA Frowein, 'Solange II, (BVerfGE 73, 339) Constitutional Complaint Firma W' (1988) *Common Market Law Review* 201–06; I Canor, 'My Brother's Keeper? Horizontal Solange: "An Ever Closer Distrust among the Peoples of Europe' (2013) *Common Market Law Review* 383–421.

[51] See, eg, C Costello, 'The Bosphorus Ruling of the European Court of Human Rights: Fundamental Rights and Blurred Boundaries in Europe' (2006) *Human Rights Law Review* 87–130; G Harpaz, 'The European Court of Justice and its Relations with the European Court of Human Rights: The Quest for Enhanced Reliance, Coherence and Legitimacy' (2009) *Common Market Law Review* 105–41.

A. Finding of Compatibility between Legal Orders

In most cases the CJEU endeavours to develop a reasoning in pursuit of a finding of compatibility between EU and international law. The delicate exercise consists in firmly asserting the specificity of EU law against the backdrop of international law obligations of both the EU and its Member States. As the friction between EU law and international law increases and solutions become more difficult to find, the CJEU however seems to be less inclined to accommodate arguments relating to the sole position of the Member States, at least if this would render the finding of a compatibility with EU law more precarious.[52]

A major difficulty resides in the fact that the reference frame to conclude to a compatibility, or not, between the two legal orders is necessarily international law. This implies that it is primarily the CJEU that has to incorporate elements of international law into EU law, and to do so to a sufficient extent, rather than vice versa.[53] But the CJEU is only a domestic court of the EU and not an international court, so it is not in a position to render an authoritative 'international' interpretation of international law. Its interpretations of international law are only for domestic use, merely binding on the EU and its Member States within the context of EU law applications. It is important, therefore, that the CJEU is as much as possible 'seen' to defer appreciations of international law to international treaties and in particular as interpreted by the competent international courts, such as the ECtHR and ICJ. Where no such firmly established external benchmark is at hand, the CJEU is most vulnerable to exposing itself to critique of having wrongfully asserted jurisdiction and misinterpreted international law.[54]

The express references already made by the CJEU early on to the ECHR and to the case law of the ECHR, at a time when the EU Treaties were silent in this respect, are clear and early examples of this preferred solution. Such references to a foreign legal order and to rulings of a foreign court, in the absence of membership of the EU to the ECHR, illustrate the understanding of the CJEU that the new and autonomous EU legal order cannot function in complete and splendid legal isolation. Instead, symbiotic and complementary systems of law had to be set up. It is interesting to point out that a similar approach seemed to be shared by the ECtHR in its famous *Bosphorus* judgment.[55] After scrutiny of the case law of the

[52] See below at section III. C.

[53] Although a certain extent of mutual influence may be noted, for instance when the ECHR refers CJEU case law.

[54] Such as in relation to the rather blunt assertion of the CJEU in the *Racke* case that the procedural provisions in the Vienna Convention on the Law of Treaties is not part of customary international law, Case C-162/96 *Racke* ECLI:EU:C:1998:293 at para 59. For a case comment, see J Klabbers, 'Case C-162/96, A Racke GmbH & Co v Hauptzollamt Mainz judgment of 16 June 1998, nyr' (1999) *Common Market Law Review* 179–89.

[55] ECtHR *Bosphorus Hava Yollari Turizm ve Ticaret Anonim Siketi v Ireland* 2005-VI 42 EHRR 1 (*Bosphorus*). See inter alia T Lock, 'Beyond Bosphorus; The European Court of Human Rights' Case

CJEU in terms of judicial protection and protection of fundamental rights, the ECHR introduced a legal presumption of 'equivalent protection' in the EU which can only be rebutted in case of manifest deficiencies.[56] The ECHR is also seen to refer to case law of the CJEU to support its own legal arguments.[57]

More recent examples concern the deference to customary international law principles and case law of the ICJ, first tentatively in the *Racke*[58] case and more openly since the *ATAA*[59] case. This follows earlier case law where the CJEU already stated that the EU is necessarily bound to respect international law and not just the agreements which the EU itself has concluded.[60] As a consequence, in its legality control of secondary acts of the EU the CJEU will no longer hesitate to take into consideration the need for the EU to respect principles of customary international law, even if those are codified in agreements to which the EU is not a party.[61] This is however to be distinguished from compatibility with international agreements in two respects.

First, it may be more difficult to determine what precisely constitutes a principle of customary international law. As the *ATAA* case illustrates, the CJEU will defer to express rulings of the ICJ where they are at hand.[62] It will also be rather precautious in assessing whether there are any divergent views among the Member States and the EU institutions as to the existence of a generally accepted qualification as principle of customary international law.[63]

Second, and somewhat related to the first point, the CJEU has pointed out that

> since a principle of customary international law does not have the same degree of precision as a provision of an international agreement, judicial review must necessarily be limited to the question whether, in adopting the act in question, the institutions of the European Union made manifest errors of assessment concerning the conditions for applying those principles.[64]

Law on the Responsibility of Member States of International Organisations under the European Convention on Human Rights' (2010) *Human Rights Law Review* 529–45; P Gragl, 'An Olive Branch from Strasbourg? Interpreting the European Court of Human Rights' Resurrection of Bosphorus and Reaction to Opinion 2/13 in the Avotiņš Case: ECtHR 23 May 2016, Case No 17502/07, Avotiņš v Latvia' (2017) *European Constitutional Law Review* 551–67.

[56] Yet rebuttable in case of manifest deficiencies.

[57] On the interaction between the two courts before and after Opinion 2/13, see F Fabbrini, J Larik, 'The Past, Present and Future of the Relation between the European Court of Justice and the European Court of Human Rights' (2016) *Yearbook of European Law* 145–79.

[58] *Racke* (n 54).

[59] Case C-366/10 *Air Transport Association of America (ATAA)* ECLI:EU:C:2011:864.

[60] [1] See Joined Cases 21/72 to 24/72 *International Fruit Company* ECLI:EU:C:1972:115.

[61] Such as the Chicago Convention in the *ATAA* case, or the Vienna Convention on the Law of Treaties in the *Racke* case.

[62] *ATAA* (n 59) at para 104.

[63] *ATAA* (n 59) at para 105–106. In casu the CJEU found that three out of the four principles were not contested and withheld as principles of customary international law. However the fact that both Germany and the UK had disputed that the 4° principle, namely that aircraft overflying the high seas are subject to the exclusive jurisdiction of the State in which they are registered, led the CJEU to conclude there was 'insufficient evidence' to establish this as a principle of customary international law.

[64] *ATAA* (n 59) at para 110.

On the other hand, even though the nature of judicial review enacted by the CJEU will thus necessarily be limited to a marginal judicial review, the CJEU has accepted that principles of customary international law may also be invoked by individuals to contest the validity of secondary EU law.[65] This leads to a rather paradoxical finding that under certain circumstances respect for international law principles may be better enforceable through the 'prism' of the EU law balloon than in the international legal order as such.

B. Finding of Incompatibility between Legal Orders

Considering that EU law is not fully tantamount to international law, there remain of course a number of situations whereby the outcome under an EU law analysis and an international legal analysis may be different and even conflicting. It is therefore unavoidable that the CJEU might in a specific case come to a finding of EU law which is incompatible with concurrent international law obligations of the EU or the Member States. This type of case which cannot be 'absorbed' through the resilience of the autonomous EU legal order presents the highest risk of puncturing the EU law balloon.

More often than not, the CJEU seems to anticipate a frontal clash between those legal orders by providing a pragmatic intermediary solution. Where needed it may allow for the conflicting EU law obligations to be temporarily put aside in favour of meeting international obligations in the short term. The condition appears to be, however, that in the middle to long term the incompatibility is resolved in favour of meeting the specific EU law obligations. Usually such a remedy is to be effected at the sole EU and/or Member State level but, exceptionally and if need be, it may also be found at the international level with the acquiescence of the third states concerned.

Such situations will often arise when the EU has contracted international obligations on a wrong legal basis, so that in principle the agreement is null and void under EU law but perfectly valid and enforceable under international law, whereas there is no real dispute as to its content. It may then suffice to temporarily stay the effects of the judgment so as not to disrupt the EU international relations whilst allowing for the adoption of the decision concluding the agreement using the correct legal basis. The CJEU thereby often expressly points to the need to avoid creating serious disruptions or negative consequences for the Union's relationship to third countries which might arise in case the contested decision would be annulled without its effects being maintained.[66] Especially in a

[65] This is subject to two conditions: 'first, those principles are capable of calling into question the competence of the European Union to adopt that act', (...), 'and, second, the act in question is liable to affect rights which the individual derives from European Union law or to create obligations under European Union law in his regard'. See *ATAA* (n 59) at para 107.

[66] See, eg, Case C-660/13 *Council v Commission (Access by the Swiss Confederation to the internal market)* ECLI:EU:C:2016:616 at para 53: 'If the contested decision were annulled without its effects

post-Lisbon context of multiple competence-related litigation, this remedy seems to have become almost a standard practice, often granted on demand of and with agreement of all or most of the parties involved.[67] Yet, as the rationale is to allow for some time to adopt the necessary measures in order to smoothly remove the indicated incompatibility in favour of compliance with EU law, the remedy may need to be tailor-made to the international context of each case whilst avoiding unwarranted and continuing disruptions to the application of EU law. The main variations therefore relate to the duration of the remedy offered, ranging from a mandatory fixed number of months,[68] to a more open-ended phrasing such as 'the effects of that decision should be maintained until it is replaced'.[69] In other cases a somewhat in-between position is taken, whereby the CJEU maintains 'the effects of the contested decision until the entry into force, within a reasonable period of time, of a new decision to replace it',[70] thus leaving the appreciation of the duration needed to comply with EU law open-ended but not limitless.

The more problematic cases are those where such a judge-made short term remedy to avoid a clash between EU and international obligations is to no avail. Typically this would concern disputes relating to content rather than competence, which require a renegotiation of the EU position and/or the international commitments. Any solution to divert an open conflict between EU and international law obligations would then necessarily need to be approved also by the third countries involved, without there being any obligation and perhaps little incentive for the latter to do so. This is where the importance of the Advisory Opinion procedure of Article 218(11) TFEU takes its full weight.[71] As the CJEU has pointed out, the very purpose of this procedure is

> to forestall complications which would result from legal disputes concerning the compatibility with the Treaty of international agreements binding upon the Community. In fact, a possible decision of the Court to the effect that such an agreement is, either by reason of its content or of the procedure adopted for its conclusion, incompatible with the provisions of the Treaty could not fail to provoke, not only in a Community context but also in that of international relations, serious difficulties and might give rise to adverse consequences for all interested parties, including third countries.[72]

being maintained, that may give rise to serious negative consequences for the Union's relationship with the Swiss Confederation'.

[67] See, eg, C-658/11 *EP v Council (Mauritius Agreement)* ECLI:EU:C:2014:2025 at para 88: 'Both the Parliament and the Council, and the majority of the intervening Member States, request that, should the Court annul the contested decision, the effects of that decision be maintained until it is replaced'.

[68] See, eg, Case C-137/12 *Commission v Council (conditional access)* ECLI:EU:C:2013:675 at para 81: 'In the interests of legal certainty, therefore, it is appropriate for the Court to maintain the effects of that decision until the adoption, within a reasonable period which must not exceed six months, of a new decision based on the appropriate legal bases, namely Article 207(4) TFEU, together with Article 218(5) TFEU'.

[69] See, eg, Case C-263/14 *EP v Council (Tanzania Agreement)* ECLI:EU:C:2016:435 at para 86.

[70] See, eg, *Council v Commission (Access by the Swiss Confederation to the internal market)* (n 66) at para 54.

[71] For an analysis of this procedure, see S Adam, *La Procédure d'avis devant la Cour de Justice de l'Union européenne* (Bruylant, 2011).

[72] Opinion 1/75 *(Export credits)* ECLI:EU:C:1975:145 at pt A. The CJEU continues to explain: 'for the purpose of avoiding such complications the Treaty had recourse to the exceptional procedure of a prior

Stated differently, the aim of this procedure is to prevent the EU from incurring international liability for engaging into international commitments with which it will not be able to comply for breach of EU law.[73] The existence of this preventive procedure is however no guarantee that such conflicts may at all times be avoided. Article 218(11) TFEU needs first of all to be triggered by one of the EU institutions or a Member State and even so there is no standstill obligation awaiting the outcome. Political considerations may take the upper hand regardless of the potential legal consequences. The troubled legal path of the EU-USA Passenger Name Records (PNR) Agreement is a prime example in this respect, having started with an Advisory Opinion procedure to proceed to an annulment case and finally the adoption of a new agreement based on the former third pillar outside the control of the CJEU.[74] In the aftermath of the New York twin tower terrorist attack, geo-political and international security considerations thus seemed to prevail over the strict adherence to EU law obligations. In a post-Lisbon setting entailing the abolishment of the pillar structure, such matters have now firmly been brought within the EU balloon, as is illustrated by the negative opinion of the CJEU in relation to the EU-Canada PNR Agreement.[75] In order to avoid a

reference to the Court of Justice for the purpose of elucidating, before the conclusion of the agreement, whether the latter is compatible with the Treaty. this procedure must therefore be open for all questions capable of submission for judicial consideration, either by the Court of Justice or possible by national courts, in so far as such questions give rise to doubt either as to the substantive or formal validity of the agreement with regard to the Treaty'.

[73] I have argued elsewhere that the Advisory Opinion procedure is in needed of thorough revision and reflection, see I Govaere, 'Setting the International Scene: EU External Competence and Procedures Post-Lisbon Revisited in the Light of ECJ Opinion 1/13' (2015) *Common Market Law Review* 1277–1308.

[74] In particular the European Parliament (EP) and the Council were opposed in this respect as concerns the first PNR Agreement with the USA. First the envisaged EU-USA PNR Agreement was duly challenged by the EP in Advisory Opinion 1/04, but this procedure was removed from the register when the Council went ahead with the conclusion of the Agreement without awaiting the Court's advisory opinion, see OJ C69/12 from 19 March 2005. The EP then successfully imitated annulment proceedings against the EU-USA PNR Agreement, see Joined Cases C-317/04 and C-318/04 *EU v Council (EU-USA PNR Agreement)* ECLI:EU:C:2006:346. In order to avoid an open conflict between the EU and international legal orders, not to say a heads-on political clash with the USA, the CJEU stayed the effects of its judgment in the following terms at para 83: 'Given, first, the fact that the Community cannot rely on its own law as justification for not fulfilling the Agreement which remains applicable during the period of 90 days from termination thereof and, second, the close link that exists between the Agreement and the decision on adequacy, it appears justified, for reasons of legal certainty and in order to protect the persons concerned, to preserve the effect of the decision on adequacy during that same period. In addition, account should be taken of the period needed for the adoption of the measures necessary to comply with this judgment.' This agreement was replaced by an EU-USA PNR Agreement based exclusively on the third pillar – Justice and Home Affairs – thus at the time bringing it outside the democratic control of the EP and the judicial control of the CJEU, see EU-US Agreement on the processing and transfer of passenger name record (PNR) data by air carriers to the United States Department of Homeland Security, 18 July 2007 [2007] OJ L204/18, 4 August 2007. On these procedural issues, see S Adam, 'Quelques réflexions sur les relations entre les procédures a priori et a posteriori d'examen de compatibilité des accords communautaires suite à l'affaire dite de l'accord PNR' (2006) *Cahiers de Droit Européen* 657–96.

[75] Since the abolishment of the pillar structure by the Lisbon Treaty, both democratic and judicial control with respect to the area of freedom, security and justice have been firmly put at EU level in the hands of the EP and the CJEU and are thus now included in the balloon of the EU autonomous legal

potential open clash between EU and international law obligations, the EU would be well advised to review and, where need be, also renegotiate the other existing PNR agreements in the light of this Advisory Opinion.[76]

In highly exceptional cases, the EU may not of itself be in a position to remedy the incompatibility between EU and international law but will instead need to rely on the goodwill of the international community to take action at an international level. A perfect example of the latter is offered by the *Kadi* saga concerning financial sanctions imposed on individuals in the fight against international terrorism.[77] A potential conflict was clearly exposed between the respect for fundamental rights in the autonomous EU legal order and the UN respectively, which could only meaningfully be remedied at the UN level since the EU sanctions list was merely a copy and paste of the UN sanctions list. In its first *Kadi* appeal judgment, the CJEU maintained the effects of the contested sanctions regulation with regard to Mr Kadi for a maximum of three months so as to allow the Council to fix the shortcomings.[78] A remedy was found at the UN level, in the form of the introduction of a summary narrative and creation of the position of an ombudsperson,[79] but this was not in itself considered to be sufficient by the CJEU in the second *Kadi* appeal judgment.[80] In the end a situation of lasting and open conflict between the requirements under the EU and UN legal orders was diverted when the UN Security Council deleted the name of Mr Kadi from the UN sanctions list.[81] However,

order. Interestingly, in Advisory Opinion 1/15 *(PNR Agreement EU-Canada)* ECLI:EU:C:2016:656 of 26 July 2017, also brought by the EP, the CJEU held that the envisaged PNR Agreement with Canada was incompatible with EU law both because of wrong legal basis and because of breach of fundamental rights in the following terms:

> '1. The Council Decision on the conclusion, on behalf of the Union, of the Agreement between Canada and the European Union on the transfer and processing of Passenger Name Record data must be based jointly on Article 16(2) TFEU and Article 87(2)(a) TFEU.
> 2. The Agreement between Canada and the European Union on the transfer and processing of Passenger Name Record data is incompatible with Articles 7, 8 and 21 and Article 52(1) of the Charter of Fundamental Rights of the European Union in so far as it does not preclude the transfer of sensitive data from the European Union to Canada and the use and retention of that data.'

[76] It remains to be seen whether third countries would respond favourably towards such a request for renegotiation. The Commission had posted its intention to do so before Advisory Opinion 1/15 was issued, but concrete steps since then have not been reported on the website, see https://ec.europa.eu/home-affairs/what-we-do/policies/police-cooperation/information-exchange/pnr_en (last accessed 12 September 2018).

[77] For a more detailed analysis of the *Kadi* saga in terms of interacting legal orders, see also I Govaere, 'The Importance of International Developments in the Case-law of the European Court of Justice: Kadi and the Autonomy of the EC Legal Order' in M Hiscock and W van Caenegem (eds), *The Internationalisation of Law: Legislation, Decision-Making, Practice and Education* (Edward Elgar Publishing, 2010) 316–40.

[78] *Kadi I* (n 33) at para 375–76.

[79] For an assessment of this remedy, see J Kokott and C Sobotta, 'The Kadi Case – Constitutional Core Values and International Law – Finding the Balance?' (2012) *European Journal of International Law* 1015–1024.

[80] *Kadi II* (n 33) at para 163.

[81] See, among others, European Parliamentary Research Service, Briefing October 2016, 'Counter-terrorist Sanctions Regimes Legal Framework and Challenges at UN and EU Levels' at 11, www.

this was very much an ad hoc solution which prevented a pointed puncturing of the EU balloon, but it does not offer a satisfactory and structural answer in the long term.

C. Setting Aside EU Obligations in Favour of International Obligations of Member States

Another possibility for the Member States only, is to squarely set aside EU obligations including under primary EU law in order to meet conflicting international obligations. The EU Treaties have always expressly allowed for such a solution in two sets of provisions, Article 351 TFEU concerning prior agreements of the Member States and the so-called security exceptions in Articles 346–348 TFEU. Hence it was acknowledged from the start that the EU and international law obligations of the Member States may not always fully coincide. It is clear, however, that such a solution is mainly intended to avoid the Member States incurring international liability and may not be invoked by the EU itself. The EU and its institutions are unconditionally bound by the EU Treaties by which they were set up. In fact those provisions, read together with the Advisory Opinion procedure of Article 218 (11) TFEU, and, since the Lisbon Treaty, also the clear objective stated in Article 3(5) TEU, may support the point of view that according to the Treaties, the EU is meant to always act in compliance with international law obligations; at least the EU Treaties do not foresee a situation where it would not.

The first possibility laid down in Article 351 TFEU[82] allows Member States to invoke conflicting prior Treaty obligations so as to temporarily set aside the EU Treaties, in line with the international law principles on successive treaties.[83] As such the underlying idea is that the Member States should not incur international

europarl.europa.eu/RegData/etudes/BRIE/2016/589864/EPRS_BRI%282016%29589864_EN.pdf (last accessed 12 September 2018).

[82] Art 351 TFEU:

> 'The rights and obligations arising from agreements concluded before 1 January 1958 or, for acceding States, before the date of their accession, between one or more Member States on the one hand, and one or more third countries on the other, shall not be affected by the provisions of the Treaties.
>
> To the extent that such agreements are not compatible with the Treaties, the Member State or States concerned shall take all appropriate steps to eliminate the incompatibilities established. Member States shall, where necessary, assist each other to this end and shall, where appropriate, adopt a common attitude.
>
> In applying the agreements referred to in the first paragraph, Member States shall take into account the fact that the advantages accorded under the Treaties by each Member State form an integral part of the establishment of the Union and are thereby inseparably linked with the creation of common institutions, the conferring of powers upon them and the granting of the same advantages by all the other Member States'.

[83] See, eg, A Rosas, 'The Status in EU Law of International Agreements Concluded by EU Member States' (2011) 34 *Fordham International Law Journal* 5, 1304–45.

liability for setting up or having joined the EU legal order with potentially conflicting obligations. In the *Burgoa* case the CJEU stressed that

> the purpose of that provision is to lay down, in accordance with the principles of international law, that the application of the Treaty does not affect the duty of the Member State concerned to respect the rights of non-member countries under a prior agreement and to perform its obligations thereunder.[84]

Under international law the Member States and the EU each have a distinct legal personality thus potentially triggering also distinct international liability. In a post-Lisbon setting which in Article 47 TEU expressly acknowledges that 'the EU shall have legal personality', the CJEU however seems inclined to blur those distinct legal personalities into one for the sake of application of EU law. As such, contrary to Advocate General Sharpston, the CJEU stated in Opinion 2/15 on the EUSFTA, that prior Member States' agreements were simply considered to be 'replaced' by later EU agreements so that neither the application of Article 351 TFEU nor a mixed agreement in order to terminate those prior Treaty obligations was warranted.[85] It is questionable that such a reasoning is consonant with international law. Furthermore, by virtue of Article 351(2) TFEU, the obligation rests on the Member States to 'extinguish' any such incompatibility, which implies to proceed to solve the conflict in favour of compliance with EU law.[86] The CJEU seems to interpret this as an obligation as to result rather than an obligation as to means.[87] Again, such an approach may put the Member States in a difficult position vis a vis the third countries involved, in particular if the latter are unwilling to cooperate, and raise issues concerning their international liability. It may thus be questioned whether the CJEU has not at least in part forsaken the very raison d'être of this provision to the detriment of the Member States as international actors.

A second set of rules concern the so-called security exceptions of Articles 346–348 TFEU.[88] These are basically safety valves that may be triggered

[84] Case 812/79 *Burgoa* ECLI:EU:C:1980:231 at para 8. This is in line with Art 30 of the Vienna Convention on the Law of Treaties, although it should be noted that under EU law Member States may only invoke prior 'rights of third countries' and hence prior 'obligations of the Member states' *vis-à-vis* those third countries in order to set aside the EU Treaties, which is more limited than under international law.

[85] Opinion 2/15 *EUSFTA* ECLI:EU:C:2017:376 at para 254–55.

[86] See Art 351(2) TFEU.

[87] See inter alia Case C-205/06 *Commission v Austria* ECLI:EU:C:2009:118; Case C-84/98 *Commission v Portugal* ECLI:EU:C:2000:359. In the latter case, the CJEU concluded that 'by failing to denounce or adjust the agreement on merchant shipping with the Federal Republic of Yugoslavia (…) the Portuguese Republic failed to fulfil its obligations under Articles 3 and 4(1) of that regulation'. For an analysis, see J Klabbers, 'Moribund on the Fourth of July? The Court of Justice on Prior Agreements of the Member States' (2001) *European Law Review* 187–97.

[88] Art 346 TFEU:

> '1. The provisions of the Treaties shall not preclude the application of the following rules:
>
> (a) no Member State shall be obliged to supply information the disclosure of which it considers contrary to the essential interests of its security;

by Member States in case they feel that their essential security interests are at stake.[89] The Treaty expressly mentions the possibility for Member States to set aside the EU Treaties inter alia with respect to the divulgence of security related information,[90] or 'to carry out obligations it has accepted for the purpose of maintaining peace and international security'. The latter indirect reference to UN Security Council resolutions which are binding on the Member States can of course not go unnoticed and offers a solution to potentially conflicting obligations which is firmly in favour of international law. An important fact thereby is that under the security exceptions, contrary to Article 351 TFEU, the EU Treaty obligations may be set aside without an indication of duration nor the requirement to ultimately solve the conflict in favour of compliance with EU law. Not surprisingly therefore, the CJEU has ruled that the security exceptions present a 'wholly exceptional situation'[91] and do not give a free hand for the Member States to derogate from EU obligations at will. Member States have 'to show that such derogation is necessary in order to protect its essential security interests'.[92] Under Article 348 TFEU the CJEU will exercise a marginal judicial review mainly to ensure that the security exceptions are not 'misused' by the Member States or abusively triggered.[93]

(b) any Member State may take such measures as it considers necessary for the protection of the essential interests of its security which are connected with the production of or trade in arms, munitions and war material; such measures shall not adversely affect the conditions of competition in the internal market regarding products which are not intended for specifically military purposes.

2. The Council may, acting unanimously on a proposal from the Commission, make changes to the list, which it drew up on 15 April 1958, of the products to which the provisions of paragraph 1(b) apply'.

Art 347 TFEU:

'Member States shall consult each other with a view to taking together the steps needed to prevent the functioning of the internal market being affected by measures which a Member State may be called upon to take in the event of serious internal disturbances affecting the maintenance of law and order, in the event of war, serious international tension constituting a threat of war, or in order to carry out obligations it has accepted for the purpose of maintaining peace and international security'.

Art 348 TFEU:

'If measures taken in the circumstances referred to in Art 346 and 347 have the effect of distorting the conditions of competition in the internal market, the Commission shall, together with the State concerned, examine how these measures can be adjusted to the rules laid down in the Treaties.

By way of derogation from the procedure laid down in Art 258 and 259, the Commission or any Member State may bring the matter directly before the Court of Justice if it considers that another Member State is making improper use of the powers provided for in Art 346 and 347. The Court of Justice shall give its ruling in camera'.

[89] See, eg, M Trybus, 'The EC Treaty as an Instrument of European Defence Integration: Judicial Scrutiny of Defence and Security Exceptions' (2002) *Common Market Law Review* 1347–72.

[90] Which was an issue in the *Kadi* saga above.

[91] Case 222/84 *Johnston* ECLI:EU:C:1986:206 at para 27.

[92] See, eg, Case C-187/16 *Commission v Austria* ECLI:EU:C:2018:194 at para 78.

[93] For an interesting analysis of the nature of judicial review relating to the security exceptions, see the opinion of Advocate General Jacobs in the FYROM Case C-120/94 *Commission v Greece* ECLI:EU:C:1995:109, esp at para 61–72.

Both sets of rules leave the appreciation and autonomy of the EU legal order intact, whilst simultaneously allowing for Member States' compliance with conflicting international law obligations. This may in practice solve an apparent clash with Member States' mandatory compliance with UN obligations under Article 103 of the UN Charter. The CJEU has in the past expressly accepted such a solution subject to a strict necessity test, for instance in the *Centro-Com* case where the UK sought to reinforce a UN security council resolution in breach of the EU principle of mutual trust between Member States.[94] It would of course be unacceptable within the EU balloon to accommodate the UK measure by giving in on such a fundamental principle as the mutual trust between the Member States. The ultimate and perhaps more unexpected EU law solution was therefore to allow for the EU legal order balloon to be pushed aside by well identified international obligations of the Member State concerned, rather than incorporating conflicting elements of international law into the EU balloon. Also this is a necessary form of resilience in order to keep the EU law balloon afloat.

IV. Post-Lisbon: Will the Balloon Fly or Deflate?

This exercise of maintaining a sufficient degree of resilience naturally becomes all the more important, but also increasingly difficult, as the EU law balloon is inflated to its near full capacity. As a consequence, the structural pressure exponentially increases whereas the balloon membrane itself becomes more fragile and vulnerable to puncturing. The crucial question to determine the viability of the autonomous EU legal order in the long run is therefore whether the balancing trick performed by the CJEU between a hermetically closed system, but with sufficient resilience to avoid conflicts with international law, is still adequate and/or sufficient in a post-Lisbon setting.

The challenges which the CJEU and the EU legal order at large face in this respect are not to be underestimated. Opinion 2/13 especially has triggered much criticism, calling upon the CJEU to be more open to interaction with international law. Such a reaction seems to be somewhat misguided though, as the insertion by the Lisbon Treaty of the express reference to accession of the EU to the ECHR has not raised for the first time, but only fundamentally altered, the nature of the possible interaction between those two legal orders. Prior to the Lisbon Treaty this interaction was found, as mentioned above, in accommodating and even openly integrating ECHR elements into the formulation of EU law, so as to render both legal systems compatible as well as complementary. The post-Lisbon quest to find the proper modalities for accession of the EU to the ECHR for the first time raises new and important issues specifically relating to the structural autonomy of the

[94] Case C-124/95 *Centro-Com* ECLI:EU:C:1997:8.

EU legal order in relation to the ECHR. Little or no guidance is currently offered in Opinion 2/13, nor in legal doctrine, on how the EU may accede to the ECHR without losing out on the specificities of the autonomous EU legal system and potentially thus puncturing the balloon.

The occurrence of such fundamentally conceptual legal problems is not, however, limited to the relationship between the EU and the ECHR legal systems. The structural pressure necessarily shifts and triggers concerns for the autonomy of the EU legal order whenever legal issues that before were kept outside the EU balloon are gradually integrated into EU law. As such, for instance also the extension of the scope of the Common Commercial Policy (CCP)by the Lisbon Treaty to include foreign investments now raises fundamental issues relating to the compatibility, or not, of the ISDS provisions in important trade agreements such as CETA and EUSFTA with the autonomy of the EU legal order. The recent *Achmea*[95] case further fuels this debate in relation to Member States' bilateral investment treaties (BITs).

Besides those newly emerging structural issues inherent to the dynamic process of inflating the EU balloon, due attention should also continue to be given to increasing the resilience of the EU legal order so as to avoid open clashes with international law. Also in this respect some troublesome remnants of inconclusively or unsatisfactorily resolved issues remain on the table in a post-Lisbon setting. Among those it may suffice to raise the following questions which are likely to emerge in the future. How to avoid a clash with international obligations of the EU in case the CJEU finds that the conclusion of an EU agreement is incompatible with EU law, but where no easy EU law solution is possible due to lack of consensus on the expediency or content of the agreement? It will be interesting to follow up on the above mentioned PNR Agreements saga in this respect in a renewed post-Lisbon setting, whereby the pillar structure was abolished and the content of the EU balloon enlarged to include the area of freedom, security and justice. Similarly, what would be the impact in case the removal of an incompatibility by international means is not deemed sufficient to align to EU law obligations? It may suffice here to recall the *Kadi* saga which was ultimately solved but only through an 'ad hoc' international remedy, namely the pointed removal of the name of Kadi from the UN sanctions list.

Ideally, the procedural remedies in the Treaties to avoid a clash between EU and international law, the so-called 'bridges' between EU and international law, would prevent the occurrence of difficult practical legal issues related to conflicts between legal systems. In order for the balloon to continue flying, it might be beneficial for the CJEU to revisit and further explain those mechanisms. Article 351 TFEU essentially seeks to shield Member States from incurring international liability for joining the EU, whereas the primary aim of the advisory opinion

[95] *Achmea* (n 31).

procedure of Article 218(11) TFEU is to prevent the EU from incurring international liability for contracting international law obligations which are contrary to EU law.

As mentioned above, a matter of concern for the Member States is that the EU law obligation to 'extinguish' the incompatibility of prior agreements in favour of EU law pursuant to Article 351(2) TFEU may in practice prove difficult to align to their international law obligations. More radical even was the position taken by the CJEU, in Opinion 2/15 on the EUSFTA, that prior Member States' agreements are simply replaced by later EU agreements so that neither the application of Article 351 TFEU nor a mixed agreement in order to terminate those prior Treaty obligations was warranted. There seems to be a sense of urgency in forging a renewed reflection on how to smoothly interconnect legal orders whilst avoiding Member States potentially incurring international liability for complying with EU law obligations.

Similarly, the CJEU has consistently held that the Advisory Opinion procedure of Article 218(11) TFEU serves to 'forestall' complications that might arise if an EU agreement were later on found to be incompatible with EU law. The crucial condition thereto is of course that this advisory opinion procedure is duly triggered in case of doubt. The Treaty thus contains merely a mechanism but no guarantee that such liability can at all times be avoided. A second issue concerns the expected outcome in case a negative opinion is formulated by the CJEU. The CJEU seems to have understood in the aftermath of Opinion 2/13 on the accession of the EU to the ECHR that merely concluding to an incompatibility between legal orders is not necessarily perceived as the most constructive and forward looking solution. In the later Opinion 1/15 on the EU-Canada PNR Agreement, it proceeded to indicate more concrete and substantive solutions for the removal of the established incompatibility in terms of fundamental rights protection.[96] Yet other than merely

[96] Opinion 1/15 (n 75). The CJEU held: 'The Agreement between Canada and the European Union on the transfer and processing of Passenger Name Record data must, in order to be compatible with Art 7 and 8 and Art 52(1) of the Charter of Fundamental Rights:

(a) determine in a clear and precise manner the PNR data to be transferred from the European Union to Canada;
(b) provide that the models and criteria used in the context of automated processing of PNR data will be specific and reliable and non-discriminatory; provide that the databases used will be limited to those used by Canada in relation to the fight against terrorism and serious transnational crime;
(c) save in the context of verifications in relation to the pre-established models and criteria on which automated processing of Passenger Name Record data is based, make the use of that data by the Canadian Competent Authority during the air passengers' stay in Canada and after their departure from that country, and any disclosure of that data to other authorities, subject to substantive and procedural conditions based on objective criteria; make that use and that disclosure, except in cases of validly established urgency, subject to a prior review carried out either by a court or by an independent administrative body, the decision of that court or body authorising the use being made following a reasoned request by those authorities, inter alia, within the framework of procedures for the prevention, detection or prosecution of crime;

pinpointing and forestalling potential conflicts, could this procedure not also be used as an important vehicle for the CJEU to better clarify the dynamics of the EU balloon and its complex interactions with international law? Admittedly, such a proposal implies more proactively using the advisory opinion procedure for an additional and explicative function. But it is one which is currently lacking and for which there appears to be much need and demand.

In a post-Lisbon setting, more than before attention has gone to the concept of the autonomous EU legal order and how it impacts on the objective to establish the EU as forceful international actor.[97] In the worst case scenario this concept would always be looming and unexpectedly pop up, as some kind of Loch Ness monster, in order to upset smooth international relations involving the EU and its Member States. Through the use of a balloon dynamics analysis, the above analysis to a large extent dispels such a perception. Instead it illustrates that the CJEU's approach to interconnecting the EU legal order with international law is much more structured and comprehensive, albeit highly complex and in urgent need of enhanced transparency.

(d) limit the retention of Passenger Name Record data after the air passengers' departure to that of passengers in respect of whom there is objective evidence from which it may be inferred that they may present a risk in terms of the fight against terrorism and serious transnational crime;
(e) make the disclosure of Passenger Name Record data by the Canadian Competent Authority to the government authorities of a third country subject to the condition that there be either an agreement between the European Union and that third country equivalent to the Agreement between Canada and the European Union on the transfer and processing of Passenger Name Record data, or a decision of the European Commission, under Art 25(6) of Directive 95/46/EC of the European Parliament and of the Council of 24 October 1995 on the protection of individuals with regard to the processing of personal data and on the free movement of such data, covering the authorities to which it is intended that Passenger Name Record data be disclosed;
(f) provide for a right to individual notification for air passengers in the event of use of Passenger Name Record data concerning them during their stay in Canada and after their departure from that country, and in the event of disclosure of that data by the Canadian Competent Authority to other authorities or to individuals; and
(g) guarantee that the oversight of the rules laid down in the Agreement between Canada and the European Union on the transfer and processing of Passenger Name Record data relating to the protection of air passengers with regard to the processing of Passenger Name Record data concerning them will be carried out by an independent supervisory authority'.

[97] See, eg, C Contartese, 'The Autonomy of the EU Legal Order in the ECJ's External Relations Case Law: From the "Essential" to the "Specific Characteristics" of the Union and Back Again' (2017) *Common Market Law Review* 1627–71; J Czuzai, 'The Autonomy of the EU Legal Order and the Law-making Activities of International Organizations: Some Examples Regarding the Council's most Recent Practice' (2012) 31 *Yearbook of European Law* 1, 452–72; S Hindelang, 'The Autonomy of the European Legal Order' in M Bungenberg and C Herrmann (eds), *Common Commercial Policy after Lisbon. European Yearbook of International Economic Law* (Springer, 2013) 187–98; JW van Rossem, 'The Autonomy of EU Law: More is Less?' in RA Wessel and S Blockmans (eds), *Between Autonomy and Dependence* (TMC Asser Press, 2013) 13–46; TS Lock, 'Walking on a Tightrope: The Draft ECHR Accession Agreement and the Autonomy of the EU Legal Order' (2011) *Common Market Law Review* 1025–54.

2

The Axiological Emancipation of a (Non-)Principle: Autonomy, International Law and the EU Legal Order

VIOLETA MORENO-LAX*

I. Introduction: A Bridge or a Wall?

The relationship between international law and EU law has long beguiled scholars. The literature on their interplay is copious.[1] And there is no scarcity of titles dealing with the notion of autonomy as applied to the relationship between the two.[2] Ever since *Van Gend & Loos*,[3] the processes of reception, compliance and contestation between the EU and international legal orders have attracted attention, with

* I am grateful to Dr Mario Méndez and Dr Paul Gragl for their helpful comments on a previous draft.

[1] See, generally, E Cannizzaro, P Palchetti and RA Wessel (eds), *International Law as Law of the European Union* (Martinus Nijhoff, 2012); P Eeckhout, *EU External Relations Law*, 2nd edn (Oxford University Press, 2011); M Evans and P Koutrakos (eds), *Beyond the Established Legal Orders* (Hart, 2011); J Wouters, A Nollkaemper and E de Wet (eds), *The Europeanisation of International Law* (TMC Asser Press, 2008); M Cremona and B de Witte (eds), *EU Foreign Relations Law* (Hart, 2008); TC Hartley, 'International Law and the Law of the European Union – A Reassessment' (2001) 71 *British Yearbook of International Law* 1; M Koskenniemi (ed), *International Law Aspects of the European Union* (Martinus Nijhoff, 1998).

[2] See, eg, T Schilling, 'The Autonomy of the Community Legal Order: An Analysis of Possible Foundations' (1996) 37 *Harvard International Law Journal* 389; JHH Weiler and UR Haltern, 'The Autonomy of the Community Legal Order – Through the Looking Glass' (1996) 37 *Harvard International Law Journal* 411; L Barents, *The Autonomy of Community Law* (Kluwer, 2004); B de Witte, 'European Union Law: How Autonomous is its Legal Order?' (2010) 65 *Zeitschrift für öffentliches Recht* 141.

[3] Case 26/62 *Van Gend en Loos* [1963] ECR 1. For a recent re-evaluation, see B de Witte, 'The Continuous Significance of Van Gend en Loos' in M Maduro and L Azoulai (eds), *The Past and Future of EU Law* (Hart, 2010) 9. *cf* I Pernice, 'The Autonomy of the EU Legal Order – Fifty Years After Van Gend' in A Tizziano, J Kokott and S Prechal (eds), *50th Anniversary of the judgment in Van Gend en Loos* (Office des publications de l'Union européenne, 2013) 55.

efforts being made to explicate the links and fissures concerning them.[4] Authors have acknowledged the limits of dichotomous accounts – relying on concepts such as 'monism' and 'dualism', from the international/domestic discourse – focusing instead on the asymmetric and constantly adjusting nature of the relationship.[5]

However, the starting point remains questioned. On one hand, international lawyers tend to assume the *Völkerrechtsfreundlichkeit* of the EU system,[6] considering the nature of the Union as a Treaty-based organisation with derivative legal personality,[7] limited conferred competences[8] and a pre-determined institutional set-up.[9] The fact that it remains subject to the ultimate will of the Member States – which retain an untouched core of sovereignty, including the powers to amend the Treaties and quit the organisation – is also of note.[10] On that basis, they take EU law as particular (*lex specialis*) international law; as a sub-system embedded within the system (of *leges generales*).[11] On the other hand, EU lawyers emphasise the distinctive, *sui generis* nature of the integration project and its supranational legal regime, focusing on its high degree of constitutional development, institutional maturity and the density of the existing *acquis*.[12]

Whatever the perspective, the Treaties are not explicit in this regard.[13] They say little about the place and ranking of international norms within the EU

[4] C Timmermans, 'The EU and Public International Law' (1999) 4 *European Foreign Affairs Review* 181; Besson, 'How International is the European Legal Order?' (2008) 5 *No Foundations* 50; B de Witte, 'Direct Effect, Primacy, and the Nature of the Legal Order' in P Craig and G de Búrca (eds), *The Evolution of EU Law*, 2nd edn (Oxford University Press, 2011) 323; and K Lenaerts, 'Direct Applicability and Direct Effect of International Law in the EU Legal Order' in I Govaere et al (eds), *The European Union in the World* (Martinus Nijhoff, 2014).

[5] KS Ziegler, 'International Law and EU Law: Between Asymmetric Constitutionalisation and Fragmentation' in A Orakhelashvili (ed), *Research Handbook on the Theory of International Law* (Edward Elgar, 2011) 268; E Cannizzaro, 'The Neo-Monism of the European Legal Order' in Cannizzaro, Palchetti and Wessel (n 1) 35; and V Moreno-Lax and P Gragl, 'The Quest for a (Fully-fledged) Theoretical Framework: Co-Implication, Embeddedness and Interdependency between Public International Law and EU Law' (2016) 35 *Yearbook of European Law* 455.

[6] E Cannizzaro, P Palchetti and RA Wessel, 'Introduction: International Law as Law of the European Union' in Cannizzaro, Palchetti and Wessel (n 1) 1; J Klabbers, '*Völkerrechtsfreundlich*? International Law and the Union Legal Order' in P Koutrakos (ed), *European Foreign Policy* (Edward Elgar, 2011) 95.

[7] Art 47, Treaty on European Union [2010] OJ C83/13 ('TEU').

[8] Art 5(2) TEU and Art 249, Treaty on the Functioning of the European Union [2010] OJ C83/47 ('TFEU').

[9] Arts 13–19 TEU.

[10] Arts 48 and 50 TEU.

[11] See, eg, A Pellet, 'Les fondements juridiques internationaux du droit communautaire' (1994) 5 *Collected Courses of the Academy of European Law* 193, 245.

[12] J Bengoetxea, 'The EU as (More than) an International Organization' in J Klabbers and A Wallendahl (eds), *Research Handbook on the Law of International Organizations* (Edward Elgar, 2011) 449. See also A Peters, 'The Position of International Law within the European Community Legal Order' (1997) 40 *German Yearbook of International Law* 9 and B de Witte, 'EU Law: Is it International Law?' in C Barnard and S Peers (eds), *European Union Law*, 2nd edn (Oxford University Press, 2017) 177.

[13] Arts 3(5) and 21 TEU are elaborated upon below. Regarding customary international law, see P Gragl, 'The Silence of the Treaties: General International Law and the European Union' (2015) 57 *German Yearbook of International Law* 375.

legal order and fail to determine their effects and functions in particular situations, whether as gap fillers, validity measures, or interpretative guidelines. In the absence of specific provisions, the systematisation of the relationship has fallen to the Court of Justice of the European Union (CJEU), which has articulated it *ad hoc* and in piecemeal fashion.

The case law is unsystematic, according power and significance depending on the type of instrument and the function it may perform in the specific circumstances.[14] Whilst the Court has reiterated its commitment to international law, retaining that the EU 'must respect [it] in the exercise of its powers',[15] and holding that provisions in agreements concluded by the organisation 'form an integral part of [the Union's] law',[16] this recognition has led to varying strategies, ranging from unswerving compliance with international norms to blatant instrumentalisation.[17] But the fact that international rules be binding and have a place within the EU system does not automatically imply that they be self-executing. Generally, the reasoning has been outcome-driven, oscillating between openness and closeness of the regime,[18] following a consequentialist approach to advance the EU cause – and preserve the Court's prerogatives.[19]

With this in mind, the Court has distinguished several degrees of intensity in the effects of international law, differentiating several methods of incorporation, each of them subject to different conditions – depending on whether international law is perceived to promote or impede EU powers. Ziegler has discerned, at least, three distinct mechanisms: direct effect; indirect effect or conform interpretation; and 'substantive borrowing'.[20] However, the gate-keeping criteria have fluctuated

[14] RA Wessel, *Close Encounters of the Third Kind: The Interface between the EU and International Law after the Treaty of Lisbon*, Swedish Institute of European Policy Studies (December 2013) www.sieps.se/en/publikationer/close-encounters-of-the-third-kind-the-interface-between-the-eu-and-international-law-after-the-treat; *cf* A Rosas, 'The European Court of Justice and Public International Law' in Wouters, Nollkaemper and de Wet (n 1) 75.

[15] Case C-286/90 *Poulsen* [1992] ECR I-6019 para 9; Case C-405/92 *Mondiet* [1993] ECR I-6133 paras 13–15; Case C-162/96 *Racke* [1998] ECR I-3655 para 45; Case C-308/06 *Intertanko* [2008] ECR I-4057 para 51.

[16] Case 181/73 *Haegeman* [1974] ECR 449 para 5; Case C-61/94 *Commission v Germany* [1996] ECR I-3989 para 52; Case C-311/04 *Dordrecht* [2006] ECR I-609 para 25.

[17] B de Witte, 'International Law as a Tool for the European Union' (2009) 5 *European Competition Law Review* 265. See also A Nollkaemper, 'The Duality of Direct Effect in International Law' (2014) 25 *European Journal of International Law* 105.

[18] On this oscillation, see BI Bonafé, 'International Law in Domestic and Supranational Settings' in J Kammehofer and J D'Aspremont (eds), *International Legal Positivism in the Post-modern World* (Cambridge University Press, 2014) 378 ff.

[19] For an elaboration, see B de Witte, 'A Selfish Court? The Court of Justice and the Design of Institutional Dispute Settlement Beyond the European Union' in M Cremona and A Thies (eds), *The European Court of Justice and External Relations Law* (Hart Publishing, 2014) 46.

[20] See Ziegler (n 5) 298–309. See also, KS Ziegler, 'The Relationship between EU Law and International Law' in D Patterson and A Södersten (eds), *A Companion to EU Law and International Law* (Wiley & Sons, 2016) 42, 45. For a classification of four main uses of *customary* international law specifically: 1) to set the limits of jurisdiction and powers of the EU and/or the Member States; 2) as aid to interpretation; 3) as gap-filler of lacunae in EU law; and 4) as validity standards, see J Wouters and D van Eeckhoutte, 'Enforcement of Customary International Law through European Community Law'

over time – with the Court holding the key to the door – from an *a priori* predisposition to the absorption of international norms, to a hostile exclusionism to guarantee the 'autonomy' of EU law.

And 'autonomy', as the remainder of this chapter will show, is not a static notion.[21] It is an elusive concept that has travelled an intricate journey through several meanings and implications.[22] It was first used to describe the distinctiveness of EU law, as the *consequence* of integration, to subsequently become the normative *cause* (or raison d'être) of the European project. Autonomy has transformed from being a key tool to denote 'the specific characteristics of the EU and EU law',[23] to implying the (normative aspiration of) closeness and self-sufficiency of the regime in its entirety. It has gone from being a (privileged) *means* securing the (formal) emancipation of EU law from its international roots, to becoming a (rootless) *end* in itself, detached from any identifiable value base – whether in the Rule of Law or in fundamental rights – despite Article 2 of the Treaty on European Union (TEU).

It will be argued that in the post Opinion 2/13 isolationist era,[24] a point of axiological vacuum has been reached, in which 'autonomy' *per se* has become a (new, if not *the* ultimate) value of the EU legal order. The objectivisation of 'autonomy' (and its veneration) means not only that EU law has been (substantively) detached from international law (and its principles), but also that the system as a whole has been emptied of the values on which 'the Union is founded',[25] posing grave problems of legitimacy and self-justification.[26] This chapter will, therefore, contest the nature of autonomy as a principle and challenge its axiological emancipation as being contrary to the Rule of (EU) Law.

in JM Prinssen and A Schrauwen (eds), *Direct Effect: Rethinking a Classic of EC Legal Doctrine* (Europa Law Publishing, 2002) 183.

[21] Speaking of a 'pattern' in the defence and promotion of autonomy by the CJEU, see A Łazowski and RA Wessel, 'When Caveats turn into Locks: Opinion 2/13 on Accession of the European Union to the ECHR' (2015) 16 *German Law Journal* 179.

[22] For an alternative classification of the 'meanings' of autonomy within the EU legal framework, see KS Ziegler, 'Autonomy: From Myth to Reality – or Hubris on a Tightrope? EU Law, Human Rights and International Law' in S Douglas-Scott and N Hatzis (eds), *Research Handbook on EU Human Rights Law* (Edward Elgar, 2017) 267. *cf* T Molnár, 'Revisiting the External Dimension of the Autonomy of EU Law: Is There Anything New Under the Sun?' (2016) 57 *Hungarian Journal of Legal Studies* 178, distinguishing different 'types' of autonomy: relative/full, derivative/original.

[23] Opinion 2/13 *EU Accession to the ECHR* [2014] ECLI:EU:C:2014:2454 para 174.

[24] ibid. For a critique, see P Gragl, 'The Reasonableness of Jealousy: Opinion 2/13 and EU Accession to the ECHR' (2015) *European Yearbook of Human Rights* 27.

[25] Art 2 TEU.

[26] For an overview of this problématique, see J Klabbers, 'The Changing Image of International Organisations' in JM Coicaud and V Heiskanen (eds), *The Legitimacy of International Organisations* (United Nations University Press, 2001) 221. See also B Simma and D Pulkowski, 'Of Planets and the Universe: Self-Contained Regimes in International Law' (2006) 17 *European Journal of International Law* 483.

II. Chronicle of Autonomy's Phases: From Distinctiveness to (Strategic) Isolation

Since the Lisbon Treaty came into force in 2009, mixed agreements are said to be 'binding upon the institutions of the Union and on its Member States'.[27] And it is also an explicit objective of the Union to 'uphold and promote' its values in its relations with the wider world, thereby contributing not only to 'the strict observance', but also to 'the development of international law'.[28] The EU, therefore, according to the very wording of Article 3(5) TEU, should emerge not only as a passive recipient, but also as an active shaper *and* guarantor of international norms.[29] The relationship between the two regimes has, however, been put under constant strain, both pre- and post-Lisbon, mediated by the fluidity of 'autonomy'. The next sub-sections will show how, progressive tightness in the case law of the CJEU has, paradoxically, developed in the wake of the more international law-friendly language introduced by the Lisbon Treaty, tracking the evolution of 'autonomy' and the different roles it has played through the ages of European integration, from a quasi-empirical descriptor to a full normative notion, hailed as a sort of meta-principle of EU law in its latest incarnation.

A. The Early Days of the 'New Legal Order': Autonomy as Descriptor?

At the time of the Union's inception, as the European Coal and Steel Community in 1952 and the European Economic Community in 1957 respectively, the inextricable bond between the EU and international law went uncontested. Because this new legal construct had been established by sovereign States (as 'masters of the Treaties') via international agreements, there was no doubt that the Communities were creatures of international law, embedded in the general regime.[30] Yet, the supervening times saw crucial developments, which raised questions regarding the EU's legal nature. The CJEU pursued an ever-deepening integration by pronouncing EU law supreme,[31] and having direct effect within the Member States' legal systems under certain conditions,[32] also elevating the Treaties as

[27] Art 216(2) TFEU. Note, however, that there is no corresponding provision regarding customary law.

[28] Art 3(5) TEU. See also Art 21(1) TEU.

[29] For a thorough account, see D Kochenov and F Amtenbrink (eds), *The European Union's Shaping of the International Legal Order* (Cambridge University Press, 2013).

[30] JHH Weiler, 'The Transformation of Europe' (1991) 100 *Yale Law Journal* 2403, 2413.

[31] Case 6/64 *Costa v ENEL* [1964] ECR 585, 594.

[32] *Van Gend en Loos* (n 3) 13.

'the basic constitutional charter' of the Union.[33] Consequently, the EU became an entity, which no longer was a 'pure' international organisation, but an increasingly 'constitutionalised' legal order.[34]

Whilst the CJEU pursued an integrating approach towards Member State law, it concurrently sought to differentiate EU law from its external basis in public international law. Although the Court still considered the then-Community a 'new legal order *of international law*' in *Van Gend en Loos*,[35] it soon dropped the 'international law' qualifier, determining instead that, '*[b]y contrast with ordinary international treaties*, the EEC Treaty has created its own legal system…'.[36] Autonomy in this context – which was not referred to in that way until the 1990s[37] – served to denote the distinctiveness of EU law, as an empirical as well as legal reality, describing how the EU, as a separate, special and 'autonomous' regime, pursued 'its own particular objectives'.[38] The stance at that point appeared to reflect the 'certain autonomy' predicated by the International Court of Justice of (*all*) international organisations, as independent subjects of international law.[39]

Normative consequences also follow from such characterisation – arguably, as would also occur with other instruments of international law.[40] The CJEU indeed subsequently held that (other) international agreements cannot affect the autonomy of Union law,[41] that 'the validity of any [Union] measure … must be considered to be the expression … of a constitutional guarantee stemming from the [EU] Treaty as an autonomous legal system',[42] and that treaties concluded by the Union must not alter the functional nature and competences of its organs, including those of the Court of Justice.[43] Autonomy thus emerged as an

[33] Case 294/83 *Les Verts* [1986] ECR 1339 para 23.

[34] JHH Weiler, *The Constitution of Europe* (Cambridge University Press, 1999) 12. See also T Lock, 'Why the EU is Not a State' (2009) 5 *European Competition Law Review* 345, 407–20; and ML Jones, 'The Legal Nature of the European Community' (1984) 17 *Cornell International Law Journal* 1. *cf* K Nicolaïdis, 'We, the Peoples of Europe…' (2004) 83 *Foreign Affairs* 97; and JA Caporaso, 'The European Union and Forms of State: Westfalian, Regulatory, or Post-modern?' (1996) 34 *Journal of Common Markets Studies* 29.

[35] *Van Gend en Loos* (n 3) 12 (emphasis added). For a theorisation, see K Culver and M Giudice, 'Not a System but an Order' in J Dickson and P Eleftheriadis (eds), *Philosophical Foundations of EU Law* (Oxford University Press, 2012) 54.

[36] *Costa v ENEL* (n 31) 593 (emphasis added).

[37] Mapping this evolution, see S Szurek, 'Du particularisme à l'autonomie? Esquisses des rapports du droit international et du droit communautaire' (2007) 5 *Annuaire du droit européen* 57.

[38] Opinion 1/91 *European Economic Area* [1991] ECR I-6079 para 30.

[39] *Legality of the Use by A State of Nuclear Weapons in Armed Conflict (Advisory Opinion)* [1996] ICJ Rep 19.

[40] This is precisely why the *pacta tertiis* principle was codified in Art 34 of the Vienna Convention on the Law of Treaties [1969] 1155 UNTS 331 ('VCLT'); to ensure that '[a] treaty does not create either obligations or rights for a third State without its consent'.

[41] Case C-459/03 *Commission v Ireland (Mox Plant)* [2006] ECR I-4635 para 123. *cf* Art 344 TFEU.

[42] Joined Cases C-402/05 P and C-415/05 P *Kadi and Al Barakaat International Foundation v Council and Commission* ('*Kadi I*') [2008] ECR I-6351 para 282.

[43] Opinion 1/09 *European and Community Patents Court* [2011] ECR I-1137 paras 76–89. See also Opinion 1/00 *European Common Aviation Area* [2002] ECR I-3498 para 12 ff; and Opinion 1/76 *Inland Waterways* ECLI:EU:C:1977:63.

operational-constitutional factor, characterising the independent functioning of the EU as per the founding Treaties.[44] Functionalism explained autonomy (at least in part), capturing the political, institutional and policy-making self-standingness of the EU as an international organisation in relation to both its Member States and other international actors.[45]

But the Court went a step further. By separating EU law from the rest of international law, it privileged the application of Union law within the legal systems of the Member States, *in lieu of* general international law, thereby consolidating its supremacy. The separation was tactical. The consequence for Member States was that they could no longer oppose or nullify the effectiveness of EU law through the invocation of domestic rules on the incorporation of 'classic' international law. The Court appropriated the instruments of its creation and 'liberated' the Union from such contingencies. It moved the source of its validation from international law to its own legal order and transformed the Treaties into the *Grundgesetz* of the EU's constitution.[46] Autonomy in this framework played a primarily 'internal' role; the emancipation of EU law from international law was an instrument to claim the direct penetration of EU rules within the domestic systems of the Member States. There was no *a priori* animosity vis-à-vis international law implicit in the term. The description of EU law – and the normative re-configuration that ensued – as an autonomous form (of international law) served the purpose of a constitutional (and hierarchical) 'fusion' with Member State law.[47]

B. The External Facet of Autonomy: Towards *Kadi* Dualism

While the EU 'withdrew' from its international legal sources and was gradually 'autonomised', in the earlier days of integration it still displayed a 'monist' openness towards the international legal order. It allowed binding international norms to become *ipso facto* and without further transposition part of the Union legal regime, whether they took the form of international agreements,[48] concluded by its own institutions,[49] or of customary law – including principles from the law

[44] There was also external recognition of EU law as a 'special legal order', not least by the Strasbourg Court. See European Court of Human Rights ('ECtHR'), *Moustaquim v Belgium*, Application No 12313/86, 18 February 1991, para 49. For other examples, refer to Molnár (n 22) 186.

[45] On this point, see further R Collins and ND White, 'International Organisations and the Idea of Autonomy: Introduction and Overview' in R Collins and ND White (eds), *International Organizations and the Idea of Autonomy* (Routledge, 2011) 1. Generally on 'functionalism' and international organisations, see J Klabbers, *An Introduction to International Organizations Law*, 3rd edn (Cambridge University Press, 2015); and N Blokker, *International Institutional Law*, 6th edn (Brill, 2018).

[46] N Tsagourias, 'Conceptualizing the Autonomy of the European Union' in Collins and White (n 45) 339, 340.

[47] Case 106/77 *Simmenthal* [1978] ECR 629.

[48] *Haegeman* (n 16) para 5; and Case 104/81 *Kupferberg* [1982] ECR 3641 para 11, see further below. Most recently, see also Case C-266/16 *Western Sahara* EU:C:2018:118 paras 45–46.

[49] RA Wessel and S Blockmans, 'Between Autonomy and Dependence: The EU Legal Order under the Influence of International Organizations – An Introduction' in RA Wessel and S Blockmans (eds), *Between Autonomy and Dependence* (Springer, 2013) 1.

of treaties,[50] nationality awards,[51] norms governing the obligation of States to allow access to their territory by their own nationals,[52] the immunities applicable to heads of State,[53] and the extent of jurisdictional powers,[54] which were quasi-automatically absorbed.[55]

Even regarding a treaty the EU was not a party to, but to which all its Member States had acceded, such as the 1947 General Agreement on Tariffs and Trade (GATT), did the Court consider the Union to be bound by virtue of the doctrine of 'functional succession'.[56] The GATT had been adopted before the Communities came into existence. And, in *International Fruit*,[57] the Court considered the Union subject to the agreement to the extent that it had assumed powers previously exercised by the Member States in the specific areas it regulated. Yet, it soon became clear that this did not amount to accepting that EU measures could be challenged, without more, on grounds of incompatibility with GATT norms. Similarly to the test for direct effect of EU law, the provisions at stake needed also to be capable of conferring rights, for which reason 'regard must be simultaneously paid to the spirit, the general scheme and the wording of the [treaty] and of the provisions concerned'.[58] On account of 'the great flexibility of its provisions', the GATT, however, was considered not to meet the mark, so it could not be invoked to challenge the lawfulness of Union law.[59] The same applied to WTO provisions

[50] *Racke* (n 15) paras 25 ff; Case C-70/09 *Hengartner* [2010] ECR I-7233 para 36; Case C-386/08 *Brita* [2010] ECR I-2189 paras 44 ff; Case T-115/94 *Opel Austria* [1998] ECR II-2739 para 77.

[51] Case C-200/00 *Chen* [2004] ECR I-9925 para 37; Case C-135/08 *Rottmann* [2010] ECR I-1449 paras 39 ff; *Poulsen* (n 15) (nationality of ships).

[52] Case 42/74 *Van Duyn* [1974] ECR 1337 para 22.

[53] Case C- 364/10 *Hungary v Slovakia* ECLI:EU:C:2012:630 para 44.

[54] Joined Cases 3, 4 and 6-76 *Kramer* [1976] ECR 1279 paras 30–33; Joined Cases 89, 104, 114, 116, 117 and 125-129/85 *Ahlström* [1988] ECR 5193 para 18; Case C-366/10 *Air Transport Association of America* ('*ATAA*') ECLI:EU:C:2011:864 para 114 ff.

[55] Méndez speaks of a model of 'automatic incorporation'. See M Méndez, 'The Application of International Law by the Court of Justice of the European Union' in CA Bradley (ed), *The Oxford Handbook of Comparative Foreign Relations Law* (Oxford University Press, forthcoming). See further Wouters and van Eeckhoutte, 'Giving Effect to Customary International Law through European Community Law' in Prinssen and Schrauwen (n 20) 183; and T Konstadinides, 'When in Europe: Customary International Law and EU Competence in the Sphere of External Action' (2012) 13 *German Law Journal* 1177.

[56] This is in spite of the wording of what has become Art 351 TFEU, according to which: 'The rights and obligations arising from agreements concluded before 1 January 1958 … between one or more Member States on the one hand, and one or more third countries on the other, shall not be affected by the provisions of the Treaties. To the extent that such agreements are not compatible with the Treaties, the Member State or States concerned shall take all appropriate steps to eliminate the incompatibilities established …'.

[57] Joined Cases C-21-24/72 *International Fruit Company* [1972] ECR 1219. For elaboration and critique, see CD Ehlermann, 'Application of GATT Rules in the European Community' in M Hilf et al (eds), *The European Community and GATT* (Kluwer, 1986) 127; EU Petersmann, 'Application of GATT by the Court of Justice of the European Communities' (1983) 20 *Common Market Law Review* 397; and KJ Kuilwijk, *The European Court of Justice and the GATT Dilemma* (Nexed, 1996).

[58] Case 87/75 *Bresciani* [1976] ECR 129 para 16. For commentary, see S Riesenfeld, 'The Doctrine of Self-Executing Treaties and Community Law: A Pioneer Decision of the Court of Justice of the European Communities' (1973) 67 *American Journal of International Law* 504.

[59] *International Fruit Company* (n 57); and Case C-280/93 *Germany v Council* [1994] ECR I-4973 para 112. *cf Fediol* and *Nakajima*, allowing for very limited exceptions, whereby EU measures could be

and decisions of its dispute settlement body, once the GATT was replaced by the World Trade Organisation (WTO) – even if the Union itself acceded to the treaty.[60] This position was hence taken as a break from the Court's previously predominantly 'monist' perspective.[61]

Subsequent cases confirmed the rupture. *Intertanko* restrained the criteria for direct effect of international agreements, refusing the review of legality of a Directive which practically incorporated an – albeit for the EU not formally binding – international convention (MARPOL) into EU law, on the basis that there had not been 'functional succession' entailing a full transfer of powers from the Member States in the areas at stake.[62] It also denied the relevance of the UN Convention on the Law of the Sea (UNCLOS) – which the EU had ratified – invoking the 'nature and structure' as well as the 'broad logic' of the treaty. Hitherto, EU courts had only precluded reliance on such grounds solely with regard to the GATT/WTO Agreement.[63] Otherwise, where the relevant provision(s) were sufficiently clear, precise and unconditional – mirroring the criteria for direct effect of internal EU rules – international treaties concluded by the Union were deemed fit for purpose.[64] Yet, UNCLOS was said not to confer rights on individuals, but rather on vessels via their flag State. And that prevented its use for validity review. The Court painted a picture of a pure inter-state agreement, disconnected from the rights that individuals (more or less directly) derived therefrom.

The *ATAA* case then made the annulment of EU legislation on the basis of international customary law nearly impossible – at least for non-privileged applicants.

challenged for incompatibility with GATT rules, where the EU measure concerned referred expressly to specific GATT provisions, or where the EU intended to implement a precise GATT obligation. See Case 70/87 *Fediol* EU:C:1989:254; and Case C-69/89 *Nakajima* EU:C:1991:186. Yet, there has not been any application of the *Fediol* and *Nakajima* doctrines, with the *Petrotub* ruling being the only exception. See Case C-76/00 P *Petrotub* EU:C:2003:4 *cf* Méndez (n 55), positing the decision is rather an example of 'a particular species of consistent interpretation' rather than a direct application of the *Nakajima* test.

[60] Case C-149/96 *Portugal v Council* [1999] ECR I-08395; and Case C-377/02 *Van Parys* [2005] ECR I-01465. For commentary, see S Griller, 'Judicial Enforceability of WTO Law in the European Union: Annotation to case C-149/96 Portugal v. Council' (2000) 3 *Journal of International Economic Law* 441; and J Jackson, 'International Law Status of WTO DS Reports: Obligation to Comply or Option to "Buy-Out"?' (2004) 98 *American Journal of International Law* 109.

[61] P Eeckhout, 'The Domestic Legal Status of the WTO Agreement: Interconnecting Legal Systems' (1997) 34 *Common Market Law Review* 11, 28–29. See also G de Búrca, 'The European Court of Justice and the International Legal Order after Kadi' (2010) 52 *Harvard International Law Journal* 1, 44 ff; and Méndez (n 55).

[62] Case C-308/06 *Intertanko* [2008] ECR I-4057 paras 49–50. See also International Convention for the Prevention of Pollution from Ships 1340 *UNTS* 61 and 1341 *UNTS* 3 ('MARPOL Convention'); and UN Convention on the Law of the Sea 1833 *UNTS* 3 ('UNCLOS'). For a critique, see Eeckhout (n 1) 398–400.

[63] On the evolution of the Court's approach, see M Méndez, *The Legal Effects of EU Agreements* (Oxford University Press, 2013) and C Hillion and P Koutrakos (eds), *Mixed Agreements Revisited* (Hart Publishing, 2010).

[64] *cf* the more relaxed approach in *Biotech* and *IATA*, where the Court seems to do away with a rights-based analysis to establish the invocability of international treaty provisions for validity review of EU law. Case C-377/98 *Netherlands v Parliament and Council* (*Biotech*) EU:C:2001:523; and Case C-344/04 *IATA* EU:C:2006:10. See also Case C-213/03 *Pêcheurs de l'étang de Berre* [2004] ECR I-07357.

Thereafter, the conditions for individuals to fulfil require that 'first, *those principles* [of customary law] *are capable of calling into question the competence of the European Union to adopt that act*', beside that 'the act in question is liable to affect rights which the individual derives from European Union law ….'[65] The scope of review was, in addition, limited to establishing any '*manifest errors* of assessment concerning the conditions for applying those principles',[66] which further reduced any chances of success.

The *Kadi* saga, where the CJEU annulled a Regulation implementing a United Nations Security Council Resolution, because of its infringement of fundamental rights (*Kadi I*)[67] – a stance the Court confirmed, despite considerable, yet still insufficient, developments for the protection of due process guarantees at the UN level (*Kadi II*)[68] – consolidated the trend. The Court adopted a stark 'dualist' stance; not only vis-à-vis customary or conventional international law of a particular kind, whether directly effective or not, but on a more general basis, proclaiming the Union an 'internal and autonomous legal order'.[69] The move allowed Luxembourg to set aside international norms as irrelevant, to focus on the constitutionality assessment of the *EU* measure at hand as per the standards of *EU* law – others have praised the stance as one challenging the adequacy of the UN terrorist listing system; they consider that the upholds *international* human rights standards and contributes to their consolidation as universal values,[70] but even in this light such upholds is achieved through the medium of *EU* fundamental rights, ie by first 'Europeanising' *international* human rights.

These judgments show the CJEU's growing reluctance to ensuring compliance with international law *as such*,[71] from building bridges to raising a 'dualist' wall with international law,[72] in a bid to safeguard the Union's autonomy.[73] Autonomy, however, takes on a new meaning in this phase, based on pragmatic and teleological arguments on the proper functioning of the EU and the achievement of Treaty goals. The Court provides it with a normative anchor in fundamental constitutional tenets: 'the principles of liberty, democracy and respect for human rights', which allow no departure therefrom under any circumstances.[74] Autonomy is thus

[65] *ATAA* (n 54) para 107 (emphasis added).

[66] *ATAA* (n 54) para 110 (emphasis added). The ruling has also been criticised for further limiting the scope of the 'functional succession' doctrine. See eg J Wouters, J Odermatt, and T Ramopoulos, 'Worlds Apart? Comparing the Approaches of the European Court of Justice and the EU Legislature to International Law' in Cremona and Thies (n 19) 249.

[67] *Kadi I* (n 42).

[68] Joined Cases C-584/10 P, C-593/10 P and C-595/10 P *Commission and Others v Yassin Abdullah Kadi* ('*Kadi II*') ECLI:EU:C:2013:518.

[69] *Kadi I* (n 42) para 317.

[70] *cf* Eeckhout (n 1) 420–21.

[71] F Casolari, 'Giving Indirect Effect to International Law within the EU Legal Order: The Doctrine of Consistent Interpretation' in Cannizzaro, Palchetti and Wessel (n 1) 395.

[72] A Skordas, '*Völkerrechtsfreundlichkeit* as Comity and the Disquiet of Neoformalism: A Response to Jan Klabbers' in Koutrakos (n 6) 126.

[73] G de Búrca, 'The ECJ and the International Legal Order: A Re-Evaluation' in G de Búrca and JHH Weiler (eds), *The Worlds of European Constitutionalism* (Cambridge University Press, 2012) 108.

[74] *Kadi I* (n 42) para 303.

presented as the *consequence* of the (substantive) hierarchy of norms within the EU legal order;[75] it constitutes a (formal or procedural) 'means to an end' for the preservation of the (substantive) integrity of the most basic values of the system. In fact, *Kadi II* omits any reference to autonomy per se, deploying its 'dualist' logic exclusively from the perspective of the constitutional superiority of fundamental rights.[76]

Autonomy in the *Kadi* jurisprudence is preoccupied with the axiological 'foundation of the Union',[77] from where the legitimacy of the order derives. It constitutes its vehicle and not (yet) an end in itself. Autonomy serves to introduce the notion of a hierarchy *within* EU primary law, justifying limits to the possibility of according priority to (conflicting) international law as a result, so that '... obligations imposed by an international agreement cannot have the effect of prejudicing the constitutional principles of the [EU] Treaty, which include the principle that all [EU] acts must respect fundamental rights ...'.[78] *Kadi* thus installs a sort of 'principled dualism' grounded in a special breed of 'super-primary' constitutional norms conveying the values of the organisation.[79] As a result, while market freedoms (*qua* 'ordinary' primary law) may exceptionality be derogated from in accordance with today's Article 351 of the Treaty on the Functioning of the European Union (TFEU), 'any derogation from ... Article [2 TEU values]' is strictly forbidden.[80] No (extraneous) source of (international) law – be it the UN Charter or imperative Security Council Resolutions – can force an interpretation of EU law in contravention of fundamental rights.

Yet, as the next section reveals, the journey of autonomy did not terminate here. There is a further shift, from form to substance, which emptied the notion of its normative justification.

C. Opinion 2/13: The Autonomisation of Autonomy

The Charter of Fundamental Rights – which after Lisbon produces legally binding effects[81] – can be taken to give expression to the founding values of the organisation mentioned in *Kadi*, translating in concrete terms the generic allusion to

[75] Rather than the *cause* – in diametrical opposition to Opinion 2/13 (see next section below).

[76] *Kadi II* (n 68) para 66.

[77] *Kadi I* (n 42) para 303; see also paras 283 ff, 326 and 330.

[78] *Kadi I* (n 42) para 285.

[79] For a similar approach, shielding the more protective EU asylum rules from the influence of international humanitarian law (IHL) in situations regarding 'war refugees', see Case C-285/12 *Diakité* ECLI:EU:C:2014:39, drawing on Case C-465/07 *Elgafaji* [2009] ECR I-921. For analysis, see V Moreno-Lax, 'Systematising Systemic Integration: "War Refugees", Regime Relations and a Proposal for a Cumulative Approach to International Commitments' (2014) 12 *Journal of International Criminal Justice* 907; and V Moreno-Lax, 'Of Autonomy, Autarky, Purposiveness and Fragmentation: The Relationship between EU Asylum Law and International Humanitarian Law' in JF Durieux and D Cantor (eds), *Refuge from Inhumanity* (Brill, 2014) 295.

[80] *Kadi I* (n 42) para 303.

[81] Art 6(1) TEU. Charter of Fundamental Rights of the European Union [2010] OJ C83/02 ('CFR').

'human rights and fundamental freedoms' enclosed in Article 2 TEU. It actually 'reaffirms' and is, therefore, based on the shared constitutional traditions of the Member States and their *common* international obligations.[82] Its final goal is to *strengthen* the protection of human rights – 'Europeanised' qua *fundamental* rights – within the EU legal order.[83]

Post Lisbon, the Charter has become the primary reference point in cases involving fundamental rights disputes.[84] When the rights and freedoms recognised in the Charter are at stake, the instrument provides the reference framework for analysis, so that recourse to external sources (such as the European Convention on Human Rights (ECHR)[85]) is no longer the priority.[86] However, the Charter is not self-sufficient. It is *by design* embedded in international human rights law, from which it borrows substance and legitimacy. This is clear from the multiple references to other instruments in the Charter Explanations,[87] from the text of certain clauses,[88] from the way in which the horizontal provisions have been articulated,[89] and from its relationship to general principles.[90]

In Opinion 2/13, the Court, nonetheless, failed to acknowledge the organic interlocking of international human rights law and EU fundamental rights. Despite the structural permeability of EU law being constitutionally scheduled in Articles 6 TEU and 52 of the Charter of Fundamental Rights of the European Union (CFR), the CJEU omitted its recognition as one of the 'specific characteristics of the EU and EU law'[91] – by which the Court itself is presumably bound.[92]

[82] Recital 5, Preamble CFR.

[83] Recital 4, Preamble CFR (emphasis added).

[84] For a detailed review, see S Iglesias Sánchez, 'The Court and the Charter' (2012) 49 *Common Market Law Review* 1565.

[85] European Convention on Human Rights [1950] *ETS* 5 ('ECHR').

[86] Opinion of AG Cruz Villalón, Case C-70/10 *Scarlet* ECLI:EU:C:2011:255, delivered on 14 April 2011, para 30. For a critique of this approach, see G de Búrca, 'After the EU Charter of Fundamental Rights: The Court of Justice as a Human Rights Adjudicator?' (2013) 20 *Maastricht Journal of European and Comparative Law* 168.

[87] This includes the European Convention on Human Rights and Biomedicine [1997] *ETS* 164, as part of the normative grounding of Art 3 CFR, on the right to the integrity of the person; the International Covenant on Civil and Political Rights ('ICCPR') [1969] 999 *UNTS* 171, regarding Art 19 CFR, on the protection in the event of removal, expulsion or extradition, and Art 49 CFR, concerning the principles of legality and proportionality of criminal offences and penalties; and the International Convention on the Rights of the Child, [1989] 1577 *UNTS* 3, within the remit of Art 24 CFR, on the rights of the child. See Explanations Relating to the Charter of Fundamental Rights [2007] OJ C303/02, 18, 24, 25 and 30. Recall that, according to Art 52(7) CFR, the explanations provide 'guidance in the interpretation of this Charter' and thus '*shall* be given due regard by the courts of the Union and of the Member States' (emphasis added).

[88] See, eg, Art 18 CFR explicitly referring to the Convention on the Status of Refugees ('Geneva Convention') [1951] 189 *UNTS* 150.

[89] According to Art 52(3) CFR, in particular, '[i]n so far as this Charter contains rights which correspond to rights guaranteed by the [European] Convention for the Protection of Human Rights and Fundamental Freedoms, the meaning and scope of those rights *shall be the same* as those laid down by the said Convention' (emphasis added).

[90] *cf* Case C-64/16 *Associação Sindical dos Juízes Portugueses* ECLI:EU:C:2018:117 para 29 ff.

[91] Opinion 2/13 (n 23) para 174.

[92] Art 19(1) TEU: 'The Court of Justice … shall ensure that in the interpretation and application of the Treaties the law is observed'.

Instead, the Court invoked and distorted the role of 'autonomy', tipping the balance towards its most exclusionary form.[93] Although independence does not require autarky and isolation, this was perceived as the only way to discard the compatibility of the Draft Accession Agreement to the ECHR with EU law and maintain its exclusive jurisdiction to adjudicate upon it.

Accession was not to affect the Union's competences, nor was it to alter the constitutional architecture and especial features of EU law. Among these, the Court mentioned the 'structured network of principles, rules and mutually interdependent relations [engaging] the EU and its Member States … in a "process of creating an ever closer union among the peoples of Europe"'.[94] The integration project was considered 'the *raison d'être* of the EU itself';[95] its ultimate aim. The legal structure supporting that process of integration was, in turn, said to be 'based on the fundamental premise that each Member State shares with all other Member States … a set of common values on which the EU is founded' which 'implies and justifies the existence of mutual trust between the Member States that those values will be recognised and … that the law of the EU that implements them will be respected'.[96]

Fundamental rights do belong in that 'set of common values', but unlike the preeminent place accorded to them in *Kadi*, in Opinion 2/13 the Court sees them as subordinate to 'the structure and objectives of the EU'; they must be 'interpreted and applied within the EU in accordance with [its] constitutional framework'.[97] So, fundamental rights appear to descend from their super-primary law position to a plain ordinary-primary law rank. Rather than providing the EU regime with its underpinning axiological basis, providing substantive, value justification to the structure and objectives of the EU, there seems to be an evolution of fundamental rights becoming a sub-set of rules that remains constrained by the constitutional dynamics (and inertia) of the system.[98]

And the Court notes that within this set-up, the (newly found) 'principle' of mutual trust 'is of fundamental importance in EU law'. The Court ties in

[93] Ziegler speaks of 'aggressive formalistic constitutionalism' to characterise the stance. See KS Ziegler, 'Beyond Pluralism and Autonomy: Systematic Harmonization as a Paradigm for the Interaction of EU Law and International Law' (2016) 35 *Yearbook of European Law* 667, 668. *cf* P Eeckhout, 'Opinion 2/13 on EU Accession to the ECHR and Judicial Dialogue: Autonomy or Autarky?' (2015) 38 *Fordham International Law Journal* 955, 989 and 991–92, presenting it rather as a form of 'radical legal pluralism'.

[94] Opinion 2/13 (n 23) para 167.

[95] Opinion 2/13 (n 23) para 172.

[96] Opinion 2/13 (n 23) para 168.

[97] Opinion 2/13 (n 23) paras 169–70 and 177.

[98] The pro-autonomy interpretation it seems to imply constitutes the EU equivalent of the much criticised *in dubio mitius* approach under international law, maximising State sovereignty over the effectiveness of contracted obligations. For a critique, see Lauterpacht, 'Restrictive Interpretation and Effectiveness in the Interpretation of Treaties' (1949) 26 *British Yearbook of International Law* 48. See also A Orakhelashvili, *The Interpretation of Acts and Rules in Public International Law* (Oxford University Press, 2008) 414.

fundamental rights to compliance with that principle[99] – instead of the other way round – stating that it 'requires' Member States 'save in exceptional circumstances, to consider all the other Member States to be complying … with the fundamental rights recognised by EU law' – regardless of whether this is the case in practice or not. Indeed, the Court insists that, 'when implementing EU law, the Member States may … be required to *presume* that fundamental rights have been observed by the other Member States, so that … they may not check whether that other Member State has actually, *in a specific case*, observed the fundamental rights guaranteed by the EU'[100] – the compatibility of this reading with the principle of effective judicial protection gone unheeded.

This frontally contradicts findings by the Strasbourg Court in *MSS* and *Tarakhel*,[101] where the Strasbourg Court found that an effective remedy requires scrutiny of compliance with human rights protection by the receiving State *before* a person can be transferred or deported there, regardless of whether that State is a Party to the ECHR or, even, a Member State of the EU. The stance also disputes the key principle of effective judicial protection of individuals' rights under EU law, 'referred to in the second subparagraph of Article 19(1) TEU [and] stemming from the constitutional traditions common to the Member States … *enshrined in Articles 6 and 13 [ECHR]*, and which is *now reaffirmed by Article 47 of the Charter*'.[102]

The Luxembourg judges do acknowledge the conflict of this interpretation with ECHR standards. But they consider those (apparently higher) ECHR standards to be problematic, stating that

> in so far as the ECHR would … require a Member State to check that another Member State has observed fundamental rights, *even though EU law imposes an obligation of mutual trust between those Member States*, accession is liable to upset the underlying balance of the EU and undermine the autonomy of EU law.[103]

[99] This was seen to a lesser extent in Joined Cases C-411/10 and C-493/10 *NS & ME* ECLI:EU:C:2011:865; and in Case C-399/11 *Melloni* ECLI:EU:C:2013:107, where the Court balances both. For an appraisal, see Spreeuw, 'Do As I Say, Not As I Do: The Application of Mutual Recognition and Mutual Trust' (2012) 8 *Cambridge Yearbook of European Legal Studies* 505.

[100] Opinion 2/13 (n 23) paras 191–92 (emphasis added). *cf* Joined Cases C-404/15 and C-659/15 PPU *Aranyosi and Căldăraru* ECLI:EU:C:2016:198 paras 90–98, tempering the approach in the context of the European Arrest Warrant and requiring that there be an assessment in the specific case, stating, nonetheless, that 'a finding that there is a real risk of inhuman or degrading treatment by virtue of general conditions of detention in the issuing Member State cannot lead, in itself, to the refusal to execute a European arrest warrant' (para 91). In such situation, 'the execution of that warrant must be postponed but it cannot be abandoned' (para 98).

[101] ECtHR, *Tarakhel v Switzerland*, Application No 29217/12, 4 November 2014, paras 92–93. See also ECtHR, *MSS v Belgium and Greece*, Application No 30696/09, 21 January 2011.

[102] *Associação Sindical dos Juízes Portugueses* (n 90) para 35 (emphasis added). See also C-279/09 *DEB* ECLI:EU:C:2010:811 paras 29–33 (post-Lisbon); and C-432/05 *Unibet* ECLI:EU:C:2007:163 para 37 (pre-Lisbon).

[103] Opinion 2/13 (n 23) para 194 (emphasis added).

Yet, the issue is whether EU law may objectively impose an obligation of mutual trust that discounts fundamental rights, making them ineffective (and even un-invocable) in the particular case.

Autonomy here seems to be re-conceptualised by the Court as unhindered self-rule, when considering that

> the Member States have, by reason of their membership of the EU, accepted that relations between them as regards the matters covered by the transfer of powers … to the EU are governed by EU law *to the exclusion, if EU law so requires, of any other law.*[104]

The 'autonomy' of the EU legal order is, hence, asserted both 'in relation to the laws of the Member States and in relation to international law', including the ECHR.[105] But can EU law disconnect Member States *inter se* relations from international law en bloc,[106] in such a categorical and unqualified a way – without even reserving international rules a subsidiary role to play as mere fallback regime?[107]

In this particular instance, isolation requires the revisiting of the relationship between the Charter and the ECHR first. Not only is the Charter taken as the primary source of human rights within the EU legal order, but the ECHR appears relegated to the position of 'any other international agreement'.[108] The Court acknowledges that 'fundamental rights, as guaranteed by the ECHR, constitute general principles of the EU's law', but its 'particular significance', recognised in past jurisprudence,[109] is no longer mentioned in this context. Nor is the fact that the Charter and the Treaties, albeit not formally, effectively incorporate the substance of the Convention into EU law – via Article 6 TEU and Article 52(3) CFR.[110] On the contrary, the Court underlines that 'as the EU has not acceded to the ECHR, the latter does *not* constitute a legal instrument which has been formally incorporated into the legal order of the EU'.[111] The Court distances itself further from the ECHR, by suggesting that it would only be *after* accession that the ECHR, '*like any other* international agreement concluded by the EU', would 'form an integral part of EU law', citing the *ATAA* case to support the claim.[112] Curiously, the CJEU omits any reference to Article 52(3) of the Charter to articulate the relationship between it and the ECHR. It appeals instead to Article 53, but re-drafting its text,

[104] Opinion 2/13 (n 23) paras 193 and 212 (emphasis added).

[105] Opinion 2/13 (n 23) para 170.

[106] *cf* Eeckhout (n 93) 977, suggesting that disconnection clauses may be acceptable in certain policy domains, but it being inappropriate as a wholesale approach to the entirety of EU law.

[107] *cf* International Court of Justice (ICJ), *Jurisdictional immunities of the State (Germany v Italy: Greece Intervening)*, Application by Germany of 23 December 2008, para 6: 'Outside the specific framework [of the EU Treaties] … the [Member States] continue to live with one another under the regime of general international law'.

[108] Opinion 2/13 (n 23) para 180.

[109] Joined Cases 46/87 and 227/88 *Hoechst* [1989] ECR 2852 para 13.

[110] Eeckhout (n 93), 960 and 964. See also (n 89).

[111] Opinion 2/13 (n 23) para 179 (emphasis added).

[112] Opinion 2/13 (n 23) para 180 (emphasis added).

mentioning that 'nothing therein is to be interpreted as restricting or adversely affecting fundamental rights as recognised, in their respective fields of application, by EU law and international law' and, then, inserting a mention to the effect of '*including the ECHR*'.[113]

Relying on that provision, the Court seems to over-write the *lex specialis* in Article 52(3), which literally requires that, in case of matching rights, the ECHR provide the 'leading standard', as a minimum floor of protection, with the Charter potentially 'providing more extensive protection'. The Court reverses the relationship between Charter/ECHR in the name of the autonomy of EU law. When assessing the effect of Article 53 ECHR, allowing Contracting Parties to maintain or introduce a higher level of human rights protection within their domestic system than the one provided for in ECHR provisions, the Luxembourg Court posits that that power, as regards Contracting Parties that are also Member States of the EU, should be 'limited … to that which is necessary to ensure that the level of protection provided for by the Charter', so that the 'primacy, unity and effectiveness of EU law are not compromised'. Sidelining Article 52(3) CFR, the coordination between the two instruments is purported to affect the reading of 'the rights recognised by the Charter that correspond to those guaranteed by the ECHR'.[114]

What the Court ultimately achieves is the reversal of the means-ends relationship between fundamental rights and the primacy, unity and effectiveness of EU law. Autonomy, encapsulating *these* 'specific characteristics of the EU and EU law',[115] is emptied from the normative foundation that fundamental rights, as per the *Kadi* paradigm, could/should provide it with. In turn, fundamental rights are prevented from going too far, if that is perceived to impinge upon the primacy, unity and effectiveness (or 'autonomy' for short) of EU law. Drawing on what has been called a 'formalistic',[116] 'free-standing teleological interpretation',[117] autonomy is ultimately 'autonomised' by the Court to defend a (selective) set of 'special characteristics' of EU law, without identifying any particular reason or its justification – while 'respect for human rights' is an explicit founding value of the Union, nowhere is 'mutual trust' mentioned in the Treaties, let alone as core grounding of integration.[118] It becomes an abstract principle, flexible enough to

[113] Opinion 2/13 (n 23) para 187 (emphasis added).

[114] Opinion 2/13 (n 23) para 189. *cf Melloni* (n 99).

[115] Opinion 2/13 (n 23) para 174.

[116] Editorial, 'The EU's Accession to the ECHR – a "NO" from the ECJ!' (2015) 52 *Common Market Law Review* 1, 11.

[117] Ziegler (n 22).

[118] To the contrary, although the CJEU reiterates the crucial character of 'mutual trust' as the backbone principle of the Area of Freedom, Security and Justice, the truth is that, according to Art 67 TFEU, the establishment of the AFSJ 'shall' (ie must) be undertaken 'with respect for fundamental rights'. Concurring: Eeckhout (n 93) 970; and S Peers, 'The EU's Accession to the ECHR: The Dream Becomes a Nightmare' (2015) 16 *German Law Journal* 213. In this regard, see also S Douglas-Scott, 'The EU's Area of Freedom, Security and Justice: A Lack of Fundamental Rights, Mutual Trust and Democracy?' (2008–2009) 11 *Cambridge Yearbook of European Legal Studies* 53.

close off EU law at will, disallowing not only any external interference from international law into the EU legal order, but also denying subjection to the internal value-related constraints imposed by (EU) fundamental rights themselves.

Autonomy in Opinion 2/13 is 'objectivised', representing the 'sovereignitisation' of the Union and its legal order;[119] becoming a (substantive) principle of its own, but without any axiological anchor. The consequences of this abstraction have become all too visible in subsequent case law.

D. The Legacy of Non-accession to the ECHR: Venerating Autonomy as Such

One may think that Opinion 2/13 was peculiar to the specific, thorny question submitted to the Court, which would entail a complete redesign of the institutional and constitutional framework of the EU legal order, by opening the system to external scrutiny by a non-EU body, thus (potentially) challenging the autonomy of the regime and the ultimate authority of the CJEU within it – though the Member States did not appear to share such perception when inserting Article 6(2) TEU into the Lisbon Treaty. It was certainly plausible to expect that there would have been no reflection in subsequent case law of the re-configuration of the place and effect of fundamental rights within the system of sources of EU law. This, however, has not been the case. There has been a wave of decisions that consolidate the exclusionary trend.

After Opinion 2/13, a (hollow) suprematised 'autonomy' of EU law has become an *end* in and of itself, to be cherished and pursued for its own sake. It is no longer the procedural rule allowing EU law to perform its functions and achieve its aims; nor is it a mere empirical descriptor of the system, part of the legal tapestry of integration. Autonomy thereafter is directly based on a reciprocal belief in the *fiction* of compliance with common standards across Member State jurisdictions, regardless of *actual* observance of fundamental rights on the ground. The inadequacy of replacing *real* compliance with *erga omnes* obligations (creating individual rights), with an inter-State *presumption* designed to accelerate expulsions and deportations (regardless of those same rights) has been neglected by the Court. Instead, autonomy has been mobilised to prevent appeals to reality beyond that assumed by the EU *acquis* – as interpreted by the Court – with the principle of loyal cooperation forcing Member States into compliance.[120]

This version of mutual confidence, as defined in Opinion 2/13, is not only independent from effective realities, but also shapes and constrains the content and extent of fundamental rights, which can thenceforth only be interpreted and

[119] Assessing autonomy as a claim to sovereignty in disguise, see JWC van Rossem, 'The Autonomy of the EU: More is Less?' in Wessel and Blockmans (n 49) 13, 25–17.

[120] Art 4(3) TEU.

applied 'in accordance with the constitutional framework [of the EU]' and on account of its *sui generis* 'structure and objectives'.[121] The cart has been put before the horses. EU objectives are no longer subservient to, and achievable within the margins of, compliance with fundamental rights – as checks on the possible excesses of power. The reverse is now true. Fundamental rights have instead been put at the service of Treaty goals; taken down the apex of the hierarchy of EU sources and substituted with a canon of near-blind trust in Member State performance. Instead of providing a normative *basis*, they have become a *means* of integration like any other, a *tool* within the body of the *acquis*, subjected to the imperatives (and whims) of constitutionalisation. If taken to its logical exhaustion, the reasoning leads to the justification of a 'market bias' in the realisation of EU fundamental rights, mediated (and limited) by the notion of autonomy.[122]

Autonomy appears to have subsumed the 'new kind of legal order' of the EU in its entirety,[123] like an untold mystical source that translates the 'intrinsic nature' of the Union – as per the interpretation of its exclusive oracle, the Court – making the whole of EU law sacrosanct.[124] As symbolic shorthand for (a specific collection of) EU objectives and structures, it incarnates 'the process of integration that is the *raison d'être* of the EU itself',[125] and must *as such*, therefore, be revered and 'preserved'[126] – presumably even above and beyond the actual rights of the individuals for the benefit of whom integration is said to be enacted.[127] The main preoccupation is to protect (this elevated version of) 'the underlying balance of the EU' and offset any threats that may 'undermine the autonomy of EU law'.[128] Under this optic, fundamental rights are no longer the vehicle or inspiration of integration, but a potential obstacle to overcome when mutual trust and autonomy so demand.

Against this background, international human rights treaties – just as the ECHR in Opinion 2/13 – rather than recognised intrinsic value, as suppliers of general principles, Article 2 TEU foundations, or content-fillers of Charter entitlements, have been treated 'like any other international agreement'.[129] The approach to the Convention on the Rights of Persons with Disabilities,[130] which

[121] Opinion 2/13 (n 23) paras 177 and 170.

[122] Concurring: Ziegler (n 22) and D Kochenov, 'EU Law without the Rule of Law: Is the Veneration of Autonomy Worth It?' (2015) 34 *Yearbook of European Law* 74.

[123] Opinion 2/13 (n 23) paras 158 and 183.

[124] Opinion 2/13 (n 23) para 193. Concurring: Ziegler (n 22). This is not to deny that via Art 351 TFEU the Court has, at times, protected some Member State agreements vis-à-vis EU law. See eg J Klabbers, *The European Union in International Law* (Pedone, 2012) 60–67; *cf* P Koutrakos, *EU International Relations Law*, 2nd edn (Hart Publishing, 2015) 324–41. But the exception does not invalidate the rule.

[125] Opinion 2/13 (n 23) para 172.

[126] Opinion 2/13 (n 23) para 174.

[127] *Van Gend en Loos* (n 3) 12.

[128] Opinion 2/13 (n 23) para 194.

[129] Opinion 2/13 (n 23) para 180.

[130] Convention on the Rights of Persons with Disabilities ('CRPD') [2006] 2515 *UNTS* 3.

the Union has ratified, and to the Convention on the Status of Refugees,[131] directly incorporated in the body of the Treaties, offer particularly telling examples of this approach.[132]

The line of cases regarding the former, including *HK Danmark*[133] and *Glatzel*,[134] culminated on 18 March 2014 in *Z*, a Grand Chamber judgment treating the Convention as any other 'international agreement concluded by the European Union' (on whatever subject).[135] The reasoning was later repeated in *FOA*, delivered on the same date as Opinion 2/13.[136]

In *Z*, the Court concluded that, since ratification by the EU, the Disability Convention must be considered to have become 'an integral part of the European Union legal order' and, therefore, 'capable of being relied on for the purposes of *interpreting* Directive 2000/78 [on equal treatment in employment]', especially for the purposes of defining the concept of 'disability' contained therein – which is not defined in EU law.[137] The interpretative function of the Convention is thus accepted. But, when it comes to establishing whether the Convention can be relied upon to challenge the *validity* of the Directive, rather than 'Europeanising' the international disability rights it enshrines as part of the EU fundamental rights *acquis* (through the medium of Charter provisions, the general principles doctrine, or via direct application), the Court assimilates the instrument to the general category of international agreements and, rather than embracing the 'direct absorption' or embeddedness approach seen in past case law in relation to other international human rights norms, it relies on the *Intertanko* and *ATAA* criteria to establish whether it may produce direct effect.

Surprisingly, the conclusion reached by the Court is that the provisions of the Convention – in spite of the instrument explicitly seeking to 'promote, protect and ensure the full and equal enjoyment of all human rights and fundamental freedoms by all persons with disabilities, and to promote respect for their inherent dignity',[138] that is, aiming at the creation of an individual right to equality,

[131] Geneva Convention (n 88).

[132] A similar approach has been followed in relation to the Aarhus Convention on Access to Information, Public Participation in Decision-Making and Access to Justice in Environmental Matters [1998] 2161 *UNTS* 447, and investment treaties to which the EU is party, reaffirming (either explicitly or *de facto*) the autonomy of EU law against individual rights clauses therein. See Joined Cases 401/12 and 403/12 P *Vereniging Milieudefensie* ECLI:EU:C:2015:4; Joined Cases C-404/12 P and C-405 P *Natuur en Milieu* ECLI:EU:C:2015:5 and Case C-284/16 *Achmea* ECLI:EU:C:2018:158. For critical accounts see, respectively, S Gáspár-Szilágyi, 'The Relationship between EU Law and International Agreements: Restricting the Application of the Fediol and Nakajima Exceptions in *Vereniging Milieudefensie*' (2015) 52 *Common Market Law Review* 1059 and A Dimopoulos, '*Achmea*: The Principle of Autonomy and its Implications for Intra and Extra-EU BITs' (*EJILTalk!*, 27 March 2018) www.ejiltalk.org/author/adimopoulos/.

[133] Joined Cases C-335/11 and C-337/11 *HK Danmark* ECLI:EU:C:2013:222.

[134] C-356/12 *Glatzel* ECLI:EU:C:2014:350.

[135] Case C-363/12 *Z* ECLI:EU:C:2014:159 para 72.

[136] Case C-354/13 *FOA* ECLI:EU:C:2014:2463.

[137] *Z* (n 135) paras 73, 75 and 76 (emphasis added).

[138] Art 1 CRPD.

entailing the obligation to remove any obstacles thereto – 'are not, as regards their content … unconditional and sufficiently precise within the meaning of [*Intertanko* and *ATAA*]' to produce direct effect. Therefore, 'the validity of Directive 2000/78 [on equal treatment in employment] cannot be assessed in the light of the Convention'.[139]

There is no article-by-article assessment or any detailed analysis of the concrete content of the Convention to buttress this finding. The only support the Court adduces to sustain its claim is that, 'in so far as the obligations imposed by that Convention are addressed to Contracting Parties', in the sense that it is Contracting Parties that bear the responsibility of adopting 'all appropriate … measures for the implementation of the rights recognised in that Convention' – as it happens with essentially every Treaty, since individuals have no treaty-making powers of their own under international law and no independent capacity to implement international commitments – the international agreement shall be considered 'programmatic'.[140] The *non sequitur* nature of this logic is ignored by the Court.[141] It is not that an international instrument be concluded and addressed to States (and the Union, in this case) as Contracting Parties that renders it programmatic. And what 'programmatic' actually means remains equally obscure. The Court relies on the general implementation clause of the Convention, in Article 4(1)(a) thereof, to deny invocability. Should the specification that 'States Parties [are subject to] adopt all appropriate legislative, administrative and other measures for the implementation of the rights recognised in the … Convention' have been absent from the text, the Court would have been at pains to sustain its reasoning. The specification does no more than translate the general *pacta sunt servanda* principle to the Convention's terrain, according to which 'every treaty in force [programmatic or not] is binding upon the parties to it [including the Union and *all* its institutions] and *must be performed by them* in good faith'[142] – including through the means expressly enumerated in Article 4(1)(a). In a sense, all international commitments – including those considered to be self-executing and/or conferring individual (human) rights – require practical observance and a form of real implementation on the ground to be effective. So, if taken to its ultimate conclusion, reliance on this point would virtually amount to a wholesale denial of invocability of *all* international law due to its 'programmatic' nature.[143]

[139] *Z* (n 135) para 90.

[140] *Z* (n 135) para 88.

[141] *cf* the very deferential approach of the CJEU towards privileged applicants under Art 263 TFEU, allowing them to rely on the Convention for Biological Diversity (presumably equally programmatic in substance) to review the legality of secondary law, even if the agreement was said not to produce direct effect, for it did not create subjective rights on private parties, in the *Biotech* case (n 64).

[142] Art 26 VCLT. Regarding the applicability of the *pacta sunt servanda* maxim to international organisations, the ICJ has famously held that, as subjects of international law, they 'are bound by any obligations incumbent upon them under general rules of international law, under their constitutions, or under any international agreements to which they are parties'. See *Interpretation of the Agreement of 25 March 1951 between the WHO and Egypt* (Advisory Opinion) [1980] ICJ Rep 73, 89–90.

[143] The absurdity of this position is illustrated by the Aarhus Convention litigation (n 132), wherein the CJEU rejects that Art 9(3), enshrining an access to justice provision within the Convention,

The same dismissive approach towards international human rights law treaties has been adopted vis-à-vis the 1951 Refugee Convention in the inadmissibility decision of the *Qurbani* case, prolonging the shift of Opinion 2/13.[144]

Up to *Qurbani*, the 1951 Refugee Convention had been considered an example of the 'integration/embeddedness approach' to human rights.[145] The instrument is mentioned in a Treaty provision, Article 78 TFEU, requiring the Union to adopt a common asylum policy 'ensuring compliance with the principle of *non-refoulement*' and in full 'accordance with the [1951] Geneva Convention'. The Convention has thus been described as a 'direct standard of decision',[146] compliance with which is required *as a matter of EU law*.[147] This has meant that, in interpreting the common asylum *acquis* and in establishing its legality, the CJEU has taken the Refugee Convention as a main reference point and as a direct source of EU fundamental rights, mandating the Union and the Member States, when acting within the scope of EU law, to make sure 'the right to asylum [is] guaranteed with due respect for the rules of the Geneva Convention'.[148] The Convention acts as a minimum floor of protection in refugee matters – akin to the function assumed by the ECHR within EU law at large under Article 52(3) CFR. The instrument has indeed been acknowledged to constitute 'the cornerstone of the international legal regime for the protection of refugees', to which *all* preambles of *all* legislative acts adopted by the Union in the field of asylum law explicitly refer.[149] What is more, legislation forming the Common European Asylum System

be sufficiently clear and unconditional to produce direct effect and substantiate the review of EU action. Further on the collision course the Court has placed the EU in relation to its international obligations, as interpreted by the Aarhus Convention Compliance Committee, see Méndez (n 55).

[144] Case C-481/13 *Qurbani* ECLI:EU:C:2014:2101.

[145] P Eeckhout, 'Human Rights and the Autonomy of EU Law: Pluralism or Integration?' (2013) 66 *Current Legal Problems* 169 (see further below).

[146] H Battjes, *European Asylum Law and International Law* (Martinus Nijhoff, 2006) 101.

[147] For a full theorisation, see V Moreno-Lax, *Accessing Asylum in Europe* (Oxford University Press, 2017) Ch 7.

[148] Art 18 CFR. In this connection, the CJEU has established, in *Abdulla*, that '[u]nder Article 13 of the [Qualification] Directive, the Member State is *required to grant* refugee status to the applicant if he qualifies …' (emphasis added). See Joined Cases C-175, 176, 178 and 179/08 *Abdulla* [2010] ECR I-1493 para 62. The same applies, as per *M'Bodj*, with regard to Art 18 of the Qualification Directive (n 149), according to which 'Member States *are to grant* that status to a third country national eligible for subsidiary protection' (emphasis added). See Case C-542/13 *M'Bodj* ECLI:EU:C:2014:2452 para 29.

[149] See Common Recital 3 of Directive 2011/95/EU of the European Parliament and of the Council of 13 December 2011 on standards for the qualification of third-country nationals or stateless persons as beneficiaries of international protection, for a uniform status for refugees or for persons eligible for subsidiary protection, and for the content of the protection granted [2011] OJ L337/9 ('Qualification Directive'); Directive 2013/32/EU of the European Parliament and of the Council of 26 June 2013 on common procedures for granting and withdrawing international protection [2013] OJ L180/60 ('Asylum Procedures Directive'); Directive 2013/33/EU of the European Parliament and of the Council of 26 June 2013 laying down standards for the reception of applicants for international protection [2013] OJ L180/96 ('Reception Conditions Directive'); and Regulation (EU) No 604/2013 of the European Parliament and of the Council of 26 June 2013 establishing the criteria and mechanisms for determining the Member State responsible for examining an application for international protection lodged in one of the Member States by a third-country national or a stateless person [2013] OJ L180/31 ('Dublin III Regulation').

(CEAS), especially the Qualification Directive,[150] is deemed to have been 'adopted to guide the competent authorities … in the application of that Convention', for which reason, the Directive 'must … be interpreted in the light of its general scheme and purpose, *while respecting the [Refugee] Convention* …'[151] – a caveat absent from case law regarding other international treaties. So, up until *Qurbani*, the 1951 Convention was the ECHR equivalent (prior to Opinion 2/3) within the EU asylum system.

But just like Opinion 2/13 upsets the standing of the ECHR within the EU legal order, so does *Qurbani* in relation to the asylum *acquis*. The decision revisits the entire set-up and turns it upside down, assimilating the Refugee Convention to the 'normal' range of 'international agreements', which, if 'concluded' by the EU, would 'form an integral part of its legal order'.[152] Because this is not the case – and due to the inadequate way in which the questions from the referring court had been worded, omitting any clear connection between Article 31 of the Convention, on the non-penalisation of refugees for their illegal entry into a country of asylum, and the EU rules on the admissibility of applications and border procedures – the Court declares to lack jurisdiction to interpret the Convention *as such*. The power of the CJEU 'extends only to rules which are part of EU law', the Court rightly asserts.[153]

This is in spite of past jurisprudence and other key factors acknowledged by the Court itself – including many of the above: that several pieces of EU legislation have been adopted in the field to which the Convention applies,[154] that Article 78 TFEU provides that the common policy on asylum must be in accordance with the Convention,[155] and that Article 18 of the Charter makes clear that the right to asylum is to be guaranteed with due respect for the Convention.[156] The wider links to the Schengen *acquis*, establishing the rules applicable to admission in the Schengen area (as well as the relevant asylum-based exceptions),[157] the Dublin implications of such *non liquet* conclusion,[158] and the possible influence of, and on, the Returns Directive,[159] are all disregarded.

[150] Qualification Directive (n 149). For analysis, see S Peers, V Moreno-Lax, M Garlick, and E Guild, *EU Immigration and Asylum Law*, 2nd edn (Brill, 2015) Vol 3, 65.

[151] See, eg, *Abdulla* (n 148) paras 51–53; Case C-31/09 *Bolbol* [2010] ECR I-5539 paras 36–38 and Joined Cases C-57 and 101/09 *B and D* [2010] ECR I- 979 paras 76–78 (emphasis added).

[152] *Qurbani* (n 144) para 22.

[153] *Qurbani* (n 144) para 21.

[154] *Qurbani* (n 144) para 24.

[155] *Qurbani* (n 144) para 25.

[156] *Qurbani* (n 144) para 25.

[157] Referring especially to Arts 3(b), 4, and 14(1), Union Code on the rules governing the movement of persons across borders (Schengen Borders Code) [2016] OJ L77/1. For a thorough account, see Moreno-Lax (n 147) Part II.

[158] Dublin III Regulation (n 149).

[159] Directive 2008/115/EC of the European Parliament and of the Council of 16 December 2008 on common standards and procedures in Member States for returning illegally staying third-country nationals [2008] OJ L348/98 ('Returns Directive').

The Court adopts a very formalistic approach to disclaim jurisdiction. It is bizarre how it discounts the importance of Article 14(6) of the Qualification Directive, which expressly refers to Article 31 of the Geneva Convention – as the Court itself notes.[160] The need to ensure the effectiveness and uniformity in the interpretation and application of EU asylum law are not enough to convince the judges,[161] notwithstanding the diametrically opposed position they adopted in analogous judgments. As the Court acknowledges, in *Bolbol* and *El Kott*,[162] on Palestinian refugees, Luxembourg 'did indeed accept that it had jurisdiction to interpret the provisions of the Geneva Convention to which EU law made a *renvoi*'.[163]

Accepting that matters of formulation may rightly lead to a request for a preliminary ruling to be rejected, what is most worrisome is not the rejection per se, but the reasoning the CJEU (unnecessarily) deploys to substantiate its dismissal – as if preparing the ground for Opinion 2/13 and its aftermath – undermining the rank and significance of the Refugee Convention within the CEAS.

Qurbani could have been an unfortunate one-off case. Yet, its effects continue to be felt today. On the same day as Opinion 2/13, the Grand Chamber adopted two controversial decisions in defiance of international standards, isolating the CEAS, and lowering the level of EU asylum protection with regard to two seriously ill subsidiary protection claimants.[164] And in February 2015, in *Shepherd*, the Court unduly narrowed down the scope of the definition of 'persecution', relying on a purely self-referential (and purportedly *contra legem*) interpretation of Article 9 of the Qualification Directive, in disregard of global trends and UNHCR materials on refugee status of conscientious objectors opposing military service.[165] The self-referential, close-circuit approach to the interpretation of CEAS instruments that the Court has continued to pursue thereafter, relying pre-eminently on (a very textual reading of) secondary law, bear witness to the long-lasting legacy of Opinion 2/13.[166]

III. Internal, External and Axiological Autonomy: Rule of Law-less Emancipation

Before Lisbon and Opinion 2/13, 'substantive borrowing' was the technique of penetration of international human rights law into EU law preferred by the

[160] *Qurbani* (n 144) para 27.
[161] *Qurbani* (n 144) para 26.
[162] Case C-31/09 *Bolbol* ECLI:EU:C:2010:351 and Case C-364/11 *El Kott* ECLI:EU:C:2012:826.
[163] *Qurbani* (n 144) para 28.
[164] *M'Bodj* (n 148) and Case C-562/13 *Abdida* ECLI:EU:C:2014:2453.
[165] Case C-472/13 *Shepherd* ECLI:EU:C:2015:117.
[166] See further, V Moreno-Lax, 'Paradise Lost – From *Elgafaji* to *Qurbani*: Towards the Hyper-Autonomy of the Common European Asylum System?' (in progress).

Court. The method was also employed, for instance, as regards norms of general international law on matters not regulated by (and arguably laying beyond the scope of) EU law, eg rules on the delimitation of State jurisdiction.[167] These were adopted and applied quasi-automatically – sometimes *qua* general principles of EU law[168] – without the Court analysing whether direct or indirect effect was possible or appropriate. At that point, (international/constitutional) human rights were 'Europeanised' as 'fundamental rights' and internalised or 'embedded' in the rest of the EU legal framework.[169]

Up to the adoption of the Charter, the EU lacked its own catalogue of rights. Instead, the CJEU 'transformed' international (and Member State constitutional) standards into internal EU law, borrowing from instruments, which were not formally binding on the Union. It was in *Internationale Handelsgesellschaft* where it was first established that 'respect for fundamental rights [as such and without further caveats] forms *an integral part* of the general principles of [EU] law protected by the Court of Justice', not necessitating an official act of incorporation.[170] And, as general principles, unlike treaty law or international custom, fundamental rights were raised to the (highest) category of primary law. This was subsequently codified in Article 6(3) TEU and elevated to the status of 'founding values' of the Union in Article 2 TEU.

'[I]nternational treaties for the protection of human rights on which the Member States have collaborated or of which they are signatories' were considered key sources of 'inspiration' from which general principles were drawn. In particular, they supplied 'guidelines which should be followed within the framework of [EU] law'.[171] Again, although not formally binding on the Union, the ECHR was recognised to bear 'particular significance' in this context.[172] But there are other examples: the Universal Declaration of Human Rights,[173] the International Covenant on Civil and Political Rights,[174] as well as the International Covenant on Economic, Social and Cultural Rights,[175] among other instruments, were also taken into account.

[167] *Kramer* (n 54) paras 30–33; *Ahlström* (n 54) para 18; *ATAA* (n 54) para 114 ff.

[168] See, for instance, *Racke* (n 15) para 49 (*pacta sunt servanda*). See also Joint Cases C-120/06 P and C-121/06 P *FIAMM and Fedon* [2008] ECR I-6513 para 92 and Joined Cases C-20/01 and C-28/01 *Commission v Germany* [2003] ECR I-3609 para 24.

[169] Eeckhout (n 145).

[170] Case 11/70 *Internationale Handelsgesellschaft* [1970] ECR 1125 para 4 (emphasis added).

[171] Case 4/73 *Nold* [1974] ECR 491 para 13.

[172] *Hoechst* (n 109) para 13; Case C-260/89 *ERT* [1991] ECR I-2925 para 41; Case C-299/95 *Kremzow* [1997] ECR I-2629 para 14; Case C-274/99 P *Connolly* [2001] ECR I-1611 para 37; Case C-94/00 *Roquette Frères* [2002] ECR I-9011 para 25.

[173] Case C-135/08 *Rottmann* [2010] ECR I-1449 para 53, referring to the Universal Declaration on Human Rights, UNGA Res 217A (III), UN Doc A/810, 71 (1948).

[174] Case C-244/06 *Dynamic Medien* [2008] ECR I-505 para 39 ff; Case C-540/03 *Parliament v Council* [2006] ECR I-5769 para 37, referring to the ICCPR (n 87).

[175] Case C-73/08 *Bressol* [2010] ECR I-2735 para 85 ff, referring to the International Covenant on Economic Social and Cultural Rights [1969] 993 *UNTS* 3.

Fundamental rights *qua* general principles were set to fulfil a dual function, providing a means of interpretation and a standard of validity and review of EU rules.[176] One could argue that these were (and are), *prima facie*, the same functions (potentially) performed by other international law sources. The difference, though, is that human rights are first internalised and operate from within, *as a matter of EU law*. Any incompatibility of an act of the Union with human/fundamental rights becomes thus one of internal inconsistency with the own constitutional values of the organisation.

Nevertheless, since the entry into force of the Charter, the relationship with international human rights law instruments has progressively been rarefied. Notwithstanding the 'bridges' to the ECHR in Article 52(3) CFR and to other relevant treaties in Article 53 CFR,[177] the 'internal' catalogue of EU fundamental rights has displaced the 'external' listings enshrined in parallel international human rights covenants, with the Court fostering a solipsistic reading of Charter rights – especially after Opinion 2/13, as elaborated above. Yet, there is no good reason for such a stance. The substance of Charter rights, as already stated, originates in common human rights obligations of the Member States, stemming from the shared constitutional traditions and joint international commitments the Charter 'reaffirms',[178] and which *continue* to penetrate the EU legal order as both general principles and founding values of the organisation, even after the CFR codification.[179]

This is why the Opinion 2/13 paradigm can only be understood to represent an unwarranted emancipation of the EU legal order not only from external referents of human rights protection, but also from its own internal fundamental rights core. The form of *a*-axiological autonomy it propounds has drained the Union system of the substantive stratum pertaining to the Rule of Law.[180] Kochenov explains this well.[181] He enlists the *jurisdictio-gubernaculum* binomial to designate the two main components of the principle. While *gubernaculum* represents the *legality* of the *acquis* of rules made in accordance with pre-established legal procedures, *jurisdictio* denotes 'the law above the law' to which the rulers are

[176] Opinion 2/94 [1996] ECR I-1759 para 34.

[177] See, eg, K Lenaerts, 'Exploring the Limits of the EU Charter of Fundamental Rights' (2012) 8 *European Competition Law Review* 375, 394, conceiving of Art 53 CFR as a 'stand-still' clause, precluding regressive interpretations of Charter rights in light of developments occurring in international (and constitutional) law. *cf Melloni* (n 99).

[178] Recital 5, CFR Preamble.

[179] Art 6(3) TEU and Art 2 TEU. On this co-existence of the Charter with general principles, see, eg, Case C-144/04 *Mangold* [2005] ECR I-9981 (pre-Lisbon); Case C-555/07 *Kücükdeveci* [2010] ECR I-365 (post-Lisbon) and *Associação Sindical dos Juízes Portugueses* (n 90) (post-Opinion 2/13).

[180] Generally, on the rule of law function of human rights, see L Lixinski, 'Taming the Fragmentation Monster through Human Rights? International Constitutionalism, "Pluralism Lite" and the Common Territory of the Two European Legal Orders' in V Kosta, N Skoutaris, and VP Tzevelekos (eds), *The EU Accession to the ECHR* (Hart, 2014) 231. See also E Voyakis, 'International Law and the Objectivity of Value' (2009) 22 *Leiden Journal of International Law* 51.

[181] Kochenov (n 122).

subject (and that 'made them king'[182]). It is the compendium of value-related standards from which legality derives its *legitimacy* – the 'spiritual heart', in Allott's words, of the legal system; inimical to the untrammelled exercise of power.[183] The two elements taken together encapsulate the duality of the law at the centre of the Rule of Law ideal.[184]

The neglect of *jurisdictio*, through a notion of autonomy that embraces only the legality component, constitutes an impoverished vision of the Rule of Law. It confounds the Rule of Law with the mere lawfulness of rules, whatever their axiological justification – it takes over the ideal of Justice inscribed in the Rule of Law absorbing its normativity away.[185] What is more, in Opinion 2/13 the idea of *jurisdictio* reining in *gubernaculum* is simply not tolerated.[186] In fact, the *EU* Rule of Law it profiles has been reduced to mean that *gubernaculum* (or 'autonomy') reigns supreme. Hailing legality over legitimacy in this way pre-empts any *jurisdictio*-based questioning from within, making any challenge of the *acquis* well-nigh impossible. Apparently, this (autopoietic version postulated by the Court of the *EU*) Rule of Law is precisely mobilised to deactivate contestation.[187]

Yet, authority – including that of the Court – should remain bound by *jurisdictio* outside its own control – in order to prevent miscarriages of justice.[188] No system governed by the Rule of Law can free itself from human (or fundamental) rights as ultimate demarcation between the legitimate use and abuse of power.[189] The opposite makes the autonomous system of the EU emerge as a formally coherent legal order, bound by nothing else than the day-to-day norms of its own creation, with no higher aspiration beyond being shielded from external influence. To achieve this aim, *human* rights are first abstractly exscinded from their *fundamental* rights counterparts and then externalised – made into exogenous rules outside the internal legal order and rejected as extraneous means of validation.

[182] M Krygier, 'Inside the Rule of Law' (2014) 3 *Rivista di filosofia del diritto* 77, 84.

[183] P Allott, 'The European Community is not the True European Community' (1991) 100 *Yale Law Journal* 2485, 2499.

[184] G Palombella, 'The Rule of Law as an Institutional Ideal' in L Morlino and G Palombella (eds), *Rule of Law and Democracy* (Brill, 2010) 3. See also G Palombella, 'The Rule of Law at its Core' in G Palombella and N Walker (eds), *Relocating the Rule of Law* (Hart Publishing, 2009) 17 and G Palombella, 'Beyond Legality – before Democracy: Rule of Law Caveats in the EU Two-level System' in L Closa and D Kochenov (eds), *Reinforcing Rule of Law Oversight in the European Union* (Cambridge University Press, 2016) 36.

[185] L Fuller, *The Morality of Law* rev edn (Yale University Press, 1969). See also J Raz, *The Authority of Law: Essays on Law and Morality* (Clarendon Press, 1979) and RH Fallon, 'Rule of Law as a Concept in Constitutional Discourse' (1997) 97 *Columbia Law Review* 1.

[186] Kochenov (n 122) 94.

[187] Kochenov (n 122) 95.

[188] Art 2 TEU. See also S Douglas-Scott, 'Justice, Injustice and the Rule of Law in the EU' in D Kochenov, G de Búrca, and A Williams (eds), *Europe Justice's Deficit* (Hart Publishing, 2015) 51.

[189] M Adams, A Meuwese and EH Ballin (eds), *Constitutionalism and the Rule of Law* (Cambridge University Press, 2017). *cf* A Williams, *The Ethos of Europe* (Cambridge University Press, 2010).

The idea of autonomy the CJEU embraces is a remarkably reductionist notion, exclusively focused on negative protections from external (and externalised) restraint. It views it as pure self-determinism and unmolested self-action, suggesting the Union legal order should be considered autonomous 'for its own sake'. The Court fails to acknowledge the fallacy of complete independence – especially in an 'ever closer Union' precisely based on 'the *universal* values of the inviolable and inalienable rights of the human person, freedom, democracy, equality and the rule of law'.[190] A self-determined choice to cooperate with others or to comply with outside standards that become internalised within the system does not amount to non-autonomy.

Autonomy does not need to involve splendid isolation by treating self-determinism as an entirely internal self-referential process. It may actually involve a reduction of independence or a decision to become dependent in certain situations. Autonomy is relational – predicated vis-à-vis *another* system, rule or entity. Co-legislation and co-validation through shared ideals, if freely self-imposed, constitutes as much an expression of autonomous will as the embracement of the purest form of autarky.

Willkür – in the Kantian sense – provides an escape from zero-sum games and a perception of autonomy in absolutising 'either/or' terms, refocusing attention on issues of legitimacy and the expression of common values reflective of mutual public reason. Autonomy in this light is not limited to its negative dimension, as solely meaning 'free from' dependence and 'exclusive of' external influence. It rather connotes a *volonté distincte*; a form of self-determinism, ensuring the capacity for autonomous choice in a system of joint production of rules and values. The ensuing normative principles of Dignity, Justice and intrinsic human worth are thereby co-generated as 'autonomous' standards, imposing common (external/internalised) constraints that are universally valid and restrict the freedom of everyone within the system (both the rulers and the ruled).[191] Those standards provide the *jurisdictio*, the moral justification, to the *gubernaculum* originating in institutional conduct – whether of the Court or somebody else.

IV. Conclusion: 'Like Ships in the Night'

The construal of autonomy *qua* autarky as a matter of course, as Luxembourg does in Opinion 2/13 and its sequels, is not tenable. There is no *a priori* determinism of what autonomy entails. And this is exemplified by the very evolution of the term in the Court's own case law that the foregoing sections have analysed – first, (implicitly) taking autonomy as a functional consequence of the Union being

[190] Recitals 2 and 13, Preamble TEU (emphasis added).

[191] For further analysis and references, see GW Brown, 'The Idea of Autonomy' in Collins and White (n 45) 104.

constituted as an (independent) actor of international law; then, as a mechanism of emancipation from the Member States and as a tool to claim primacy and direct effect within their legal systems; later still, as a vehicle of constitutionalisation vis-à-vis international law (to preserve fundamental rights); to finally become detached from the EU founding values (to protect the entire legal order, and particularly the CJEU's jurisdiction within it, from any possible interference).

Autonomy should simply be the 'door' to the external world – the line of communication between orders, rules and values. Whether the door is then kept open or closed is a different issue. There is no necessary implication for autonomy to mean isolation. Reading into autonomy a predetermined substantive choice of insularity is not warranted. The decision is not fixed by autonomy itself. The notion does not automatically demand that 'the [EU] legal order and the international legal order pass by each other like ships in the night'.[192] Internationalism and constitutionalisation are not mutually exclusive by definition, especially when it comes to human/fundamental rights.[193]

The decision to open or close the system can well be based on *gubernaculum* alone. But then the system as a whole requires *jurisdictio* to keep the power behind such decision in check and for compliance with its ultimate source of validation. External/internalised constraints are an essential feature of governance by law.[194]

The conversion of EU law into an autonomous island risks becoming self-destructive. Therein the Rule of Law becomes contingent and human/fundamental rights relative and alienable; left at the mercy of the naked authority of the Luxembourg Court.[195] The CJEU judges should, therefore, revisit their approach – the principle of loyalty (or 'mutual trust') applies to them too, enjoining them to engage in 'sincere cooperation' to assist the Union and its legal order 'in carrying out tasks which flow from the Treaties'.[196] The Treaties' choice to embed (universal) rights into EU law binds the Court and must inform its (re-)interpretation.[197] Autonomy *qua* axiological emancipation from the very values of a 'community based on the rule of law'[198] is unsustainable. It amounts to denying 'the ultimate purpose of all law'.[199]

[192] Opinion of AG Maduro in Joined cases C-402/05 P and C-415/05 P *Kadi* ECLI:EU:C:2008:11, delivered on 16 January 2008, para 22.

[193] Concurring: Ziegler (n 22).

[194] HE Allison, *Kant's Theory of Freedom* (Cambridge University Press, 1990) 103. See also G Postema, 'Law's Autonomy and Public Practical Reason' in RP George (ed), *The Autonomy of Law* (Oxford University Press, 1996) 79 and P Capps, 'Autonomy in Kant's Philosophy of International Law' in Collins and White (n 45) 48.

[195] Eeckhout (n 93) 992.

[196] Art 4(3) TEU. See also Art 13(2) TEU.

[197] *cf* On the especial rank of human rights in international law, see S Gardbaum, 'Human Rights as International Constitutional Rights' (2008) 19 *European Journal of International Law* 749; ID Seiderman, *Hierarchy in International Law: The Human Rights Dimension* (Intersentia, 2001) and MT Kamminga and M Scheinin (eds), *The Impact of Human Rights Law on General International Law* (Oxford University Press, 2009).

[198] *Les Verts* (n 33) para 23.

[199] H Lauterpacht, *International Law: Collected Papers* (Cambridge University Press, 1975) Vol 2, 47.

3

Studying International and European Law: Confronting Perspectives and Combining Interests

RAMSES A WESSEL

I. Introduction

European law is international law, albeit perhaps a special branch in which, in particular, the link with domestic legal systems is further developed and the states have shown more willingness to transfer some of their competences to an international organisation. The fact that European law does not exist in isolation, but is very well connected to other areas and levels of international law has become more apparent over the years. Part of the reason is to be found in the development of the European Union's so-called external relations, that is: the relations it has with non-EU member states and other international organisations. This development, which became even clearer with the focus of the 2009 Lisbon Treaty on the role of the EU as a global actor,[1] underlines two dimensions of the interface between international and European law.

The first one is the effect of international law on the EU legal order. While the idea of the 'autonomy' of the EU legal order is still seen as a cornerstone for its functioning[2] – perhaps in particular where the application and interpretation of EU law is concerned[3] – many studies focussed on the ways in which international

[1] See for instance the various contributions to B Van Vooren, S Blockmans and J Wouters (eds), *The EU's Role in Global Governance: The Legal Dimension* (Oxford, Oxford University Press, 2013); as well as, in particular, Arts 3(5), 21 and 22 of the Treaty on European Union (TEU).

[2] Among the many publications on the autonomy of the EU, see for instance T Molnár, 'The Concept of Autonomy of EU Law from the Comparative Perspective of International Law and the Legal Systems of Member States' (2015) *Hungarian Yearbook of International Law and European Law* 433–59; as well as C Contartese, 'The Autonomy of the EU Legal Order in the CJEU's External Relations Case-Law: From the "Essential" to the "Specific Characteristics" of the Union and Back Again' (2017) *Common Market Law Review* 1–46.

[3] In Opinion 2/13, the Court of Justice of the European Union (CJEU) confirmed the complexities related to the EU's submission to external judicial scrutiny; Opinion 2/13 of the Court of 18 December 2014: *Accession by the Union to the European Convention for the Protection of Human*

law is received in the Union's legal order (often applying domestic constitutional analogies involving terms such as monism and dualism), or on the hierarchical position of international law among other norms (often concluding that it was placed somewhere between primary and secondary EU law).[4] The overall consensus seems to be that, as a matter of principle – and despite what has been viewed as a 'tormented relationship' or 'a source of great confusion'[5] – the EU's order is open to international law; international commitments of the EU do have an effect internally and may even set aside secondary EU rules. And, on some occasions the EU has simply no choice but to accept international law in exercising its role as a global actor among states.[6]

The second dimension of the interface between international and European law is the influence of the EU on the international legal order (and on the domestic order of third states). Political science, in particular, has underlined and studied the role of the EU as a global normative actor,[7] in particular in the promotion of its own values and by influencing global policy-making. More recently, the question of the external impact of EU rules and the ways in which these could form a

Rights and Fundamental Freedoms, ECLI:EU:C:2014:2454. See more generally M Cremona, A Thies and RA Wessel (eds), *The European Union and International Dispute Settlement* (Oxford, Hart Publishing, 2017).

[4] See for instance (and for further references) the contributions to E Cannizzaro, P Palchetti and RA Wessel (eds), *International Law as Law of the European Union* (Leiden/Boston, Martinus Nijhoff Publishing, 2011); RA Wessel, *Close Encounters of the Third Kind: The Interface Between the EU and International Law after the Lisbon Treaty* (Sieps Report, 2013); K Ziegler, 'International Law and EU law: Between Asymmetric Constitutionalisations and Fragmentation' in A Orakhelashvili (ed), *Research Handbook on the Theory and History of International Law*' (Cheltenham, Edward Elgar, 2011) 268; K Ziegler, 'The Relationship between EU Law and International Law', University of Leicester School of Law Research Paper No 15-04. See also V Moreno-Lax and P Gragl, 'Introduction: Beyond Monism, Dualism, Pluralism: The Quest for a (Fully-Fledged) Theoretical Framework: Co-Implication, Embeddedness, and Interdependency between Public International Law and EU Law' (2016) *Yearbook of European Law*; as well as the various other contributions to that special issue on *EU Law and Public International Law: Co-implication, Embeddedness and Interdependency*.

[5] Respectively J Wouters, 'The Tormented Relationship between International Law and EU Law' in PHF Bekker, R Dolzer, and M Waibel (eds), *Making Transnational Law Work in the Global Economy: Essays in Honour of Detlev Vagts* (Cambridge, Cambridge University Press, 2010) 98–221; and J Klabbers, *Treaty Conflict and the European Union* (Cambridge, Cambridge University Press, 2009) ix.

[6] An example is formed by the 'contracting-in' strategy of the EU in international diplomatic law in relation to the functioning of its representatives abroad and the so-called Union Delegations. See further below, as well as J Wouters and S Duquet, 'The EU and International Diplomatic Law: New Horizons?' (2012) *Hague Journal of Diplomacy* 31–49.

[7] See, for instance, I Manners, 'Normative Power Europe: A Contradiction in Terms?' (2002) 40 *Journal of Common Market Studies* 235–58; H Sjursen, 'The EU as a Normative Power: How Can This Be?' (2006) 13 *Journal of European Public Policy* 235–51; R Whitman (ed), *Normative Power Europe: Empirical and Theoretical Perspectives* (Palgrave, 2011); and T Forsberg, 'Normative Power Europe, Once Again: A Conceptual Analysis of an Ideal-type' (2011) 49 *Journal of Common Market Studies* 1183–1204, at 1183. See also some chapters in N Witzleb, A Martínez Arranz, P Winand (eds), *The European Union and Global Engagement: Institutions, Policies and Challenges* (Edward Elgar, 2015). See for a critical assessment of political theories on this point, for instance, H Sjursen, 'Normative Theory: An Untapped Resource in the Study of European Foreign Policy' in KE Jørgensen, ÅK Aarstad, E Drieskens, K Laatikainen and B Tonra (eds), *The SAGE Handbook of European Foreign Policy, Vol. 1 & 2* (Sage, 2015) 197–213.

legitimate source of international law, has also been picked up by legal scholars.[8] This may first of all have been triggered by the clear (some would perhaps prefer 'neo-colonialist') manner in which the EU treaties these days present the organisation's ambitions to 'uphold and promote its values and interests' in the wider world and to be guided by 'the principles which have inspired its own creation' (Articles 3(5) and 21(3) of the Treaty on European Union (TEU)). Furthermore, these provisions make no mistake about not only the Union's intention to respect and observe international law, but also its promise to contribute to 'the development of international law'.[9]

In that respect, earlier legal studies already addressed the question of the 'Europeanisation of international law', understood as dealing with the way in which international law is 'Europeanised' when it becomes part of the EU legal order (leading to questions on the emergence of a distinct European system of international law or the consequences of this 'Europeanisation' for the unity and coherence of public international law),[10] as well as the normative aspects of making international law more 'European'.[11]

While the mutual influence of international and EU law thus seems to be generally acknowledged, EU law remains special. After all, it is not just law *between*

[8] See E Fahey, *The Global Reach of EU Law* (Abingdon and New York, Routledge, 2016); D Kochenov and F Amtenbrink (eds), *The European Union's Shaping of the International Legal Order* (Cambridge, Cambridge University Press, 2013); J Odermatt, *The European Union as a Global Actor and its Impact on the International Legal Order*, PhD thesis, University of Leuven, 2016; P Nevill, 'The European Union as a Source of Public International Law' (2013) *Hungarian Yearbook of International Law and European Law* 281–95 (Eleven International Publishing, 2014); F Hoffmeister, 'The Contribution of EU Practice to International Law' in M Cremona (ed), *Developments in EU External Relations Law* (Oxford, Oxford University Press, 2008) 37–127; RA Wessel, 'Flipping the Question: The Reception of EU Law in the International Legal Order' (2016) *Oxford Yearbook of European Law*; and in the same volume T Konstadinides, 'Means of Interaction between EU and International Law: Customary International Law as a Source of EU Law: A Two-Way Fertilization Route?' (2016) *Yearbook of European Law*.

[9] Whether or not the EU is successful in that respect is also debated. See for instance KE Smith, 'The European Union at the Human Rights Council: Speaking with One Voice but Having Little Influence' (2010) *Journal of European Public Policy* 224–41; J Wouters, A-L Chané and J Odermatt, 'Improving the EU's Status in the UN and the UN System: An Objective Without a Strategy?, KU Leuven Centre for Global Governance Studies, Working Paper No 133 – March 2014.

[10] See J Wouters, A Nollkaemper and E de Wet (eds), *The Europeanisation of International Law: The Status of International Law in the EU and its Member States* (The Hague, TMC Asser Press, 2008).

[11] See, on the idea of the EU as a 'model' for the international legal order, for instance, A Cassese, 'Towards a Moderate Monism: Could International Rules Eventually Acquire the Force to Invalidate Inconsistent National Laws?' in A Cassese (ed), *Realizing Utopia: The Future of International Law* (Oxford, Oxford University Press, 2012) at 187; A-M Slaughter and W Burke-White, 'The Future of International Law Is Domestic (or, the European Way of Law)' (2006) *Harvard International Law Journal* No 2, 327–52 at 327; M Weller, 'The Struggle for an International Constitutional Order' in D Armstrong (ed), *Routledge Handbook of International Law* (Routledge, 2009) 179–94 at 181. It has even been suggested that 'the European example is now most often cited by international lawyers not by way of contrasting public international law regimes but by way of suggesting the probable or desired trajectory of some of the more specialized international law regimes'. See JE Alvarez, *International Organizations as Law-Makers* (Oxford, Oxford University Press, 2006) at 468.

states, but also *within* states.[12] It is characterised by a number of elements that are often absent in other branches of international law: *inter alia*, primacy and direct effect, quite well-developed systems of political and judicial supervision, a directly elected parliament and, perhaps above all, a clear and quite extensive transfer of competences. All of this has turned the EU into something that is much more than a regular international organisation and an entity that is increasingly assuming state-like functions.[13]

It is this 'specialness' of the EU that lies at the basis of the continued separation between the study of international law and EU law. Let's face it: in most educational programmes, international law and European law are taught in different courses. And in the event that they are combined, course outlines usually show different weeks for international and EU law. Textbooks in which international and EU law are combined in any conceptual fashion hardly exist.[14] The same separation is visible in the research communities. International law scholars would generally be hesitant to teach EU law and *vice versa*, even at a very basic level. And, at conferences of the European Society of *International Law* (ESIL), the present author meets a completely different crowd than at the conferences of the Fédération Internationale pour le *Droit Européen* (FIDE). While 'EU external relations' used to be the area where international and EU law would necessarily be combined, even that field has developed into a subject area of its own, with its own circle of specialists that have become more focussed on EU case law and questions of competence division than on learning to combine insights from both disciplinary perspectives.[15] Indeed, few fora allow for an exchange of thoughts between international and European law and few journals would be interested in publishing in both areas.

Yet, the links between the two areas are obvious, as also reflected in the other contributions to this book. The European Union was established by a treaty concluded by sovereign states and many international law issues recur within the EU. One may think of methods for the interpretation of treaty provisions, questions on the legal personality of EU Institutions or agencies, or the need to respect commitments in good faith. Also other issues, such as the rules on the Stability Pact, the voting arrangements in the Council, the late implementation

[12] See already the early statement that the EU 'cannot be fitted into traditional categories of international or constitutional law'; HL Mason, *The European Coal and Steel Community: Experiment in Supranationalism* (Dordrecht, Martinus Nijhoff, 1955) 126.

[13] C Eckes and RA Wessel, 'The European Union: An International Perspective' in T Tridimas and R Schütze (eds), *The Oxford Principles of European Union Law – Volume 1: The European Union Legal Order* (Oxford, Oxford University Press, 2017).

[14] To overcome this, the present author co-wrote a new Dutch textbook that was initially quite well used at Dutch universities offering a course on 'international and European law'. After a few years, however, the integrated approach offered by the book proved to be difficult to match the course outlines, which preferred to deal with the issues separately. See WG Werner and RA Wessel, *Internationaal en Europees recht: Een verkenning van grondslagen en kenmerken*, 3rd edn (Groningen, Europa Law Publishing, 2011).

[15] *cf* J Larik, 'EU Foreign Relations Law as a Field of Scholarship' (2017) *AJIL Unbound*, 111, 321–25.

of EU legislation by Member States or the relatively limited competences of the European Parliament are understandable only with some knowledge of the nature and structure of the international system.

This contribution does not aim to add to the extensive body of knowledge on the relationship between international and European law, to which the present volume contributes in such an excellent way. Rather, it raises a meta question by asking to what extent – given the non-contested interrelationship between international and EU law – both disciplines could benefit from each other's insights. It is argued that to better understand EU law, it would also make sense for students to be confronted with the interface with international law rather than with the mere 'specialness' of their object of study; and to better understand international law, it may be useful to keep an eye on the way it develops in and around the EU. As argued by Ličková on the separate study of international and EU law: 'Such partial inquiries are useful, but they remain incomplete because both legal orders intervene and interplay when normative conflicts between them appear.'[16] Admittedly, the same holds true for other academic sub-disciplines. Thus, findings in national constitutional law should be compared more with global and European constitutional developments,[17] and knowledge of private law helps one understand the logic of treaty law and the law of responsibility.[18] More generally, the 'triangular relationship between EU law, international law and the EU Member States'[19] forces us to continue to study international, EU and domestic law with an open mind to the increasing opportunities of legal systems to influence each other.[20] Yet, the present chapter will focus on international and EU law only. The aim is even more modest, as the available space merely allows for a first inquiry, allowing for future research to further analyse and develop the various themes. This chapter will start by confronting the perspectives both academic disciplines have on each other. The risk that the presentations of these disciplines result in the creation of strawmen (as classifications may be based on this author's own

[16] *cf* M Ličková, 'European Exceptionalism in International Law' (2008) *European Journal of International Law* 463–90 at 465.

[17] *cf* Ziegler, 'The Relationship between EU Law and International Law' (n 4): 'the Court of Justice of the EU (CJEU) adopts a strong constitutionalist approach which assimilates the relationship between EU law and international law in many respects to the relationship between international law and national law. The EU's approach to international law may be motivated by inward-looking (constitutional) considerations that may be instrumental to its own dynamics, constitutional narrative and trajectory.' *cf* the transnational dimensions of the constitutional debate N Walker, *Intimations of Global Law* (Cambridge, Cambridge University Press, 2014).

[18] *cf* S Kadelbach, 'From Public International Law to International Public Law: A Comment on the "Public Authority" of International Institutions and the "Publicness" of their Law' in A von Bogdandy, R Wolfrum, J von Bernstorff, P Dann and M Goldmann (eds), *The Exercise of Public Authority by International Institutions* (Berlin/Heidelberg, Springer, 2010) 33–49.

[19] Ziegler, 'The Relationship between EU Law and International Law' (n 4).

[20] *cf* the contributions to A Føllesdal, RA Wessel and J Wouters (eds), *Multilevel Regulation and the EU: The Interplay between Global, European and National Normative Processes* (Leiden/Boston, Martinus Nijhoff Publishers, 2008); as well as E Nijman and A Nollkaemper (eds), *New Perspectives on the Divide Between National and International Law* (Oxford, Oxford University Press, 2007).

perceptions)[21] will, hopefully, be mitigated by a number of references to different sources. The confrontation of perspectives will be followed by mapping a number of areas of potential common interest. Finally, this chapter will try and answer the question of whether it makes sense to study both disciplines in a more integrated fashion.

II. Mutual Perspectives

A. An International Law Perspective on the European Union

As an international entity, the European Union can obviously be studied from the perspective of international law.[22] Yet, international law's focus is mainly on states. Only states are vested with 'original rights' and hence are 'primary subjects' of international law.[23] And even though other international actors accept that the Union takes at times a state-like position, 'the EU is, under international law, precluded by its very nature from being considered a State'.[24] At the same time, international law also deals with international organisations, and the EU can be classified as one.[25] Nevertheless, the special relationship with its Member States is unique in the law of international organisations and even in that field, the EU is often set apart.

Indeed, it has been argued that the EU is 'an international legal experiment'.[26] Few would argue that the EU is a state;[27] many would evade the question and say that it is an international entity *sui generis*.[28] International law, however, only

[21] Indeed, a priori perceptions matter and do influence the debate as well as the conclusions. As recently held by Binder and Hofbauer: 'In particular the classification of the EU as a subsystem of international law, as a *de facto* domestic order, or as a *sui generis* legal order predetermines which conflict rules and reconciliatory techniques find application.' C Binder and JA Hofbauer, 'The Perception of the EU Legal Order in International Law: An In- and Outside View' (2017) *European Yearbook of International Economic Law* 139–203 at 142.

[22] See also Eckes and Wessel (n 13). Some arguments in this section are derived from that paper.

[23] A Carty, *Philosophy of International Law* (Edinburgh, Edinburgh University Press, 2007) Ch 3, 'International Legal Personality' 81. See also International Court of Justice (ICJ), *Reparation For Injuries Suffered In The Service Of The United Nations*, Advisory Opinion of 11 April 1949 (the Reparations case, ICJ Reports, 1949, 174), discussed below.

[24] CJEU, Opinion 2/13 of 18 December 2014, para 156.

[25] At best as a particular type of international organisation that enjoys additional rights in certain contexts, a regional economic integration organisation (REIO). See further below.

[26] B De Witte, 'The European Union as an International Legal Experiment' in G De Búrca and JHH Weiler (eds), *The Worlds of European Constitutionalism* (Cambridge, Cambridge University Press, 2011) 19–56.

[27] As noted above this was (for the first time) underlined by the CJEU in Opinion 2/13, para 156. Yet, it can be argued that there are close resemblances with federations; see further below.

[28] Yet, see the (rightful) critique on the use of the 'sui generis' notion by R Schütze, 'On "Federal" Ground: The European Union as an (Inter)national Phenomenon' (2009) *CMLR* 1069–1105, at 1091–92. Republished in R Schütze, *Foreign Affairs and the EU Constitution: Selected Essays* (Cambridge, Cambridge University Press, 2014) Ch 1.

works when it is applied across the board for certain categories of international actors. Its rationale is to offer clarity and set the conditions for a smooth cooperation between different subjects. At the same time, it is of course possible to create special rules for special entities. The clauses on Regional Economic Integration Organizations (REIOs) in some multilateral agreements[29] are a good example.

To deal with the fact that the EU is more than a regular international organisation, the term 'integration organisation' is often used, implying that from the perspective of international law, the Union is an international organisation that at times requires adaptation of the usual paradigms applied to international organisations and that the sovereignty of Member States has not been taken away but has adapted. The Union may not possess original sovereign rights, except for from its own perspective, but it has been successful in changing the international position and the self-conception of its Member States.[30] Indeed, EU membership has transformed States into Member States, both internally and externally.

Yet, international lawyers would argue that '[f]rom an international law perspective, there is no reason to *per se* "detach" the EU from the international legal framework'.[31] Irrespective of the difficulty to classify the EU from the perspective of international law, there is agreement that, as an international actor, the EU is subject to international law in its relations with third states and international organisations.[32] It is bound by the international agreements to which it is a party as well as to customary international law.[33] More recent developments show that international law is indeed capable of taking the differences between

[29] A REIO is commonly defined in UN protocols and conventions as 'an organization constituted by sovereign states of a given region to which its member states have transferred competence in respect of matters governed by [...] convention or its protocols and [which] has been duly authorized, in accordance with its internal procedures, to sign, ratify, accept, approve or accede to it [the instruments concerned]'. See, eg, the 2004 Energy Charter Treaty (Art 3). See also E Paasivirta and PJ Kuijper, 'Does One Size Fit All?: The European Community and the Responsibility of International Organisations' *Netherlands Yearbook of International Law*, 2005 (The Hague, TMC Asser Press, 2007) 169–226 at 205. In the new Convention on the Rights of Persons with Disabilities, the REIO clause seems to have evolved to a RIO (Regional Integration Organisation) clause, which does justice to the large scope of activities of the EU these days (see Art 44: '"Regional integration organisation" shall mean an organisation constituted by sovereign States of a given region, to which its member States have transferred competence in respect of matters governed by this Convention').

[30] On the latter see C Bickerton, *European Integration* (Oxford, Oxford University Press, 2012). See more extensively Eckes and Wessel (n 13).

[31] Binder and Hofbauer (n 21) at 141. Compare also B Simma and D Pulkowski, 'Of Planets and the Universe: Self-Contained Regimes in International Law' (2006) *European Journal of International Law* 483–529 at 516: 'The continuous assertion of the Community's sui generis character [...] does not by itself create an 'own legal order'. From a public international law perspective, the EC legal system remains a suborder of international law.'

[32] See for a survey of the many facets of the relationship between international and EU law: RA Wessel, *Close Encounters of the Third Kind: The Interface Between the EU and International Law after the Lisbon Treaty* (Stockholm Sieps Report, 2013).

[33] More extensively, ibid, 106. See also clearly the judgment of the CJEU in Case C-366/10 *Air Transport Association of America, American Airlines Inc., Continental Airlines Inc., United Airlines Inc v Secretary of State for Energy and Climate Change*, 2011.

states and international integration organisations into account.[34] This is particularly relevant as in recent years the EU has been taking up 'state-like functions' in more areas than before.[35] This is partly due to the fact that the introduction of the European External Action Service (EEAS)[36] led to a professionalisation of the EU's diplomatic network around the world. The EU's physical presence through its delegations is based on Article 221(1) of the Treaty on the Functioning of the European Union (TFEU): 'Union Delegations in third countries and at international organisations shall represent the Union.' Indeed, distinctions with states representations are increasingly blurred. Heads of Delegations *de facto* act as 'EU ambassadors', and the EU adapts international diplomatic law to be able to 'play along'.[37]

The EU is also quite visible in international law as it regularly concludes international agreements with third countries, ie non-Member States.[38] Its international legal personality was confirmed in the current Treaties.[39] Since the entry into force of the Lisbon Treaty, the Union has succeeded the Community and taken over all international obligations flowing from the latter's treaty-making activities over the first decades. This separate legal status in international law also confirmed a separate role of the EU in international institutions, mostly alongside its Member States. Thus, the EU is a full member of a number of international organisations, including the World Trade Organisation (WTO), the Food and Agriculture Organisation (FAO),[40] the *Codex Alimentarius*, as well as of most fisheries organisations;[41] and an observer to many other international organisations. Indeed, its engagement with a large number of international organisations has made it a visible actor in the international legal order.[42]

[34] Respectively to be found at http://untreaty.un.org/ilc/texts/instruments/english/conventions/1_2_1986.pdf and http://untreaty.un.org/ilc/texts/instruments/english/draft%20articles/9_11_2011.pdf. Obviously, the extent to which these instruments successfully take the complex position of international organisations into account may be subject to debate.

[35] See more extensively RA Wessel, 'Can the European Union Replace its Member States in International Affairs? An International Law Perspective' in I Govaere, E Lannon, P Van Elsuwege, S Adam (eds), *The European Union in the World: Essays in Honour of Marc Maresceau* (Leiden/Boston, Martinus Nijhoff Publishers, 2013) 129–47; as well as Wouters and Duquet (n 6).

[36] M Gatti, *European External Action Service: Promoting Coherence through Autonomy and Coordination* (Leiden/Boston, Brill/Nijhoff, 2016); J Bátora and D Spence (eds), *The European External Action Service: European Diplomacy Post-Westphalia* (Basingstoke, Palgrave MacMillan, 2015).

[37] Wouters and Duquet (n 6); see also F Fenton, 'EU Ambassadors: A New Creed?' in P Quinn (ed), *Making European Diplomacy Work: Can the EEAS Deliver?* (College of Europe, EU Diplomacy Paper 08/2011) 26–30; P Kerres and RA Wessel, 'Apples and Oranges? Comparing the European Union Delegations to National Embassies' (2015) *Centre for the Law of EU External Relations (CLEER) Papers*, No 2.

[38] For an overview see https://treaties.un.org/.

[39] Article 47 TEU 'The Union shall have legal personality'.

[40] Articles II (8)-(11) FAO Constitution.

[41] See RA Wessel, 'The Legal Framework for the Participation of the European Union in International Institutions' in S Oberthür, KE Jorgenson and J Shahin (eds), *The Performance of the EU in International Institutions* (London/New York, Routledge, 2013) 23–37 (also published in *Journal of European Integration*, 2011).

[42] See RA Wessel and J Odermatt (eds), *Research Handbook on the EU's Engagement with International Organizations* (Edward Elgar Publishing, forthcoming in 2019).

Apart from the claim for autonomy by EU law, which may lead to fragmentation and an undermining of the international dispute settlement system (see below),[43] most problematic perhaps from an international law perspective is the complex division of competences between the EU and its Member States.[44] The starting point is given in treaty law, pursuant to which an international organisation may not invoke the rules of the organisation as justification for its failure to perform a treaty (Article 27(2), 1986 Vienna Convention). Article 46 (2) of the 1986 Convention adds that an international organisation may not invoke the fact that its consent to be bound by a treaty has been expressed in violation of the rules of the organisation regarding competence to conclude treaties as invalidating its consent unless that violation was manifest and concerned a rule of fundamental importance. Article 46(3) specifies that a violation is manifest if it would be objectively evident to any State or any international organisation conducting itself in the matter in accordance with the normal practice of States and, where appropriate, of international organisations and in good faith.[45] Given the manifold international relations and the dynamic and extensive competences of the Union, the question comes up to what extent the division of competences should be objectively evident to other international actors. It has been argued that once this division is made known, the rules are no longer purely internal, but may form part of the international agreements, or at least form a source for interpretation.[46] This would in particular be true in cases where a 'declaration of competence' has been issued by the EU.[47] The division of competences and its consequences under international law will be returned to in some of the analyses below.

B. A European Law Perspective on the International Legal Order

EU legal scholars would generally see international law as less complex, less technical and perhaps even closer to politics than to law. They wonder what the

[43] See extensively on these issues Binder and Hofbauer (n 21).

[44] See, among the many studies in this topic, recently S Garben and I Govaere (eds), *The Division of Competences between the EU and the Member States: Reflections on the Past, the Present and the Future* (Oxford, Hart Publishing, 2017).

[45] This seems to have been accepted by the European Court of Justice as well. See for instance the cases C-327/91 *France v Commission* [1994] ECR I-3641 and the passenger name records (PNR) cases in Joined Cases C-317/04 and C-318/04 *European Parliament v Council and Commission* [2006] ECR I-04721.

[46] 'European Union External Action and International Law', *CAVV Advisory Report* No 24, 2014; http://cms.webbeat.net/ContentSuite/upload/cav/doc/CAVV_Advisory_Report_EU_External_Action_and_International_Law(1).pdf.

[47] See for an overview of 'Agreements with a declaration of competence by the EU' the website of the EU Treaties Office: http://ec.europa.eu/world/agreements/viewCollection.do. See on the declarations also J Heliskoski, 'EU Declarations of Competence and International Responsibility' in M Evans and P Koutrakos (eds), *International Responsibility: EU and International Perspectives* (Oxford, Hart Publishing, 2013) 189–212; and more recently A Delgado Casteleiro, *The International Responsibility of the European Union: From Competence to Normative Control* (Cambridge, Cambridge University Press, 2016).

International Court of Justice (ICJ) judges are doing the entire day with so few cases to handle and how international law scholars spend their day without having to deal with events on a daily basis. Obviously, they deny the fact that law is not just about case law or legal instruments that are adopted on a constant basis, but also, or perhaps mainly, about interpretation. And that is not so different from what they do in EU law. International law is based on many international agreements and on custom and, apart from the ICJ, there are many more tribunals involved in international dispute settlement.[48] And, is treaty law, the law of responsibility, or international trade or environmental law – to name just a few – really less 'technical' and less complex than EU law?

It is well-known that EU legal scholars have a tendency to stress the 'specialness' (and related 'autonomy') of the EU. Obviously, the early case law of the Court had set a trend in that respect. We all remember the famous qualification by the Court in *Van Gend & Loos* of the Community as 'a new legal order of international law for the benefit of which the states have limited their sovereign rights, albeit within limited fields and the subjects of which comprise not only member states but also their nationals'.[49] There has been some debate on whether *Van Gend & Loos* should be seen as a logical follow-up to choices made in the Treaties and earlier case law of the Court,[50] or that it 'should be understood as a decisive turning point in the history of the ECJ and of European law in general'.[51] In the latter view,

> The judgment constituted at the most fundamental level an attempt to differentiate European law from what was perceived as traditional international public law. A process completed when the ECJ in the *Costa v. E.N.E.L.* judgment termed the European legal order merely as a 'new legal order'.[52]

[48] In a recent study, Alter counted 17 international courts with the competence to settle disputes; see KJ Alter, *The New Terrain of International Law: Courts, Politics, Rights* (Princeton/Oxford, Princeton University Press, 2014) Ch 5. See also on different forms of international dispute settlement, L Boisson de Chazournes, MG Kohen, JE Vinuales (eds), *Diplomatic and Judicial Means of Dispute Settlement* (Leiden/Boston, Martinus Nijhoff Publishers, 2013).

[49] Case 26/62 *NV Algemene Transport- en Expeditie Onderneming van Gend & Loos v Netherlands Inland Revenue Administration* ECLI:EU:C:1963:1.

[50] See, eg, JHH Weiler, 'Rewriting *Van Gend en Loos*: Towards a Normative Theory of ECJ Hermeneutics' in O Wiklund (ed), *Judicial Discretion in European Perspective* (The Hague, Kluwer Law International, 2003) 150 at 150–51: '*Van Gend en Loos* and its progeny are not the result of a new hermeneutics and that the decision would, or at least could, be the same under the traditional rule of interpretation of public international law.' Compare also D Edwards, 'Judicial Activism–Myth or Reality? *Van Gend en Loos, Costa v ENEL* and the *Van Duyn Family* Revisited' in AIK Campbell and M Voyatzi (eds), *Essays in the Honour of Lord Mackenzie-Stuart* (Hampshire, Trenton Publishing, 1996) 29.

[51] M Rasmussen, 'Revolutionizing European Law: A History of the *Van Gend en Loos* Judgment' (2014) 12 *International Journal of Constititutional Law* 1, 136–63.

[52] ibid. See on different analyses of the case also A Tizzano, J Kokott, S Prechal (eds), *50th Anniversary of the judgment in Van Gend en Loos*, 1963–2013 (Luxembourg, European Court of Justice, 2013).

While all of this may have resulted in 'a partly autistic approach of the EU Institutions towards international law',[53] it remains worth noting that the Court itself 'never sought to develop a doctrine affirming the specific *and* non-international nature of the EU'.[54] The separation between the two disciplines is largely a scholarly invention.

There are good arguments to continue viewing EU law as part of international law. After all, it is based on treaties that were concluded under international law and the chosen form of institutional cooperation was (and is) made possible by international law.[55] Yet, with the continued integration process, the divide between international and EU law studies deepened and distinctions rather than similarities dominated the debate.[56] As one observer held 'even if the EEC did conform to the status of international organizations in its early days (which is unlikely) it has now moved well beyond that'.[57] Or,

> [I]n the eyes of the European Court and the majority of European scholars, the normative force of European law derives no longer from the normative foundations of international law. The ultimate normative base within the European Union – its 'originality hypothesis' or 'Grundnorm' – is the Rome Treaty as such.[58]

Notions like these have seriously influenced the EU's self-perception in relation to international law.

EU scholars have increasingly made comparisons to 'statehood', rather than to 'organisationhood'.[59] Notions like the one by the Court in *Van Gend & Loos* that '[i]ndependently of the legislation of member states, community law […] not only imposes obligations on individuals but is also intended to confer upon them rights which become part of their legal heritage', seem to have steered EU law scholarship in that direction. Rather than viewing EU law as a special branch of international law, EU scholarship turned to state-like metaphors.[60] Thus, analyses have

[53] Binder and Hofbauer (n 21) at 155.

[54] B de Witte, 'EU Law: Is it International Law?' in C Barnard and S Peers (eds), *European Union Law*, 2nd edn (Oxford, Oxford University Press, 2017) 177–97 at 182.

[55] ibid at 178.

[56] For an early and influential publication in that respect, see P Pescatore, 'International Law and Community Law – A Comparatice Analysis' (1970) *CMLR* 167.

[57] S Douglas-Scott, *Constitutional Law of the European Union* (London, Longman, 2002) at 260; as well as JHH Weiler and UR Haltern, 'Constitutional or International? The Foundations of the Community Legal Order and the Question of Judicial Kompetenz-Kompetenz' in A-M Slaughter, A Stone Sweet and JHH Weiler (eds), *The European Courts and National Courts: Doctrine and Jurisprudence* (Oxford, Hart Publishing, 1998) 331 at 342; but many more similar quotes can be found.

[58] R Schütze, 'On "Federal" Ground: The European Union as an (Inter)national Phenomenon' (2009) *CMLR* 1069–1105 at 1082. Republished in R Schütze, *Foreign Affairs and the EU Constitution: Selected Essays* (Cambridge, Cambridge University Press, 2014) Ch 1. In the last sentence quoting Madison, *The Federalist No 39* in Hamilton, Madison, and Jay (eds), *The Federalist* (Cambridge, Cambridge University Press, 2003) at 187.

[59] *cf* GF Mancini, 'Europe: The Case for Statehood' (1998) *European Law Journal* 29.

[60] See, for a short analysis of the various notions, including 'supranational organisation', 'Statenverbund', or 'constitutional order of States', also de Witte (n 54) at 191.

assessed the EU as a confederation,[61] or even in federal terms.[62] The federative argument was for instance presented by Schütze when he argued in relation to the EU that:

> Its formation was clearly international and its amendment still is. However, its international birth should not prejudge against the 'federal' or 'constitutional' status of the EC Treaty. [...] The fact remains that the European legal order has adopted the 'originality hypothesis' and cut the umbilical cord with the international legal order. The Treaty as such – not international law – is posited at the origin of European law. Functionally, then, the European Union is based on a 'constitutional treaty' that assumes and stands on federal middle ground.[63]

It has also been argued that 'the EU has combined a confederal foundation with some crucial federate reinforcements in its constitutional superstructure'.[64] As indicated earlier, only recently the EU Court for the first time expressly stated that the EU is not a state.[65]

All in all, the debate in the EU has been focused much more on its nature and on the relations with its Member States (and the related division of powers) than on a comparison with international law. Since this original conception of permanently transferred sovereign rights, the Court and the Treaties, have hand in hand, pushed forward a process of fortifying the European construction.

III. Mutual Interests

The purpose of the present contribution is not to deny the above findings, but to map areas in which international and EU law can – nevertheless – learn from each

[61] A Cuyvers, 'The Confederal Comeback: Rediscovering the Confederal Form for a Transnational World' (2013) 19 *European Law Journal* 711–38. See also his thesis defended at the University of Leiden: *The EU as a Confederal Union of Sovereign Member Peoples: Exploring the Potential of American (Con) federalism and Popular Sovereignty for a Constitutional Theory of the EU*, Meijers-series no MI-227 (Leiden, Wohrmann / Meijers, 2014).

[62] See, eg, M Cappelletti, M Secombe and JHH Weiler (eds), *Integration through Law – Europe and the American Federal Experience* (De Gruyter, 1986) Vol I; K Lenaerts, 'Federalism: Essential Concepts in Evolution – the Case of the European Union' (1998) 21 *Fordham International Law Journal* 746; A von Bogdandy, 'The European Union as a Supranational Federation: A Conceptual Attempt in the Light of the Amsterdam Treaty' (2000) 6 *Columbia Journal of European Law* 27; R Schütze, 'On "Federal" Ground: The European Union as an (Inter)National Phenomenon' (2009) 46 *Common Market Law Review* 1096; JHH Weiler, 'The Transformation of Europe' (1991) *Yale Law Journal* 2403–84; G De Baere and K Gutman, 'Federalism and International Relations in the EU and the US: A Comparative Outlook' in E Cloots, G De Baere, S Sottiaux (eds), *Federalism in the European Union* (Oxford, Hart Publishing, 2012) 131–66. And, as a warning against too much federalism: SJ Boom, 'The European Union After the Maastricht Decision: Will Germany Be the Virginia of Europe?' (1995) *American Journal of Comparative Law* 177–226 at 208.

[63] Schütze, ibid, at 1089. Republished in R Schütze, *Foreign Affairs and the EU Constitution: Selected Essays* (Cambridge, Cambridge University Press, 2014) Ch 1; in the last sentence quoting Madison, *The Federalist No 39* in Hamilton, Madison, and Jay (n 58) 187.

[64] Cuyvers (n 61) at 712.

[65] Opinion 2/13 of the Court of 18 December 2014, para 49.

other and where a dialogue should continue. The list below is by no means meant to be exhaustive; it merely aims to give an indication of possible mutual interests.

A. The Nature of the Legal System

One of the popular differences between international and EU law is the different nature of their legal orders (see also above: law *between* states or (also) law *within* states). Yet, international law has also moved from just being inter-state law, to law that can have an effect on the relations between governments and their individuals. Obvious examples include human rights law and international criminal law. International law seems to have realised that many problems are domestic and that – in the words of Slaughter and Burke-White –

> To create desirable conditions in the international system, from peace, to health to prosperity, international law must address the capacity and the will of domestic governments to respond to these issues at their sources. In turn, the primary terrain of international law must shift – and is already shifting in many instances – from independent regulation above the national state to direct engagement with domestic institutions.[66]

These authors have argued that what international law needs is 'a direct emphasis on shaping or influencing political outcomes within sovereign states in accordance with international legal rules' and a 'European way of law' should be at the basis of a transformation of international law.[67] In particular agreeing on objectives (in 'Directives'), while leaving the (most suitable form of) implementation to the states, would better help international law attain many of its goals. The authors look somewhat jealously to 'the EU's "soft" intervention in the "domestic affairs" of EU member states' on an almost daily basis.[68] Furthermore, the EU is not seldomly mentioned as a blueprint for other regions in the world and comparisons with the African Union, ASEAN (the Association of Southeast Asian Nations) or MERCOSUR (the Southern Common Market in Latin America) are often made to see whether the 'European way of law' could be helpful in other areas of the world as well. The EU itself has even claimed that these forms of integration 'make an important contribution to a more orderly world'.[69]

While there are certainly lessons to draw from the way in which European law interacts with domestic legal orders, it is obvious why many of the starting points are hardly translatable to a wider context. The European Union started with a few states only and in a very specific period in time. Sixty years and 22 more members later, the limits of the project are becoming more visible.

[66] Slaughter and Burke-White (n 11) at 328.
[67] Slaughter and Burke-White (n 11).
[68] Slaughter and Burke-White (n 11) at 133.
[69] 2003 European Security Strategy, 'A Secure Europe in a Better World'.

B. Constitutionalism and Effects on Individuals

The nature of the two legal orders is closely related to another development which is prominent in both international and EU law: a constitutional approach. This approach, with a focus on checks and balances and the rights of individuals, has of course been part and parcel of EU-studies from the outset.[70] These days it is also no longer uncommon to view the international legal order in constitutional terms, and 'international constitutional law' has slowly become a special area of study.[71] As in European Union law, the effects of rules and legislation on individuals also triggered this development in international law. The proliferation and law-making,[72] or even legislative,[73] functions of many international organisations made us aware of the existence of – perhaps not the emergence of a world government[74] – but at least of global governance 'beyond the state'[75] in what is sometimes normatively framed in 'communitarian' terms that sound familiar to EU lawyers: a 'world community'.[76]

The trigger may very well have been formed by the sanctions regimes of the United Nations Security Council,[77] but the study of the effects on individuals was

[70] See, eg, A Stone Sweet, *Govering with Judges: Constitutional Politics in Europe* (Oxford, Oxford University Press, 2000); J Weiler and M Wind (eds), *European Constitutionalism beyond the State* (2003); N Walker, 'European Constitutionalism in the State Constitutional Tradition' in C Holder, C O'Cinneide and C Campbell-Holt (eds), *Current Legal Problems* (Oxford, Oxford University Press, 2006) 51–89.

[71] Among the many publications in this area B Fassbender, *The United Nations Charter as the Constitution of the International Community* (Leiden/Boston, Brill, 2009) in particular Chapter 2, 'The Transfer of the Constitutional Idea to the Sphere of International Law: Different Approaches'; A Paulus, 'The International Legal System as a Constitution' in JL Donoff and JP Trachtman (eds), *Ruling the World? Constitutionalism, International Law and Global Governance* (Cambridge, Cambridge University Press, 2009) 69–109; J Klabbers, A Peters and G Ulfstein (eds), *The Constitutionalization of International Law* (Oxford, Oxford University Press, 2009); E De Wet, 'The International Constitutional Order' (2006) *International and Comparative Law Quarterly* 51–76; R St J MacDonald and DM Johnston, *Towards World Constitutionalism – Issues in the Legal Ordering of the World Community* (Leiden/Boston, Martinus Nijhoff Publishers, 2005); as well as Christine EJ Schwöbel, *Global Constitutionalism in International Legal Perspective* (Leiden/Boston, Brill, 2011).

[72] See for a recent analysis ND White, 'Lawmaking' in J Cogan, I Hurd and I Johnston (eds), *Oxford Handbook of International Organizations* (Oxford, Oxford University Press, 2016); as well as the various contributions to C Bröllman and Y Radi (eds), *Research Handbook on the Theory and Practice of International Lawmaking* (Cheltenham/Northhampton, Edward Elgar Publishing, 2016).

[73] This discussion primarily took place in relation to the UN Security Council. See or instance *cf* PC Szasz, 'The Security Council Starts Legislating' (2002) *American Journal of International Law* 901–05; S Talmon, 'The Security Council as World Legislature' (2005) *American Journal of International Law* 175–93; B Elberling, 'The Ultra Vires Character of Legislative Action by the Security Council' (2005) *International Organizations Law Review* 337–60; M Akram, and SH Shah, 'The Legislative Powers of the United Nations Security Council' in MacDonald and Johnston (n 71) 431–55.

[74] Yet, see JP Trachtman, *The Future of International Law: Global Government* (Cambridge, Cambridge University Press, 2013).

[75] *cf* BS Chimni, 'International Institutions Today: An Imperial Global State in the Making' (2004) *European Journal of International Law*.

[76] But see M Koskenniemi, 'The Subjective Dangers of Projects of World Community' in Cassese (n 11) 3–13; as well as the other contributions in Part 1 of this volume under the heading 'Can the World become a Global Community?'

[77] *cf* C Eckes, *EU Counter-Terrorist Policies and Fundamental Rights: The Case of Individual Sanctions* (Oxford, Oxford University Press, 2009).

much broader and has led to new areas such as Global Administrative Law.[78] In general, where traditionally the 'contractual' relations between states were at the forefront, the 'publicness' of public international law is gaining more attention.[79] Obviously, this development raised new questions – not only related to the constitutionalisation of the international legal order, but also to the legitimacy of the decisions or the accountability of the actors.[80] While 'constitutionalism' is a more general theme in current international legal discourse[81] the increasing autonomy of international organisations (or at least the perception that this is the case) has triggered a new stream of literature, which basically aims to apply (variations of) constitutional and similar state-oriented notions related to the rule of law, such as 'administrative governance',[82] to international organisations.[83]

In general, it has been argued that international law benefits from its more evolved, more constitutionalised parts. International organisations could be seen as 'laboratories of international law'.[84] The EU in particular has 'experimented' with supranational rule-making, compulsory jurisdiction, strong enforcement mechanisms and a strong subjectivity of the individual.[85] Indeed, over the years, the EU developed quite sophisticated ways to allow individuals affected by EU law to address these issues, either before their domestic courts or before the European Court. Targeted sanctions regimes, such as the ones at stake in the *Kadi* cases,[86] in particular, made us aware that similar notions were needed at the international

[78] Among the many publications in this area, one to mention is perhaps N Krisch, 'The Pluralism of Global Administrative Law' (2006) *European Journal of International Law* 262–74.

[79] See Kadelbach (n 18); as well as RA Wessel, 'Revealing the Publicness of International Law' in C Ryngaert, EJ Molenaar, and S Nouwen (eds), *What's Wrong With International Law? – Liber Amicorum AHA Soons* (Leiden/Boston, Martinus Nijhoff Publishers, 2015) 449–66. Recently also A von Bogdandy, M Goldmann and I Venzke, 'From Public International to International Public Law: Translating World Public Opinion into International Public Authority' (2017) *European Journal of International Law* 115–45.

[80] See also J Klabbers, 'Law-Making and Constitutionalism' in Klabbers, Peters and Ulfstein (n 71) at 12, arguing that non-state actors have 'started to compete with states for the scarce resource of politico-legal authority (i.e. the power to set authoritative standards)'. In general, the book discusses international constitutionalism as a framework within which further normative debate on a legitimate and pluralist constitutional order can occur (Klabbers, ibid, at 10). But see also J Pauwelyn, RA Wessel and J Wouters, 'When Structures Become Shackles' (2014) *European Journal of International Law* 733–63, where we have argued that the effects on legitimacy should not be overestimated as the traditional 'thin state consent' is replace by a 'thick stakeholder consensus'.

[81] See for instance Klabbers, Peters and Ulfstein (n 71); and A Peters, 'Are we Moving toward Constitutionalization of the World Community' in Cassese (n 11) 118–35.

[82] See PL Lindseth, 'Supranational Organizations' in Cogan, Hurd and Johnston (n 72) 152–70. Lidseth argues that an 'administrative' approach, rather than the 'constitutionalisation' approach is more helpful in classifying international organisations along an intergovernmental-supranational axis.

[83] See the various chapters on Legitimacy (Dominik Zaum), Participation (Patrizia Nanz and Klaus Dingwerth), Accountability (Mathias Koenig-Archibugi) and Transparency (Jonas Tallberg) in Cogan, Hurd and Johnston (n 72).

[84] C Walter, 'International Law in a Process of Constitutionalization' in Nijman and Nollkaemper (n 20) 191 at 214.

[85] Ziegler, 'The Relationship between EU Law and International Law' (n 4) at 2.

[86] See for instance Eckes (n 77); as well as RA Wessel, 'The *Kadi*-case: Towards a More Substantive Hierarchy in International Law?' (2008) *International Organizations Law Review* 323–27.

level and have been picked up and analysed by studies on the 'direct effect' of decisions of international organisations on individuals.[87]

C. Democracy and Legitimacy

Irrespective of these developments – or, indeed, as a result of them – another trend is visible as well: back to the state. The reason is that global and EU initiatives are less easily accepted by citizens – as is exemplified by the debates on large regional trade and investment initiatives such as the Transatlantic Trade and Investment Partnership with the United States (TTIP), the Comprehensive Economic and Trade Agreement with Canada (CETA), but also by Association Agreements concluded by the EU[88] or, indeed, by 'Brexit' ('taking back control'). The developments indeed seem to be connected. Fahey has argued that 'the merger of sovereignty, territoriality and jurisdiction in a global world is an emerging matter for EU law'.[89] At the same time effects of 'post-nationalism' or 'post-sovereignty' increasingly lead to popular protest: 'An aggrandizement of EU influence, competence, scope and even territory may increasingly score lowly in terms of social legitimacy, both inside and outside the EU.'[90]

Both international and EU law are currently struggling with keeping the populations onboard in the ongoing process of globalisation and Europeanisation. The idea of representing the people in parliaments at international organisations is of course best implemented at the EU, but is also visible in a number of other international organisations.[91] More generally, the struggle for legitimacy is something that the EU and other international fora share and where best (and worst) practices may be shared.

D. The Autonomy of International Organisations and International Responsibility

The already mentioned development in which international organisations have increasingly become international actors in their own right,[92] also leads to questions that have been part of EU legal doctrine. The division of competences between

[87] See, recently, P Schmitt, *Access to Justice and International Organizations: The Case of Individual Victims of Human Rights Violations* (Cheltenham (UK)/Northampton (USA), Edward Elgar Publishing, 2017).

[88] G Van der Loo, 'The Dutch Referendum on the EU-Ukraine Association Agreement: Legal Implications and Solutions' (2017) *Netherlands Yearbook of International Law 2016*.

[89] Fahey (n 8) at 12.

[90] Fahey (n 8) at 15.

[91] See www.internationaldemocracywatch.org/index.php/international-parliamentary-assemblies.

[92] ND White and R Collins (eds), *International Organizations and the Idea of Autonomy: Institutional Independence in the International Legal Order* (Routledge, 2011).

the EU and its Member States is a fact that has to be recognised by third parties, both when they wish to conclude international agreements and when issues of international responsibility emerge. In the words of Ličkóva:

> The complexity of the EU legislation that incidentally generates international consequences makes the international situation of the Member States more difficult every day. For this reason, the EU and its members have introduced legal tools that, if consented to by third parties, endow the international obligations of the EU states with flexibility. It seems that third parties have indeed paid attention to the peculiar nature of the EU legal order and to the specific legal position in which the EU states often operate. A generalized understanding has emerged that whenever an EU Member State comes to the international-negotiation table, the European-law implications will be part of the agenda. Accordingly, third parties adjust to this state of affairs, and the question today is whether this EU-friendly treatment has reached the status of an international custom.[93]

Indeed, the introduction in the international legal order of an entity of which the members are also international legal persons in their own right and where competences and responsibilities are divided among them,[94] already had an impact on the traditional view in international law that 'domestic' arguments are usually not so relevant in assessing international obligations.

As the 2011 Articles on the Responsibility of International Organisations (ARIO) reveal,[95] a division of competences between international organisations and their member states has become a more general issue. The complexity of the division of competences between the EU and its Member States remains unique, but at the same time other international organisations (including the UN) have shown difficulties in establishing a clear line of demarcation when questions of international responsibility occur. While the EU has been struggling for quite a while to clarify its internal division of competences to third states (eg through the use of so-called 'Declarations of competence'),[96] the recent 'Srebrenica' cases before courts in The Netherlands exemplify the increasing problem of drawing clear lines of demarcation between, in this case, the United Nations' and Member State responsibilities.[97]

[93] Ličková (n 16) at 464.

[94] *cf* RA Wessel, 'The European Union as a Party to International Agreements: Shared Competences, Mixed Responsibilities' in A Dashwood and M Maresceau (eds), *Law and Practice of EU External Relations – Salient Features of a Changing Landscape* (Cambridge, Cambridge University Press, 2008) 145–80.

[95] See on the specific position of the EU, PJ Kuijper and E Paasivirta, 'Further Exploring International Responsibility: The European Community and the ILC's Project on Responsibility of International Organisations' (2004) *International Organizations Law Review*, 111; as well as in general on the ARIO, the special issue of the same journal, 2009, No 1.

[96] See on this issue and on EU international responsibilities in general Delgado Casteleiro (n 47).

[97] See for instance P Palchetti, 'Attributing the Conduct of Dutchbat in Srebrenica: The 2014 Judgment of the District Court in the Mothers of Srebrenica Case' (2015) 62 *Netherlands International Law Review* 2279–94.

E. Statehood, Territoriality and Legal Personality

As mentioned above, the EU is assuming more and more state-like functions. At the same time, as a non-state actor there is only so much the EU can do to participate in a state-based system. Yet, even territorial questions do seem to come up even in EU law – including the Court's case law[98] – and a connection with doctrinal issues on that point seems helpful as notions of territory and jurisdiction are central in international law. Buxbaum argued that sovereignty, territory and jurisdiction are the greatest challenge of law across borders in the global legal age.[99] Indeed, state sovereignty implies that states are the sole rule makers and rule enforcers within a jurisdiction that is closely linked to their territory. The question of whether in the case of international organisations one may speak of a 'territory' is somewhat unsettled in international law.[100] During the process of drafting the Convention on the Law of Treaties, the International Law Commission had difficulties in accepting the existence of a 'territory of the organization'.[101] Despite its 'state-like' characteristics, the case of the European Union is not too different. At the same time, its competences to make and enforce rules within a given 'territorial space' are undisputed. While territorial issues have always been prominent in debates on the application of EU law in its overseas countries

[98] The Court of Justice has been faced with questions of territorial scope on a number of occasions. To mention some examples: *Anastasiou* (Case C-432/92; ECLI:EU:C:1994:277) was a case concerning Cyprus, before it became an EU Member State. The CJEU refused to recognise export certificates from authorities other than those belonging to the Republic of Cyprus (that is to say, those which bear the name 'Turkish Republic of Northern Cyprus') under the EC-Cyprus agreement. In *Brita* (Case C-386/08; ECLI:EU:C:2010:91) the Court was faced with a similar but more complex question of whether goods originating from the West Bank could be included within the EU's free trade agreement signed with the State of Israel and benefit from the preferential treatment allowed for Israeli products in the EU. Other issues came up in the *Front Polisario* case (Case T-512/12; ECLI:EU:T:2015:953)).

[99] See H Buxbaum, 'Territory, Territoriality and the Resolution of Jurisdictional Conflict' (2009) *American Journal of Comparative Law* 631. See also H Buxbaum, 'Transnational Legal Ordering and Regulatory Conflict: Lessons from the Regulation of Cross-Border Derivatives' (2016) 1 *UC Irvine Journal of International Law, Transnationals Law and Comparative Law* 91.

[100] Art 29 (on the 'Territorial scope of treaties') of the 1986 Vienna Convention basically copied Art 29 of the 1969 Convention and provides: 'Unless a different intention appears from the treaty or is otherwise established, a treaty between one or more States and one or more international organizations is binding upon each State party in respect of its entire territory.' It is interesting to note that, while international agreements concluded by international organisations are included, the obligations are imposed on 'each State party' only.

[101] The 1982 ILC Commentary explains this choice in the following terms: 'Is it possible to imagine a parallel provision concerning the obligations of international organizations? Despite the somewhat loose references which are occasionally made to the 'territory' of an international organization, we cannot speak in this case of 'territory' in the strict sense of the word. However, since this is so and since account must nevertheless be taken of the variety of situations which the multiple functions of international organizations may involve, it seemed preferable to avoid a formula which was too rigid or too narrow. If the draft articles said that, in the case of an international organization which is a party to a treaty, the scope of application of the treaty extended to the entire territory of the States members of that organization, the draft would diverge from Art 29 of the Vienna Convention by raising the question of the scope of application of a treaty, which is not expressly covered by that Convention.'

and regions,[102] these days we are witnessing an extension of that 'territorial space'. This is obviously also as a consequence of the enlarged membership of the EU, but more importantly because of the 'global reach' of EU law,[103] and its extra-territorial effects.[104] Ever more studies have stressed the importance of this phenomenon as well as its impact on international law. As phrased by Joanne Scott: the EU

> makes frequent recourse to a mechanism that may be labelled 'territorial extension.' The practice of territorial extension enables the EU to govern activities that are not centered upon the territory of the EU and to shape the focus and content of third country and international law.[105]

This may also lead to jurisdictional questions, eg with respect to international law notions of the concept.[106]

While it is not completely alien to the Court to refer to the 'territory of the EU',[107] the many references to 'territory' in the EU Treaties are mainly related to the Member States' territories.[108] Nevertheless, it has been claimed that 'it is clearly

[102] See, inter alia, J Ziller, 'Outermost Regions, Overseas Countries and Territories and Others after the Entry into Force of the Lisbon Treaty' in D Kochenov (ed), *EU Law of the Overseas* (The Hague, Kluwer Law International, 2011) 69; J Ziller, 'Flexibility in the Geographical Scope of EU Law: Diversity and Differentiation in the Application of Substantive Law on Member States' Territories' in G de Búrca and J Scott, *Constitutional Change in the EU* (Oxford, Bloomsbury, 2000) at 119; D Kochenov, 'The Application of EU Law in the EU's Overseas Regions, Countries, and Territories After the Entry into Force of The Treaty of Lisbon' (2012) 20 *Michigan State International Law Review* 669.

[103] Fahey (n 8).

[104] *cf* J Scott, 'Extraterritoriality and Territorial Extension in EU Law' (2014) 62 *American Journal of International Law* 87–126; J Scott, 'The New EU Extra-territoriality' (2014) 51 *Common Market Law Review* 1343.

[105] Scott, ibid, at 89. In this paper, Scott is actually challenging the notion of 'extraterritoriality' as it commonly used in the literature, and draws attention to 'territorial extension': 'a measure will be regarded as extraterritorial when it imposes obligations on persons who do not enjoy a relevant territorial connection with the regulating state. By contrast, a measure will be regarded as giving rise to territorial extension when its application depends upon the existence of a relevant territorial connection, but where the relevant regulatory determination will be shaped as a matter of law, by conduct or circumstances abroad' (ibid at 90). For the present contribution it suffices to note that both notions are relevant to underline the need to understand both international and EU law systematics.

[106] A case in point was formed by the *Ebony Martime* case, where the question arose of the compatibility of an EU Regulation on the enforcement of sanctions and the freedom of the high seas under international law. See Case 177/95 *Ebony Maritime SA and Loten Navigation Co Ltd v Prefetto della Provincia di Brindisi and others* ECLI:EU:C:1997:89.

[107] See for instance the frequent use of the term 'Community territory' in *Ebony Maritime*, ibid. Other cases in point may be Case C-34/09 *Gerardo Ruiz Zambrano v Office national de l'emploi* ECLI:EU:C:2011:124 and Case C-434/09 *Shirley McCarthy v Secretary of State for the Home Department* ECLI:EU:C:2011:277. *cf* D Kochenov, 'A Real European Citizenship; A New Jurisdiction Text; A Novel Chapter in the Development of the Union in Europe' (2011) 18 *Columbia Journal of European Law* 56.

[108] See extensively as well as much more in detail on these provisions, D Kochenov, 'European Union Territory from a Legal Perspective: A Commentary on Articles 52 TEU, 355, 349, and 198-204 TFEU' in M Kellerbauer, M Klamert and J Tomkin (eds), *The EU Treaties and the Charter of Fundamental Rights – A Commentary* (Oxford, Oxford University Press, forthcoming in 2019); University of Groningen Faculty of Law Research Paper 2017-05; available at SSRN: https://ssrn.com/abstract=2956011.

possible to speak of the emergence of the concept of Union territory, given the autonomous demarcation of the territorial application of EU law defined in the Treaties'.[109] Indeed, one may find some hints at the possible existence of an 'EU territory', in particular in relation to 'economic, social and territorial cohesion', which intends to view the territories of the Member States as a whole.[110] With regard to third country nationals (TCNs), the EU's common immigration policy (Article 79 TFEU) provides other arguments to start viewing the territories of the EU Member States as one 'EU territory'. More generally, the internal market rules seem to point to the, at least 'virtual' existence of a common EU territory. Clearer notions of a possible 'EU territory' can be found when the 'territorial application' of the Treaties in concerned. First of all, the Treaties apply to the EU Member States (which are all mentioned by name).[111] This is further specified in relation to the so-called countries and territories overseas, which leads to an extension of the territorial scope of the EU.[112] At the same time, the existence of overseas territories may have territorial implications under, for instance, the law of the sea, in particular where these territories may result in an additional economic exclusive zone (EEZ) to be used for fishing and possible mining activities. Thus, while EU law is not (fully) applicable to Greenland, its location is of interest to the EU in debates on the future of the arctic area.

Finally, the present author's – admittedly – mild obsession with the notion of legal personality,[113] warrants a few lines on that issue. First of all, international law perspectives have been used in EU law scholarship to answer the question of the EU's own legal personality or the legal status of its agencies.[114] These notions have been important to establish the EU's separate legal status as a global actor alongside its Member States. Furthermore, more recently the EU also seems to give its own interpretation to the notion. A recent case in point is the

[109] Kellerbauer, Klamert and Tomkin, ibid, at 3.

[110] Thus, Article 3(3) TEU refers to the Union's objective to 'promote economic, social and territorial cohesion, and solidarity among Member States'. At the same time 'It shall respect its rich cultural and linguistic diversity, and shall ensure that Europe's cultural heritage is safeguarded and enhanced'. References like these are meant to create some unity while preserving the diversity, and the objective of 'territorial cohesion' has merely been the driver behind the allocation of the so-called cohesion funds aimed at 'reducing disparities between the levels of development of the various regions and the backwardness of the least favoured regions' (Art 174 TFEU).

[111] Art 52 TEU.

[112] Art 355 TFEU.

[113] See for instance RA Wessel, 'Reparation for Injuries Suffered in the Service of the United Nations' in C Ryngaert, IF Dekker, RA Wessel and J Wouters (eds), *Judicial Decisions on the Law of International Organizations* (Oxford, Oxford University Press, 2016) 11–18; or in the same volume RA Wessel, 'Legal Status (Personality)' 6–10; NM Blokker and RA Wessel, 'Revisiting Questions of Organizationhood, Legal Personality and Membership in the OSCE: The Interplay Between Law, Politics and Practice' in M Platise Steinbrück, C Moser, A Peters (eds), *Revisiting the Legal Status of the OSCE* (Cambridge, Cambridge University Press, 2018); or earlier RA Wessel, 'Revisiting the International Legal Status of the EU' (2000) *European Foreign Affairs Review* 507–37 and RA Wessel, 'The International Legal Status of the European Union' (1997) *European Foreign Affairs Review* 109–29.

[114] See for references the final two publications in the previous footnote.

Front Polisario case,[115] which dealt with the territorial application of a trade agreement between the EU and the Kingdom of Morocco.[116] Indeed, the case has 'fascinating international law aspects'.[117] Apart from the territorial questions, the case also dealt with the recognition of the claimant, the Polisario Front – a national liberation movement (NLM) that claims sovereignty for Western Sahara – as a natural or legal person under Article 264(4) TFEU. Both the General Court, and on appeal the CJEU, combined international as well as EU law arguments to decide on the NLM's legal personality and questions of territorial application.[118] In the further definition and development of international legal personality, both EU and international law scholarship will find new material in cases like these.

F. Citizenship and Nationality

There is a clear link between territory, nationality and citizenship. While nationality is usually related to a particular state, citizenship can also be granted to others living on the territory of that state. European citizenship is a key element in the process of European integration. Article 30(2) TFEU inter alia provides: 'Citizens of the Union shall enjoy the rights and be subject to the duties provided for in the Treaties. They shall have [...] the right to move and reside freely within the territory of the Member States'. Indeed, the territory of *all* Member States; the rights of European citizens have largely been harmonised and European citizenship is frequently used by the Court of Justice of the EU to rule on extensive rights for individuals. Citizenship has thus become an essential element in the right to seek or accept jobs, to start a business or to provide cross-border services. At the same time, European citizenship entails

> the right to enjoy, *in the territory of a third country* in which the Member State of which they are nationals is not represented, the protection of the diplomatic and consular authorities of any Member State on the same conditions as the nationals of that State [...].[119]

[115] Case T-512/12 *Front Polisario* (n 98).

[116] 2010 EU-Morocco Agreement on agricultural, processed and fisheries products.

[117] See Geraldo Vidigal, 'Trade Agreements, EU Law, and Occupied Territories – A Report on Polisario v Council' (*EJIL Talk!*, 1 July 2015), available at www.ejiltalk.org/trade-agreements-eu-law-and-occupied-territories-a-report-on-polisario-v-council/. See also FG Nicola, 'Of Pirates, Occupied Territories and Oil companies: The Quiet Diplomacy of the European Court of Justice' paper presented at the Workshop Workshop *EU Trade Law and Policy: Current Developments and Challenges*, Università LUISS Guido Carli, Rome, Italy, 10 April 2017.

[118] Case T-512/12 *Front Polisario* (n 98). In the appeals case (C-104/16 P; ECLI:EU:C:2016:973), the CJEU held that products originating from Western Sahara did not fall within the territorial scope of the agreement and that the provision that determined the territorial scope of the agreement ought to be construed in a way that contradicted the practice followed by the parties, in order to be compatible with the international peremptory principle of self-determination. See also A Rasi, 'Front Polisario: A Step Forward in Judicial Review of International Agreements by the Court of Justice?' (2017) 2 *European Papers* 3, and other contributions to the dialogue in that journal issue.

[119] Art 23 TFEU (emphasis added).

Hence, outside the EU a European citizen may rely on the help of another EU Member State. Thus, the traditional national diplomatic and consular assistance is extended to an EU-wide system of protection of European citizens abroad. Links with international diplomatic and consular law become ever more visible.[120]

While, currently, the idea of 'supranational citizenship'[121] can most easily be seen as a dimension of the European integration process, it has been argued that the existence of the phenomenon could allow for a more general separation between states and (single) citizenship:

> This belonging to a polity, expressed in purely legal terms, is the real novelty of the European model, replicable in other geographical areas or global organizations – which could generate – one day – their one partial citizenships – and it opens the door to multiple and cumulative citizenships, not conflicting among each other, to communities partially overlapping.[122]

At the same time, it is clear that EU citizenship does not endow the EU with competences states would generally have under international law to protect their nationals. In international diplomatic and consular law, the notion of nationality remains crucial. New developments in EU diplomacy reveal at least an ambition of the EU to act on behalf of its Member States in situations of diplomatic protection and consular assistance. This clearly highlights the parallels between being a national of a state and a European citizen.

G. Legal Instruments and the Hierarchy of Norms

A classic difference between EU and international law is perceived to be found in the availability of legal instruments. Under EU law, 'legally binding' decisions can be taken, that – in most cases – can even be enforced before a court of law. International law would have to rely on politics and persuasion rather than on legal instruments. Obviously, this is a caricature of both EU and international law. Large parts of the European integration process are based on 'softer' instruments, including all kinds of 'green or white papers' of the European Commission, resolutions by the European Parliament, Declarations by the European Council or instruments such as the 'open method of coordination'.[123] The main source of

[120] S Duquet, *The Contribution of the European Union to Diplomatic and Consular Law*, PhD thesis, University of Leuven, 2018; Kerres and Wessel (n 37); Wessel (n 35) 129–47; RA Wessel and B Van Vooren, 'The EEAS' Diplomatic Dreams and the Reality of International and European Law' (2013) *Journal of European Public Policy* 9 1350–67.

[121] See F Strumia, *Supranational Citizenship and the Challenge of Diversity: Immigrants, Citizens and Member States in the EU* (Leiden/Boston, Brill/Nijhoff, 2013).

[122] S Cafaro, 'Peculiarities of a Supranational Citizenship', 21 November 2016, available at www.linkedin.com/pulse/peculiarities-supranational-citizenship-susanna-cafaro.

[123] *cf* A von Bogdandy, F Arndt and J Bast, 'Legal Instruments in European Union Law and their Reform: A Systematic Approach on an Empirical Basis' (2004) *Yearbook of European Law* 91–136;

international law, on the other hand, is formed by the thousands of (legally binding) treaties concluded between states and international organisations; and quite a few international organisations have the competence to enact binding decisions.[124] While enforcement possibilities indeed differ, one can hardly maintain that the daily practice in the EU is based on legally binding instruments and the daily practice in international law is not. Both international and EU law have a variety of (legal) instruments at their disposal and – given the above-mentioned similar questions they are faced with – there are no a priori reasons to study the use and effects of these instruments in complete isolation.

A different, yet related, question concerns the hierarchy between international, EU and domestic legal norms as well as their inter-relationship. While the principle of 'primacy' of EU law over the law of its Member States is rightfully seen as a cornerstone of the EU's legal system, in practice the difference with international law norms may be less clear. It is easy to point to some differences (eg under EU law domestic courts seem to have to accept the primacy of EU law even within their own legal order), but it is perhaps more interesting to assess some of the parallels (eg international law is also binding on states and, domestically, they may also be forced to find solutions to square possibly conflicting national and international norms).[125] Moreover, in finding solutions for potentially conflicting norms in a situation of 'multilevel regulation',[126] both EU and international law use similar techniques, such as 'treaty conform interpretation' or 'consistent interpretation' to allow for norms at different levels to coincide without conflict.[127] A comparison of the practical application of these principles in EU, international and domestic law may very well lead to new insights in the way in which legal norms have an effect in different legal orders.

IV. Conclusion: Towards a More Integrated Study of International and EU Law?

First reactions to presentations of drafts of this contribution where telling and ranged from disapproval to almost sheer panic. Was I really suggesting to get rid

M Ruffert, 'The Many Faces of Rule-Making in the EU' in E Fahey (ed), *The Actors of Postnational Rule-Making: Contemporary Challenges of European and International Law* (Abington/New York, Routledge, 2016) 47–66. See on soft law in the EU for instance, F Terpan, 'Soft Law in the European Union: The Changing Nature of EU Law' (2014) *European Law Journal* 40.

[124] *cf* IF Dekker and RA Wessel, 'Governance by International Organisations: Rethinking the Source and Normative Force of International Decisions' in IF Dekker and W Werner (eds), *Governance and International Legal Theory* (Leiden/ Boston, Martinus Nijhoff Publishers, 2004).

[125] *cf* Nijman and Nollkaemper (n 20).

[126] Føllesdal, Wessel and Wouters (n 20).

[127] See for instance DT Björgvinsson, *The Intersection of International Law and Domestic Law: A Theoretical and Practical Analysis* (Edward Elgar, 2015) Ch 6.

of the distinction between international and EU law in our curriculae? Did I not see that the two fields of study were so different that combining them would not do justice to their respective peculiarities? Did I deliberately ignore the fact that for both sub-disciplines it is already impossible to find generalists and that combining them could only lead to superficial analysis? Of course I am aware of all this. In fact, the gap between international and EU law I witnessed while teaching at various universities in Europe formed exactly the reason to look for bridges. Once students have chosen their specialisation, they tend to lock themselves up in their new disciplinary cage. And, frankly, we help them do so by not drawing attention to the interactions between different legal systems. It is not unusual for graduate students to respond: 'I'm sorry I'm doing EU law, I know nothing about public international law' (and vice versa), while their undergraduate courses in these fields where only one or two years ago.

In reaction to these somewhat defensive statements, a useful reassurance may be that – as phrased by Bruno de Witte – 'qualifying EU law as international law does not imply that the Treaties should be understood and interpreted from an intergovernmental perspective and that limitations of sovereignty should be narrowly construed'.[128] The many specific, and valuable, characteristics of the EU, and of the European integration process more generally, are undeniable and warrant a continued in-depth study. The mere aim of the present contribution was to draw attention to a number of areas in which the study of both international and EU law should remain aware of doctrinal developments. True, it is hardly possible in any of these two areas to remain a generalist, given the advanced and often quite complex and technical details that by now characterise most sub-disciplines in international and EU law. A plea to try and even go beyond that may be wishful thinking and perhaps, indeed, even result in far too superficial analyses. After all, any comparison becomes easier at a higher level of abstraction.

The aim of this contribution is therefore more modest. Noticing a deepening of the divide between international and EU law scholarship and the reflection of this in our educational programmes, the question was whether we could indicate issues in one discipline of which it makes sense to be included in analyses of the other. While there are certainly exceptions, it is quite strange that in EU law programmes hardly any attention is paid to treaty law, trade law, statehood, the law of international responsibility, international organisations law or (these days) diplomatic law. Similarly, why do courses on the law of international organisations mostly continue to exclude the EU and the institutional developments in that organisation? And, why do we hardly see a comparison to EU enforcement mechanisms, negotiations and decision-making, institutional solutions, democratic experiments or variations of legal acts in general courses on international law?

This contribution briefly analysed the mutual perspectives of international and EU law and mapped a number of areas in which these disciplines can continue

[128] De Witte (n 54) at 196.

to learn from each other. While admitting the somewhat EU-centric locus of the plea,[129] both the study of the further institutionalisation of the international legal order and the study of the internal and external relations of the EU may benefit from that exchange of thoughts. As a result of the increasing global interests of the EU, the mutual influence of international and EU law on each other's development seems to be getting more attention in recent academic research. This may form a logical momentum to get reacquainted and renew the dialogue.

[129] Indeed, the entire discussion is far less relevant for law students in Asia, Africa or the Americas.

PART II

The Interaction between EU and International Law in Selected Areas

4

Integrated Rights Protection in the European and International Context: Some Reflections about Limits and Consequences

CHRISTINA ECKES*

I. Introduction

The universal claim of human rights and the cultural and political dimension of fundamental rights stand in an apparent tension. So do different regimes of fundamental rights that govern the same substantive situations within the same territory. An integrated rights protection must ideally be able to put these tensions at work in order to attain a justified and adequate level of protection in the European, national and international context.

Courts of different jurisdictions, ie the Court of Justice of the European Union (CJEU), the European Court of Human Rights (ECtHR), and national constitutional courts, have offered their interpretations of how the different legal regimes protecting fundamental rights in Europe relate to each other. Each of them considers these relationships from the perspective of their own legal order and aims to integrate external legal norms in ways that give priority to the internal coherence of their own legal order. While the different claims can be compared and contrasted with regard to the protection of fundamental rights, ie in terms of scope and substance, the different points of departure, ie each court from the perspective of its own legal order, make it impossible to weigh the underlying systemic considerations.

What are the roles of the CJEU, national constitutional courts and the ECtHR in ensuring that the different legal regimes protecting rights work together to achieve a justifiable and adequate level of protection? How much *integration* of

* Special thanks to Minke de Haan and Sophie Dura for their research assistance.

fundamental rights protection is justifiable and adequate? How much room for *variation* in *fundamental* rights (protection) is justifiable and adequate? Does the argument differ within the EU legal order and internationally?

This paper argues that the courts make claims that can be justified within the logic of their different legal orders but that studying judicial practice does not help in finding an answer to the question of how the different regimes should relate and to what extent they should integrate for a justified and adequate level of rights protection. A search for the answer to this question must turn to theoretical considerations.

The increasing EU competence in human rights sensitive areas, mainly within the Area of Freedom, Security and Justice (AFSJ), ie criminal law, asylum law, securing the external borders, will more prominently bring to the fore questions about the harmonisation or integration of rights protection within the EU legal order, as well as tensions between EU law and international rights instruments. It will make it essential to find a satisfactory and workable answer to the question of who should interpret fundamental rights. This trend is strengthened by the normalisation of the AFSJ, in particular the full jurisdiction of the court over these policy areas since the end of the transition period in December 2014.

This paper is structured as follows. Section two sets out why fundamental rights are substantively different from other fields of law. Section three engages with the practice of how the different rights regimes in Europe relate to each other. It does so on the basis of a study of the codified law and case law of the relevant courts. Section four zooms in on the plausibility of the CJEU's autonomy concern, which led it to declare the draft agreement on the EU's accession to the European Convention on Human Rights (ECHR) incompatible with EU law. Section five makes the central argument which theoretical considerations should guide the interrelations between different fundamental rights regimes. Section six draws conclusions for the adequate level of integration between the different rights regimes.

II. Prelude: Why are Rights a Special Case?

Human rights are a special case when it comes to the interaction of different legal spheres. I would go as far as claiming that fundamental rights constitute the most difficult area when pondering questions of resilience, autonomy and porosity of one legal sphere *vis-à-vis* another. The following five substantive reasons support this position. They also explain why institutionally rights have proven so problematic within the history of EU integration.

Firstly, human rights are by definition a '*horizontal*' policy, in that they deploy their effects across all substantive policy areas. This makes it impossible to limit the effects of any given ruling to a particular policy area. Not only aspects of a ruling that relate to the scope and substance of rights but also aspects relating to the division of competence between the national and EU actors. At the same time it may also be undesirable that the scope and substance of rights protection is determined purely and from the perspective of the individual seemingly arbitrarily by institutional and competence considerations.

A concrete example of the tensions that this may create is the headscarves rulings by the CJEU of 14 March 2017.[1] For a long time EU law has made illegal discrimination on the basis of gender and discrimination of *EU citizens* on grounds of nationality. Since 2000, EU law also covers discrimination on grounds of ethnicity[2] and discrimination at work on grounds of disability, age, sexual orientation or religion.[3] The CJEU regularly ruled on the first three of these grounds in the work environment. The recent headscarves cases were the first occasion for the CJEU to rule on non-discrimination at work on religious grounds. In its rulings, the CJEU on the one hand accepted the possibility of a general ban on religious symbols. On the other hand it ruled out that the wish of a particular client could justify relying on the occupational requirement exception.[4] Because of the competence division between the EU and its Member States, EU law does not regulate other aspects of religious freedom, outside of the occupational environment. Consequently the CJEU could not for example rule on the religious symbols in an educational setting, as the ECtHR has in the past.[5] At the same time, the CJEU could rule on discrimination on grounds of ethnicity across the board, since the Racial Equality Directive is not limited to the work environment. The particular limitation of the CJEU's powers with regard to religious symbols follows from the institutional and constitutional set-up of the EU. This makes it difficult to justify this limitation in terms of substantive rights considerations. On the contrary, a consistent approach to the interpretation of the right to wear religious symbols could be expected to contribute to legal certainty and equality before the law.

Fragmentation of the competence to rule on the scope and substance of a particular right highlights in several ways the relevance of who rules on a particular fundamental rights issue. First, the power of framing an issue carries legal and political significance. In the headscarves ruling of March 2017 the CJEU chose, differently to its own ruling in *Nikolova*,[6] not to engage with the political context

[1] Case C-157/15 *Samira Achbita v G4S Secure Solutions NV* ECLI:EU:C:2017:203 and Case C-188/15 *Asma Bougnaoui v Micropole SA* ECLI:EU:C:2017:204.

[2] Directive 2000/43/EC implementing equal treatment irrespective of racial or ethnic origin ('Racial Equality Directive) [2000] OJ L180/22.

[3] Council Directive 2000/78/EC establishing a general framework for equal treatment in employment and occupation [2000] OJ L303/16.

[4] See Art 4 of Directive 2000/43 (n 2), specifically in *Bougnaoui* (n 1), paras 34 ff.

[5] *Lautsi and others v Italy* [GC] No 30814/06 ECHR 2011; *Aktas v France* No 43563/08; *Bayrak v France* No 14308/08; *Gamaleddyn v France* No 18527/08; *Ghazal v France* No 29134/08; *J Singh v France* No 2546/08 *and R Singh v France* No 27561/08; *Dogru v France* No 27058/05 and *Kervanci v France* No 31645/04 ECHR 4 December 2008; *Kurtulmus v Turkey* No 65500/01 ECHR 2006-II; *Leyla Sahin v Turkey* No 44774/98, ECHR 2005-XI; *Köse and 93 Others v Turkey* No 26625/02 ECHR 2006-II; *Dahlab v Switzerland* No 42393/98 ECHR 2001-V. For full summaries see www.echr.coe.int/Documents/FS_Religious_Symbols_ENG.pdf.

[6] Case C-83/14 *CHEZ razpredelenie Bulgaria AD v Komisia za zashtita ot diskriminatsia* ECLI:EU:C:2015:480, concerned the practice of CHEZ, the largest electricity company in Bulgaria, to

of growing islamophobia in Europe. There may be many reasons for this but it does not open the door to a debate on the *legal* and political significance of this growing trend of othering Muslims. Second, the CJEU considers any fundamental rights issue within the logic of EU law. This necessarily introduces considerations relating to regulation and integration into the debate, such as prominently considerations of uniformity and effectiveness. This is very different before the ECtHR. The Strasbourg Court has the exclusive mandate to ensure minimum protection of human rights. It is not guided by a broader responsibility of ensuring a functioning legal order of a supranational nature. This point also relates to the overconstitutionalisation of EU law,[7] which leaves little room for contestation or the co-existence of alternative models. The CJEU's involvement may hence arguably be expected to result in uniformisation of rights protection – at least in this particular way. Competence considerations and the particular legal framework, in which a particular case may determine whether it is argued as a case of discrimination (EU law) or human rights (ECHR). This may lead to different forms of fragmentation. Not only are the norms then interpreted by different actors. Also substantively the framing as a discrimination case, usually working with comparators, or a human rights case, usually working without a comparator, but balancing different rights, makes a significant difference.

Second, fundamental rights have a particular *cultural* dimension. While a general convergence and integration of rights norms between different legal contexts may be observed,[8] the differences in terms of interpretation and application often go to the core of what members of a polity see as choices that define their identity.[9] Freedom to religion is a good example in this context. While France is a state with a very strong commitment to secularity, Ireland or Poland for example emphasise the relevance of God or religion and both permit religious references in the oaths of public servants.[10] All three make clear commitments to the freedom of religion; yet, when the specific question is posed of whether a

place electricity meters in districts where the majority was of Roma ethnicity at a height of 7 meters, which made it impossible for the inhabitants to monitor their electricity consumption. The practice only occurred in districts where the majority was Roma, which continued for nearly a quarter of a century. According to the Court, 'the compulsory, widespread and lasting nature of the practice at issue suggests (…) that the inhabitants of that district, which is known to be lived in mainly by Bulgarian nationals of Roma origin, are, as a whole, considered to be potential perpetrators of such unlawful conduct'. Accordingly, this made the practice offensive and stigmatising. See paras 84 ff.

[7] D Grimm, 'Does Europe Need a Constitution' (1995) 1 *European Law Journal* 282.

[8] See E de Wet and J Vidmar, 'Conflicts between International Paradigms: Hierarchy versus Systemic Integration' (2013) 2 *Global Constitutionalism* 196.

[9] For eg regarding issues such as abortion in the public debate surrounding the Constitutional Treaty.

[10] See, eg, Article 44 of the Irish Constitution: 'The State acknowledges that the homage of public worship is due to Almighty God. It shall hold His Name in reverence, and shall respect and honour religion.' See also the more balanced Preamble of the Polish Constitution: 'We, the Polish Nation – all citizens of the Republic, Both those who believe in God as the source of truth, justice, good and beauty, As well as those not sharing such faith but respecting those universal values as arising from other sources, …'.

civil servant may wear a religious symbol, the answer may very well be different. An interesting case study in practical terms of the effects EU membership has on the scope and substance of national fundamental rights will be Brexit. Once the UK leaves the EU the EU Charter of Fundamental Rights will cease to apply within the legal order of the UK. The UK Equality Act 2010 will continue to exist as primary UK legislation. However, this does not mean that there are no changes in interpretation expected or that it is protected from being repealed in part or in full.[11]

Third, minimum standards of rights are difficult to maintain. Fundamental rights cases often require a specific determination of how to strike the balance between different rights and, hence, a weighing of different rights against each other. This results in a fairly precise determination of the scope of manoeuvre left for public policy makers. It often does not allow protecting one right at a higher level because this would result in an infringement of interpretation of another right by the competent judicial authority.[12]

Fourth, rights catalogues usually give rights to individuals. The EU is the best example of how powerful and effective centrally controlled yet decentralised enforcement by private individuals may be. In the EU legal order this enforcement is based on the combination of primacy and direct effect with the preliminary ruling procedure. It is fundamentally based on the market freedoms but may also serve as a warning to the transformative potential of fundamental rights. International human rights instruments have already been declared as examples of great interference with state sovereignty.[13] Yet, they should be considered as a hybrid in this regard. Consider for example the ECHR, which is built on a two-tier system of rights of individuals that individuals can assert before the ECtHR and an enforcement stage, after a country has failed to give effect to the ECtHR's ruling that may end with state responsibility.[14]

Fifth, human rights are necessarily formulated in a particularly open-textured manner. They require interpreting and developing codified law further to allow application to the individual case. This interpretation is usually understood to be at least partially based on value choices. From a democratic perspective, such

[11] R Wintemute, 'Goodbye EU Anti-Discrimination Law? Hello Repeal of the Equality Act 2010?' (2016) 27 *King's Law Journal* 387; S Fredman, A Davies, M Freedland, J Fudge and M Campbell, 'The Potential Challenges to Equality Law in the UK' (Oxford Human Rights Hub, 2016).

[12] In the context of the Charter of Fundamental Rights, see D Gudmundsdóttir, 'A Renewed Emphasis on the Charter's Distinction between Rights and Principles: Is a Doctrine of Judicial Restraint more Appropriate?' (2015) 52 *Common Market Law Review* 685. S Greer, 'The Margin of Appreciation: Interpretation and Discretion under the European Convention on Human Rights' (Human Rights Files No 17, Council of Europe Publishing, 2000).

[13] See for the debate, J Delbruck, 'International Protection of Human Rights and State Sovereignty' (1982) 57 *Indiana Law Journal*, article 3. See also, J Donnelly, 'State Sovereignty and International Human Rights' (2014) 28 *Ethics and International Affairs* 225. However, this argument is made in the context of state intervention by Mohammed Ayoob, 'Humanitarian Intervention and International Society' (2001) 7 *Global Insight* 225.

[14] Art 46 of the ECHR.

determination of the specific interpretation and application of rights by unelected judges may be and is seen as particularly problematic if those judges are external to the legal order whose norms are deemed to stand in conflict with a given fundamental right.

These particularities of rights go a long way in explaining why courts of different legal spheres have chosen to keep external rights control at bay in one way or another. Conferring the power to interpret and apply rights to an external legal sphere, including an external judicial authority, whose rulings are then binding within the domestic legal sphere in a potentially hierarchically superior manner, is seen as highly problematic. They also explain why fundamental rights have played and continue to play an important role in the debate on EU legal integration. On the one hand, national courts have pressured the EU to protect fundamental rights as a condition for them to accept the primacy of EU law. On the other hand, EU fundamental rights protection is a way of constitutionalising the European legal order, which is largely perceived as happening at the expense of national sovereignty. Fundamental rights remain the subject of continuous tug-of-war matches between the CJEU and the German Federal Constitutional Court (GFCC).[15]

III. Judicial Practice: Convergence at Distance

A. EU Law and the ECHR

The ECHR is highly relevant for the determination of fundamental rights under EU law. The constitutional status of the ECHR within the EU legal order is codified in the EU Treaties. Article 6(3) TEU stipulates that the EU's general principles are based on the ECHR, together with the constitutional traditions of the Member

[15] In 2013, for eg, the CJEU decided Case C-617/10 *Åklagaren v Hans Åkerberg Fransson* ECLI:EU:C:2013:105 paras 19–21, explaining that the EU Charter of Fundamental Rights is applicable to Member States' actions within the 'scope of EU law'. The GFCC in *Counter-Terrorism Database*, 1 BVerfGE 1215/07, warned the CJEU not to interpret 'scope of EU law' too broadly (C, para 91: 'for the questions … which only concern German fundamental rights, the European Court of Justice is not the lawful judge according to Art 101 sec 1 GG. The ECJ's decision in the case *Åkerberg Fransson* does not change this conclusion. As part of a cooperative relationship between the Federal Constitutional Court and the European Court of Justice (*cf* BVerfGE 126, 286 <307>), this decision must not be read in a way that would view it as an apparent ultra vires act or as if it endangered the protection and enforcement of the fundamental rights in the Member States (Art 23 sec 1 sentence 1 GG) in a way that questioned the identity of the Basic Law's constitutional order (*cf* BVerfGE 89, 155 <188>; 123, 267 <353 and 354>; 125, 260 <324>; 126, 286 <302 et seq>; 129, 78 <100>). The decision must thus not be understood and applied in such a way that absolutely any connection of a provision's subject-matter to the merely abstract scope of Union law, or merely incidental effects on Union law, would be sufficient for binding the Member States by the Union's fundamental rights set forth in the EUCFR.'). Source (available in English and German) www.bundesverfassungsgericht.de/SharedDocs/Entscheidungen/EN/2013/04/rs20130424_1bvr121507en.html. The CJEU confirmed its position in Case C-418/11 *Texdata Software* ECLI:EU:C:2013:588 paras 72–73.

States. The ECHR is also closely interlinked with the Charter of Fundamental Rights (CFR), which is the EU's binding catalogue of fundamental rights at primary law level. Indeed, Articles 52(3) and 53 CFR underline the particular relevance of the ECHR for the interpretation of the Charter. They declare that a Charter right that corresponds to a right under the Convention has the same meaning and scope as laid down by the ECHR and that nothing in the Charter may adversely affect rights protected under the Convention. Furthermore, while the Charter only refers to the Convention itself and not to the case law of the ECtHR (except in its Preamble),[16] the CJEU ruled in *J McB v LE* that where rights in the Charter correspond to rights in the ECHR, it will follow the case law of the ECtHR.[17] Hence, the ECHR as interpreted by the ECtHR is in many ways the prime source for EU fundamental rights, determining their scope and interpretation. Secondary law regularly refers to the ECHR.[18]

B. Convergence on Substance

Convergence in terms of substance is visible even in areas where differences have emerged and resulted in an avalanche of scholarship on the potential of a clash between the CJEU and the ECtHR and of contradictory obligations of the Member States.[19] An example of this is the case law of the ECtHR, the CJEU and the UK Supreme Court on the limits of the principle of mutual recognition/trust in a series of cases concerning the Common European Asylum System.

In 2011, in the *M.S.S.* case,[20] the ECtHR found Belgium in violation of Article 3 ECHR for sending an asylum seeker back to Greece where their rights under the Convention were blatantly infringed. The ECtHR made clear that the obligations under the Convention impose limits to the principle of mutual recognition/trust

[16] Art 52(3) of the Charter of Fundamental Rights.

[17] Case C-400/10 PPU *J McB v LE* ECLI:EU:C:2010:582. S Douglas-Scott interprets 'correspond' as 'the same' or 'identical', in 'The European Union and Human Rights after the Treaty of Lisbon' (2011) 11 *Human Rights Law Review* 655, 655–56. This seems to be an overly strict reading. Indeed, the explanations to the Charter offer a list of 'corresponding rights'. This appears to offer a good interpretation of the scope of the Court of Justice's ruling.

[18] eg Recital 1, Council Directive 2000/78/EC (n 3); Recital 1, Directive 2016/343/EU on the strengthening of certain aspects of the presumption of innocence and of the right to be present at the trial in criminal proceedings [2016] OJ L65/1. Recital 5 ff, Directive 2012/13/EU on the right to information in criminal proceedings [2016] OJ L142/1.

[19] S Gáspár-Szilágyi, 'Joined Cases Aranyosi and Căldăraru. Converging Human Rights Standards, Mutual Trust and a New Ground for Postponing a European Arrest Warrant' (2016) 24 *European Journal of Crime, Criminal Law and Criminal Justice* 197. A Lübbe, 'Systemic Flaws' and Dublin Transfers: Incompatible Tests before the CJEU and the ECtHR?' (2015) 27 *International Journal for Refugee Law* 135. W Weiss, 'Human Rights in the EU: Rethinking the Role of European Convention on Human Rights After Lisbon' (2011) 7 *European Constitutional Review* 64. S Morano-Foadi and S Andreadakis, 'The Convergence of the European Legal System in the Treatment of Third Country Nationals in Europe: The ECJ and ECtHR Jurisprudence' (2011) 22 *European Journal of International Law* 1071.

[20] *M.S.S. v Belgium and Greece* Reports of Judgments and Decisions (2011) Application No 30696/09.

under EU law, which establishes a presumption of compliance with EU fundamental rights. Shortly after, in the cases of *N.S.* and *M.E.*, the CJEU followed *M.S.S.* and reconciled EU law with the ECtHR's ruling by declaring that the transferring Member State was obliged to examine the asylum application itself in cases such as *M.S.S.*, where numerous clear indications pointed at a violation of the ECHR. In light of the wording of the Dublin-II-Regulation, this is quite a stretch, but it allowed Member States to reconcile their obligations under the Convention and under EU law. Two years later, in 2013, the CJEU introduced a higher threshold to justify departure from the Dublin II rules. In the case of *Abdullahi*, a national court requested the CJEU to clarify the procedure for determining responsibility for asylum applications under the Common European Asylum System. The CJEU replied that when two Member States agreed which of them was the state that was responsible for the application under the Dublin II Regulation, the asylum seeker could 'only' challenge that decision by 'pleading *systemic deficiencies* in the asylum procedure and in the conditions for the reception of applicants for asylum' in the responsible Member State.[21]

Again one year later, in 2014, an Afghan family brought an application to the ECtHR challenging their transfer from Switzerland to Italy amongst others on the grounds that in Italy they would be treated in a way that violated Article 3 ECHR (*Tarakhel*).[22] The Strasbourg Court accepted by a majority of 14 to 3 that Switzerland had indeed breached Article 3 ECHR. The Court relied on its usual test, which assumes that Article 3 ECHR stands in the way of a transfer if 'substantial grounds have been shown for believing' that a 'real risk' exists of treatment contrary to that article in the state of destination.[23] In the following case of *Aranyosi*, the CJEU brought its position again much more in line with the ECtHR by emphasising the 'real risk' test, which also places emphasis on the specific situation of the applicant rather than only systemic deficiencies.[24]

This line of case law should be taken as evidence of the mutual willingness to avoid an open clash. In its development it demonstrates how mutual approximation in terminology and focus can lead to convergence that bridges the actual or putative differences.

C. Keeping Interpretational Distance

Opinion 2/13 on the EU's accession to the ECHR gave the CJEU the opportunity to engage with the potential tension between the EU principle of mutual trust

[21] Case C-394/12 *Shamso Abdullahi v Bundesasylamt* ECLI:EU:C:2013:813 at para 60 (emphasis added).

[22] *Tarakhel v Switzerland* [GC] No 29217/12 ECHR 2014.

[23] See *Soering v the United Kingdom* No 14038/88 ECHR 1998-VII, Series A No 161.

[24] Joined Cases C-404/15 and C659/115 PPU *Pál Aranyosi and Robert Căldăraru v Generalstaatsanwaltschaft Bremen* ECLI:EU:C:2016:198 para 88.

and obligations under the ECHR at an abstract level, unrestrained by the concrete facts of a particular case.[25] The Opinion could be considered the clearest and most consequential expression of the CJEU's attempts to keep the ECHR at a *distance* to the EU legal order.[26]

In Opinion 2/13, the CJEU found that the agreement setting out the legal framework for EU accession to the ECHR was incompatible with EU law, essentially because it endangered the autonomy of the EU legal order.[27] Indeed, the CJEU treats the concern over autonomy as a second-order reason in the Razian sense of a meta-consideration that displaces all first-order reasons.[28] In other words, in the view of the CJEU, the protection of the autonomy of the EU legal order must be ensured, not on a balance of interests but as an absolute value. By autonomy the CJEU understands that EU law is valid in itself without the intervention or recognition of national or international law. The CJEU regards protecting the autonomy of the EU legal order as identical to protecting its own ability to maintain *from the authoritative perspective of EU law* that EU law 'stems from an *independent source of law*'.[29] This unilateral claim of the CJEU, while remaining unconfirmed by national courts, is central to the balance of powers within the EU legal order. The mutually agreed suspension of the decision over the 'last word' between the CJEU on the one hand and national constitutional and supreme courts on the other depends on the ability of each of the judicial actors (the CJEU and the national constitutional courts) to make their own claims within the logic of their own legal order. If the CJEU's absolute claim of original validity of EU law could be challenged, not only from the perspective of national and international law, but *within the logic of EU law*, this would allow national courts to end the suspension and make a universally valid claim.

In fact post-accession, the CJEU could reasonably expect greater pressure from the highest national courts if it was legally bound and had to enforce external determinations of fundamental rights standards that clashed with the internal, national and/or European interpretations of these rights. Yet with regard to the determination of the scope or substance of rights the EU's position is not

[25] Opinion 2/13 *Accession of the EU to the ECHR* ECLI:EU:C:2014:2454.

[26] See on the pre-accession distance, C Eckes, 'EU Accession to the ECHR: Between Autonomy and Adaptation' (2013) 76 *Modern Law Review* 254.

[27] See also N Jaaskinen and A Sikora, 'The Exclusive Jurisdiction of the Court of Justice of the European Union and the Unity of the EU Legal Order' in M Cremona et al (eds), *The EU and International Dispute Settlement* (London, Hart Publishing, 2016); T Lock, 'The Not So Free Choice of EU Member States in International Dispute Settlement' in Cremona et al, ibid.

[28] Raz calls first-order considerations: 'reasons for action' that have been drawn directly from 'considerations of interest, desire or morality' and second-order considerations: 'reason[s] to act on or refrain from acting on a reason', see J Raz, *Practical Reason and Norms* (Oxford, Oxford University Press, 1975) at 34 and 39, respectively. Raz's framework of first and second-order considerations is often used in the human rights context as an argument against balancing and a justification for giving rights priority over other considerations, see, eg, RH Pildes, 'Avoiding Balancing: The Role of Exclusionary Reasons in Constitutional Law' (1994) 45 *Hastings Law Journal* 711.

[29] Opinion 2/13 (n 25) para 166 (emphasis added).

essentially different from the position of states. The margin of appreciation may equally ensure the EU's autonomy to make interpretative choices of substance. The great difference between the position of the EU and a state pertains to the ECtHR's ability to make a binding determination of the hierarchical relations between norms belonging to different legal spheres, and thus interfere with the power relations within the EU.[30]

D. European and International Rights Instruments in National Law

In the EU's compound legal order, not only the CJEU but also, and even primarily, national courts are confronted with the task of delimiting and reconciling the different obligations that flow from different legal expressions of rights, such as the Universal Declaration of Human Rights (UDHR), the ECHR, the EU Charter and national bills of rights. This section will turn to some examples of how national constitutional courts choose the approach of convergence at distance.

An example of convergence at distance is the interpretative value given to the EU Charter under Spanish constitutional law. Both the Romanian Constitution and the Spanish Constitution expressly give the UDHR interpretative value and align their corresponding constitutional provisions to this instrument.[31] The Spanish Constitutional Court extended this rule to EU law and held that even if EU law lacked constitutional status EU law provisions that have fundamental status (including the Charter) should be treated the same way as the sources that have formally been vested with interpretive value.[32]

The UK Supreme Court dealt in 2014, only two months after the above-discussed case of *Abdullahi*, with the exact question of whether and to what extent national authorities are required to check the circumstances of asylum seekers after their transfer to another Member State. The Supreme Court held in the case of *EM* that, irrespective of whether 'systemic deficiencies' existed in the reception system for asylum seekers in Italy, the Court of Appeal should examine on a case-by-case basis the risk that appellants would be subjected to treatment contrary to

[30] See for more detail the next subsection below, which examines the plausibility of the CJEU's autonomy concern.

[31] Art 20(1) of the Romanian Constitution: 'Constitutional provisions concerning the citizens' rights and liberties shall be interpreted and enforced in conformity with the Universal Declaration of Human Rights, with the covenants and other treaties Romania is a party to.'

[32] Art 10(2) of the Spanish Constitution: 'The principles relating to the fundamental rights and liberties recognized by the Constitution shall be interpreted in conformity with the Universal Declaration of Human Rights and the international treaties and agreements thereon ratified by Spain.' M de Visser, 'National Constitutional Courts, the Court of Justice and the Protection of Fundamental Rights in a Post-Charter Landscape' (2014) 15 *Human Rights Review* 39, 43 (the case is not translated to English).

the Convention if they were returned to Italy.[33] The parties had based their arguments on the case law of the ECtHR but had not referred to the case law of the CJEU at all. The UK Supreme Court did not mention *Abdullahi* either. This case demonstrates the important role that national courts play in giving authority to the reading of either the ECtHR or the CJEU.

The GFCC has for a long time made much noise about the relationship between fundamental rights protected under national and EU law. The GFCC has a tradition of, on the one hand, encouraging the CJEU to protect fundamental rights[34] and, on the other, delimiting the applicability of the EU Charter of Fundamental Rights and the case law of the CJEU.[35] It consistently excludes that constitutional complaints could be based on a violation of the ECHR or the Charter, but limits the application of these instruments to situations where they are invoked in conjunction with a violation of a fundamental right protected under the German Constitution.[36]

In 2013, the CJEU had linked Article 51(1) CFR, which sets out that the provisions of this Charter are addressed to [...] the Member States only when they are *implementing* Union law, to the CJEU's pre-Charter case law on when Member States are bound by EU fundamental rights and interpreted it to mean 'applicable in all situations governed by European Union law' (*Ackerberg Fransson*).[37] The GFCC considered in the same year whether *Ackerberg Fransson* was *ultra vires*, came to the conclusion that it was not and that it did not violate the constitutional identity of the German basic law. In this ruling the GFCC explained that *Ackerberg Fransson* cannot be understood in a way that

> absolutely any connection of a provision's subject-matter to the merely abstract scope of Union law, or merely incidental effects on Union law, would be sufficient for binding the Member States by the Union's fundamental rights set forth in the EUCFR. Rather, the European Court of Justice itself expressly states in this decision that the European fundamental rights under the Charter are 'applicable in all situations governed by European Union law, but not outside such situations'.[38]

In other words, the GFCC demonstrated that it considers itself the arbiter of whether the CJEU acts *ultra vires* and also set out how the case law of the CJEU could not be interpreted because *if the CJEU did so*, it would act *ultra vires*. A large body of case law confirms the GFCC's self-understanding as an autonomous guardian of fundamental rights protection in Germany, which even has the

[33] *R (on the application of EM (Eritrea)) (AE (FC) (Appellant)) v Secretary of State for the Home Department (Respondent)* [2014] UKSC 12.

[34] *Internationale Handelssgesellschaft mbH v Einfuhr- und Vorratsstelle für Getreide und Futtermittel*, BVerfGE 37, 271 *(Solange I)*; *Re Wünsche Handelsgesellschaft*, BVerfGE 3 *CMLR* 225 *(Solange II)*.

[35] See *Counter-Terrorism Database* (above n 15) on the constitutionality of a counter-terrorism database.

[36] BVerfG, 1 BvR 2329/15. Available in German at www.bundesverfassungsgericht.de/SharedDocs/Entscheidungen/DE/2015/10/rk20151015_1bvr232915.html.

[37] See *Åkerberg Fransson* (n 15) para 19.

[38] See *Counter-Terrorism Database* (n 15).

obligation of holding the CJEU at distance. The GFCC held for example in another case that it was reasonable for the Federal Supreme Court (*BGH*) to establish that Article 50 CFR was to be interpreted in the same way as Article 54 of the Schengen Convention without making a reference to the CJEU, because the Explanations to the Charter state that Article 50 CFR corresponds to Articles 54 to 58 of the Schengen Convention.[39] In yet another case the GFCC elaborated on the obligations of national courts to contribute to an effective fundamental rights protection under Union law, including their obligation to interpret national provisions adopted to give effect to EU law in light of the Charter. It emphasised its own role as the guardian which ensures that national courts apply the Charter and safeguard fundamental rights protection.[40]

The EU Charter also has interpretative influence beyond the scope of EU law.[41] One illustrative example is a recent case, in which the Spanish Constitutional Court supported that a minor is able to carry his mother's family name in the first place (rather than the name of his father) with the CJEU's ruling case of *Sayn Wittgenstein*[42] that the name of a person is part of an individual's identity and privacy, despite the fact that the case at hand was missing any link to EU law.[43]

[39] BVerfG, 2 BvR 148/11. Available in German at www.bundesverfassungsgericht.de/SharedDocs/Entscheidungen/DE/2011/12/rk20111215_2bvr014811.html.

[40] BVerfG, 1 BvR 1585/13. Available in German at www.bundesverfassungsgericht.de/SharedDocs/Entscheidungen/DE/2016/05/rs20160531_1bvr158513.html paras 120–24.

[41] Bulgaria: Supreme Cassation Court/1524/2014 (Court used Art 1 CFR besides universal declarations to establish that the obligation to constitute every person as an accused before starting the investigation does not violate the private sphere of the accused); Czech Republic: Constitutional Court/II.ÚS 164/15 (The Czech Constitutional Court used Art 24 CFR in order to conclude that the prohibition of an anti-abortion demonstration near an elementary school was lawful); The Supreme Court/30 Cdo 3223/ 2011 (besides the UDHR, the Court used Art 1 CFR to establish that the protection of human dignity is not lower for disabled persons); Denmark: High Court/ B – 1753 – 08 (Arts 1 and 3 CFR do not include the right of persons to have a sign prohibiting nude bathing); Italy: Constitutional Court/ Judgment No 178/2015 (Measures restricting the collective bargaining for civil servants is in breach with Art 39 Italian Constitution, international law and Art 30 CFR); Court of Cassation (Labour Section)/ 41 *CV v Radio dimensione suone* (Court established that the case was outside the scope of EU law but the Italian Court used Art 30 CFR as a source of 'free interpretation'); Lazio Regional Administrative Tribunal/ Judgment No 201509411 (Court used Art 41 CFR in conjunction with national rules to establish that a decision of the Ministry of Justice did not comply with the minimum conditions of transparency necessary to act understandable for citizens and ensure the right to justice and good administration – need to state reasons – a decision concerning the bar examination board); Lithuania: Supreme Administrative Court of Lithuania/A-82281265/2014 (The Supreme Court used Art 41 CFR as 'an additional source of interpretation' to annul an administrative provision because the right to be heard was infringed.); Poland: Appellate Court in Wrocław/I ACa 1337/11 (Proceedings between an individual and her health insurance, the Polish Court used the EU Charter together with international charters (eg Art 11 European Social Charter) to stress the importance of the correspondent constitutional right); Appellate Court in Białystok/II AKzw 665/13 (interruption of 25-year prison sentence to receive medical treatment outside the prison, the Court used Art 4 CFR and Art 3 ECHR to stress the importance of the relating Polish Constitutional right); Portugal: Constitutional Court / 578/2014 (Court used CFR to stress the importance of the freedom of thought, religion and conscience in a case concerning compulsory moral and religious education in school).

[42] C-208/09 *Sayn-Wittgenstein* ECLI:EU:C:2010:806.

[43] Spanish Constitutional Tribunal 167/2013.

Hence, the CJEU's ruling on the permissibility of a general ban on religious symbols may in this very way have effects beyond the actual scope of EU law. It is likely to have an influence on how German courts assess similar cases. Until now the understanding had been that religious symbols could not be banned from the workplace, except for safety considerations. It will be interesting to see how national courts square this with the ECtHR's decision in *Eweida*, in which the Strasbourg Court found that a rule must be appropriate and necessary and a fair balance must be struck between the wish of an employee to wear a cross at the workplace in order to manifest her religious belief and the employer's wish to protect a neutral corporate image.[44]

E. The Plausibility of the CJEU's Autonomy Claim[45]

The core reason why the CJEU holds the ECtHR at distance is the CJEU's concern for the autonomy of the EU legal order and its own monopoly of jurisdiction. Accession could indeed be a threat for the EU's autonomy for three interconnected reasons. First, the ECtHR enjoys an exceptional status within the EU legal order. It is not only one of the sources of the general principles of EU law, but has over time been vested with an elevated status that requires that the EU Treaties are interpreted in conformity with the ECHR. Second, EU law is of international origin. This makes the relationship between the ECHR and EU law different from the relationship between the ECHR and national law in that the 'domestic nature' of EU law is contested. Both the foundations of the EU legal order and the CJEU's claim to dualism are essentially contested and contestable. Third, the EU is a compound rather than unitary actor, with numerous internal parts. From the perspective of international law and the ECtHR, all states are monolithic while the EU can ultimately be dissolved into its Member States, which all possess full international personality and may equally contest the original validity of EU law.

As to the first point, the ECHR enjoys a supreme status within the EU legal order. As explained above,[46] the Treaties codify the ECHR's constitutional status and the CJEU has extended it to the case law of the ECtHR. Moreover, EU fundamental rights, which are not only inspired but interpreted in line with the ECHR and the case law of the ECtHR, are part of the 'foundations' of EU law. In the case of *Kadi I* the Court ruled that these foundations constitute a layer of law that is hierarchically superior to the rules codified in the Treaties.[47] This particular case

[44] *Eweida and Others v the United Kingdom* No 48420/10 ECHR 2013 para 94.

[45] This section draws from C Eckes, 'International Rulings and the EU Legal Order: Autonomy as Legitimacy?' (CLEER Papers 2016/2, TMC Asser Institute, 2016).

[46] See section III. A. above.

[47] Joined Cases C-402/05 P and C-415/05 P *Yassin Abdullah Kadi and Al Barakaat International Foundation v Council of the European Union and Commission of the European Communities* ECLI:EU:C:2008:461 *(Kadi I)* paras 303–04.

concerned the right of Member States to derogate from EU law under Article 351 of the Treaty on the Functioning of the European Union (TFEU), which the Court held to be limited by these foundations. As a consequence, the foundations are vested with a status supreme to 'ordinary' primary law. This reading of the legal hierarchy between the foundations of the Union and EU primary law is confirmed by the *Cresson* and *Ocalan* cases.[48] In both cases, the CJEU held that EU primary law must be read in the light of the ECHR.

Post accession, the ECHR would be legally binding on the EU and the EU institutions, both under international and EU law. Furthermore, the ECtHR's rulings in cases to which the EU is a party would become directly binding on the EU. In practice, national courts take account of the ECtHR's case law more broadly, not only in cases to which their state was a party. For the Member States, in addition to their international legal obligations, the ECHR would become binding as a matter of EU law. Applying the same hierarchy developed by the CJEU, the EU courts, as well as national courts, would have to enforce the ECHR and the binding decision of the ECtHR above EU law.[49] At the same time, the CJEU would, of course, continue to hold the monopoly of judicial interpretation over the EU fundamental rights and the foundations of EU law. Technically, this would allow the CJEU to insist on an interpretation that lowers the status of the ECHR within the EU legal order. Yet in the light of the clear choices of Article 6(3) TEU and Articles 52(3) and 53 CFR, as well as the high level of acceptance of the ECHR's authority, it would be difficult for the CJEU to change its position on the elevated status of the ECHR.

As to the second point, the 'domestic' nature of the EU legal order, its 'separateness' from international law and its 'original validity' claim are constructions of the CJEU. The CJEU and most EU legal scholars conceive of the EU legal order as a (quasi-)constitutional system.[50] By contrast, international law and international legal scholars understand EU law as a special and potentially self-contained subsystem of public international law.[51] Moreover, while the primacy of EU law is in practice widely accepted, national constitutional and supreme courts, national governments and national legal scholars dispute the Court's original validity claim. This constellation, in which the international legal framework imposes limits and national actors call the autonomy of EU law into question, makes the EU legal order as constructed by the CJEU, including its dualist approach *vis-à-vis* international law, *essentially contested and contestable*.

[48] Case C-432/04 *Commission of the European Communities v Édith Cresson* ECLI:EU:C:2006:455 para 112; Case C-229/05 P *Osman Ocalan, on behalf of the Kurdistan Workers' Party (PKK) and Serif Vanly, on behalf of the Kurdistan National Congress (KNK) v Council of the European Union* ECLI:EU:C:2007:32 conclusion in para 83.

[49] Art 46(1) ECHR; see the discussion of the status of the ECHR within the EU legal order above.

[50] For the CJEU, see *Kadi I* (n 47); Case 294/83 *Parti écologiste 'Les Verts' v European Parliament* ECLI:EU:C:1986:166. For legal scholars, see, eg, R Schütze, *European Constitutional Law* (Cambridge, Cambridge University Press, 2012).

[51] See, eg, the attempts to accommodate the EU in the Draft Articles on the International Responsibility of International Organisations (ARIO).

As to the third point, the EU's claim to autonomy from international law is further *legally limited* by the fact that the Member States collectively have the power to amend the treaty framework. Individually Member States can be subject to state responsibility claims and be brought before the ECtHR. They can hence be forced to take a legally binding stand in an external forum on how they construct the relationships between international, EU and national law. The situation of the EU is in this regard very different from the situation of federal states. While federate units may politically challenge the federal level, they are part of a hierarchical legal and judicial structure and cannot essentially contest the federal structure *within its own logic*. Moreover, they do not – as long as they are part of the federation – enjoy an independent status as subjects of international law for purposes of state responsibility. On the contrary, under international law (including before the ECtHR) federal states are treated as one unitary unit. This also means that federate units cannot actively rely on international law to challenge the status or existence of the federal level.

In practice, the different *essentially irreconcilable* positions of what the EU legal order is, have amounted to a delicate system of checks by national constitutional and supreme courts and balances of different political forces, in which all actors 'bark but not bite'.[52] This delicate equilibrium of irreconcilable claims to sovereignty and autonomy functions because none of the actors holds the *monopoly* of interpreting the nature of EU law or the relationship between the different legal spheres. None of the actors is able to legally bind the other within their own legal order. Each actor can only make claims reasoned on the terms of their own legal order, which are consequently only valid within the logic of their own legal order. This of course does not exclude *persuasive* powers beyond this legal order.

This separation of logical frameworks for legal reasoning would change after accession. The ECtHR sees the EU as an 'international organisation' to which the states 'have transferred part of their sovereignty'.[53] It refers to EU law as 'international legal obligations' of the contracting parties.[54] Indeed, the core of its argument in *Bosphorus*, justifying the presumption of equivalent protection, is based on a view of the CJEU as an 'international machinery for supervising fundamental rights'.[55] Hence, the ECtHR's deference to the CJEU is closely interlinked with its understanding that EU law is of an international nature. Indeed, the ECtHR accepts 'that compliance with European Union law by a Contracting Party constitutes a legitimate general-interest objective'.[56] Post accession, the *Bosphorus*

[52] See differently N Petersen, 'Karlsruhe Not Only Barks, But Finally Bites – Some Remarks on the OMT Decision of the German Constitutional Court' (2015) 15 *German Law Journal* 321.

[53] *Bosphorus Hava Yollari Turizm veTicaret AS v Ireland* No 45036/98 ECHR 2005-VI para 154 and following case law.

[54] ibid.

[55] For example *Michaud v France* No 12323/11 ECHR 2012.

[56] *Bosphorus* (n 53) paras 150–51.

doctrine would, logically, no longer be applicable,[57] but this does not mean that it should be expected that the ECtHR changes its reading of EU law as international law. Already at present (pre-accession) Member States and, in particular, national courts, can rely on international law (including rulings of the ECtHR) in order to challenge the CJEU's construction of the EU legal order. Post-accession, rulings of the ECtHR that challenge the CJEU's perspective of the EU as an autonomous legal order would be an exceptionally powerful tool in the hands of the Member States and national courts. National courts could use these rulings, including those directly binding on the CJEU, to challenge the EU legal order from within. Hence the core difference is that the ECtHR's view of EU law as international law, with the attached consequences both for the relation between EU law and international law (no dualism possible) and EU law and national law (dualism possible), would be directly binding on the CJEU in cases to which the EU is a party. This would potentially allow national courts to drive a wedge into the judicial construction of the EU as an autonomous legal order.

By way of conclusion, after accession the ECtHR would exercise constitutional review over fundamental political choices made by the EU institutions. Human rights under the ECHR not only allow the ECtHR to make value choices, but with their indeterminacy they even *require* such choices. Yet, even more relevant for the autonomy of the EU is the fact that the ECtHR would also rule on the relationship between legal spheres, which is interpreted very differently by the ECtHR (EU law as international law) and the CJEU (autonomous domestic legal order). Post accession, the ECtHR's interpretation would be *binding on the EU and the CJEU* and in principle even enjoy *an elevated status within the EU legal order*. This would allow national courts to challenge the core relationship between national, international and EU law from *within the logic of EU law*. This would also allow national courts to undermine the CJEU's monopoly of interpretation of EU law by relying on rulings on the ECtHR, which are part of the EU legal order.

All this brings me to the conclusion that accession, because it allows national courts to rely in a very different fashion on international law and the case law of the ECtHR, would impact on the delicate equilibrium of irreconcilable claims to sovereignty and autonomy within the EU legal order. I must hence agree with the CJEU that making the ECHR and the case law of the ECtHR directly binding on the EU has the potential to undermine the status quo of the suspended irreconcilable claims to sovereignty and autonomy. This would challenge the CJEU's ability to interpret EU law as if the EU legal order was a domestic and autonomous legal order. I should add that I do not argue that the CJEU's reading of the original validity of EU law is any more convincing than the national or international narratives. I only argue that its internal validity appears necessary

[57] Eckes (n 26). Considering the application of *Bosphorus* post-accession as uncertain: L Besselink, 'The Protection of Fundamental Rights Post-Lisbon: The Interaction between the EU Charter of Fundamental Rights, the European Convention on Human Rights (ECHR) and National Constitutions' (*FIDE*, 2012). Available at www.fide2012.eu/index.php?doc_id=94.

to maintain the *status quo*, which is built on an equilibrium of irreconcilable claims about the nature of EU law. It would be sufficient to threaten the system if several national supreme or constitutional courts, such as those of Germany, Poland or the Czech Republic, made a credible and serious threat that they start challenging the EU from within. It would by no means require a challenge by all national systems.

The Commission seems to be keenly aware of the challenges. Its suggestion to treat EU law as domestic law in international trade agreements, which has already been incorporated in EU-Canada Comprehensive Economic and Trade Agreement (CETA),[58] is one step in addressing these tensions. Establishing an explicit understanding that EU law is domestic law and can take a dualist position *vis-à-vis* international law which is binding both on the external court (ie the ECtHR) and on the Member States, may help to address the described threat to the EU's autonomy.

IV. Theories of Rights

The moral appeal of human rights at a certain level of abstraction is difficult to dispute. They have a universal vocation and presume that people have rights unconditionally by virtue of their human nature. Fundamental rights by contrast are community specific and defined within and for a particular polity and jurisdiction. The latter require at least prima facie a justification that goes beyond the human nature. This discussion can be conducted in isolation from specific legal expressions of rights, ie the EU Charter of Fundamental Rights, the ECHR or national bills of rights, if rights are understood as *moral*[59] demands rather than *legal* rights. Furthermore, if the existence of certain rights, or even their specific stipulation, is agreed, this still leaves room for genuine and reasonable disagreement on how these rights are to be interpreted or applied in the specific case, or how they are weighed against each other. Similarly, genuine and reasonable disagreement is likely on which standard of protection, ie which fundamental rights catalogue, should prevail where different standards of protection are agreed that overlap in substantive and territorial scope, as it is for example the case for the Charter, the ECHR and national rights instruments. Besides legal disagreement, which is contingent on starting from the perspective of one legal sphere or order, there can hence be moral disagreement about in which context rights should be determined and filled with meaning.

[58] See Article 8.31(2) CETA: 'The Tribunal shall not have jurisdiction to determine the legality of a measure, alleged to constitute a breach of this Agreement, under the *domestic* law of the disputing Party' (emphasis added).

[59] Moral and ethical are here used in a way broadly following Habermas and Dworkin, ie that moral indicates an independent justification, while ethical is ultimately connected to a conception of the good.

I argue that since contingent legal decisions do not help us to decide in which contexts rights should be determined, it is useful to turn to theory. Theories of rights may indeed be useful in determining the scope within which genuine disagreements can be reasonably argued. In order to support this argument it is necessary to identify and explicate at least in a rudimental fashion the consequences of different theories of rights for the question of how different rights catalogues and their authoritative interpretations should be reconciled.

Any theory of (human) rights is to some extent a function of what its objective is. Theories of human rights must above all justify human rights' claim to universality and ability to trump other considerations. Fundamental rights theories must additionally justify the existence of rights that are developed and applicable within a certain polity rather than to all humans because they are humans. They hence face different challenges to justify their universality and relativism respectively.

This is not the place to give even a concise overview of different human rights theories. It suffices to point out that human rights theories have tackled an array of questions from foundational to categorical ones: whether rights are based on duties or whether duties derive from rights;[60] whether natural rights exist;[61] the distinction and relationship between moral rights and legal rights;[62] the distinction between rights and interests;[63] the relevance of a taxonomy between positive and negative rights;[64] the distinction between rights to freedom and social contract rights, and how they relate to principles of distributive justice;[65] the relative importance of rights *vis-à-vis* principles and rules; their inherent authority over competing political values;[66] and the relationship between group and individual rights.[67] Some broad strands can be identified, such as those based on a utilitarian understanding;[68] those based on an ethical understanding;[69] and a legal understanding which considers 'human rights' to be a term of art under positive law.[70] Many of the debates about the nature and origin of rights are relevant for

[60] See, eg, P Montague, 'Two Concepts of Rights', J Waldron, 'Rights in Conflict' and F Kamm, 'Conflicts of Rights: Typology, Methodology, and Nonconsequentialism' all in CL Ten (ed), *Theories of Rights, The International Library of Essays on Rights* (Aldershot, Ashgate Publishing Ltd, 2006).

[61] As is well known, T Hobbes; J Locke; HLA Hart prominently argued in favour of natural rights; challenged eg by J Bentham, 'Anarchical Fallacies' in J Waldron (ed), *Nonsense Upon Stilts: Bentham, Burke and Marx on the Rights of Man* (New York, Methuen, 1987) 53: 'Natural rights is simply nonsense: natural and imprescriptible rights, rhetorical nonsense, nonsense upon stilts'.

[62] See, eg, Waldron (n 60).

[63] See, eg, J Raz, 'On the Nature of Rights' in Ten (n 60).

[64] Kamm (n 60).

[65] R Peffer, 'A Defense of Rights to Well-Being' in Ten (n 60).

[66] R Dworkin, *Taking Rights Seriously* (Harvard University Press, 1977); see also R Dworkin, *Justice for Hedgehogs* (Belknap Press, 2011).

[67] See, eg, P Jones, 'Group Rights and Group Oppression' in Ten (n 60).

[68] J Bentham, 'Anarchical Fallacies' (1824) in J Bowring (ed), *The Works of Jeremy Bentham* (Edinburgh, 1843) Vol II.

[69] See, eg, J Griffin, *On Human Rights* (Oxford, Oxford University Press, 2008). A Sen, 'Elements of a Theory of Human Rights' (2004) 32 *Philosophy & Public Affairs* 315.

[70] C Tomuschat, *Human Rights: Between Idealism and Realism*, 3rd edn (Oxford, Oxford University Press, 2013). HLA Hart, 'Are there any Natural Rights?' (1955) 64 *Philosophical Review* 175.

their interpretation and existence, but do not necessarily give any guidance to the question of who should interpret them, who should apply them, or when several differing codifications exist in different legal spheres how these should relate to each other. Yet, none of the different approaches gives us appropriate guidance on how the different legal spheres should relate and which standard of integration may be seen as adequate as a result. Considerations of a utilitarian nature can – as a matter of principle – be applied to all the different spheres or polities – the national, European, and even the international. On a simplified level it may be read as justifying a focus on the legal sphere that governs the greater number (ie international law) to increase the benefits from human rights for a greater number. Human rights theories grounded in an ethical understanding presuppose an agreement on what the good life is (contenders would be happiness, well-being, autonomy). This is in fact difficult to establish in either context – national, European or international. The positive law approach is subject to the same limitations explained above for the judicial practice. I hence argue that in particular those theories of rights that link rights to public reasoning[71] or justification[72] are most capable of giving us guidance on how the different legal spheres should relate to each other.

The positive law as expressed in the common traditions of national constitutions and the EU Treaties makes a clear and express commitment to the principle of democracy. It could further be argued that even international law and international relations make a commitment to (democratic) self-determination, albeit in a far weaker manner.[73] This makes the choice for a theory of rights that links rights to public reasoning and justification sit coherently with the law. This also makes such theory particularly apt to give guidance on how the different legal spheres should connect.

Rainer Forst has developed a theory of human rights as originating in a right to justification.[74] His theory falls into the strand of theories that point to human dignity as the common underlying reason for the existence of rights that all persons enjoy because they are humans. Forst understands dignity as a relational concept and argues that the core of the human rights discourse is the understanding that being a person ('*Personsein*') depends on being treated as a being with a right to justification ('*Rechtfertigungswesen*').[75] This creates the necessity to accept all individuals as persons to whom one owes reasons[76] and requires that all individuals be treated as persons whose rights and interests are respected both in the process

[71] Sen (n 69).

[72] J Cohen, 'Minimalism about Human Rights' (2004) 12 *Journal of Political Philosophy* 190.

[73] C Eckes, 'The Reflexive Relationship between Internal and External Sovereignty' (2015) 18 *Irish Journal of European Law* 33.

[74] R Forst, *Kritik der Rechtfertigungsverhältnisse. Perspektiven einer kritischen Theorie der Politik* (Berlin, Suhrkamp Verlag, 2011) 54.

[75] ibid 67.

[76] ibid 66.

of decision-making and in the substantive decision.[77] Reflexiveness is at the core of what distinguishes Forst's theory from other human rights theories.[78] It in fact makes it a theory of fundamental rather than human rights within the meaning of these words as they are used in this paper.[79]

Accepting a reflexive right to justification as the origin of all rights has consequences for the present discussion of the justifiable and desirable level of harmonisation and variation. As a consequence of the right to justification, those exercising public power in a way that restricts rights have to offer their citizens legitimate reasons.[80] Human rights play in this reason-giving process the role of a language of critique ('*Sprache der Kritik*'), which protects citizens from unjustified societal and political circumstances of oppression.

The choice between universal human rights and jurisdiction-bound fundamental rights is an expression of the choice between universalism and relativism. It imposes a hierarchy between the standard of a cosmopolitan or at least more inclusive moral community and the standard of one's own cultural home community. Forst considers his theory as a matter of theory agnostic on the question of what the appropriate political or societal framework for realising rights is.[81] He maintains that 'the question at issue between globalists and statists have to be decided elsewhere, namely with reference to a conception of transnational justice […]'.[82] However, I would argue that in lack of even emerging political structures at the international level that allow meaningful participation or even communication structures that could make justification possible, it seems difficult to imagine a reflexive discourse that allows realisation of human rights in the way Forst appears to imagine it. I would hence further argue that Forst's theory speaks in favour of political structures that are built on democratic legitimacy and participation.

Standards of human rights and fundamental rights differ, both in law and in practice. I propose to analyse the relevance of these differences or variations on the basis of a distinction between the existence of rights, their interpretation and their implementation.[83] The three categories of variations stand in a hierarchical relationship with each other: existence and wording of a right set the limit to differences in interpretations, interpretation sets the limits for differences in implementation. Variation in the existence and wording of rights is limited by the reason of existence for these rights, which is here understood as ultimately being

[77] ibid 77.

[78] R Forst, 'The Justification of Human Rights and the Basic Right to Justification: A Reflexive Approach' (2010) 120 *Ethics* 711.

[79] See also R Forst, 'The Justification of Basic Rights: A Discourse-Theoretical Approach' (2016) 3 *Netherlands Journal of Legal Philosophy* 7.

[80] ibid 76.

[81] Forst, 'A Reflexive Approach' (n 78) at 738.

[82] Forst, 'A Reflexive Approach' (n 78) at 738.

[83] This distinction is borrowed from J Donnelly, 'Cultural Relativism and Universal Human Rights' (1984) 6 *Human Rights Quarterly* 400 at 402.

a right to justification. The core question is what the limits of these variations and deviations are. Any deviation not only from universal human rights but arguably more inclusive fundamental rights standards and practice must be justified in this light in order to be legitimate. Forst's theory leaves room for justified variation between rights standards. It can even explain such variation. Rights, understood as ultimately based on a moral right to justification, link the determination of the precise interpretation and content of these rights to the process of reason-giving in any given polity. The processes of reason-giving may then come to different outcomes in different polities and in different contextual settings. This may justify some room for variation in fundamental rights protection.

The most problematic case in this regard are fundamental rights standards and practices that may be and are justified within a particular jurisdiction pursuant to the internal standard, but are not the most defensible choice in light of an external evaluation. Pursuant to Forst's theory, this only becomes problematic if this leads to domination or oppression. As long as all rights-holders are also norm-givers any particular choice does not have to be the 'most-defensible' and the theory that grounds rights in a right to justification rejects external standards of what is 'good'.

Human rights are an expression of a moral standard. The three categories of variation: substantive rights, interpretation and implementation start from the highest level of hierarchy and generality, moving to the hierarchically inferior and more specific. The more specific any universal prescription is the closer it moves to a claim of moral objectivity. Moral relativism by contrast is concerned with cultural differences and sets limits to the legitimacy of imposing contingent norms across the boundaries of jurisdictions. A distinction must be made between the possibility, depending on authority, and the legitimacy, ie moral defensibility of imposing such standards. The discussion here is concerned with the latter. In short, a moral reason to justify departure from a more inclusive standard is self-determination. Self-determination is a human right accepted both by moral relativists and moral universalists. The reading that the very reason for the existence of human rights is the justification of the exercise of power, ie the imposition of limits on behaviour, shifts the focus to those to whom the rights are owed. This connects to Forst's theory that treating individuals as persons to whom reasons are owed is the common ground justifying the existence of human rights.

V. Conclusions

Positive law within the compound European legal order contains a number of procedural mechanisms and substantive clauses in order to avoid clashes between different conceptions of fundamental rights. Examples under EU law are the preliminary ruling procedure and Articles 51 to 53 CFR. Section III demonstrated that in practice national courts within the compound European legal order, as well as the CJEU *vis-à-vis* international law (ECHR) opt, when they are confronted with external rights systems, for a combination of substantive convergence and keeping autonomous control, ie a monopoly of interpretation within their own legal system.

The plausibility of the CJEU's autonomy concern confirms with regard to the specific relationship of the EU legal order and the ECHR that it may be justified to keep at distance an external legal sphere that may impose a binding interpretation of fundamental rights. This may even be required to protect not only the internal choices of how fundamental rights should be interpreted, but necessary to maintain the autonomy of the whole legal order. The specific example of the EU's accession to the ECHR was also discussed to place a question mark behind the reasoning that more integration of fundamental rights is necessarily better (ie resulting in a higher level of protection). Essentially it justifies a certain level of distance between different instruments protecting fundamental rights with the possibility of resulting in variation. Rights are inter alia means to ensure inclusiveness. Yet inclusiveness is not determined, or at least not exclusively determined, by the number of humans that are governed by any given legal sphere. Problematic in this context are also institutional limitations. Jurisdictional limitation and the principle of conferral do not allow the CJEU to develop a coherent level of protection across different policies.

Studying judicial practices does not allow us to draw a conclusion on what particular level of integration is desirable from a rights perspective. Each court justifies its decisions within the logic and on the terms of its own legal order. Any decision is strongly influenced not only by rights considerations but also by structural considerations particular to the individual legal order. The different institutional starting points limit discourse and make convergence a matter of judicial choice. This justifies turning to theory for finding guidance on the most desirable level of fundamental rights integration from a rights perspective. Forst's theory of rights originating in a right to justification is particularly well suited in this context because it builds on the Kantian tradition of individual agency, which is also reflected in the positive legal structures of the compound European legal order.

The aim of this paper was not to offer answers to the questions of who should determine rights and what variations are justified. The aim was to argue in favour of a particular way of thinking about these questions, namely starting from theory rather than judicial practices.

In light of a theory of rights that presumes that a right to justification lies at the core of all other rights, the level of integration that is justified and adequate cannot be established in abstract. More integration is not necessarily more adequate. The level of integration should depend on the ability of the political structures to make reflexive *justification* possible. An *interactive process of reason-giving* is necessary to allow for justification. This is only rudimentary in the international context, in which decision-making is based on representation through governments, a large number of which do not internally meet any standard of justification, but stay in power through oppression and coercion. As a matter of principle this is possible in the state context within modern democracies. I would further argue that the European Union not only possesses structures that would allow for reflexive justification but that it could make a credible argument that it is better suited to include those who are affected by the externalities of the political decisions within any given state within a globalised world. Indeed, the EU's enhanced ability to address rights relevant consequences that occur external to the legal order, in which the political decision for a particular measure is taken, ie the national context, could speak in favour of the EU context for the deliberation of fundamental rights standards.

5

A Balloon Dynamic in the Area of Social Rights

SACHA GARBEN*

I. Introduction

Fundamental rights have been, and continue to be,[1] pivotal in defining the relationship between the international, EU and national legal orders. As discussed in more detail by Christina Eckes in her contribution to the present book in chapter 4, it is on this issue that national constitutional courts,[2] the Court of Justice of the European Union (CJEU) as well as the European Court of Human Rights, all claim a certain measure of final authority, which may theoretically be reconcilable as '*constitutional pluralism*'[3] but nevertheless leads to an uncomfortable state of affairs both from the perspective of the international rule of law and from a more practical point of view. While these issues are now subject to a flourishing literature, the position of fundamental *social* rights in this respect has remained slightly overlooked.[4] This is all the more remarkable considering that

* Sacha Garben is currently on leave from the European Commission. All views expressed in this paper are entirely personal and do not in any way represent those of the European Commission. This chapter builds on some of the views presented in S Garben, 'The Problematic Interaction between EU and International Law in the Area of Social Rights' (2018) 7/1 *Cambridge International Law Journal* 77.

[1] See for instance Case C-399/11 *Stefano Melloni v Ministerio Fiscal* [2013] ECLI:EU:C:2013:107. For discussion, see L Besselink, 'The Parameters of Constitutional Conflict after Melloni' (2014) 39 *European Law Review* 531.

[2] For instance, BVerfG, Order of January 14, 2014 – 2 BvR 2728/13 et al, para 29. For recent discussion, see A Bobic, 'Constitutional Pluralism is Not Dead: An Analysis of Interactions between Constitutional Courts of Member States and the European Court of Justice' (2017) 18 *German Law Journal* 1395.

[3] N Walker, 'The Idea of Constitutional Pluralism' (2002) 65 *Modern Law Review* 317; N Walker, 'Constitutional Pluralism Revisited' (2016) 22 *European Law Journal* 333.

[4] There are, of course, notable exceptions, such as C Barnard, 'The Protection of Fundamental Social Rights in Europe after Lisbon: A Question of Conflicts of Interest' in S de Vries, U Bernitz

over the past decade, a number of high-profile frictions have appeared between national, EU and international social rights. Serving as a powerful illustration of the '*balloon dynamic*' as set out by Inge Govaere in the first chapter of this book, it will be explained that these frictions have arisen mainly because of the rapidly inflating balloon of European integration in the 2000s, both in terms of the EU's territorial expansion and its substantive influence, resulting in (and aggravating) structural internal and external pressures. After critically examining the nature and extent of these frictions, the chapter will examine possible solutions. It will be argued that EU accession to the European Social Charter, which has been proposed as a possible way forward, is not a viable or desirable option, as it would most likely be ineffective and would pose problems for the autonomy of the EU legal order (ie puncture the balloon). Instead, the chapter argues for, first, a stronger emphasis on the individual and collective responsibility of the Member States in causing and managing the frictions between EU and international social law, and, second, a more reconciliatory accommodation of international law concerns by the key European institutions in this area: the CJEU and the European Commission,[5] to guarantee sufficient elasticity of the EU balloon membrane.

II. Setting the Scene: Recent Frictions between International and EU Social Law

To provide a baseline for the analysis in the rest of this chapter, the present section will map the current sources of international and EU social law and will describe the main frictions that have appeared recently.

and S Weatherill (eds), *The Protection of Fundamental Rights in the EU After Lisbon* (Oxford, Hart Publishing, 2013) 37, 50 and more recently: M Rocca, 'Enemy at the (Flood) Gates: EU "Exceptionalism" in Recent Tensions with the International Protection of Social Rights' (2017) 7 *European Labour Law Journal* 52; A Kornezov, 'Social Rights, the Charter, and the ECHR: Caveats, Austerity, and Other Disasters' in F Vandenbroucke, C Barnard and G De Baere (eds), *A European Social Union after the Crisis* (Cambridge, Cambridge University Press, 2017) 407; U Khaliq, 'The EU and the European Social Charter: Never the Twain Shall Meet?' (2017) 15 *Cambridge Yearbook of European Legal Studies* 169; C O'Cinneíde, 'The European Social Charter and EU Labour Law' in A Bogg, C Costello and A Davies, *Research Handbook on EU Labour Law* (Cheltenham, Edward Elgar, 2016) 191; M Dawson, 'Governing Fundamental Social Rights' in M Dawson, *The Governance of EU Fundamental Rights* (Cambridge, Cambridge University Press, 2017).

[5] The European Parliament, and national parliaments equally, should furthermore be given a drastically enhanced role in the decision of socio-economic questions in the internal market on the one hand and economic governance on the other hand. This ties in to the argument on democratisation of socio-economic questions that I have made elsewhere (S Garben, 'Restating the Problem of Competence Creep, Tackling Harmonisation by Stealth and Reinstating the Legislator' in S Garben and I Govaere (eds), *The Division of Competences between the EU and the Member States: Reflections on the Past, the Present and the Future* (Oxford, Hart Publishing, 2017)). I have applied that argument to the context of the incompatibilities between EU and international social law in Garben (n *), which will not be repeated here.

A. International and EU Sources of Social Law and Policy

The two most important international sources of social rights are the Council of Europe's European Social Charter (ESC) and the UN's International Labour Organisation (ILO) with its several conventions.

The ESC guarantees a broad range of human rights related to employment and working conditions, housing, education, health, medical assistance and social protection. These rights are additional to the civil and political rights enshrined in the European Convention on Human Rights and, like the latter, have their origin in the Universal Declaration of Human Rights. The ESC is based on an *à la carte* ratification system, which enables signatory states, under certain conditions, to choose the provisions they are willing to accept as binding international legal obligations. While all EU Member States are party to either the 1961 Social Charter or the Revised Social Charter, not all of them have accepted both or all provisions contained in the European Social Charters. For the signatory states that have accepted the reporting system[6] and the collective complaints system,[7] the European Committee of Social Rights (ECSR) monitors compliance through collective complaints lodged by the social partners and other non-governmental organisations and through national reports drawn up by States Parties. The decisions of the ECSR must be respected by the States concerned, by force of international law. The Committee of Ministers intervenes in the last stage of the ESC's monitoring mechanism through the adoption of Resolutions and Recommendations, ensuring the follow-up of the conclusions and decisions adopted by the ECSR.

The second important source of international social rights is the ILO, a UN tripartite agency bringing together governments, employers and workers representatives of 187 countries (which includes all EU Member States), to set labour standards and policies promoting decent work. Its conventions are binding international treaties on a range of social/labour issues. Those that have been ratified by all 28 EU Member States are most notably the eight 'fundamental' conventions: the Freedom of Association and Protection of the Right to Organise Convention; the Right to Organise and Collective Bargaining Convention; the Forced Labour Convention; the Abolition of Forced Labour Convention; the Minimum Age Convention; the Worst Forms of Child Labour Convention; the Equal Remuneration Convention; and the Discrimination (Employment and Occupation) Convention. In terms of enforcement, several systems coexist. The regular system of supervision entails examination by the ILO (Committee of Experts and Tripartite Committee) of periodic reports submitted by Member States on the

[6] Articles 21–29 of the 1961 Charter, and Protocol amending the European Social Charter, CETS No 142, ratified by 19 EU Member States.

[7] Additional Protocol to the European Social Charter Providing for a System of Collective Complaints, CETS No 158, currently ratified by 14 EU Member States.

measures they have taken to implement the provisions of the ratified Convention. In addition, there are three special procedures: (i) a representations procedure which allows industrial associations of employers or of workers to present a representation, upon which a tripartite committee of the Governing Body may be set up and will issue recommendations; (ii) a complaints procedure whereby complaints can be brought by another Member State, an ILO Conference delegate or the Governing Body, upon which the ILO may form a 'Commission of Inquiry' and may recommend action to be taken by the Conference; and (iii) a special procedure for the enforcement of Convention Nos 87 and 98 on freedom of association and collective bargaining, where a Committee on Freedom of Association examines complaints about violations of freedom of association (brought by employers' and workers' organisations), whether or not the country had ratified the conventions.

In turn, Article 3 of Treaty on European Union (TEU) describes the EU as 'a social market economy'[8] aiming at full employment and social progress, and provides that it 'shall combat social exclusion and discrimination, and shall promote social justice and protection'. This 'social mandate' as defined in the Treaties enables and requires the EU to adopt policies ensuring social progress and improvement in living and working conditions. In the most general terms, it is a mission to preserve and foster the European Social Model, which can generally be understood as a commitment to social and employment rights, a universal and fair social protection system, inclusive labour markets, strong social-dialogue, high quality public services and high levels of social inclusion and cohesion.[9] Since the Treaty of Lisbon, the EU Charter of Fundamental Rights is the most important reference point for social rights in the EU legal order, as it has the same primary law legal value as the Treaties. The Charter recognises a wide range of social rights, such as the prohibition of forced labour (Article 5), freedom of association (Article 12), the right to equal treatment (Article 21), the right to information and consultation within the undertaking (Article 27), the right of collective bargaining and action (Article 28), the right to protection in the event of unjustified dismissal (Article 30), the right to fair and just working conditions (Article 31), the prohibition of child labour and protection of young people at work (Article 32), and the entitlement to social security and assistance (Article 34). In accordance with Article 51 of the Treaty on the Functioning of the European Union (TFEU), these rights are primarily addressed to the EU Institutions and only apply to the Member States when they act in the scope of EU law. However, many of these rights find more concrete expression in secondary legislation adopted on the basis of the provisions of the TFEU's Social Policy

[8] On the significance of this concept, see F Scharpf, 'The Asymmetry of European Integration, or Why the EU Cannot Be a "Social Market Economy"' (2010) 8/2 *Socio-Economic Review* 211.

[9] See European Commission, White Paper on Social Policy, COM(94) 333; D Vaughan-Whitehead (ed), *The European Social Model in Crisis, Is Europe Losing its Soul?* (Edward Elgar Publishing, 2015) 1–10.

Title, thereby indeed binding the Member States in their implementation of these measures.[10] The legislation adopted on this basis is limited to setting minimum standards, leaving the Member States free to provide higher levels of social protection. In addition to this, a range of legal measures impacting on social policy have been adopted on the basis of the internal market provisions, such as Article 114 TFEU, like the measures concerning the posting of workers,[11] the protection of workers in the event of structural changes in the company (insolvency, collective redundancies,[12] transfer of undertakings),[13] and the first directives on safety and health at work. Last but not least, the EU plays an increasingly important role in Member States' social policies through coordination processes such as the Open Method of Coordination and especially the European Semester (the EU's yearly cycle of economic policy coordination).

B. Recent Frictions between EU and International Social Law

Since the 2000s, a number of discrepancies have emerged between these various EU and international social standards,[14] and while, as we shall see, they are not all equally problematic, they nevertheless present a certain degree of friction between the EU and the international level.

First, it has transpired that the minimum standards set in EU secondary law adopted on the basis of the Social Policy Title are not always protective enough in accordance with the case law of the ECSR or the ILO Convention Committee. This means that EU Member States that are also signatories to the ESC or the ILO convention in question are therefore required in their national law to go beyond the minimum standards set in EU law. Examples of these divergences include the issue of maximum weekly working time, where under the EU Working Time Directive[15] an individual opt-out is possible with the consent of the worker

[10] Directives on non-discrimination, occupational health and safety, working time (general, sectoral, young people), non-standard forms of employment (temporary agency, fixed term and part time), information and consultation of workers, social security coordination.

[11] Directive 96/71/EC of the European Parliament and of the Council of 16 December 1996 concerning the posting of workers in the framework of the provision of services ('Posting of Workers Directive') [1997] OJL18/1–6; Directive 2014/67/EU of the European Parliament and of the Council of 15 May 2014 on the enforcement of Directive 96/71/EC concerning the posting of workers in the framework of the provision of services and amending Regulation (EU) No 1024/2012 on administrative cooperation through the Internal Market Information System ('the IMI Regulation') ('Posting Enforcement Directive') [2014] OJ L159/11–31.

[12] Council Directive 98/59/EC of 20 July 1998 on the approximation of the laws of the Member States relating to collective redundancies ('Collective Redundancies Directive') [1998] OJ L225/16–21.

[13] Council Directive 2001/23/EC of 12 March 2001 on the approximation of the laws of the Member States relating to the safeguarding of employees' rights in the event of transfers of undertakings, businesses or parts of undertakings or businesses ('Transfer of Undertaking Directive')[2001] OJ L82/16–20.

[14] See also the literature cited above in n 4.

[15] Directive 2003/88/EC of the European Parliament and of the Council of 4 November 2003 concerning certain aspects of the organisation of working time [2003] OJ L299/9–19.

which could imply an average weekly working time well above the maximum of 60 hours required by the ESC[16] as interpreted by the Committee,[17] and the right to family reunification regulated in Directive 2003/86, which allows a minimum residence period for the migrant workers to be joined by their family for more than a year and which excludes social assistance from the calculation of the income of the migrant worker for the purposes of the right to reunification.[18] In such cases, there is no outright conflict between EU and international norms, and Member States are perfectly able to simultaneously comply with the duties arising under both instruments. Still, it reflects poorly on the EU standard if it is not considered sufficient to fulfil the minimum international level of social rights protection and, at the same time, it risks detracting from the credibility of the international norm as a core minimum standard, and of the universality of human rights more generally.[19]

Second, difficulties have arisen in the context of the EU's austerity policy pursued in the context of the economic crisis and, more specifically, through the national reforms that had to be executed in countries in return for receiving financial assistance in accordance with so-called Memorandums of Understanding signed by the European Commission and the national government. The legal status of these instruments under EU law is unclear[20] but even if they were to be considered EU norms, they would not be subject to the direct scrutiny of either the ECSR or the ILO enforcement bodies, as the EU is not a signatory to these instruments. As such, it is only the compliance of the national measures implementing the Memoranda that can be brought under review. On several occasions, the ECSR has held that the national implementing measures infringed the ESC. It upheld the complaint of Greek trade unions against the introduction of special apprenticeship contracts for young workers, which provided for a minimum wage lower than the poverty line, did not provide three weeks' paid annual leave and did not mandate any type of training, as being contrary to Articles 4(1), 7(7), 10(2) and 12(3) of the ESC.[21] It also upheld the complaint against compensation-free dismissal during a one-year trial period as being in breach of Article 4(4)[22] and

[16] Arts 2(1) and 4(2) of the Revised European Social Charter.

[17] *Confédération Générale du Travail (CGT) v France* (Complaint) European Committee of Social Rights No 55/2009 (23 June 2010) and many related cases.

[18] Council Directive 2003/86/EC of 22 September 2003 on the right to family reunification [2003] OJ L251/12; Art 19(6) of the Charter. See Council of Europe, *The Relationship between European Union Law and the European Social Charter* (2014) European Committee of Social Rights Working Paper, 22 https://rm.coe.int/16806544ec, 24.

[19] See also, on this latter point, the contribution by C Eckes in chapter 4.

[20] C Kilpatrick, 'Are the Bailouts Immune to EU Social Challenge Because They Are Not EU Law?' (2014) 10 *European Constitutional Law Review* 393, 406; M Schwarz, 'A Memorandum of Misunderstanding – The Doomed Road of the European Stability Mechanism and a Possible Way Out: Enhanced Cooperation' (2014) 51 *Common Market Law Review* 389.

[21] *General Federation of Employees of the National Electric Power Corporation (GENOP-DEI) and Confederation of Greek Civil Servants' Trade Unions (ADEDY) v Greece* (Complaint) ECSR No 66/2011.

[22] *General Federation of Employees of the National Electric Power Corporation (GENOP-DEI) and Confederation of Greek Civil Servants' Trade Unions (ADEDY) v Greece* (Complaint) ECSR No 65/2011.

against pension reforms.[23] With regard to the argument of the Greek Government that it had no choice as it was due to comply with the Memorandum, the Committee noted that 'the fact that the contested provisions of domestic law seek to fulfil the requirements of other legal obligations does not remove them from the ambit of the Charter'.[24] Similarly, the ILO's Committee on Freedom of Association has condemned certain austerity measures taken in Greece under Troika auspices. It noted that 'while deeply aware that these measures were taken within a context qualified as grave and exceptional, provoked by a financial and economic crisis', the Committee found that there were 'a number of repeated and extensive interventions into free and voluntary collective bargaining and an important deficit of social dialogue'.[25] The Committee warned that:

> the elaboration of procedures systematically favouring decentralized bargaining of exclusionary provisions that are less favourable than the provisions at a higher level can lead to a global destabilization of the collective bargaining machinery and of workers' and employers' organizations and constitutes in this regard a weakening of freedom of association and collective bargaining contrary to the principles of Conventions Nos 87 and 98.[26]

Finally, the most problematic case of conflict arises where a binding EU norm *requires* measures that infringe international standards. In such a situation, the Member State in question is placed in the position where observance of the EU norm implies an infringement of its international obligations and vice versa. Such a situation is clearly damaging to the EU's reputation, legitimacy and credibility. However, it is also detrimental to the ESC and/or ILO and its standing. When there is such outright conflict, it is likely that a Member State will choose to comply with the EU standard rather than the international one as the enforcement mechanisms in the EU legal order are more developed and effective than those in international law and can imply, in case of non-compliance with a CJEU judgment, financial sanctions. The instances of such outright conflict are rare but they have occurred, particularly in relation to the well-known and controversial judgments of the CJEU in *Viking* and *Laval*.[27] In these judgments, the CJEU considered collective action undertaken by workers to protect their interests to be a prima facie restriction on

[23] *Federation of Employed Pensioners of Greece (IKA-ETAM) v Greece* (Complaint) ECSR No 76/2012.

[24] *Pensioners' Union of the Athens-Piraeus Electric Railways (ISAP) v Greece* (Complaint) ECSR No 78/2012, p 10.

[25] ILO, 'ILO Calls on Greece to Bring its Labour Relations System Back to Fundamental Rights' (International Labour Organisation, 15 November 2012) www.ilo.org/brussels/press/press-releases/WCMS_193308/lang--en/index.htm (last accessed 18 September 2018).

[26] Governing Body of the International Labour Office (316th Session) Reports of the Committee on Freedom of Association: 365th Report of the Committee on Freedom of Association (Geneva, 1–6 November 2012) para 997.

[27] Case C-438/05 *International Transport Workers' Federation and Finnish Seamen's Union v Viking Line ABP and OÜ Viking Line Eesti* [2007] ECR I-10779; and Case C-341/05 *Laval un Partneri Ltd v Svenska Byggnadsarbetareförbundet, Svenska Byggnadsarbetareförbundets avdelning 1, Byggettan and Svenska Elektrikerförbundet* [2007] ECR I-11767.

companies' free movement rights enshrined in the EU Treaties.[28] While in *Viking*, the CJEU left it open to the national court to consider whether the restriction could be justified, in *Laval* it held that it could not. In response to the judgment, the Swedish Government adopted the so-called *Lex Laval*, a package of measures to bring Swedish law into compliance with EU law as interpreted by the CJEU in *Laval*. In response to the ensuing complaint lodged with the ECSR, the Committee stated that:

> the facilitation of free cross-border movement of services and the promotion of the freedom of an employer or undertaking to provide services in the territory of other States – which constitute important and valuable economic freedoms within the framework of EU law – cannot be treated, from the point of view of the system of values, principles and fundamental rights embodied in the Charter, as having a greater a priori value than core labour rights, including the right to make use of collective action to demand further and better protection of the economic and social rights and interests of workers.[29]

The Committee upheld the complaint and while only directly condemning the Swedish measures and not the CJEU judgment, it cast another shadow over that controversial case law. As Rocca notes,[30] the importance of the violation and connection to EU law was confirmed by the Report of the Secretary General of the Council of Europe on the State of Democracy, Human Rights and the Rule of Law in Europe, which mentions the ESC decision and the need to find 'pragmatic solutions to settle conflicts between the two sets of standards'.[31] The *Viking* and *Laval* saga also caused friction with the ILO. In a case concerning collective action taken by the British Air Line Pilots' Association against its employer's plans to launch a new subsidiary airline, which British Airways held to be contrary to the *Viking* doctrine, the ILO Committee of Experts denied the application of the principle of proportionality to the right to strike and wished to make clear that while 'its task is not to judge the correctness of the ECJ's holdings in Viking and Laval [...] but rather to examine whether the impact of these decisions at national level are such as to deny workers' freedom of association rights under Convention No. 87', nevertheless 'the doctrine that is being articulated in these [...] judgments

[28] In *Viking*, ibid, the CJEU held that collective action initiated by a trade union against the re-flagging of the Finnish ship the Rosella to Estonia in order to incur lower wage costs was considered a restriction of the company's freedom of establishment that could only be justified if it did not go beyond what was necessary to protect the jobs and conditions of employment of the members of that union. In *Laval*, ibid, the CJEU held that collective action by a Swedish trade union in the form of a blockade of Swedish construction sites in order to force a building company established in Latvia posting Latvian workers to Sweden to pay their workers the wages applicable under the Swedish collective agreements in the building sector, constituted an unjustified restriction of the freedom to provide services.

[29] *Swedish Trade Union Confederation (LO) and Swedish Confederation of Professional Employees (TCO) v Sweden* (Complaint) ECSR No 85/2012 (3 July 2013), para 122.

[30] Rocca (n 4) 67.

[31] Report by the Secretary General of the Council of Europe, 'State of Democracy, Human Rights and Rule of Law in Europe' (2014) SG (2014)1-Final, 41.

is likely to have a significant restrictive effect on the exercise of the right to strike in practice in a manner contrary to the Convention'.[32]

III. The Cause of the Frictions: The (Over-)Inflated Balloon of EU Integration in Social Law and Policy through EU Enlargement and Economic Governance Post-Crisis

As will be argued in this section, the main cause of the above frictions lies in the significant inflation of the balloon of EU integration. Contrary to what one might expect, however, this is not so much because of the EU's increasing development of its own social rights and policy as such, but instead through, on the one hand, the Eastern enlargement of the EU that has increased the socio-economic divergence between the Member States and, on the other hand, the EU's growing involvement in Member States' social policies through its economic governance since the Euro-crisis. These developments have resulted in internal and external structural pressures that are at the heart of the increasingly fraught relationship between the EU and international social standards and actors.

To start at the beginning, the Treaty of Rome already contained a Social Policy Title, although its provisions were mostly rhetorical and programmatic in nature, and did not confer much by way of either legal basis for Community action or direct rights for individuals.[33] Common action was mostly directed at promoting non-binding cooperation between the Member States.[34] The most powerful provision was Article 119 (now 157 TFEU) on equal pay, which the CJEU held to be directly effective in the landmark *Defrenne* case.[35] EU law-making competence in this area developed very gradually since then, with the inclusion by the Single European Act of the health and safety of workers (ex Article 118a of the EEC Treaty), via the Treaty of Maastricht's annexed 'social chapter', comprising the Social Policy Agreement and the Social Policy Protocol which excluded the UK, to the current Social Title as essentially founded by the Treaty of Amsterdam. To a certain extent, the EU's initially rather limited role in social rights can be explained by the idea that other international actors, such as indeed the Council of Europe and the United Nations, were better placed in that area. The EU's purview was that of economic integration, and social issues were either left to the Member States, or to the ILO and Committee of Social Rights, a view initially

[32] ILO, *Report of the Committee of Experts on the Application of Conventions and Recommendations: Report III (Part 1A), General Report and Observations Concerning Particular Countries* (International Labour Office, 2010) 209.

[33] C Barnard, *EU Employment Law*, 4th edn (Oxford, Oxford University Press, 2012) 2.

[34] Joined Cases 281, 283, 285, 287/85 *Germany, UK and Others v Commission* ECLI:EU:C:1987:351.

[35] Case 149/77 *Defrenne v Sabena* ECLI:EU:C:1978:130.

actively fostered by those international actors. ILO experts drafted the influential 'Ohlin report' that provided 'the theoretical basis for the social policy chapter of the Rome Treaty'[36] and indicated that the creation of the European Economic Community did not require the harmonisation of labour standards.[37]

However, as the balloon of European integration further inflated, the EU's role in social issues became more pronounced and more needed. At the very least, it became clear that a certain degree of harmonisation of social and labour law and policy was needed as a corollary to the internal market. Social policy was necessary to ensure an 'equal level playing field' for economic actors in the internal market. Without certain minimum common labour rules, for instance, (companies in) countries with high levels of protection would potentially suffer a competitive disadvantage and these countries would thereby be incentivised to lower their standards to prevent the loss of competitiveness of domestic companies and to attract foreign business. To prevent such 'social dumping' as a result of regulatory competition, the EU should adopt minimum standards to prevent 'a race to the bottom' and instead promote competition on other factors, such as the quality of goods and services. There is a tight relationship between social and economic objectives in this approach, and legal measures adopted in pursuit of these goals can therefore also be adopted on the basis of the internal market provisions, such as Article 114 TFEU. Indeed, an important part of the EU social *acquis* consists of measures that were (at least initially) adopted on the basis of the internal market provisions rather than the social legal basis now contained in Title X, such as the measures concerning the posting of workers,[38] the protection of workers in the event of structural changes in the company (insolvency, collective redundancies,[39] transfer of undertakings),[40] and the first directives on safety and health at work. This explains how, even before the Treaties contained a fully-fledged social legal basis, a significant body of secondary law in this area could emerge. Furthermore, EU action on social issues is no longer limited to this economic rationale. As we have seen in the previous section, EU primary law now clearly bestows a social mission on the EU, with the EU Charter of Fundamental Rights as well as a range of legislative measures providing minimum levels of social and employment protection, making up a rich social *acquis*.

This evolution of EU social rights took place alongside the continuing existence and development of international social rights, particularly in the context of the ESC and the ILO conventions. One might therefore think that this is in itself the cause of the increased friction between the EU and international level. However, for a long time, this growing overlap presented a largely unproblematic state of affairs. Generally, international social standards were seen as a minimum

[36] Rocca (n 4) 55.

[37] ILO, 'Social Aspects of European Economic Co-operation' Report by a Group of Experts (1956) 74 *International Labour Review* 99–123.

[38] Posting of Workers Directive (n 11), Posting Enforcement Directive (n 11).

[39] Collective Redundancies Directive (n 12).

[40] Transfer of Undertaking Directive (n 13).

floor of protection that the EU's actions in all areas would respect and would go beyond whenever it intervened actively on social rights. The EU could furthermore act as a catalyst for the adoption and enforcement of the international standards through its external action, particularly its accession policy. EU law and international social norms could therefore peacefully co-exist in the same legal space, and perhaps even establish positive synergies. More specifically, the EU legal order explicitly accommodates, and thus to a certain extent internalises, these international social instruments, particularly the ESC. Prominently referenced in the Preamble of the TEU[41] and Article 151 TFEU,[42] the ESC is further mentioned in the Preamble of the EU Charter of Fundamental Rights, which 'reaffirms' 'the rights as they result, [...] from the Social Charters adopted by the [...] Council of Europe'. Although the non-regression clause of Article 53 of the Charter only explicitly mentions the European Convention on Human Rights (ECHR) and not the ESC, the CJEU refers to the ESC[43] as well as the case law of the Committee of Social Rights[44] as a source of inspiration for the interpretation of EU law.[45] Sometimes, secondary EU law makes explicit reference to the ESC.[46] Similarly, EU law also occupies a special position in the context of the ESC. For instance, the Revised Charter contains amendments to the original Charter of 1961 that builds on higher standards included in EU law, such as concerning gender equality, young workers and collective redundancies.[47]

[41] The Member States confirm 'their attachment to fundamental social rights as defined in the European Social Charter signed at Turin on 18 October 1961'.

[42] 'The Union and the Member States, having in mind fundamental social rights such as those set out in the European Social Charter signed at Turin on 18 October 1961 and in the 1989 Community Charter of the Fundamental Social Rights of Workers, shall have as their objectives the promotion of employment, improved living and working conditions, so as to make possible their harmonisation while the improvement is being maintained, proper social protection, dialogue between management and labour, the development of human resources with a view to lasting high employment and the combating of exclusion'.

[43] Joined Cases C-395/08 and C-396/08 *Istituto nazionale della previdenza sociale (INPS) v Tiziana Bruno and Massimo Pettini and Daniela Lotti and Clara Matteucci* [2010] ECLI:EU:C:2008:677, para 31; Case C-579/12 RX-II *Réexamen European Commission v Guido Strack* [2013] ECLI:EU:C:2013:570. See also Case C-201/15 *Anonymi Geniki Etairia Tsimenton Iraklis (AGET Iraklis) v Ypourgos Ergasias, Koinonikis Asfalisis kai Koinonikis Allilengyis* [2016] ECLI:EU:C:2016:429, Opinion of AG Wahl, para 60.

[44] See recently Case C-190/16 *Werner Fries v Lufthansa CityLine GmbH* [2017] ECLI:EU:C:2017:225, Opinion of AG Bobek, fn 37.

[45] However, according to Case C-67/96 *Albany International BV v Stichting Bedrijfspensioenfonds Textielindustrie* [1999] ECR I–5751, Opinion of AG Jacobs, para 146 in relation to the right to bargain collectively recognised by Article 6 ESC, 'the mere fact that a right is included in the [European Social] Charter does not mean that it is generally recognized as a fundamental right. The structure of the Charter is such that the rights set out represent policy goals rather than enforceable rights, and the States parties to it are required only to select which of the rights specified they undertake to protect'.

[46] See, eg, Council Directive 2011/36/EU of 5 April 2011 on preventing and combating trafficking in human beings and protecting its victims and replacing Council Framework Decision 2002/629/JHA [2011] OJ L101/1; Council Directive 2003/109/EC of 25 November 2003 concerning the status of third-country nationals who are long-term residents [2004] OJ L16/44; Council Directive 2003/86 (n 18).

[47] See Council of Europe, *The Relationship between European Union Law and the European Social Charter* (2014) European Committee of Social Rights Working Paper, 22 https://rm.coe.int/16806544ec

As regards the ILO and its conventions, the situation has always been slightly more complicated. First, disagreement already occurred early on about the respective powers of Member States and the (then) Community concerning the negotiation and conclusion of ILO conventions.[48] The matter came before the CJEU in the early 1990s concerning Convention No 170 on safety in the use of chemicals at work, which the Court held to concern a matter falling within the joint competence of the Member States and the EC.[49] More importantly, around the same time, an issue of substantive divergence between EU and ILO law arose concerning night work. In the *Stoeckel* judgment, the CJEU condemned a French provision prohibiting the employment of women to do night work as contrary to Article 5 of Directive 76/207 on equal treatment.[50] In a subsequent preliminary reference, the French national court pointed out that the contested provision resulted from ILO Convention No 89, which prohibits night work by women. In its corresponding judgment,[51] the CJEU considered that while equal treatment of men and women constitutes a fundamental right recognised by the EC legal order, its implementation has been gradual, and has been achieved by means of directives that allow certain derogations. In those circumstances, the national court was allowed to apply the conflicting national provision in order to comply with an obligation under an earlier international agreement, observance of which is safeguarded by (now) Article 351 TFEU.

Although this interpretation of EU law would allow Member States to comply with both ILO and EU obligations, France denounced the ILO Convention,[52] as did many other EU Member States, leaving Romania as the only EU Member State

(last accessed 19 September 2018), according to which the Charter was revised to make 'changes in women's rights so as to ensure full equality between men and women (with the sole exception of maternity protection measures), which draw directly on EU law; the minimum age for employment in certain occupations regarded as dangerous or unhealthy, which was not specified in the 1961 Charter, but was set at 18 years of age in the Revised Charter [stemming] from Council Directive 94/33 on the protection of young people at work; Article 29 providing that the states must impose on employers and obligation of information and consultation of employee representatives in collective redundancy procedures, which is inspired inter alia by Directive 92/56 on [...] collective redundancies'.

[48] The issue first arose in the late 1970s in connection with Convention No 153 on working hours and rest periods in road transport, an issue on which EC Regulation 543/69 on the harmonisation of certain social legislation relating to road transport [1969] OJ L77/49–60 was in force. It reared its head again in the preparation of Convention No 162 concerning safety in the use of asbestos, an area covered by four EC directives. After some difficulty, agreement was reached about the division of responsibilities in cases coming within exclusive EC competence, by means of a Council decision. See Opinion 2/91 of the CJEU of 19 March 1993 [1993] ECR I–1061, which discusses these issues in detail.

[49] ibid. The Court confirmed that, although the EC cannot itself conclude conventions under the ILO Constitution, its external competence may be exercised through the Member States acting jointly in the EC's interest.

[50] Case C-345/89 *Criminal Proceedings against Alfred Stoeckel* [1991] ECR I-04047.

[51] Case C-158/91 *Criminal Proceedings against Jean-Claude Levy* [1993] ECR I–4287.

[52] However, it initially maintained the national provision. The Court of Justice accordingly condemned France and only after the Commission brought an action against France for complying with that judgment and seeking a fine, France amended its labour code. Case C-197/96 *Commission of the European Communities v French Republic* [1997] ECR I–1489.

still subject to it.[53] This demonstrates the willingness of both the CJEU and the EU Member States to avoid conflicts between EU and ILO obligations, and thus of the 'elasticity' of the EU balloon, although from a social rights perspective the resulting reduction in protection against night work was perhaps not the best solution. From this standpoint, a more fruitful interaction between EU and ILO norms concerning night work, and working conditions more generally, was established by virtue of Recital 6 to the EU Working Time Directive 2003/88, providing that '[a]ccount should be taken of the principles of the [ILO] with regard to the organization of working time, including those relating to night work'. As Hugh Collins et al note, this presents a 'formidable commitment', considering that there are over 30 conventions dealing directly with working time.[54] The CJEU has applied this commitment to the right to paid annual leave laid down in Article 7 of the Working Time Directive in *KHS*, where it relied on ILO Convention No 132 concerning Annual Holidays with Pay to the calculation of the minimum carry-over period of annual leave not taken due to sick leave.[55] This is all the more interesting considering the fact that not all EU Member States have ratified this Convention. By internalising ILO standards in this way, EU law thus acted not only to enforce but also to expand the scope of application of ILO law.

The upshot of the foregoing account is that although there was an increasing risk of overlap between the EU and international level in the area of social rights because of the EU's progressive development of its own social *acquis*, which occasionally resulted in some coordination problems and diverging minimum standards, overall there was still a great degree of convergence and fruitful interaction between the various sources of social rights. There, apparently, was sufficient resilience and elasticity of the EU balloon, as well as the international one. This situation changed fundamentally as the EU balloon was suddenly rapidly and strongly inflated by two landmark events in the 2000s: the 2004 Eastern Enlargement[56] and the 2008 economic crisis and its aftermath. Both events are closely related to one of the EU's most important internal structural pressures: the socio-economic divergence between the Member States. The 2004 Enlargement is itself responsible for widening and deepening this divergence, whereas the economic crisis has shone further light on it (and by some accounts was partially caused by it, and in any event has been the driver behind a range of measures and policies aimed at turning this divergence into convergence). It is this internal structural pressure of socio-economic divergence caused by an (over)inflated EU balloon, and the EU's attempts to mitigate it by even further inflating it, that are

[53] Current ratification status available at: www.ilo.org/dyn/normlex/en/f?p=1000:11300:0::NO:11300:P11300_INSTRUMENT_ID:312234 (last accessed 19 September 2018).

[54] H Collins, K Ewing and A McColgan, *Labour Law* (Cambridge, Cambridge University Press, 2012) 271.

[55] Case C-214/10 *KHS AG v Winfried Schulte* [2011] ECR I-11757, paras 41–42.

[56] See on this issue P Copeland, 'EU Enlargement, the Clash of Capitalisms and the European Social Model' (2012) 10 *Comparative European Politics* 476, 482.

also at the heart of the external pressure that we are examining here: the most important frictions with international social law.

Indeed, the *Viking* and *Laval* cases cannot be considered without taking into account the Enlargement context. While levels of socio-economic development have diverged between the EU Member States from the outset, which could be argued to form part of the very logic behind an internal market of goods, services and labour, the 2004 expansion of EU membership brought about an entirely new degree of intra-EU socio-economic divergence. The difference in salary levels and costs of living has increased, while at the same time all kinds of practical hurdles to the mobility of both people and services have fundamentally decreased. These circumstances create the ideal conditions for what some would call a more 'efficient allocation of economic factors and resources' and what others would call 'social dumping' and a 'race to the bottom' type of regulatory competition. The difficulty here is that what is 'social' may differ very much according to which standpoint one adopts: the posting of Latvian workers to Sweden under Latvian wage conditions provides Latvian workers with employment and could be argued to be in their socio-economic interest. On the other hand, the undercutting of Swedish wage standards by this posting can be considered detrimental for the socio-economic interests of Swedish workers. Similarly, the reflagging of the Rosella from Finland to Estonia may have led to lower social standards for staff but at the same time might have saved their jobs (as the ship was running at a loss). Furthermore, regardless of the question whether the internal market rights in play have a social dimension, they are the cornerstone of the internal market *id est* the European construction, and form the foundation of the political and constitutional settlement in the context of which the Enlargement deliberately and consciously took place. The point here is not so much to defend the *Viking* and *Laval* case law, of which this author remains critical indeed,[57] but to highlight the important role played by the increased structural pressure in the enlarged EU balloon since 2004 to explain and contextualise this case law – and so too the conflict with international social norms that it has given rise to.

The second paradigmatic shift in EU integration that is relevant for understanding the root causes of the increased friction with international social law is the 2008 global economic crisis and the string of financial, sovereign-debt and EURO-crises that ensued in its wake. Both the *ad hoc* financial assistance measures to countries on the verge of bankruptcy under strict conditionality and the fundamentally reformed permanent economic governance framework for all EU Member States (the European Semester) have greatly increased the involvement of the EU in matters of social and employment policy (as well as other areas such as education and public health), where previously the EU's role had been limited because of restrictions on its direct, legislative competences.

[57] S Garben, 'The Constitutional (Im)balance between "the Market" and "the Social" in the European Union' (2017) 13/1 *European Constitutional Law Review* 23.

The 'competence coup'[58] that has taken place in this respect may be defendable and understandable in light of the gravity of the crisis and the fundamental need for increased socio-economic convergence that it arguably demonstrated, it has clearly also raised a number of constitutional and democratic concerns[59] as well as given rise to frictions with the international level. Although (as will be elaborated on in the following section) not every measure condemned by the ILO and ECSR can directly or even indirectly be attributed to the EU's austerity policy, and while many of the political choices made in the EU's post-crisis governance may be regrettable from a social perspective but do not as such constitute infringements of minimum social standards (at either EU or international level), meaning that the degree of outright normative conflict is limited, it shall nevertheless be clear that the EU's crisis policy has aggravated the problems in the relationship between the EU and international social law and actors which started a few years earlier with *Viking* and *Laval*.

IV. Possible Solutions: More Responsibility, more Elasticity

As already mentioned, the discrepancy between EU norms and international social law poses a number of problems. The EU's credibility suffers whenever it transpires that the norms it adopts are at a lower standard than those of the internationally recognised minima; and its legitimacy is compromised when it appears that its norms are in outright conflict with these international standards. Even if there is not a direct legal incompatibility, because the EU is not a signatory to either the ILO conventions or the ESC, it does raise fundamental concerns under the international rule of law when a Member State is subject to two conflicting sets of higher norms – where compliance with the one means infringing the other. From the viewpoint of an individual citizen this is even more problematic, as it becomes impossible to establish with any degree of certainty the content of the rights and obligations to which s/he is subject. Such a state of affairs is harmful for the coherence and standing of the transnational legal order, the universal claim of human rights and the actors responsible for respecting and promoting them; as such, it should be in the interests of both the EU and the international organisations to try to find a constructive solution to ensure a more harmonious and consistent legal framework.

This chapter argues that while the discussed frictions are an important issue that should be resolved, it is not necessary to revise the Treaties or for the EU to accede to any of these international instruments to do so. Although the internal structural pressures as set out in the preceding section are fundamental, and

[58] ibid.
[59] ibid.

cannot be rolled back, the resolution of the most important instances of friction as reported here is actually surprisingly manageable and does not require structural changes to the EU legal order. By and large, as explained in more detail below, it will suffice to, on the one hand, stress the ownership and responsibility of the Member States a little more and, on the other hand, for the EU Institutions to adopt a slightly more accommodating approach. This is not to say that, as I have argued elsewhere, the present situation does not also call for a fundamental reflection on the relationship between national, EU and international law as well as the balance at all levels between constitutionalism and democracy.[60] Indeed, a question that goes to the heart of the controversies described in this chapter is whether by entrenching socio-economic issues in supranational, constitutional norms (fundamental economic and social rights, the Treaty provisions on 'no-bail outs' and conditionality), they have not been unduly removed from the democratic process and instead illegitimately relocated to the international/EU judiciary and executive.[61] Having said that, the approach taken here is a more pragmatic one, to indicate two relatively modest and practicable changes along the lines of Inge Govaere's balloon theory: to stress the responsibility of those who inflate the balloons (Member States) and to ensure the EU balloon membrane's elasticity (CJEU and Commission).

A. Member States as 'Masters of the Balloons'

First, it should be emphasised that in most cases, including where there is apparent friction, there actually does exist a way for the national governments to comply with both the EU and international standards. For instance, as regards the austerity measures in Greece, the first Memorandum of Understanding provided that Greece was 'following dialogue with social partners, government to adopt legislation on minimum wages to introduces sub-minima for groups at risk such as the young and long term unemployed', but it did not specifically require the adoption of the apprenticeship contract with its regressive terms, for which Greece was condemned by the Committee of Social Rights, as such.[62] Similarly, while the Memorandum did specify that Greece was to 'extend the probationary period for new jobs to one year', it did not require these to be without any protection against unjustified dismissal. This means that the cases of outright conflict between EU and international norms are, perhaps, even rarer than generally assumed, and that the fault instead lies with the Member States' interpretation of the various norms.

[60] Garben (n *).

[61] Garben (n *). See also Garben (n 57). If one was to also apply the 'balloon imagery' to the question of constitutionalism and democracy, one could say that a better ratio between the oxygen of the democratic process and the helium of fundamental rights is warranted.

[62] Directorate-General for Economic and Financial Affairs, European Commission, *The Economic Adjustment Programme for Greece: Occasional Papers 61 May 2010* (European Union, 2010) 80.

In such situations, the current relationship between EU and international social law – and the institutions tasked with enforcement – can arguably be defended. The EU and the CJEU formulate their requirements in which economic concerns tend to play a very important role and may sometimes trump social concerns, but this is counter-balanced by the ILO and the ESC, which have social rights as their main concern. This leaves it to the Member States to formulate their policy in the admittedly narrow space between these competing requirements. This certainly is a demanding exercise and places a high burden on the national democratic process. However, it is at the same time an important reminder that ultimately, it is the Member States that carry this responsibility – indirectly because they are the (co-)authors of both EU and international law and more directly because there is usually a way for them to comply with both EU and international law at the same time. The phenomenon whereby Member States blame the EU/international level for all their woes is well-known – and it is destructive and corrosive. While it may be tempting for scholars to stress the responsibility of the EU in these situations, it could also be argued that such a narrative is insufficiently nuanced if it does not also underline the role of the Member States in that context (they are the EU) and risks becoming counterproductive in the long term as it may serve the Member States' blame game in deflecting responsibility.

That being said, there remain a few instances where the Member States did not, *de jure* or *de facto*, have sufficient space for manoeuvre to comply with all sets of norms, and these cases need to be recognised as problematic from the perspective of the international rule of law. These include, first, the *Viking* and *Laval* saga and, second, a limited number of the structural reforms in Greece passed under Troika auspices. For these cases, discussed below, additional solutions are needed. Still, it remains a valid point to also stress the responsibility of the Member States in these situations. As said, they are the most important (co-)authors of both EU and international (as well as national) norms and policies. In other words, they are the ones that inflate the balloons and tie them together.

B. *De Jure* Outright Conflict in *Viking* and *Laval*: More Elasticity Needed from the CJEU

The decisions of the ILO and ECSR directly concerned the *Viking* and *Laval* case law, even if they officially only had the power to condemn the national implementing measures. It is clear that the CJEU's case law itself is considered irreconcilable with the international social minimum standards concerning collective bargaining and worker protection and as such it is difficult to see how a Member State could meet all applicable sets of obligations simultaneously. While it is not necessarily problematic that the CJEU considers strike action a potential hindrance to free movement rights, its strict application of the proportionality test especially in *Laval* cannot be reconciled with the ILO and ESC requirements. Although the underlying Treaty norms that the CJEU interprets are ultimately the responsibility of the Member States, the CJEU's strict stance is not necessarily supported, let alone required, by the text of these provisions.

This latter consideration, ie that the text of the Treaties does not preclude a different interpretation of the free movement provisions that would better accommodate international social norms, means that the solution to this conflict is potentially straightforward: the CJEU could revisit its case law. To some extent, the CJEU already seems to be moving in this direction, recently readjusting its position to the benefit of national social regulatory autonomy.[63] For instance, in *Elektrobudowa*, the CJEU was asked to (re-)interpret the Posting of Workers Directive like it had done in *Laval*.[64] The case concerned 186 Polish workers posted to Finland, who considered that they had received insufficient pay. They assigned their claims to a Finnish trade union which went to a national court. The national court asked the CJEU for guidance on what the employer would be obliged to pay the workers under host State rules. The Court, in a remarkably generous judgment, sided with the trade union, confirming that it is possible for workers to assign their wage claims to unions if the host Member State law so provides, regardless of whether home State law permits this. Even more importantly, the Court gave a broad interpretation of what host States could consider as part of the mandatory 'minimum rates of pay' under Article 3(1) of the Directive. Contrary to the Attorney General, who followed a strict interpretation of the *Laval* doctrine, the CJEU held that minimum wages could be calculated by categorising workers into pay groups based on criteria such as qualifications, training, experience and type of work and could include a posting-specific flat-rate daily allowance. The Court also considered that the cost of the accommodation provided by the employer and meal vouchers could not be deducted from the minimum rates of pay payable to the workers. This important shift was followed in the *RegioPost* ruling.[65] Contrary to the position of the Commission, the CJEU held that the award of public contracts may be made subject by law to a minimum wage.

Other recent case law is also promising in light of the conflict with the ESC, as the Court seems willing to engage more actively with international social standards. In December 2016, the Court ruled in *AGET Iraklis* that Greek protections concerning collective redundancies, entailing that prior authorisation had to be obtained from a Greek authority before executing such redundancies, were contrary to the freedom of establishment.[66] While this judgment again may be considered as favouring economic over social interests,[67] both the tone of the judgment and its consequences are more accommodating of social rights than

[63] For a more extensive discussion of all the relevant case law in this respect, see Garben (n 57) 23.

[64] Case C-396/13 *Sähköalojen ammattiliitto ry v Elektrobudowa Spółka Akcyjna* [2015] ECLI:EU:C:2015:86.

[65] Case C-115/14 *RegioPost GmbH & Co KG v Stadt Landau in der Pfalz* [2015] ECLI:EU:C:2015:760.

[66] Case C-201/15 *AGET Iraklis* ECLI:EU:C:2016:972.

[67] S Garben, 'The European Pillar of Social Rights: Effectively Addressing Displacement?' (2018) 19 *European Constitutional Law Review*.

in *Viking* and *Laval*.[68] For one, in these latter judgments the CJEU, while recognising the fundamental nature of the right to take collective action as laid down in the ESC, did not refer to the case law developed by the Committee of Social Rights.[69] This 'recalcitrance' to refer to 'other sources of human rights law and "jurisprudence"'[70] on the part of the CJEU has been lamented more generally.[71] In *AGET*, by contrast, AG Wahl referred explicitly to the ESC in his Opinion, considering that an alternative to the Greek system where criteria for the authorisation of collective redundancies applied by the national authorities were formulated in very general and imprecise terms 'might have consisted in listing the types of dismissals considered to be unjustified, as in the case of the list which appears in paragraph 3 of the section of the Appendix to the Social Charter relating to Article 24 thereof'.[72] Some may oppose this type of use of the ESC's minimum standards, which would de facto be used to set a ceiling to the level of protection that can be provided against dismissal, but it would allow a narrow space for compliance with both EU law and the ESC, which was lacking in *Laval*, and constitute a compromise between economic and social interests.

While the CJEU in its recent case law therefore seems more accommodating of (international) social concerns, strictly speaking it has not overturned *Laval* on the point of collective action aimed at preventing a deterioration of working conditions as a consequence of a company exercising its free movement rights. Another step is therefore needed. But it need not be a leap. The Court could apply the proportionality assessment slightly more leniently, closer to what it did in *Viking*, and recognise that collective action in the interest of workers may not always be rational and proportionate in a strict sense, and may indeed try to prevent a company relocating to another Member State where this is done with a view to lowering labour protections.

Such an adjustment of the case law to comply with the ESC and ILO standards would increase the elasticity of the EU balloon and not puncture it. By relieving the external pressure from the ILO and ESC it would in fact help preserve the balloon's membrane and integrity. It is true that the internal market provisions are part of the EU's fundamental principles and, as such, could perhaps be argued to be part of the EU's '*constitutional core values*'[73] in the sense of the *Kadi* judgment, that should be upheld regardless of any contradicting international obligations. However, such a radical position should surely only apply to the very essence of these provisions (which, one could imagine, turns on overt

[68] M Markakis, 'Can Governments Control Mass Layoffs by Employers? Economic Freedoms vs Labour Rights in Case C-201/15 AGET Iraklis' (2017) 13 *European Constitutional Law Review* 724, 743.

[69] Rocca (n 4) 64.

[70] Rocca (n 4) 65.

[71] Barnard (n 4) 50; G de Búrca, 'After the EU Charter of Fundamental Rights: The Court of Justice as a Human Rights Adjudicator?' (2013) 20 *Maastricht Journal of European and Comparative Law* 168.

[72] *AGET Iraklis* (n 66) para 71.

[73] J Kokott and C Sobotta, 'The Kadi Case – Constitutional Core Values and International Law – Finding the Balance?' (2012) 23/4 *The European Journal of International Law* 1015.

protectionism and nationality-discrimination by the State) and not to any of their precise applications and interpretations in specific circumstances under the Court's own expansive doctrines on horizontal application of the provisions, potential restrictions and equally applicable measures. And especially where the market freedoms are balanced against human rights, it would seem that there is sufficient scope and reason to recalibrate the balancing, perhaps leaving more space to the national level to find the narrow space of compatibility between the internal market provisions on the one hand, and social standards on the other hand, without injuring the autonomy or integrity of the internal market and EU legal order as a whole.

In fact, as noted by Inge Govaere in chapter one in a more general sense, the CJEU could do this without conceding any territory to the international level, simply by internalising the external norms that are leading to friction. This should not be too difficult; we have already discussed the special position that the ESC occupies in the EU Treaties, as well as the EU's growing role in social rights with the EU Charter of Fundamental Rights. More recently, the EU has furthermore adopted the European Pillar of Social Rights.[74] I have argued elsewhere that while the Pillar can have important positive effects on the 'social output' of the EU, it does not fundamentally address the imbalance between economic and social values in the EU legal order and the democratic deficit connected to it. That remains true, but at the same time the Pillar may provide the EU institutions, including the CJEU, with additional impetus to revalue and upgrade social interests in the EU's overall framework of norms and values. In light of the only very gradual development of EU social law and policy and the EU's initially limited mandate in this respect, it is understandable that the CJEU may at times have to be alerted by external actors to the fact that it has insufficiently incorporated social rights into EU law. In the overall constructive attitude that it has taken in other areas of substantive friction,[75] it is not unlikely that it will take its cue and decide to accommodate the concerns through an explicit or implicit adjustment of its doctrine, for which it would now find support in a high-level Inter-Institutional Proclamation about the importance of social rights in the EU.

C. *De Facto* Outright Conflict with the Greek Austerity Measures: More Elasticity Needed from the European Commission

As stated above, not all the measures that were taken by the Greek Government in the context of the Eurozone crisis and that were condemned by the ECSR and the

[74] For comprehensive discussion, see Garben (n 67).

[75] See the discussion on the divergent interpretations by the CJEU and the ECHR on human rights in a migration context, as discussed by Cristina Eckes in chapter 4, as well as T Tridimas, 'Competence, Human Rights, and Asylum: What Price Mutual Recognition?' in Garben and Govaere (n 5).

ILO were the direct 'implementation' of stipulations by the Troika in the Memorandums of Understanding. Nevertheless, in some cases, it would seem that the 'creditors' did not realistically leave much room for manoeuvre for the Greek Government to comply with its conditionalities and still comply with international social norms. While these conditionalities do not constitute 'EU law' *stricto sensu*, a slightly thicker and less formalistic notion of political responsibility would include the EU's (and particularly the Commission's) role in the formulation of these requirements. They may have lacked binding force but the impending threat of bankruptcy would seem a more effective enforcement mechanism than any formal judicial proceedings could be. As such, this situation could be considered a *de facto* outright incompatibility between the EU legal/political order and the international one.

The recent Decision of the ECSR in *Greek General Confederation of Labour (GSEE) v Greece*[76] would seem to confirm this approach. It is noteworthy that the Commission itself, in its observations presented in the case, seemed to accept a direct link between the Eurozone crisis measures and the disputed Greek legislation. The Decision notes that the Commission did not dispute that the legislation adopted between 2010 and 2014 in response to the economic and financial crisis has affected the rights guaranteed by the 1961 Charter and that the 'legislation reflects the conditions laid down by the "Troika"'.[77] The ECSR considered that 'the pressure of the creditor institutions was considerable by prescribing in such detail measures which affected notably the right to work, the minimum wage and working time for both adult and young workers, dismissal protection, information and consultation in the workplace and collective bargaining' and that these measures 'resulted in a dismantling of important parts of labour law and the employment system in Greece'.[78] This, more than in previous decisions, implicates the responsibility of the Troika.

The Committee upheld the complaint on grounds of violation of the rights to work, to just conditions of work, to fair pay, to protection for children and young persons against hazards, and to participate in decision-making processes on working conditions established in the 1961 ESC and the 1988 Additional Protocol. It stated that it took 'due account of the scale and severity of the economic and financial crisis of which the population of Greece, especially workers, are victims', but that the violations of the 1961 Charter are particularly serious due to the large number of provisions concerned and the effects on persons protected by the rights violated, the number of victims of these violations that made up a significant part of the population, and the persistent nature of some of these violations, already identified in the examination of previous complaints. The Committee noted that it:

> underlines that the legislature's inaction, under strong pressure from the creditor institutions, with respect to amending the laws for a period from April 2012 until

[76] *Greek General Confederation of Labour (GSEE) v Greece* (Complaint) European Committee of Social Rights No 111/2014 (23 March 2017).
[77] ibid para 80.
[78] ibid para 86.

> September 2015 despite the violations of the Charter to which they gave rise, has led to a worsening of the situation over the years, contrary to the obligation for States Parties to undertake both legal and practical measures that will allow the full exercise of the rights recognised by the Charter. The Committee insists that these violations do not simply concern the persons protected by the rights which have been infringed or their relationship with the respondent state. They also pose a challenge to the interests of the wider community and to the shared fundamental standards of all the Council of Europe's member states, namely those of human rights, democracy and the rule of law.[79]

Considering the sweeping nature of, on the one hand, the structural reforms executed under Troika auspices and, on the other hand, the Committee's condemnation thereof, it may seem that there are no easy solutions to this particular friction. However, while some may insist that each and every part of the reforms were absolutely necessary, it seems unlikely that respect of the international minimum of social rights would really have made stabilisation of the Greek economy recovery impossible. Otherwise, how can we ever maintain the credibility of these universal norms as international minima? While speculative, it seems that if at that time a genuine social impact assessment had been carried out on the Memorandums, and if international social rights had been used as (one of) the standards of assessment in that respect, many if not all of the frictions could have been prevented. Politically, it may be difficult to admit this, but if this finding is accepted it does provide us with the solution. The internalisation of international social standards not just by the CJEU but also by the other institutions, such as in this case the European Commission and the European Council, would once again have been an effective way to resolve any friction between the EU and international legal orders. And while, because of the ambiguous legal status of the Memorandums in the context of the European Stability Mechanism, it is difficult for the CJEU to legally impose such internalisation,[80] the Court has nevertheless created a safety net of sorts in its landmark *Ledra* ruling. In this judgment it considered that Memorandums of Understanding may constitute a serious infringement of EU law by the Commission and the European Central Bank when they are incompatible with the EU Charter of Fundamental Rights, engaging the EU's non-contractual liability under Article 340 TFEU.[81] Under this new approach, it is up to the Court to decide to what extent the ESC and the ILO Conventions and their respective case law should feed into the interpretation of the relevant EU Charter rights to establish such a breach, but this clearly provides an avenue to effectively and elegantly resolve the frictions, upholding the international rule of law and preserving the integrity and autonomy of the EU legal order at the same time.

[79] ibid para 250.

[80] Cases C-105/15 P to C-109/15 P *Mallis and Others v Commission and ECB* [2016] EU:C:2016:702.

[81] Cases C-8/15 P to C-10/15 P *Ledra Advertising and Others v Commission and ECB* [2016] EU:C:2016:701.

D. Accession to the ESC: Puncturing the EU Balloon

Upholding the international rule of law whilst preserving the integrity and autonomy of the EU legal order would *not* be achieved if another solution that has been under discussion were to be followed, namely for the EU to accede to the ESC.

Authors have presented an in itself appealing case for such accession[82] as a way to resolve the frictions discussed in this chapter, and the view is shared by the European Parliament[83] and the ECSR.[84] The idea would be that accession would subject the EU, including the CJEU's judgments, directly to the high social standards[85] of the ESC and would constitute a clear political commitment. Making EU law subject to the ESC could potentially resolve the *Laval* conflict as well as the Greek austerity controversy in favour of the standards featured in the ESC (as well as the ILO more indirectly).

However, the option of ESC accession seems unfeasible at the moment, both politically and legally. The same concerns that led the CJEU to deny the possibility of EU accession to the ECHR[86] would apply *mutatis mutandis*. As the CJEU held in relation to the ECHR, through accession the ESC would, by virtue of Article 216(2) TFEU, be binding upon the institutions of the EU and on its Member States and would therefore form an integral part of EU law,[87] and the EU would be subject to external control,[88] in particular to the decisions of the Committee. While the CJEU considered that such external control, in principle, would not be incompatible with EU law, it added that this was the case 'particularly' where 'the conclusion of such an agreement is provided for by the Treaties themselves'[89] which, contrary to the ECHR, is not the case for the ESC or ILO. Moreover, the Court held that Article 344 TFEU entailed that any external jurisdiction over disputes between Member States or between Member States and the EU in relation to the application of the ECHR within the scope *ratione materiae*

[82] See O de Schutter, 'L'Adhésion de l'Union Européenne à la Charte Sociale Européenne' (2015) 102 *Revue Trimestrielle des Droits de l'Homme* 259.

[83] Such accession has been envisaged on various occasions, ever since the 'Spinelli' Treaty on the European Union of 1984 and the European Parliament has unequivocally expressed itself in favour. See Directorate General for Internal Policies, 'The European Social Charter in the Context of the Implementation of the EU Charter of Fundamental Rights' (2016) European Parliament, Policy Department C: Citizens' Rights and Constitutional Affairs www.europarl.europa.eu/RegData/etudes/STUD/2016/536488/IPOL_STU(2016)536488_EN.pdf (last accessed 19 September 2018).

[84] See Council of Europe, *The Relationship between European Union Law and the European Social Charter* (2014) European Committee of Social Rights Working Paper, 22 https://rm.coe.int/16806544ec (last accessed 19 September 2018) para 82.

[85] On the comparison between the level of protection of the ESC and EU law, see O de Schutter, 'Le statut de la Charte sociale dans le droit de l'Union européenne', J-F Akandji-Kombé, 'Charte sociale et droit communautaire' in J-F Akandji-Kombé and S Leclerc (eds), *La Charte sociale européenne* (Bruylant, 2001).

[86] Case C-2/13 *Opinion of the Court (Full Court) of 18 December 2014* [2014] ECLI:EU:C:2014:2454.

[87] ibid para 180.

[88] ibid para 181.

[89] ibid para 182.

of EU law should be excluded, which would apply equally to the jurisdiction of the Committee. In essence, the autonomy of the EU legal order as interpreted by the CJEU requires that only the CJEU can interpret EU law; and since accession would make the ESC an integral part of EU law, the CJEU should have exclusive jurisdiction in any dispute between the Member States, and between those Member States and the EU regarding compliance with the ESC where EU law is at issue.[90] This makes it very hard to see any legal possibility for the EU to participate in the collective complaint system. And it would seem that the CJEU's stipulations preclude precisely the situation where the Committee would rule on the balance between EU internal market rights and the social rights under the ESC, which would all but defeat the purpose of accession in the first place.

As regards the crisis-measures, apart from the fact that the ESC could not be retroactively applied to previous Greek Memoranda, their ambiguous legal status means that it is not certain whether the EU as such could be held accountable for the infringements of the ESC. And if they would be qualified as legal acts subject to judicial review and interpretation, it should only be for the CJEU to carry out such a review and interpretation, as explained above.

Accession to the ESC therefore does not seem legally feasible. Politically, too, it is doubtful that there is any appetite on the part of the Member States which, in any event, have not all accepted all provisions of both Social Charters. But perhaps most importantly, as this chapter has argued, it is not necessary. We have at our disposal a perfectly workable solution to mediate tensions between EU and international law in the form of internalisation. As set out in the previous subsections, this option is available both in the context of the *Laval* doctrine, and in Euro-crisis governance. The EU could, and indeed should, invest slightly more in this effort in the area of social rights. Such limited additional effort, however, would be absolutely worthwhile, as it would have a very beneficial outcome for both the international legal order and the EU one. Perhaps the real value of the proposal of ESC accession and the enthusiasm with which it is received in some corners, is that it warns the EU institutions that if they do not sufficiently internalise external minimum norms, either because of a lack of awareness or unilateralism, they risk being faced with far more intrusive scenarios, which will puncture the EU balloon – unnecessarily.

V. Concluding Remarks

The area of social law is particularly interesting to analyse in the context of the theme of the present book, since it is an area where there has been a consistent increase in overlapping activities between EU and European/international action

[90] ibid para 204.

over the past half-century, and over the past decade some high-profile divergences in interpretation have emerged between these different legal orders. This chapter has reflected, first of all, on the causes of these frictions, locating them – in line with Inge Govaere's theory – in the (over)inflation of the balloon of European integration. However, importantly, it is not so much the EU's development of its own social rights, but instead the 2004 Eastern Enlargement and the EU's expanded economic governance powers since the 2008 economic crisis that has led to this problematic over-inflation. At the heart of both developments is the structural internal pressure of profound socio-economic divergence and the EU's attempts (legally, politically) to increase convergence in response. This, in turn, leads to external pressures, in the form of frictions with international social norms and actors.

The chapter has also tried to encourage a critical reflection as to what extent such divergences are just inconvenient, or fundamentally problematic. I have argued that only in cases of outright conflict, where a Member State is placed in the *de jure* or *de facto* situation that it cannot comply with the EU norm and the international norm at the same time, that there is such a fundamental problem with the international rule of law that we need to somehow remedy the divergence, for otherwise we risk puncturing the EU balloon. In all other cases, it seems sufficient to stress the responsibility of the Member States to adopt policies that are in line with the EU and international commitments that they have entered into and often co-authored. This responsibility also exists in cases of outright conflict, but there it seems that additional reconciliatory action is necessary.

As we have seen, the main instances of such conflict, between EU law/policy on the one hand and ESC and ILO law on the other, are (i) the CJEU's *Viking* and *Laval* case law, and (ii) a limited number of the Greek austerity measures. As regards (i), a part of the solution here seems to lie in both a more conciliatory approach by the CJEU, to apply a less rigid proportionality assessment thereby better accommodating international norms (as well as internal social values). Recent case law in fact suggests that the CJEU is moving in that direction. As regards (ii), the de facto outright conflict has been vividly highlighted recently by the Decision of the ECSR in Complaint 111/2014. This chapter has argued that such conflict can, however, be avoided relatively easily if the EU institutions were to carry out a genuine social impact assessment when formulating such measures, using international minimum standards as the basis for that assessment.

In sum, a better internalisation of the ESC and ILO standards by the CJEU, the Commission and the Council would resolve the frictions discussed in this chapter. That would avoid having to go down the route supported by the European Parliament, of EU accession to these international instruments (particularly the ESC). Such accession would be problematic, especially in light of the CJEU's exclusive jurisdiction on the interpretation of EU law. It would thus, from an EU perspective, be a counter-productive move, as in order to avoid a puncturing of the balloon by external frictions, we would puncture it by sacrificing the autonomy of the EU legal order.

6

The Interplay of International and EU Environmental Law

NICOLA NOTARO AND MARIO PAGANO*

This chapter will present the parallel historical development of International and EU environmental law, showing their mutual influences as well as their divergences. In that context, the role of the US and of the EU, as key players in the development of environmental law, will be analysed with a view to explaining if, when, how and why they have been able to demonstrate global environmental leadership. After that, two examples of the interconnected developments of International and European environmental law will be analysed. First, the focus will be on the parallel birth of the Bern Convention and of European legislation on nature protection to understand mutual influences or divergences. Second, the Aarhus Convention on access to information, public participation and access to justice in the environmental field will be introduced to underline its impact on the EU legal order and the gaps in its transposition within the EU, particularly in relation to access to justice. The recent decision of the Aarhus compliance committee to fail the EU for its incomplete implementation of the access to justice provisions will be studied to anticipate the possible impact on the EU legal order.

I. Environmental Legal Orders

A. From International to European

The history of International and European environmental law is closely intertwined and mutual influences are common and have increased over time. We have discussed elsewhere[1] how the main milestones in the historical development of

* Dr Nicola Notaro authored parts I–IV of this piece and the views expressed here are the author's only. Mario Pagano authored the remainder of this piece.

[1] N Notaro, 'International and European Environmental Law: Mutual Supportiveness for Improving "Green Governance"' in P Demaret, I Govaere and D Hanf (eds), *30 Years of European Legal Studies at the College of Europe* (2005) 2 College of Europe Studies.

International and European environmental law provide ample evidence of the cross-fertilisation between the two bodies of law.

To recall a major example, the preparatory process leading to the 1972 UN Stockholm Conference on the Human Environment[2] and the Conference itself increased the environmental awareness of European leaders considerably. This is reflected in the very flexible and broad interpretation of the objective of the EC Treaty that the Heads of State of the EC provided in their October 1972 Paris Summit. By including the notion of 'environment' in their reading of the EC Treaty objective of 'economic expansion', they gave de facto birth to European environment policy, in spite of the lack of an environmental legal base in the Treaty.[3]

A similar inter-connection and parallelism can be noticed with regard to the development of the notion of sustainable development at the International and European levels. In 1987 the Brundtland Report entitled 'Our Common Future' gave a definition of sustainable development as a means to reconcile environmental protection and economic growth and provided a major input to the development of International environmental law.[4] It is not hard to imagine that (at least some of) the drafters of the Single European Act,[5] who introduced in 1987 for the first time in the EC Treaty an environmental legal basis, were knowledgeable about and sensitive to the Brundtland Report as well as to other important developments in International environmental law since the Stockholm Conference.

In the same vein, it is not surprising that the Maastricht Treaty,[6] in 1992, referred to the need to respect the environment in its objectives and mentioned explicitly the EC environment policy and the idea of sustainability. Moreover, the EC 1993 5th Environment Action Programme ('Towards Sustainability'),[7] adopted shortly after the 1992 Rio Conference on Environment and Development (UNCED),[8] already testifies in its title to the impact that the Rio Conference had on EC environment policy.

Many more examples of the central importance of international developments can be found when looking at specific sectors of EC environment policy such as climate change, the protection of the ozone layer, biological diversity and access to justice.[9]

[2] *Report of the UN Conference on the Human Environment*, Stockholm, 5–16 June 1972, UN doc A/CONF 48/14/Rev 1.

[3] See *Bulletin EC* 10-1972, 15 and JH Jans, *European Environmental Law* (London, Kluwer Law International, 1995) 1.

[4] G Bruntland, *Our Common Future: The World Commission on Environment and Development* (Oxford, Oxford University Press, 1987).

[5] Single European Act [1987] OJ L169/1.

[6] Treaty on the European Union [1992] OJ C191/1.

[7] [1993] OJ C138/5.

[8] Held in June 1992 following a decision of the UN General Assembly, UNGA Res 43/196 (1988).

[9] Notaro (n 1) 521 and ff.

B. From European to International

As the interaction between International and European legal orders is a two-way street, the contribution provided by European environmental law and policy to the development of their international counter-parts cannot be over-estimated.

The EC is a Party to a wide range of environmental agreements at global, regional and sub-regional levels.[10] The matters addressed by these agreements are very wide, and include among others the following areas: biodiversity and nature protection, climate change, protection of the ozone layer, desertification, management of chemicals and waste, transboundary water and air pollution, environmental governance (including impact assessments, access to information and public participation), industrial accidents, maritime and river protection, environmental liability.

In these fields, the EC is a leading proponent of international environmental action and co-operation, and an active player in the negotiations.

Maybe the most well-known example in this respect relates to the precautionary principle. Born in Germany as the *Vorsorgeprinzip*,[11] the precautionary principle was enshrined in the EC Treaty in Maastricht in 1992. The principle empowers policy-makers to take decisions which take into account the potential environmental and health risks of particular activities, even in the absence of incontrovertible scientific evidence demonstrating their safety or their danger. It gives the right to society to choose, through its democratically elected leaders, the level of health and environmental protection that it deems appropriate: such a choice is not and should not be left to scientists alone or to multinational companies.

The precautionary principle has been recognised by the international community only with many 'caveat' as reflected in Rio Principle 15.[12] The EC has been for the last 25 years an active defender of the notion of precaution as a 'principle', including as a principle of customary international law, thereby binding under International law.

This is reflected, *inter alia*, in the negotiations that led to the adoption of the Cartagena Protocol on Biosafety[13] and of the Convention on Persistent Organic

[10] For a full list of the Treaties to which the EC is Party, see www.ec.europa.eu/environment/international_issues/agreements_en.htm.

[11] See Jans (n 3) 20.

[12] 'In order to protect the environment, the precautionary approach shall be widely applied by States according to their capabilities. Where there are threats of *serious or irreversible* damage, lack of *full* scientific certainty shall not be used as a reason for postponing *cost-effective* measures to prevent environmental degradation' (emphasis added); see Rio Declaration at www.un.org/documents/ga/conf151/aconf15126-1annex1.htm.

[13] The text of the Cartagena Protocol is annexed to the Council Decision on the conclusion, on behalf of the European Community, of the Cartagena Protocol on Biosafety to the Convention on Biological Diversity [2002] OJ L201/48. It is also available at www.cbd.int/doc/legal/cartagena-protocol-en.pdf.

Pollutants (POPs)[14] as well as in the texts of these two treaties.[15] The Cartagena Protocol in particular is often used as a paradigmatic example of the enshrinement of precaution in International law.

Also in the field of general principles of environmental law, it is worth recalling the role of the EU in promoting the polluter pays principle which aims at internalising environmental externalities by requiring those who cause pollution to bear (at least part of) its cost. The principle was first enshrined in an Organisation for Economic Cooperation and Development (OECD) recommendation from 1972[16] and then codified in European environmental policy[17] and law,[18] well before obtaining wide international recognition through Rio Principle 16 in 1992.

II. US or EU Global Environmental Leadership

To better understand the interaction between International and EU environmental law, it is worth looking into the roles of two key actors in the international arena: the US and the EU.

In the 1970s when the ancestor of the EU – the European Community (EC) – was constituted by only six Member States, the US was the undisputed international leader in the field of International law development, including environmental law.[19] This situation went on for almost two decades, during which the US was the main promoter of successful Multilateral Environmental Treaties (MEAs) such as the 1973 Washington Convention on International Trade on Endangered Species (CITES)[20] and the 1985 Vienna Convention on the ozone layer, together with its 1987 Montreal Protocol.[21]

By 1987, the EC had changed considerably as its membership had already doubled and a dedicated environmental legal basis had been added to the EC Treaty,

[14] The text of the Stockholm Convention is annexed to the Commission proposal for a Council Decision on the conclusion, on behalf of the European Community, of the Stockholm Convention on Persistent Organic Pollutants COM(2003) 331 final. It is also available at www.pops.int/TheConvention/Overview/TextoftheConvention/tabid/2232/Default.aspx.

[15] See Arts 10.6 and 11.8 of the Cartagena Protocol and 8.9 of the POPs Convention.

[16] Recommendation of the OECD Council on Guiding Principles concerning International Economic Aspects of Environmental Policies, 26 May 1972, C(72)128, available at http://acts.oecd.org/Instruments/ShowInstrumentView.aspx?InstrumentID=4&InstrumentPID=255&Lang=en&Book=False.

[17] First EC Environmental Action Programme (1973–76) [1973] OJ C112/1.

[18] Art 130r as introduced in the EC Treaty by the Single European Act [1987] OJ L169/1.

[19] See RD Kelemen and T Knievel, 'The United States, the European Union, and International Environmental Law: The domestic Dimensions of Green Diplomacy' (2015) 14/3 *International Journal of Constitutional Law* 945–65.

[20] Convention on International Trade in Endangered Species of Wild Fauna and Flora (Washington) 3 March 1973, 993 UNTS 243.

[21] Montreal Protocol on Substances that Deplete the Ozone Layer, Montreal 1987, 26 ILM (1987) 1550; added to the Vienna Convention for the Protection of the Ozone Layer, Vienna 1985, 26 ILM (1987) 1529.

giving the EC a stronger legitimacy to take action in the environmental field at both European and international level. As mentioned, the EC – and then the EU – used this prerogative on many occasions and became a Party to around 50 MEAs, quite a few of which were never ratified by the US. For instance, the EU is a Party to the 1992 United Nations Framework Convention on Climate Change (UNFCCC),[22] to its 1997 Kyoto Protocol[23] and to its 2015 Paris Agreement.[24] The role of the US in relation to climate change international law is much more inconsistent: it ratified the UNFCCC, it signed the Kyoto Protocol but then refused to ratify it; it ratified the Paris Agreement but has recently announced its intention to walk away from it.[25]

Similarly, while the EU became a Party and strong supporter of the 1992 UN Convention on Biological Diversity[26] and its Protocols (the 2000 Cartagena Protocol on Biosafety;[27] and the 2010 Nagoya Protocol on Access and Benefit-Sharing),[28] the US never ratified any of them. The EU also went on to ratify the 1989 Basel Convention on the transboundary movement of hazardous wastes and their disposal;[29] the 1998 Convention on the Prior Informed Consent Procedure for Certain Hazardous Chemicals and Pesticides in International Trade (PIC);[30] the 1998 Aarhus Convention on Access to Information, Public Participation in Decision Making and Access to Justice in Environmental Matters;[31] and the 2001 Stockholm Convention on POPs.[32] Again the US is not a Party to any of these treaties which constitute major pillars of international environmental law.

[22] UN Framework Convention on Climate Change (UNFCCC), New York 1992, 31 ILM (1992) 849.

[23] Kyoto Protocol to the UN Framework Convention on Climate Change (UNFCCC), Kyoto 1997, 37 ILM (1998) 37.

[24] https://treaties.un.org/Pages/showDetails.aspx?objid=0800000280458f37.

[25] www.nytimes.com/2017/06/01/climate/trump-paris-climate-agreement.html?mcubz=0.

[26] UN Convention on Biological Diversity (CBD), Nairobi 1992, 31 ILM (1992) 822.

[27] The text of the Cartagena Protocol is annexed to the Council Decision on the conclusion, on behalf of the European Community, of the Cartagena Protocol on Biosafety to the Convention on Biological Diversity [2002] OJ L201/48. It is also available on www.biodiv.org/biosafety/protocol.asp.

[28] The text of Nagoya Protocol is annexed to Council Decision on the conclusion, on behalf of the European Union, of the Nagoya Protocol on Access to Genetic Resources and the Fair and Equitable Sharing of Benefits Arising from their Utilization to the Convention on Biological Diversity [2014] OJ L150/231. It is also available on www.cbd.int/abs/text/.

[29] The text of the Basel Convention is annexed to the Council Decision of 1 February 1993 on the conclusion, on behalf of the Community, of the Convention on the control of transboundary movements of hazardous wastes and their disposal (Basel Convention) [1993] OJ L039/1. It is also available on www.basel.int/TheConvention/Overview/TextoftheConvention/tabid/1275/Default.aspx.

[30] The text of the PIC Convention is annexed to the Council Decision on the conclusion, on behalf of the European Community, of the Convention on the Prior Informed Consent Procedure for Certain Hazardous Chemicals and Pesticides in International Trade [2003] OJ L63/27. It is also available on www.pic.int/en/ViewPage.asp?id=104.

[31] The text of the Aarhus Convention is annexed to the Commission proposal for a Council Decision on the conclusion, on behalf of the European Community of the Aarhus Convention on Access to Information, Public Participation in Decision Making and Access to Justice in Environmental Matters COM(2003) 625. It is also available on www.unece.org/env/pp/treatytext.htm.

[32] The text of the Stockholm Convention is annexed to the Council Decision on the conclusion, on behalf of the European Community, of the Stockholm Convention on Persistent Organic Pollutants [2006] OJ L209/144. It is also available on www.pops.int/.

It has been pointed out[33] that the reasons pushing the US and the EU in opposite directions in terms of their engagement with international environmental law are multiple and often contingent upon domestic politics. The US political system in which the President needs the approval of the Senate to ratify most international agreements has clearly been a major obstacle due to the lack of majority support among the senators even during the democratic presidencies of Clinton and Obama. Moreover, the influence of the lobbies of the oil, agro-food, pharmaceutical and chemical industries has probably also played a role in the US choice to stay out of so many major international environmental commitments.

On the other hand, the EU has witnessed the opposite trend with the appearance of some influential green parties across its Member States and a growing public environmental awareness which have prompted a rise in domestic environmental standards. This in turn has motivated the EU to push its own standards to become a world-wide reference not only to protect the environment but also to ensure a level playing field for its exports.[34]

One can find signs of EU self-interest in the promotion of some MEAs such as the Cartagena Protocol on Biosafety that originated from developing countries' requests but also provides international legitimacy to the EU legal framework on genetically modified organisms. Similarly, the continued support of the EU to the Kyoto Protocol and the negotiation of the Paris Agreement are also justified by the need to ensure that the fight against climate change is not only an effort made by European countries but rather a world-wide commitment. In this respect, the EU (failed) attempt to extend the application of its Emission Trading System (ETS) to the aviation sector[35] also for flights coming to its territory from outside the EU is an example of the tension between the unilateral development of ambitious domestic standards and their extension to the rest of the international community.

However, there are also historical reasons that explain the different approaches of the US and the EU to multilateralism, including in the environmental field, in particular in the interaction of these two big actors with the developing countries. Experience of international environmental negotiations[36] shows that the EU, probably because of the load of the colonial past of several of its members, feels a stronger responsibility to cooperate and to be forthcoming to developing countries' requests. This is apparent in the negotiations and conclusion of the Convention on Biological Diversity Nagoya Protocol[37] for which it is hard to identify any possible

[33] See Kelemen and Knievel (n 19) section V.

[34] Kelemen and Knievel (n 19) section V.

[35] The EU decided to limit the scope of the EU ETS to flights within the EEA until 2017 to support the development of a global measure by the International Civil Aviation Organization (ICAO). See www.ec.europa.eu/clima/policies/transport/aviation_en.

[36] The author has represented the EC/EU in many international environmental negotiations during the period 2000–2010.

[37] Above n 28.

EU self-interest. Even outside the relationship with developing countries, the EU ratification of treaties such as the Bern Convention[38] or the Aarhus Convention is a sign of genuine commitment to environmental law.[39]

Moreover, while the EU commitment to multilateral cooperation is also partly explained by the fact that it is not a big military power as the US, it is worth recalling that the EU is the first international donor providing 55 per cent of Official Development Aid (ODA); 38 per cent of the UN regular budget and 50 per cent of UN voluntary contributions.

Nowadays, while the EU has been a lonely leader in the development of international environmental law in the last two decades, the emergence of the Trump administration in the US and its decision to withdraw from the Paris Agreement may – unexpectedly – leave room for China to clean up its reputation as a big polluter and start emerging as a new environmental leader. This would be in its economic self-interest as developing and applying clean technologies on such a large domestic scale is likely to give it an extraordinary competitive edge over the rest of the world.

III. Pan-European Environmental Law and the EU: Partnership or Hegemony?

The previous sections have shown how the entire relationship between international and European environmental law is characterised by a 'give and take' approach where the influence of the EU as a global actor is often counterbalanced by other global players. This balance, which is continuously reset at the international level on the basis of the evolution of domestic and global geopolitics, tends to fade away when looking at the interaction between Europe-wide regional environmental treaties and EU environmental law.

This is because the enlargement of the EU to 28 Member States has given it a preponderant – if not hegemonic – role in treaties concluded in the framework of the Council of Europe[40] or of the UN Economic Commission for Europe (UNECE).[41]

These treaties build a pan-European legal framework and integrate countries with economies in transition into a common legal and economic space. We will illustrate the role of the EU in this context by taking two examples: the 1979 Bern Convention on the Conservation of European Wildlife and Natural Habitats and

[38] Convention on the Conservation of European Wildlife and Natural Habitats, Council of Europe, 1979, ETS No 104.

[39] A commitment that may be dwindling as we will see below in this piece.

[40] The Council of Europe has 47 members, see www.en.strasbourg-europe.eu/member-states,44987,en.html.

[41] The UNECE has 56 members, see https://www.unece.org/oes/nutshell/region.html.

the 1998 Aarhus Convention on Access to Information, Public Participation in Decision Making and Access to Justice in Environmental Matters. The former treaty was concluded in the framework of the Council of Europe, the latter under the UNECE. Both treaties are open to ratification of non-European States under certain conditions but their membership remains mostly European.[42]

Both examples will provide evidence of positive synergies between the EU and the pan-European legal framework. However, under the Aarhus Convention an on-going and recently escalating conflict will also be analysed in depth before drawing some conclusions.

IV. The 1979 Bern Convention

The birth and development of the Bern Convention and of EU Habitats and Birds (Nature) Directives[43] are closely related. The EU Birds Directive was adopted in 1979 after almost three years of negotiation among Member States and the Bern Convention was adopted in the same year. The negotiators from the EC Member States involved in the drafting of the Bern Convention must have tried to ensure consistency between the two instruments, in spite of the fact that the Directive focuses only on birds while the Convention encompasses many plants and animal species as well as habitats protection. This is illustrated by many commonalities in the two legal texts, such as the content of Article 2 on the measures to be taken by the Member States/Parties which is almost identical in the two instruments.[44] While the negotiations of the Birds Directive have inspired the Bern Convention, the latter has had a considerable influence on the development of the EU Habitats Directive which, in 1992, complemented the Birds Directive and fully implemented the Bern Convention into the EU legal order.

The similarities between the Bern Convention and the Habitats Directive are quite striking but there are also some important differences.

Both instruments provide for the protection of habitats and habitats of species of protected flora and fauna (Article 4 Bern, Article 2 Habitats). While the Habitats

[42] For the membership of the Bern Convention see www.coe.int/en/web/conventions/full-list/-/conventions/treaty/104/signatures?p_auth=0jP7Bwmh; for the membership of the Aarhus Convention see http://www.unece.org/env/pp/aarhus/map.html.

[43] Council Directive 92/43/EEC of 21 May 1992 on the conservation of natural habitats and of wild fauna and flora [1992] OJ L206/7 and Directive 2009/147/EC of the European Parliament and of the Council of 30 November 2009 on the conservation of wild birds [2010] OJ L20/7.

[44] Bern Convention Art 2: 'The Contracting Parties shall take requisite measures to maintain the population of wild flora and fauna at, or adapt it to, a level which corresponds in particular to ecological, scientific and cultural requirements, while taking account of economic and recreational requirements and the needs of sub-species, varieties or forms at risk locally.' Birds Directive Art 2: 'Member States shall take the requisite measures to maintain the population of the species referred to in Art 1 at a level which corresponds in particular to ecological, scientific and cultural requirements, while taking account of economic and recreational requirements, or to adapt the population of these species to that level'.

Directive provides explicitly (Article 3) for the creation of Natura 2000, the EU wide network of protected areas; the Bern Convention has developed its Emerald network, that extends Natura 2000 beyond EU borders, on the basis of Parties' resolutions.[45]

Under both instruments there is a graduation in flora and fauna species' protection which ranges from strict for some groups (Appendix I and II Bern, Annex IV Habitats) to less strict and subject to exploitation/management measures for other groups (Appendix III Bern, Annex V Habitats). Those groups largely overlap under the two legal instruments.

The prohibition of means of mass killing is also reflected in very similar language in Appendix IV of the Bern Convention and Annex VI of the Habitats Directive. The provisions detailing the conditions for exemptions from the strict protection regimes are also very similar as they require the absence of satisfactory alternative solutions, the lack of impact on favourable conservation status (on the survival of the population under Bern) and both legal instruments list the public interests that may justify a derogation (Article 9 Bern, Article 16 Habitats). A requirement for transparency on the use of such derogations is equally reflected in those provisions under the Bern Convention and the Habitats Directive on the basis of reporting requirements for Parties/Member States.

Finally, both instruments are equally cautious in supporting the reintroduction of native species and regulating the introduction of non-native species (Article 11 Bern and Article 22 Habitats).

Turning to areas where there is less convergence, the Habitats Directive's Article 6 establishes a fully-fledged system of habitats/species protection and restoration with a view to achieving their favourable conservation status. This is based on the designation of protected sites, the establishment of their conservation objectives and measures, the application of a strict principle of non-deterioration/non-disturbance and the requirement to assess plans and projects with possible adverse conservation effects so that the latter are avoided, mitigated or compensated. In this regard, the Bern Convention is less sophisticated and less ambitious as it only refers, in its Article 4 on habitats protection, to the duty for Parties in their planning and development policies to have regard to the conservation requirements of the areas protected for habitat conservation, 'so as to avoid or minimise as far as possible any deterioration of such areas'.

On the other hand, the Bern Convention contains an explicit provision on Parties' cooperation in relation to the protection and management of migratory species (Article 10) which has no equivalent in the Habitats Directive and only a partial equivalent in Article 7 of the Birds Directive. This is probably due to the fact that the EU is itself a cooperation forum for its Member States and that the selection of sites of EU importance, taking into account their biogeographical value, to develop Natura 2000 as a coherent ecological network, requires a considerable amount of cooperation between Member States.

[45] Recommendation No 16 (1989) of the Standing Committee to the Bern Convention.

In one of the rare analysis of the interplay between the Bern Convention and the Habitats Directive, Epstein[46] summarises the positive effects of the interaction between the two legal instruments as increased enforcement, increased funding and coordinated research and monitoring. The author, however, criticises the EU influence as having shifted the Bern Convention focus from species to area protection, giving less attention to the former. This criticism does not seem entirely justified. The Habitats Directive, whose name is certainly misleading, creates parallel and consistent systems of species and habitats protection that support each other. Natura 2000 aims at protecting habitats which are important *per se* and as habitats for protected species. The protected species are to be protected no matter whether they are inside or outside Natura 2000. Therefore, while it is true that the EU has 'inspired' the development of the Emerald Network under Bern, extending Natura 2000 beyond the EU, the network serves species protection as much as it protects habitats.

Epstein also flags the institutional impact of EU participation on the Bern Convention which has made it difficult to amend the Convention's appendices if these amendments are not in line with the Habitats Directive. This is because the EU holds the majority of the votes under the Convention and has only amended the Habitats Directives' annexes to expand them on the occasion of subsequent EU enlargements.[47]

It is undeniable that the EU has a hegemonic role under the Bern Convention due to the number of Parties it gathers but this is an inevitable consequence of its existence and prerogatives.

It is also true that the annexes of the Habitats Directive on species protection have remained static over time since it has been considered that their amendment would not be the most cost-effective solution to enhance species protection. In other fora such as the Convention on Migratory Species, it is possible to amend the Convention's appendices against the will of the EU as the EU Member States are not the majority of the Parties under that global treaty. Then the EU enters reservations on the amendments of the appendices which are not compatible with its legislation. This legal avenue however does not seem to be available for the Bern Convention as it would require a major – and unrealistic – increase of the number of its Parties.

Thus regional conventions such as Bern – without belittling the extremely useful work that they carry out – are likely to remain an extended arm of EU environmental legislation.

[46] Y Epstein, 'The Habitats Directive and Bern Convention: Synergy and Disfunction in Public International and EU Law' (2014) 26 *The Georgetown International Environmental Law Review* 139.

[47] See www.ec.europa.eu/environment/nature/legislation/fitness_check/docs/nature_fitness_check.pdf at 62.

V. The Aarhus Convention and its Compliance Committee

In 2005 the European Union (EU) adhered to the UNECE Aarhus Convention.[48] The Aarhus Convention entered into force on 30 October 2001, establishing a number of rights of the public (individuals and their associations) with regard to the environment. In particular, the Convention provides for 'the right of everyone to receive environmental information that is held by public authorities ("access to environmental information")';[49] 'the right to participate in environmental decision-making ("public participation in environmental decision-making")';[50] and 'the right to review procedures to challenge public decisions that have been made without respecting the two aforementioned rights or environmental law in general ("access to justice")'.[51]

In particular, as far as the right to access to justice is concerned, Article 9(3) of the Aarhus Convention states that

> each Party shall ensure that, where they meet the criteria, if any, laid down in its national law, members of the public have access to administrative or judicial procedures to challenge acts and omissions by private persons and public authorities which contravene provisions of its national law relating to the environment.

This provision aims at guaranteeing to individuals and non-governmental organisations (NGOs), meeting the criteria laid down under national law, the broadest possible access to administrative or judicial procedures in environmental matters, whilst paragraph 4 of Article 9 requires each Party to the Convention to 'provide adequate and effective remedies, including injunctive relief as appropriate, and be fair, equitable, timely and not prohibitively expensive [...]'. Furthermore, Articles 15 and 16 of the Aarhus Convention establish a review of the compliance mechanism aiming at guaranteeing that the legislation of each Party fulfils the requirements laid down in the Convention itself. On the basis of this provision, at its first session (Lucca, October 2002) the Meeting of the Parties (MOP) adopted Decision I/7 on review of compliance[52] that created the Aarhus Convention Compliance Committee (ACCC).[53]

Among others, Decision I/7 specifies that review of a specific Party's compliance may also be triggered by a communication concerning a Party's compliance with the Convention submitted by members of the public. The acknowledgement

[48] See above n 31.
[49] European Commission, 'The Aarhus Convention'. See www.ec.europa.eu/environment/aarhus/.
[50] ibid.
[51] ibid.
[52] United Nations Economic Commission for Europe, Guide to the Aarhus Convention Compliance Committee, 2nd edn (draft) (2015) 6, available at www.unece.org/fileadmin/DAM/env/pp/compliance/CC_Guidance/Guide_to_the_ACCC_for_CC56_clean.pdf.
[53] ibid.

of such a right makes the compliance mechanism of the Aarhus Convention an *unicum* in international environmental law, as it allows members of the public to communicate their concerns about a Party's compliance directly to a board of independent experts.[54] The Committee adopts findings which do not have any legally binding character and if non-compliance is found, it may make recommendations either to the MOP, or, with the Party's agreement, directly to the Party concerned.[55]

A. The EU Declaration upon Signature

The Aarhus Convention is open for signature to sovereign States as well as to regional economic integration organisations (REIOs) such as the EU. Article 19 of the Convention requires REIOs and their Member States to decide on their respective responsibilities for the performance of their obligations under the Convention, as they are not entitled to exercise concurrently their rights under the Convention. Moreover, the same provision clarifies that REIOs and their Member States should declare the extent of their competence with respect to the matters governed by the Aarhus Convention, which does not include any provision precluding reservations on its obligations. Indeed, Sweden and Switzerland put forward two reservations each, while the EU limited itself to making the declaration below upon signature, which was re-stated upon approval:

> [...] Within the institutional and legal context of the Community and given also the provisions of the Treaty of Amsterdam with respect to future legislation on transparency, the Community also declares that the Community institutions will apply the Convention within the framework of their existing and future rules on access to documents and other relevant rules of Community law in the field covered by the Convention. [...][56]

This declaration, and – especially – the sentence 'the [EU] institutions will apply the Convention within the framework of their existing and future rules' can be seen as the EU's first attempt – in the frame of the Aarhus Convention negotiations – to preserve its *sui generis* character and its constitutional autonomy. Nevertheless, such a statement should be interpreted as a declaration about the EU understanding of the agreement and not as reservation on certain obligations stemming from the Convention.[57]

[54] ibid.
[55] ibid.
[56] EU declaration upon signature of the Aarhus Convention, 25 June 1998. https://treaties.un.org/Pages/ViewDetails.aspx?src=IND&mtdsg_no=XXVII-3&chapter=27&clang=_en#EndDec. The legal implications of the EU declaration will be examined in depth below.
[57] See below.

VI. Communication ACCC/C/2008/32 (Part I)[58]

On 1 December 2008, the NGO ClientEarth, supported by a number of entities and a private individual, submitted a communication to the ACCC[59] alleging a failure by the EU to comply with its obligations under Article 3, paragraph 1, and Article 9, paragraphs 2, 3, 4 and 5 of the Aarhus Convention.

In particular, ClientEarth alleged that by applying the 'individual concern' standing criterion for private individuals and NGOs that challenge decisions of EU institutions before the Court of Justice of the European Union (CJEU) and the General Court or Court of First Instance (CFI), the EU fails to comply with Article 9, paragraphs 2–5, of the Convention. The Communication further alleged that the law adopted by the EU in the form of a regulation in order to comply with the provisions of the Convention (the Aarhus Regulation),[60] fails to grant to individuals or entities, other than NGOs, such as regional and municipal authorities, access to internal review; and that the scope of this internal review procedure is limited to appeals against administrative acts of an individual nature. As a result, ClientEarth claimed that the EU had failed to comply with Article 3, paragraph 1, and Article 9, paragraph 2, of the Convention.

Following ClientEarth's communication, the ACCC reviewed the compliance of the EU with the Convention and went through a detailed analysis of the relevant case law of the CJEU.[61] In particular, the Committee explored whether the 'Plaumann test' and the following CJEU case law were in compliance with the Convention, whilst the question of compliance of the procedure for internal review of administrative acts laid down in Article 10 of the EU Aarhus Regulation was analysed in Part II of the ACCC findings.[62]

[58] Report of the Compliance Committee, findings and recommendations with regard to communication ACCC/C/2008/32 (Part I) concerning compliance by the European Union, 14 April 2011, para 94. Hereinafter 'Part I'.

[59] Communication ACCC/C/2008/30.

[60] Regulation (EC) No 1367/2006 of the European Parliament and of the Council of 6 September 2006 on the application of the provisions of the Aarhus Convention on Access to Information, Public Participation in Decision-making and Access to Justice in Environmental Matters to Community institutions and bodies [2006] OJ L264/13–19.

[61] Cases 25/62 *Plaumann & Co v Commission* ECLI:EU:C:1963:17; T-585/93 *Stichting Greenpeace Council (Greenpeace International) and Others v Commission* ECLI:EU:T:1995:147; C-321/95 P *Stichting Greenpeace Council and Others v Commission* ECLI:EU:C:1998:153; T-173/98 *Unión de Pequeños Agricultores v Commission* ('*UPA*')ECLI:EU:T:1999:296; C-50/00 P *Unión de Pequeños Agricultores v Council* ECLI:EU:C:2002:462; T-37/04 *Região autónoma dos Açores v Council of the European Union* ECLI:EU:T:2008:236; T-236/04 *EEB and Stichting Natuur en Milieu v Commission* ECLI:EU:T:2005:426; C-355/08 P *WWF-UK Ltd v Council of the European Union* ECLI:EU:C:2009:286; T-338/08 *Stichting Natuur en Milieu and Pesticide Action Network Europe v Commission* ECLI:EU:T:2012:300.

[62] See below.

A. The Plaumann Test

As far as the assessment of the 'Plaumann test' is concerned, Article 263(4) TFEU[63] establishes the conditions under which any natural or legal person may seek the annulment of an EU act. Notably, under paragraph 4, 'any natural or legal person may [...] institute proceedings against an act addressed to that person or which is of direct and individual concern to them [...]'.

In 1963, the CJEU interpreted for the first time the criterion of 'individual concern' in the *Plaumann* case.[64] In *Plaumann*, the Court held that:

> persons other than those to whom a decision is addressed may only claim to be individually concerned if that decision affects them by reason of certain attributes which are peculiar to them or by reason of circumstances in which they are differentiated from all other persons and by virtue of these factors distinguishes them individually just as in the case of the person addressed.

The criteria for standing established in this decision has since then been referred to as the 'Plaumann test'.

The CJEU used for the first time the Plaumann test in environmental matters in the *Greenpeace* case.[65] In such a case, the CFI asserted that the Plaumann test was applicable to environmental matters and refused standing to the applicants. The CJEU confirmed the CFI decision and also added that remedies were available in the national courts, based on Article 234 TEC[66] (today Article 267 TFEU) concerning preliminary rulings. The Court re-affirmed its interpretation in later cases, and in *Danielsson*[67] it clarified that such an individual concern could not be established even if the applicants suffered harm.

ClientEarth alleged that the established CJEU jurisprudence on the interpretation of Article 263(4) TFEU is more favourable towards corporations and other entities with economic objectives, than towards NGOs and private individuals with environmental objectives.[68] Furthermore, the NGO pointed out that an alternative interpretation of the 'individual concern' criterion in Article 263(4) has already been developed by the CJEU, which has granted *locus standi* to entities in the field of competition, state aid and intellectual property. According to ClientEarth, this demonstrates that a more flexible interpretation of the provision is also possible in environmental matters.

On this point, the ACCC found that – in the field of the environment –

> the EU Courts have in no case accepted standing to any individual or civil society organization unless the matter concerned a decision addressed directly to that person. In two Cases relating to the environment, ie, the *Greenpeace* Case and the *Danielsson*

[63] Treaty of the Functioning of the European Union.
[64] *Plaumann & Co v Commission* (n 61).
[65] *Stichting Greenpeace Council (Greenpeace International) and Others v Commission* (n 61).
[66] Treaty of the European Community.
[67] T-219/95 R *Danielsson and Others v Commission* ECLI:EU:T:1995:219.
[68] Part I (n 58) para 36.

> Case, the EU Courts did not grant standing to the applicant, despite the possibility of reinterpreting the provision in question.[69]

Other cases were also put forward by ClientEarth and reviewed by the ACCC – such as *UPA*, *Jégo-Quéré* and *EEB*[70] – to show that the CJEU has not endeavoured to alter its jurisprudence, in spite of the alternative interpretation provided by the CFI.[71]

As a consequence, the Committee pointed out that Article 263(4) TFEU – on which the EU judges have based their strict position on standing – is 'drafted in a way that could be interpreted so as to provide standing for qualified individuals and civil society organizations in a way that would meet the standard of Article 9(3) of the Convention'.[72] ClientEarth argued that, to be individually concerned, according to the CJEU, 'the legal situation of the person must be affected because of a factual situation that differentiates him or her from all other persons'.[73] Thus, private citizens cannot be individually concerned if the decision or regulation takes effect by virtue of an objective legal or factual situation.[74]

The consequences of applying the Plaumann test to environmental and health issues is that in effect no member of the public is ever able to challenge a decision or a regulation in such case before the CJEU.[75] The ACCC thus concluded that 'without having to analyse further in detail all the cases referred to, it is clear to the Committee that this jurisprudence established by the [CJEU] is too strict to meet the criteria of the Convention'.[76]

However, while awaiting the outcome of the *Stichting Milieu* case,[77] still pending before the CJEU, the Committee refrained from examining whether the Aarhus Regulation or any other relevant internal administrative review procedure of the EU met the Convention's requirements on access to justice. The Committee thus decided to stay its proceedings and the adoption of its findings with regard to Part II of the communication until the CJEU adopted its ruling in Joined Cases C-401/12 P to C-403/12 P and Joined Cases C-404/12 P and C-405/12 P.

For this reason, on 14 April 2011, the ACCC simply concluded that – with regard to access to justice by members of the public – if

> the jurisprudence of the EU Courts, as evidenced by the cases examined, were to continue, unless fully compensated for by adequate administrative review procedures, the Party concerned would fail to comply with Article 9, paragraphs 3 and 4, of the Convention.[78]

[69] Part I (n 58) para 83.
[70] *UPA* (n 61); C-263/02 P *Commission v Jégo-Quéré & Cie SA*. ECLI:EU:C:2004:210; *EEB* (n 61).
[71] Part I (n 58) para 83.
[72] Part I (n 58) para 86.
[73] Part I (n 58) para 86.
[74] Part I (n 58) para 86.
[75] Part I (n 58) para 86.
[76] Part I (n 58) para 87.
[77] Joined Cases C-404/12 P and C-405/12 P *Council and Commission v Stichting Natuur en Milieu and Pesticide Action Network Europe* ECLI:EU:C:2015:5.
[78] Part I (n 58) para 94.

Therefore, in Part I of its final report, the ACCC found that – at the moment in which the findings were adopted – the EU was not in breach of the Aarhus Convention. Nonetheless, the Committee considered that 'a new direction of the jurisprudence of the EU Courts [had to] be established in order to ensure compliance with the Convention'.[79]

VII. Communication ACCC/C/2008/32 (Part II)[80]

Given that the communication was submitted in 2008 and most outstanding issues were not included within the scope of the court proceedings pending before the CJEU, on 20 May 2014 ClientEarth asked the Committee to consider adopting findings on Part II, which were formally released on 17 March 2017.

The ACCC's final assessment stressed a serious non-compliance

> with Article 9 paragraphs 3 and 4 of the Convention with regard to access to justice by members of the public because neither the Aarhus Regulation, nor the jurisprudence of the CJEU implements or complies with the obligations arising under those paragraphs.[81]

The analysis of Part II of the ACCC findings and recommendations will be divided into two main blocks, discussing, respectively, compliance of Article 263(4) TFEU (after the Lisbon Treaty amendment) and of the EU Aarhus Regulation with the Aarhus Convention.

A. Article 263(4) TFEU after Lisbon

The Lisbon Treaty,[82] which substantially amended the EU Treaties, came into force in 2009, one year after ClientEarth's communication concerning compliance by the European Union was submitted to the ACCC.

The Lisbon Treaty also amended Article 263(4) TFEU by adding a new sentence empowering any natural or legal person to institute proceedings 'against a regulatory act which is of direct concern to them and does not entail implementing measures'.

In order to assess the compliance of the new formulation, the ACCC analysed the meaning behind the different main elements of the last sentence of the provision, namely the meaning of 'regulatory act', 'of direct concern', and 'does not entail implementing measures'.

[79] Part I (n 58) para 97.

[80] Report of the Compliance Committee, findings and recommendations with regard to communication ACCC/C/2008/32 (Part II) concerning compliance by the European Union, 17 March 2017. Hereinafter 'Part II'.

[81] ibid, para 123.

[82] Treaty of Lisbon amending the Treaty on European Union and the Treaty establishing the European Community, signed at Lisbon [2007] OJ C306/1–271.

The three different elements have been considered and defined by the CJEU in two relevant cases – *Inuit*[83] and *Microban*.[84] In the first one, a non-profit Canadian organisation representing over 50,000 Inuit people, challenged a regulation of the European Parliament and Council on seal products. The case was brought before the CFI, which denied *locus standi* to the NGO as the challenged regulation could not be qualified as a 'regulatory act' under Article 263(4), which should be interpreted as meaning 'act of general application other than a legislative act'.[85] Such a narrow interpretation was confirmed on appeal by the CJEU two years later.[86] This appears to be in breach of the right enshrined in Article 9(3) to have access to administrative or judicial procedures to challenge acts and omissions by private persons and public authorities which contravene provisions of national law relating to the environment.

Regarding the two other elements laid down in Article 263(4) TFEU, in *Microban*, the applicants were found to be 'directly concerned' as they bought a particular substance with peculiar properties which was regulated by the challenged measure. The substance was then used for manufacturing a product which was then placed on the market. 'Thus by being economically affected they were considered by the Court to be directly concerned.'[87] In this regard, the CFI put forward that

> that condition required that, firstly, the contested [EU] measure must directly affect the legal situation of the individual and, secondly, it must leave no discretion to its addressees, who are entrusted with the task of implementing it, such implementation being purely automatic and resulting from [EU] rules without the application of other intermediate rules […].[88]

The ACCC thus found that such an interpretation prevents Article 263(4) from implementing Article 9(3) of the Convention, as 'an NGO promoting environmental protection would not be directly concerned with a contested measure unless the measure in question directly affected the organization's legal position',[89] and no basis in the Convention allows for the exclusion of acts which include implementing measures from the scope of Article 9(3).[90]

Therefore, the analysis of the CJEU case law after Lisbon carried out by the ACCC did not provide any evidence of a 'new direction in the jurisprudence of the EU Courts that could ensure compliance with Article 9(3)(4) of the Convention'.[91]

[83] C-583/11 P *Inuit Tapiriit Kanatami and Others v Parliament and Council* ECLI:EU:C:2013:625.
[84] T-262/10 *Microban International and Microban (Europe) v Commission* ECLI :EU:T:2011:623.
[85] T-18/10 RII-INTP *Inuit Tapiriit Kanatami and Others v Parliament and Council* ECLI:EU:T:2011:419, para 56.
[86] *Inuit Tapiriit Kanatami* (n 83) para 60.
[87] Part II (n 80) para 74.
[88] *Microban* (n 84), para 27.
[89] Part II (n 80) para 75.
[90] Part II (n 80) para 79.
[91] Part II (n 80) para 81.

B. The Aarhus Regulation

In the second part of its findings, the ACCC assessed whether the Aarhus Regulation (AR) compensates for the legal gaps identified in the CJEU case law. As mentioned before, the analysis of the relevant provisions of the AR had been postponed in order to wait for the final outcome of the *Stichting Milieu* case,[92] which was decided on 13 January 2015 and concerned the provisions at stake before the Committee.

In particular, the Committee focused its attention on the first paragraph of Article 10 of the AR, allowing for the 'request for internal review of administrative acts', according to which

> any non-governmental organisation which meets the criteria set out in Article 11 is entitled to make a request for internal review to the [EU] institution or body that has adopted an administrative act under environmental law or, in case of an alleged administrative omission, should have adopted such an act.

The Committee found that the AR fails to correctly implement Article 9(3) of the Convention for a number of reasons. Namely, it only allows for internal review of administrative acts requested by NGOs, whilst the Aarhus Convention specifies 'members of the public', which clearly has a broader scope than the wording laid down in the AR.[93]

Then, the ACCC focused on the subject matter of the procedure for internal review: the notion of 'administrative act', which was at stake in the *Stichting Milieu* case. In this regard, Article 2(g) of the AR defines the term 'administrative act' as meaning 'any measure of individual scope under environmental law, taken by a [EU] institution or body, and having legally binding and external effects'. On this point, the Committee recalled the ruling of the CFI on *Stichting Milieu*, which was then reversed by the CJEU. In that ruling, the EU judges pointed out that the Convention does not provide any definition of the term 'acts'.[94] In our opinion, this deliberate choice of the Convention's drafters aimed to make it possible to challenge in administrative or judicial procedures the broadest number of acts having an impact on the environment. Similarly, the CFI stated that an internal review procedure covering only measures of individual scope would be very limited, 'since acts adopted in the field of the environment are mostly acts of general application'.[95] Furthermore, the CFI pointed out that the AR defines the term '[EU] institution or body' as meaning 'any public institution, body, office or agency established by, or on the basis of, the Treaty except when *acting in a judicial*

[92] *Council and Commission v Stichting Natuur en Milieu* (n 77).
[93] Part II (n 80) para 94.
[94] *Stichting Natuur en Milieu* (n 61) para 72.
[95] *Stichting Natuur en Milieu* (n 61) para 76.

or legislative capacity',[96] a notion which is not covered by Article 2(2) of the Aarhus Convention.[97] The EU judges thus argued that

> the possibility that measures adopted by an institution or body of the [EU] acting in a judicial or legislative capacity may be covered by the term 'acts', as used in Article 9(3) of the Aarhus Convention, can be ruled out. That does not mean, however, that the term 'acts' as used in Article 9(3) of the Aarhus Convention can be limited to measures of individual scope.[98]

The ACCC agreed with the findings of the CFI in *Stichting Milieu* and was *surprised* by the reasoning of the CJEU in the appeal case which set aside the ruling of the CFI.

i. *The* Stichting Milieu *Judgment*

In *Stichting Milieu*, the question of whether provisions of an international agreement to which the EU is a party can be relied on in support of an action for annulment of an act of secondary EU legislation was raised again.[99] The CJEU recalled its case law *Intertanko*[100] and *FIAMM*,[101] according to which it is possible to rely on those provisions when 'first, the nature and the broad logic of that agreement do not preclude it and, secondly, those provisions appear, as regards their content, to be unconditional and sufficiently precise' (direct effect).[102]

On this point, the Court confirmed what was stated in the *Slovak bear* case[103] and denied the direct effect of Article 9(3) of the Aarhus Convention, as it 'does not contain any unconditional and sufficiently precise obligation capable of directly regulating the legal position of individuals and therefore does not meet those conditions'.[104] Indeed, the EU judges argued that only members of the public who 'meet the criteria, if any, laid down in national law' are entitled to exercise the rights provided for in Article 9(3) of the Convention. Consequently,

[96] *Stichting Natuur en Milieu* (n 61) para 78 (emphasis added).

[97] Art 2(2) of the Aarhus Convention defines 'Public authority' as meaning: '(a) Government at national, regional and other level; (b) Natural or legal persons performing public administrative functions under national law, including specific duties, activities or services in relation to the environment; (c) Any other natural or legal persons having public responsibilities or functions, or providing public services, in relation to the environment, under the control of a body or person falling within subparagraphs (a) or (b) above; (d) The institutions of any regional economic integration organization referred to in art 17 which is a Party to this Convention. This definition does not include bodies or institutions acting in a judicial or legislative capacity'.

[98] *Stichting Natuur en Milieu* (n 61) paras 78–79.

[99] *Council and Commission v Stichting Natuur en Milieu* (n 77) para 33.

[100] C-308/06 *Intertanko and Others* ECLI:EU:C:2008:312.

[101] C-120/06 P *FIAMM and Others v Council and Commission* ECLI:EU:C:2008:476.

[102] ibid paras 110–20.

[103] C-240/09 *Lesoochranárske zoskupenie* ECLI:EU:C:2011:125. See below.

[104] *Council and Commission v Stichting Natuur en Milieu* (n 77) para 47.

its implementation or effects are conditional on the adoption of a subsequent national measure.[105]

Moreover, the CJEU also recalled the two *Fediol*[106] and *Nakajima*[107] 'exceptions'. Indeed, in those cases the Court recognised its competence to review the legality of the act at issue, and the acts adopted for its implementation in the light of the rules of the World Trade Organisation (WTO) agreements where (i) the EU intends to implement a particular obligation assumed in the context of the agreements concluded in the context of the WTO; or (ii) where the EU act at issue refers explicitly to specific provisions of those agreements.

However, the Court dismissed the applicability of these exceptions on the basis that they were 'justified solely by the particularities of the agreements that led to their application'.[108] As to the *Fediol* exception, it did not apply to the cases at issue since Article 10(1) of the AR did not directly refer to any specific provisions of the Aarhus Convention, nor did it explicitly confer a right to individuals.

As to the *Nakajima* exception, the factual and legal background of *Nakajima* had to be distinguished from the case at hand.[109] In *Nakajima* the dispute centred on an EU implementing act linked to the anti-dumping system, which was, according to the Grand Chamber, 'extremely dense in its design and application, in the sense that it provides for measures in respect of undertakings accused of dumping practices'.[110] As a consequence, the CJEU concluded that no implementation was at stake in the *Stichting Milieu* Case.[111] Moreover, by adopting the AR, which concerns only EU institutions and one of the remedies available to private citizens for ensuring compliance with EU environmental law, the EU was not intended to implement the obligations deriving from Article 9(3) of the Convention, within the meaning of the *Fediol* and *Nakajima* case law.[112] According to the Court reasoning, those obligations 'fall primarily within the scope of Member States law', as previously stated in the *Slovak bear* case.

[105] *Council and Commission v Stichting Natuur en Milieu* (n 77) para 47 *cf* Opinion of Advocate General (AG) Jääskinen in Joined Cases C-401/12 P to C-403/12 P *Council of the European Union and Others v Vereniging Milieudefensie and Stichting Stop Luchtverontreiniging Utrecht* ECLI:EU:C:2014:310, paras 92–95. Jääskinen points out that Art 9(3) of the Aarhus Convention is a 'mixed provision', 'since it also contains an obligation on the part of the contracting parties to ensure that there is a clearly identifiable outcome'. Therefore, the AG argued that 'the obligation to guarantee access to justice is sufficiently clear to preclude a rule which would have the object or the effect of removing certain categories of non-legislative decisions taken by public authorities from the scope of the review to be conducted by the national courts'.

[106] Case 79/87 *Fédération de l'industrie de l'huilerie de la CEE (Fediol) v Commission of the European Communities* ECLI:EU:C:1989:254.

[107] C-69/89 *Nakajima All Precision Co Ltd v Council of the European Communities* ECLI:EU:C:1991:186.

[108] *Council and Commission v Stichting Natuur en Milieu* (n 77) para 49.

[109] H Schoukens, 'Access to Justice in Environmental Cases after the Rulings of the Court of Justice of 13 January 2015: Kafka Revisited?' (2015) 31(81) *Utrecht Journal of International and European Law* 58.

[110] *Council and Commission v Stichting Natuur en Milieu* (n 77) para 51.

[111] Schoukens (n 109) 58.

[112] *Council and Commission v Stichting Natuur en Milieu* (n 77) para 52.

Therefore, on the basis of its analysis of the CJEU case law, the ACCC found that – by setting aside the ruling of the CFI in the *Stichting Milieu* case – the CJEU's more recent interpretation of the remedy laid down in Article 10(1) of the AR is not in compliance with the Aarhus Convention.[113]

ii. Article 2 of the Aarhus Regulation

The ACCC also found that Article 2 of the AR, defining 'administrative act' as meaning 'any measure of individual scope adopted under environment law […]', was in breach of the obligations stemming from Article 9(3) of the Convention, as the latter covers *any act under any law* which contravenes law relating to the environment.

The ACCC maintained that the scope of the expression 'acts adopted under environmental law' is too narrow, as Article 2(1)(f) of the AR intends 'environmental law' as including any EU legislation which, irrespective of its legal basis, contributes to the pursuit of the objectives of the EU policy on the environment as set out in the Treaty. Moreover, the Committee argued that the scope of Article 9(3) of the Convention is broader than that, since it is clear that, under the Aarhus Convention, 'an act may contravene laws relating to the environment without being adopted under environmental law within the meaning of Article 10(1)' of the AR.

In addition, the ACCC assessed whether the condition laid down in Article 2(1)(g) of the AR requiring that – in order to be challengeable in administrative or judicial procedures – an act of the EU institutions or body shall have legally binding and external effects, was in compliance with the Convention.

On this point, the statements of the Committee were more cautious and its arguments weaker, as it applied by analogy the reasoning used to motivate the non-compliance of the 'individual scope' criterion, without looking into the actual external effects of the acts at stake.[114] Besides, the Committee clearly stated it was not *convinced* that 'generally excluding all acts that do not have legally binding and external effect is compatible with Article 9(3) of the Convention'.[115]

Such a statement was supported by the arguments presented by ClientEarth, which alleged that on a number of occasions administrative review of an act was refused because of this requirement.[116] In particular, on one occasion, a NGO sought the internal review of the Commission's decision, adopting the list of candidates to be proposed to the Management Board of the European Chemicals Agency (ECHA) for the appointment by the latter of the Executive Director

[113] Part II (n 80) para 57.
[114] See below.
[115] Part II (n 80) para 104.
[116] Part II (n 80) para 103.

of the Agency.[117] The Commission denied internal review of the decision as it formed 'an integral part of the procedure whereby the Executive Director of ECHA is appointed by the Management Board thereof'.[118] The Commission thus considered that 'such staff related decisions are by their very nature to be regarded as internal to the institution or body concerned and thus incapable of "having external effects" within the meaning of the Regulation'.[119]

Nonetheless, the applicant observed that 'the fact that a decision forms part of an internal procedure does not preclude it from having external effects'.[120] The NGO alleged that the decision should have included a broader number of eligible candidates and that suitable candidates had been arbitrarily excluded in the course of the selection procedure.[121] 'Deciding which candidates are eligible to become the Executive Director of an EU agency such as ECHA inevitably has external effects'.[122] According to the NGO,

> the background and prior and existing commitments of these persons directly influences their strategic and political choices which, given their mandate, impacts on the environment. Furthermore, the decision not to include certain candidates in the list prevents these people from being nominated as Director, and that is a concrete legal external effect.[123]

Therefore, the ACCC pointed out that this kind of act[124] *might* be covered by Article 9(3) of the Aarhus Convention without actually explaining what specific criteria should be used to assess whether a decision forming part of an internal procedure produces external effects or not. Nevertheless, the Committee then declared the general non-compliance of Article 10(1) of the AR considered in its entirety.[125]

C. The ACCC Conclusions and Recommendations

The Committee concluded by acknowledging an overall failure of the EU to comply with Article 9(3)(4) of the Aarhus Convention, as neither the jurisprudence of the CJEU nor the AR implement or comply with the obligations stemming from those

[117] ClientEarth's comments on the update on the Court of Justice rulings in Cases C-401/12 P to C- 405/12 P, dated 23 February 2015, paras 62–68.
[118] ibid.
[119] ibid.
[120] ibid.
[121] ibid.
[122] ibid.
[123] ibid.
[124] Decisions forming part of an internal procedure.
[125] In addition to the review of Arts 2 and 10, the ACCC also assessed whether the exemption of administrative review as well as of the internal review procedure as an adequate and effective remedy were in compliance with the Convention. However, the analysis of these relevant sections of Part II of the findings will not be carried out here.

international provisions.[126] In line with its non-confrontational, non-judicial and consultative nature, the Committee issued four recommendations to the EU as a Party, two of which were specifically addressed to the CJEU.

First, the Committee recommended that the EU amends the AR or drafts new legislation to make it clear to the CJEU that 'that legislation is intended to implement Article 9(3) of the Aarhus Convention'.[127] Second, the Committee recommended that any new or amended legislation implementing the Aarhus Convention uses 'wording that clearly and fully transposes the relevant part of the Convention'.[128] The Committee also stressed the importance of using words or terms which do not diverge from the ones laid down in the Convention, as this would cause 'failures in implementation'.[129]

These first two recommendations are clear references to the *Fediol* and *Nakajima* exceptions, whose application to the *Stichting Milieu* case was set aside as they were 'justified solely by the particularities of the agreements that led to their application'.[130]

Regarding the two final recommendations, the ACCC advised the CJEU to (i) assess the legality of the EU's implementing measures in the light of those obligations and acts accordingly; and to (ii) interpret EU law in a way which, to the fullest extent possible, is consistent with the objectives of Article 9(3)(4) of the Convention.

Also, these two recommendations are clear references to the CJEU case law, in particular to the *Intertanko* and *Slovak bear* cases. As mentioned before, in *Intertanko* the Court was called upon to decide whether provisions of an international agreement to which the EU is a party can be relied on in support of an action for annulment of an act of secondary EU legislation,[131] whilst in the *Slovak bear* case, the Court adopted a progressive approach towards access to justice at national level. In *Slovak bear*, the EU judges stated that Article 9(3) of the Convention – despite its lack of direct effect – cannot 'be interpreted in such a way as to make it in practice impossible or excessively difficult to exercise rights conferred by EU law'.[132] Therefore,

> it is for the national court, in order to ensure effective judicial protection in the fields covered by EU environmental law, to interpret its national law in a way which, to the fullest extent possible, is consistent with the objectives laid down in Article 9(3) of the Aarhus Convention.[133]

The duty of consistent interpretation with international agreements laid down in *Slovak bear* can certainly be seen as a step further in the EU system of judicial

[126] Part II (n 80) para 123.
[127] Part II (n 80) para 125(a).
[128] Part II (n 80) para 125(b).
[129] Part II (n 80) para 125(b).
[130] See above.
[131] ibid.
[132] *Lesoochranárske zoskupenie* (n 103) para 49.
[133] *Lesoochranárske zoskupenie* (n 103) para 50.

protection. However, the ACCC underlines the ambiguous approach of the CJEU as far as access to justice at national and EU level is concerned. In other words, since the EU is also Party to the Convention, why should the CJEU itself not be required to apply the same duty of consistent interpretation with the Convention with regard to EU law?[134]

The ACCC pointed out that if the EU Courts had considered to be bound in the same way as the national courts to the obligations deriving from the Aarhus Convention, 'the EU might have moved towards compliance with Article 9(3)(4) of the Convention'.[135]

VIII. Endorsing the Findings or not? That is the Question

Certainly, the findings of the ACCC recommended amendments of *constitutional relevance* in the EU legal order and its system of judicial protection, and provided an alternative interpretation – even if not definitive – of EU law provisions.

On 13 July 2017, a few months after Part II of the ACCC findings was published, the EU Council of Ministers adopted its final decision[136] on the EU's position to be adopted at the sixth session of the MOP to the Aarhus Convention.[137]

In its decision, the Council did not endorse the original proposal of the Commission, which was to reject the findings of the ACCC as they 'challenge the system of judicial protection under EU law'.[138] From its side, the Commission was to preserve the autonomy of the EU legal order and 'the specific nature of the system of judicial review' which is 'carefully drafted in the EU Treaties, so that every Union citizen has access to justice'.[139]

In its original proposal, the Commission pointed out that

> access to judicial review of EU measures is not limited to direct actions to be lodged before the EU Courts but can occur also before a national court, which can – and in some circumstances must – raise a question of legality before the CJEU, which can declare the EU act or measure invalid.[140]

[134] JH Jans, 'Who is the Referee? Access to Justice in a Globalised Legal Order' (2011) 4 (1) *Review of European Administrative Law* 98.

[135] Part II (n 80) para 83.

[136] Draft Council decision on the position to be adopted, on behalf of the European Union, at the sixth session of the Meeting of the Parties to the Aarhus Convention as regards compliance case ACCC/C/2008/32, Brussels 13 July 2017.

[137] Budva, Montenegro, 11–13 September 2017.

[138] Statement by the Commission on the Draft Council Decision on the position to be adopted, on behalf of the European Union, at the sixth session of the Meeting of the Parties to the Aarhus Convention regarding compliance case ACCC/C/2008/32, Brussels, 17 July 2017.

[139] Proposal for a Council decision on the position to be adopted, on behalf of the European Union, at the sixth session of the Meeting of the Parties to the Aarhus Convention regarding compliance case ACCC/C/2008/32, 29 June 2017, 4.

[140] ibid.

This point had already been addressed by the ACCC in Part I of its findings, which acknowledged the *internal* relevance of the preliminary reference procedure in the EU for ensuring consistent application and proper implementation of EU law in its Member States. However, the Committee found that such a procedure 'cannot be a basis for generally denying members of the public access to the EU Courts to challenge decisions, acts and omissions by EU institutions and bodies',[141] and it thus rejected the argument.

Furthermore, the Commission recalled that the Aarhus Convention bodies had been made aware in the EU declaration upon signature of the peculiarities of the legal order of the Union. According to the declaration, the EU institutions 'will apply the Convention within the framework of their existing and future rules on access to documents and other relevant rules of [EU] law in the field covered by the Convention'.[142]

In fact, the purpose of such a declaration is not very clear. It seems to imply that the EU should not be treated as the other Parties to the Convention since the Union will apply the provisions of the agreement not *as they are*, but within the current and future relevant EU legal framework. The Committee did not take this argument into consideration. In this regard, it is our opinion that if the EU really wanted to limit the scope of Article 9(3) of the Convention in its legal order, it had to put forward a clear *reservation* upon approval. Indeed, as mentioned above,[143] two other Parties to the Convention entered reservations while the EU limited itself to make two simple *declarations*, one upon signature and another one upon approval.

The Commission concluded by saying that the Committee's findings challenge constitutional principles of EU law that are so fundamental that it is legally impossible for the EU to follow and comply with the findings. For this reason, the Commission proposed that the EU's position at the MOP should have been to reject the ACCC findings, even if this position would have not diminished the EU's commitment to the principles and objectives of the Convention.

The contradiction of the Commission seems quite evident: how could the EU reject the findings of the ACCC and, at the same time, remain fully committed to pursue the principles and objectives of the Convention?

The Council adopted a more 'cautious' approach, and proposed that the MOP should not reject the ACCC findings, but simply 'take note' of them.[144] Moreover, in view of the separation of powers in the European Union, the Council made clear that it cannot give instructions or make recommendations to the CJEU concerning its judicial activities. For this reason, it rejected the recommendations related to the Court of Justice and its jurisprudence.[145]

[141] Part I (n 58) para 90.
[142] See above.
[143] ibid.
[144] Draft Council decision (n 138), 5.
[145] Draft Council decision (n 138) 4.

The Council confirmed that the EU will continue to 'fully support the important objectives of the Aarhus Convention' but it also declared that the Union should 'explore ways and means to comply with the Aarhus Convention in a way that is compatible with the fundamental principles of the Union legal order and with its system of judicial review'.[146]

In this regard, it seems hard to identify other 'ways and means to comply' without *touching* some of the fundamental procedural rules on which the EU judicial system is based. In particular, the Plaumann test has already been *softened* in areas other than environmental law by the jurisprudence of the CJEU.[147] Therefore, the real question seems to be: why not for the environment?

As mentioned previously,[148] the CJEU has already provided alternative interpretations of the 'individual concern' criterion laid down in Article 263(4) TFEU in quite a broad range of legal areas. However, none of them deals with the protection of public interests. The protection of the environment is the ultimate 'public interest', as it can only be defended by *someone else*,[149] making the role of civil society all the more important in seeking to enforce EU law in this policy area. The reason behind the EU institutions' reticence to open access to justice could be linked to the fear of seeing any future EU act, with a direct or indirect impact on the environment, challenged in front of the EU Courts. The CJEU would be overwhelmed by thousands of new cases, making the functioning of the EU institutions almost impossible.

Nonetheless, it does not appear that such fears are justified. Indeed, the EU institutions, in particular the Commission and the CJEU, could work together – within their respective competences – on possible legal *filters*, such as the establishment of specific criteria in line with the Aarhus Convention aiming to define what kind of acts could actually be challenged, rather than shutting down any possibility for a civil society organisation to bring a case in front of the EU Courts or to ask for internal review of administrative acts adopted by EU institutions and bodies.

IX. The Decision of the MOP

The MOP's role is in line with the nature of the ACCC and it may only take non-confrontational, non-judicial and consultative measures, such as making

[146] Draft Council decision (n 138) 3.

[147] See above.

[148] ibid.

[149] 'The fish cannot go to Court. […] The environment cannot protect itself if it is threatened or harmed. It is a public good and should be supported by public voice'. AG Sharpston at the hearing of Case C-115/09 *Bund für Umwelt und Naturschutz Deutschland, Landesverband Nordrhein-Westfalen eV v Bezirksregierung Arnsberg* ECLI:EU:C:2011:289.

recommendations to the Party concerned, requesting the Party concerned to submit a strategy to the ACCC regarding the achievement of compliance with the Convention, issuing declarations of non-compliance and cautions.[150]

The fact that neither the ACCC nor the MOP can issue economic sanctions, as well as the lack of a legally binding character of the MOP measures, might imply that the EU has nothing to fear from the findings of the ACCC. The consultative nature of the Committee makes its findings no real threat for the constitutional autonomy of the EU legal system,[151] as only the CJEU would have the final say over the interpretation of EU law provisions. Nonetheless, the main consequences of the EU non-compliance with the Aarhus Convention are not legal, but political.

The EU is going through a time of political instability and democratic discredit, which is pushing the people away from the European Union. For this reason, a *partial* commitment in the implementation of one of the major environmental democracy pillars enshrined in the Aarhus Convention would put the EU's credibility as a global environmental actor into question, and reduce the relevance of the role of civil society organisations in the enforcement of international and EU environmental law.

At its sixth session which took place in Budva (Montenegro) on 11–13 September 2017, the MOP – 'considering the exceptional circumstances' – decided by consensus to 'postpone the decision-making on draft decision VI/8f concerning the European Union to the next ordinary session of the Meeting of the Parties to be held in 2021'.[152] On the other side, the EU recalled its 'willingness to continue exploring ways and means to comply with the Convention in a way that is compatible with the fundamental principles of the Union legal order and with its system of judicial review'. Such a final outcome of the sixth session of the MOP was highly criticised by civil society organisations which accused the EU of 'hypocrisy' and invited the latter, without delay, to start the process of

> revising the Aarhus Regulation which up to now, in combination with the jurisprudence of the Court of Justice of the EU, has effectively prevented NGOs from seeking access to justice in defence of the environment at the EU level in all but access to documents cases.[153]

[150] Meeting of the Parties to the Convention on Access to Information, Public Participation in Decision-making and Access to Justice in Environmental Matters, Decision I/7 – Review of compliance, 21–23 October 2002, 7.

[151] See Opinion 2/13 of the CJEU, *Access of the EU to the ECHR* ECLI:EU:C:2014:2454, paras 174–76.

[152] www.ukhumanrightsblog.com/2017/09/23/the-biter-bit-eu-does-not-like-being-criticised-by-aarhus-body.

[153] European Eco Forum statement on the role of the European Union in relation to the finding that it is in non-compliance with the Aarhus Convention, Budva, Montenegro, Thursday 14 September 2017. See www.wecf.eu/download/2017/09-September/EuropeanECOForumStatementNon-ComplianceEU.pdf.

X. Conclusions

The above analysis has demonstrated the strong interlinkages between international and EU environmental law which has most often been based on mutual supportiveness, enrichment and cross-fertilisation. It has also shown how developments in the international environmental arena are often generated under the stimulus of one or few key players and that the EU has long replaced the US in this role. However, in our fast evolving world, economic power-houses like China may soon emerge as new environmental leaders matching their economic interests and environmental protection. The EU, heavily affected by economic and social crisis, may also be facing a decline as environmental leader. The selected examples have shown that, while the EU is successfully exporting its nature protection standards at pan-European level, it faces great difficulties in 'importing' from the international arena an 'open access to justice', one of the fundamental pillars of democracy in the environmental field.

This is a major flaw. If high environmental standards are not to remain mere rhetoric, access to justice at EU level as well as in its Member States must be opened up substantially more than is the case now. Our digital interconnected society has already been the vehicle for radical changes in the EU (and global) political landscape due to new forms of citizens' organisations that have in some cases swept away traditional political parties. Thinking that citizens can be kept away from accessing legal remedies against EU legal acts is like attempting to stop the ocean with a dam.

7

Implementing International Norms through EU Procedure? The Case of Business and Human Rights

PIERRE THIELBÖRGER[1]

This chapter introduces a case in which the international and the European legal framework complement each other perfectly: while one, namely international law, has established widely accepted norms for the field of business and human rights, the other, European Union (EU) law, offers the perfect platform for the coordination of its implementation. While international law generally suffers from weak implementation, the respective shortcomings in the field of business and human rights could be addressed through a process within EU law along the lines of an Open Method of Coordination (OMC) – a policy instrument which the EU has used previously in other policy fields.

More specifically, the chapter sketches out the global governance approach behind the United Nations Guiding Principles on Business and Human Rights (UNGPs) and discusses their domestic implementation via National Action Plans (NAPs). It provides an overview of some of the EU Member States' already developed NAPs on business and human rights, critically assessing their content and drafting process along international guidelines. It is suggested that the shortcomings found in the current European NAPs are addressed through an OMC process between EU Member States – a policy proposal that has also found support within EU institutions, most notably by the EU Fundamental Rights Agency. The chapter then goes on to outline the possible contours of such OMC for business and human rights. It argues that the field of business and human rights specifically offers great potential for linking the two legal systems: first, because the issue of business and human rights is a policy issue where the main missions of both institutions, the UN with its focus on promoting human rights

[1] This chapter is a further development of D Augenstein, M Dawson and P Thielbörger, 'The UNGPs in the European Union: The Open Coordination of Business and Human Rights?' (2018) 3:1 *Business and Human Rights Journal* 1–22.

and the EU with its focus on promoting economic exchange, overlap; and second, because EU law has from early on experimented with the horizontality of its own fundamental rights and freedoms – promoting human rights obligations for businesses in international law seems nothing more than the logical extension to this existing feature of EU law. Understanding the issue of business and human rights in Europe as a joint project between the UN and the EU – with both institutions holding distinct roles – is therefore the most promising way forward to achieve real policy change.

I. Introduction

EU law and international law, in particular law under the umbrella of the United Nations (UN), have often been perceived as two very different legal creatures in competition with each other. While European lawyers accuse international law of not being properly enforceable in the first place and being too aspirational in nature, international lawyers, in particular human rights lawyers, have challenged EU law of having for too long focused on economic freedoms, thereby creating a rather economic outlook on international relations in Europe. Both legal orders have famously competed over their hierarchy in Europe with some European courts giving precedence to international law, as in the decision by the Court of First instance in *Kadi*,[2] and sometimes to European law, as in the decision by the European Court of Justice in that very same case.[3] In this way, EU law and international law have been perceived too often as rivalling legal orders rather than emphasising at the same time how they can also complement each other most effectively. This chapter will highlight an example where this is the case: the strength of one should be used to make up for the weakness of the other. In this chapter, I will show how in the specific field of business and human rights the successful implementation of internationally negotiated norms could benefit largely from mechanisms of coordination at the EU level.

First, I will briefly explain the UNGPs, particularly highlighting the position the EU has taken towards them and their implementation in Europe via NAPs. I will then, second, look into the current development of NAPs within the EU, highlighting some of their achievements, but also critiquing some of their shortcomings. I will, third, explain the advantages of involving the EU in the implementation process when addressing these shortcomings in existing NAPs, and elaborate, fourth, on how such an involvement could be designed: namely by employing an OMC for business and human rights: an approach that in the

[2] Case T-315/01 *Kadi* ECLI:EU:T:2005:332, judgment of 21 September 2005.
[3] Case C-402/05 *Kadi* EU:C:2008:461, judgment of 3 September 2008.

meantime also the EU's Fundamental Rights agency supports.[4] I will finish by pointing out reasons why specifically in the field of business and human rights the interplay of international law and European law has so much potential for cooperation and complementation.

II. The Guiding Principles on Business and Human Rights and National Action Plans

When in 2011 the United Nations Human Rights Council (UNHRC) endorsed the Guiding Principles on Business and Human Rights,[5] little did anybody know what the importance of these principles would be for the field of business and human rights one day. The UNGPs had been developed by Harvard Professor John Ruggie, former Special Representative of the Secretary-General on the issue of human rights and transnational corporations and other business entities (SRSG).[6] By now, some ten years later, the UNGPs and its underlying three pillar framework, must be considered the most comprehensively developed and most widely accepted approach to the issue of business and human rights.

In a nutshell, the UNGPs take up and further develop the SRSG's previous 'Protect, Respect and Remedy' three-pillared framework. Under this approach, States first have a *duty* to protect human rights against violations by third parties (including private companies); second, corporations have a *responsibility* to respect human rights (in particular to exercise due diligence in order to avoid human rights abuses); and third, both states and corporations have to create greater access to effective remedies (both judicial and non-judicial) for victims of corporate human rights abuse.

In 2011, the UN Working Group on the Issue of Human Rights and Transnational Corporations and Other Business Entities was tasked to promote the 'effective and comprehensive dissemination and implementation' of the UNGPs,[7] thus to make sure that this concept, developed under the umbrella of the UN, did find its way into the reality of States and businesses. One of the key tools to achieve this are so-called National Action Plans (NAPs):[8] policy documents with

[4] EU Fundamental Rights Agency, 'Improving Access to Remedy in the Area of Business and Human Rights at the EU Level', FRA Opinion 1/2017, 10 April 2017.

[5] Human Rights Council, 'Guiding Principles on Business and Human Rights: Implementing the United Nations' "Protect, Respect and Remedy" Framework' A/HRC/17/31, 21 March 2011.

[6] For a more detailed account of the evolution of the UNGPs, see P Thielbörger and T Ackermann, 'A Treaty on Enforcing Human Rights Against Business: Closing the Loophole or Getting Stuck in a Loop?' (2017) 24:1 *Indiana Journal of Global Legal Studies* 43, 46–53.

[7] Human Rights Council, 'Human Rights and Transnational Corporations and Other Business Entities' A/HRC/RES/17/4, 6 July 2011.

[8] UN Secretary-General, 'Report of the Working Group on the Issue of Human Rights and Transnational Corporations and other Business Enterprises' A/69/263, 6 August 2014.

which states outline their rather abstract national strategies to improve the issue, but also develop concrete policy tools of how to achieve what is required under the UNGPs.

The EU, like many other international actors, has expressed its full support for the UNGPs and the translation in NAPs in various forms. For instance, the 2016 Council Conclusions on Business and Human Rights expressly support the European Commission in its intention to create an EU Action Plan, sketching out a comprehensive European policy framework to further the implementation of the UNGPs within the European Union.[9] Already in 2011, the Commission had addressed the responsibilities under the second pillar of the UNGPs and developed a European strategy for corporate social responsibility (CSR).[10] Member States were encouraged to develop their NAPs by the end of 2012; the deadline was later extended until 2017.[11]

Currently, 15 EU Member States have released NAPs on business and human rights (the United Kingdom, the Netherlands, Denmark, Finland, Lithuania, Sweden, Italy, Germany, France, Poland, Spain, Belgium, Luxembourg, Czech Republic and Ireland) and four further Member States have produced drafts or have at least initiated a NAP process (Greece, Latvia, Portugal and Slovenia).[12] It is safe to say that the EU is one of the key players in developing and promoting NAPs on business and human rights worldwide today.

Two documents provide specific orientation for States on how to effectively implement the UNGPs and how to develop their NAPs: the Guidance on National Action Plans on Business and Human Rights developed by the UN Working Group on Business and Human Rights (UNWG Guidance)[13] and the Toolkit on National Action Plans on Business and Human Rights published by the Danish Institute for Human Rights in collaboration with the International Corporate Accountability Roundtable (DIHR/ICAR Guidance).[14] Generally speaking, both documents

[9] Council of the EU, 'Council Conclusion on Business and Human Rights' 10254/16, 20 June 2016.

[10] European Commission, 'Communication from the Commission to the European Parliament, the Council, the European Economic and Social Committee and the Committee of the Regions: A renewed EU strategy 2011–14 for Corporate Social Responsibility' COM(2011) 681 final, 25 October 2011.

[11] Council of the EU, 'EU Strategic Framework and Action Plan on Human Rights and Democracy' 11855/12, 25 June 2012; Council of the EU, 'Council Conclusions on the Action Plan on Human Rights and Democracy 2015 – 2019' 10897/15, 20 July 2015.

[12] Within the EU, also Scotland (as a non-State entity) will develop its own NAP. Of the European countries without EU membership, Norway published its NAP in 2015 and Switzerland in December 2016. For a global overview, see Business & Human Rights Resource Centre, 'National Action Plans', https://business-humanrights.org/en/un-guiding-principles/implementation-tools-examples/implementation-by-governments/by-type-of-initiative/national-action-plans (last accessed 25 September 2018).

[13] UN Working Group on Business and Human Rights (UNWG), 'Guidance on National Action Plans on Business and Human Rights', December 2014, www.ohchr.org/Documents/Issues/Business/UNWG_%20NAPGuidance.pdf (last accessed 24 September 2018); revised versions of the Guidance were published in November 2015 and November 2016.

[14] Danish Institute for Human Rights (DIHR) and International Corporate Accountability Roundtable (ICAR), 'National Action Plans on Business and Human Rights: A Toolkit for the Development,

emphasise that NAPs should follow three main goals, namely to enumerate state measures already existent to implement the UNGPs, to identify gaps in said implementation and outline strategies to close these and prevent potential future gaps. More specifically, the UNWG Guidance emphasises that all NAPs need to have a close link to all elements of the UNGPs and be informed by core human rights principles, that they must be country-specific (including giving special weight to important sectors within a given economy), that their drafting requires a transparent and inclusive process which takes views of affected parties (governmental and non-governmental) into account, and that a regular review process for existent NAPs should be in place.[15]

The UNWG and DIHR/ICAR also recommend that states explicitly acknowledge their commitment to the UNGPs in the NAP process, that a concrete timeline is outlined and that adequate work plans are made available.[16] Stakeholder mapping and meaningful and effective participation enabled through timely access to information are equally described as essential parts of a successful NAP process.[17] NAPs should include mandatory and voluntary, as well as national and international measures,[18] and extend to matters outside the State's territorial jurisdiction.[19] NAPs should furthermore outline SMART-actions: the suggested means should be specific, measurable, achievable, relevant and time-specific.[20] Monitoring and reporting should be ensured.[21] The implementation should be supported by a multi-stakeholder group and other institutions (including the National Human Rights Institutions (NHRIs)).[22] NAPs should be regularly reviewed, evaluated and updated to improve over time. Information and best practices should be shared within and between governments.[23]

Already, it becomes apparent from this analysis that the international expectation that States have to meet is very demanding. While – legally speaking – States are free in (if and) how they design and implement their own NAPs: if their ambition is to meet the standards described in the two guiding documents, developing and updating the NAP becomes a work-intensive endeavour that requires substantial financial and time investment (not only on the part of the States, but also by civil society).

Implementation, and Review of State Commitments to Business and Human Rights Frameworks', June 2014, https://static1.squarespace.com/static/583f3fca725e25fcd45aa446/t/5865d59fe6f2e17f4f0cb629/1483068841826/DIHR-ICAR-National-Action-Plans-NAPs-Report3.pdf (last accessed 24 September 2018).

15 UNWG Guidance (n 13) 3–10.

16 UNWG Guidance (n 13) 5–6; DIHR and ICAR (n 14) 41–42.

17 UNWG Guidance (n 13) 7–8; DIHR and ICAR (n 14) 43–44.

18 UNWG Guidance (n 13) 12.

19 DIHR and ICAR (n 14) 45.

20 DIHR and ICAR (n 14) 46.

21 DIHR and ICAR (n 14) 47.

22 UNWG Guidance (n 13) 9–10; DIHR and ICAR (n 14) 37–38.

23 UNWG Gudance (n 13) 10; DIHR and ICAR (n 14) 49.

III. Implementing the UNGPs in the EU: Evaluation of Existing NAPs in the EU

While States know the extensive guidance that is given to them, existing NAPs have almost unanimously been criticised for not adhering to the standards outlined in the two guiding documents. The critique focuses both on the process by which the NAPs were drafted as well as on the (missing) substance laid out therein.

One prominent example of such critical NAP evaluation is the 2014 assessment of the United Kingdom (UK), Dutch, Danish and Finnish NAPs (some of the first to have been published) by ICAR and the European Coalition for Corporate Justice (ICAR-ECCJ-assessment).[24] Another one is the European Network of National Human Rights Institutions assessment (ENNHRI-assessment) of existing NAPs in the EU.[25]

In terms of process, ICAR and ECCJ argue that the mapping of stakeholders and identification of existing protection gaps, as well as the quality of consultations falls clearly short of the desired standard. In terms of content, the examined NAPs would focus often too much on past actions and on voluntary rather than legally-binding measures. If commitment to future goals is identifiable at all, it remains vague without highlighting concrete next steps or the state agency responsible for them.[26] The ENNHRI-assessment of existing NAPs in the EU comes to a very similar assessment: NAPs in EU Member States were insufficiently participatory and transparent, backwards rather than forward looking, and lacking concrete commitments.[27] A study commissioned by the European Parliament has also largely confirmed these findings,[28] drawing on an even larger pool of NAPs.

As I have outlined with colleagues elsewhere in greater detail,[29] when taking a closer look at the existing NAPs, three main concrete procedural and substantive shortcomings in the development and implementation of EU Member State NAPs are identifiable: first, the lack of indicators and benchmarks (to measure success or lack thereof); second, insufficient monitoring, review and follow-up (to enable adaptation over time); and third, a misalignment of Ruggie's three pillars

[24] ICAR and European Coalition for Corporate Justice (ECCJ), 'Assessments of Existing National Action Plans (NAPs) on Business and Human Rights', November 2015, https://static1.squarespace.com/static/583f3fca725e25fcd45aa446/t/58d2bdb63a0411eedc66af79/1490206143625/ICAR-ECCJ-Assessments-of-Existing-NAPs-2015-Update.pdf (last accessed 24 September 2018).

[25] European Network of National Human Rights Institutions (ENNHRI), 'Recommendations for the Next EU Strategy on CSR', April 2015, 2, https://business-humanrights.org/sites/default/files/documents/EU%20CSR%20Communication%20ENNHRI%20Final%20Apr%202015%20(2).pdf (last accessed 24 September 2018).

[26] ICAR and ECCJ (n 24) 3–5.

[27] ENNHRI (n 25) 2.

[28] European Parliament, 'Study: Implementation of the UN Guiding Principles on Business and Human Rights' (2017) 39–42, www.europarl.europa.eu/RegData/etudes/STUD/2017/578031/EXPO_STU(2017)578031_EN.pdf (last accessed 24 September 2018).

[29] Augenstein, Dawson and Thielbörger (n 1) 6–11.

(that would enable the 'smart' use mix of voluntary and legally binding measures instruments).

First, for policy change to be traceable, governments should employ an evidence-based approach and ensure that the effects of the employed tools are measured, for instance by means of indicators and benchmarks.[30] Indicators assess whether and how far the employed policies have proven suitable to contribute to the implementation of the UNGPs. Benchmarks are quantifiable targets to be achieved within a certain timeframe. Studies suggest that indicators and benchmarks are also suitable tools for assessing business-related human rights impacts.[31]

However, current NAPs often fail to specify quantitative or qualitative indicators, and even less so set concrete benchmarks to be achieved. One exception is the German NAP which sets a benchmark of 50 per cent of German companies with more than 500 employees to have incorporated human rights due diligence by 2020.[32] However, the disappointment lies in the detail: if the target is missed, the Government announces to consider ('*prüfen*') further legislative steps[33] – thus, the NAP leaves open as to what the concrete consequence of a missed benchmark will be. Similarly, other NAPs, like the Dutch, the Danish and the Italian NAPs, often contain a list of future-looking 'action points', yet fall short of setting out indicators, benchmarks or clear time-frames to make any of these vague goals measureable.[34] Also, as the EU Fundamental Rights Agency points out, a set of agreed indicators

[30] UN General Assembly, 'Human Rights and Transnational Corporations and other Business Enterprises: Note by the Secretary-General' A/69/263, 5 August 2014, paras 20, 73.

[31] D Tromp, 'Assessing Business-Related Impacts on Human Rights: Indicators and Benchmark in Standards and Practice', INEF-Report 110/2016, December 2016, https://inef.uni-due.de/index.php?rex_media_type=ImgTypeName&rex_media_file=report110.pdf (last accessed 24 September 2018).

[32] German Government, 'Nationaler Aktionsplan: Umsetzung der VN-Leitprinzipien für Wirtschaft und Menschenrechte 2016–2020', 21 December 2016, 12, www.auswaertiges-amt.de/cae/servlet/contentblob/754690/publicationFile/222786/161221-NAP-DL.pdf (last accessed 24 September 2018).

[33] German Government (n 32) 12. Critical, see Deutsches Institut für Menschenrechte, 'Stellungnahme: "Zögerliche Umsetzung": Der politische Wille reicht nicht weiter: Deutschland setzt die VN-Leitprinzipien um – mit kleinen Schritten', 21 December 2016, www.institut-fuer-menschenrechte.de/fileadmin/user_upload/Publikationen/Stellungnahmen/Stellungnahme_Verabschiedung_NAP_Wirtschaft_und_Menschenrechte.pdf (last accessed 24 September 2018).

[34] Dutch Ministry of Foreign Affairs, 'National Action Plan on Business and Human Rights', April 2014, 41–42 www.business-humanrights.org/sites/default/files/documents/netherlands-national-action-plan.pdf (last accessed 24 September 2018); Danish Government, 'Danish National Action Plan: Implementation of the UN Guiding Principles on Business and Human Rights', March 2014, 14, 18 www.ohchr.org/Documents/Issues/Business/NationalPlans/Denmark_NationalPlanBHR.pdf (last accessed 24 September 2018); Italian Government, 'Italian National Action Plan on Business and Human Rights 2016–2021', 1 December 2016, 9, 14–15, 17–19, 21–27, 29 www.cidu.esteri.it/resource/2016/07/48254_f_NAPBHRENGOpenConsultation.pdf (last accessed 24 September 2018); Irish Government, 'National Plan on Business and Human Rights 2017–2020', November 2017, 16–19 www.dfa.ie/media/dfa/alldfawebsitemedia/National-Plan-on-Business-and-Human-Rights-2017-2020.pdf (last accessed 24 September 2018); Polish Government, 'Polish National Action Plan for the Implementation of the United Nations Guiding Principles on Business and Human Rights 2017-2020', May 2017, 26–27, 37, 50–54 www.ohchr.org/Documents/Issues/Business/NationalPlans/PolandNationalPland_BHR.pdf (last accessed 24 September 2018).

and benchmarks would make cross-country comparison possible, which is also desirable in terms of policy coherence amongst Member States.[35]

Second, the NAPs we have seen so far have also displayed weaknesses in terms of monitoring and follow-up. If monitoring and follow-up is mentioned at all in NAPs, it remains unclear which State-run (or independent) institution is responsible for it and how it can be held accountable for failing to do so. Exceptions prove the rule: the Finnish NAP orders yearly monitoring by the Finnish Committee on Corporate Social Responsibility[36] and the Danish NAP proscribes continuous update.[37] The German NAP announces a yearly evaluation and tasks a new specific inter-ministerial institution with it;[38] however, this monitoring is made conditional upon budgetary permission in the German case.[39] The Italian NAP shall be monitored periodically through an ongoing analysis of the implementation in consultation with all relevant stakeholders.[40]

The UK[41] is currently the only country to have published an updated version of its NAP. While the UK update itself does not add much to the original NAP in terms of content (apart from launching an inquiry by the UK Joint Committee on Human Rights to investigate the progress of implementation of all three pillars),[42] the 2016 update also does not contain any new information or commitment on further updates in the future.[43]

While it should be clear that review and update are essential for the success of NAPs in times of constant political and economic change – and that this change adaptation can only succeed if clear timeframes are established and the responsible institutions can be held accountable – most NAPs to date fall short of these important elements. It appears that creating a NAP has become a 'box ticking exercise' for some States rather than recognising the true value of steered and continuous policy change in the field of business and human rights through regularly revising and updating NAPs.

[35] See EU Fundamental Rights Agency (n 4) 65.

[36] See Finnish Ministry of Employment and the Economy, 'National Action Plan for the Implementation of the UN Guiding Principles on Business and Human Rights', October 2014, 32 https://tem.fi/documents/1410877/3084000/National%20action%20plan%20for%20the%20implementation%20of%20the%20UN%20guiding%20pronciples%20on%20business%20and%20human%20rights/1bc35feb-d35a-438f-af56-aec16adfcbae (last accessed 24 September 2018).

[37] See Danish Government (n 34) 22.

[38] See German Government (n 32) 33, 40–41 ('*interministerieller Ausschuss*').

[39] German Government (n 32) 41.

[40] See Italian Government (n 34) 29.

[41] UK Government, 'Good Business: Implementing the UN Guiding Principles on Business and Human Rights, Updated May 2016', May 2016, 2 www.gov.uk/government/uploads/system/uploads/attachment_data/file/522805/Good_Business_Implementing_the_UN_Guiding_Principles_on_Business_and_Human_Rights_updated_May_2016.pdf (last accessed 24 September 2018).

[42] See UK Parliament, 'Human Rights and Business Inquiry', www.parliament.uk/business/committees/committees-a-z/joint-select/human-rights-committee/inquiries/parliament-2015/inquiry/ (published report https://publications.parliament.uk/pa/jt201617/jtselect/jtrights/443/443.pdf) (last accessed 24 September 2018).

[43] See UK Government (n 41) 24.

Third, the Ruggie-approach can only be successful, if the three pillars of 'protect, respect and remedy' are aligned and if the employed measures are a smart regulatory mix. Previous NAPs have in an almost blunt manner neglected pillar three ('remedy'),[44] but also pillar one ('protect') is often not fully addressed. For instance, the Danish NAP focuses on voluntary approaches to CSR of companies and access to purely non-judicial remedies.[45] The Danish NAP relates largely to supporting and encouraging State action rather than regulatory, thereby failing to address pillars one and three[46] that have a stronger normative force than pillar two. NAPs often encourage corporations to create due diligence mechanisms or to give themselves codes of conduct, but fall short of making any regulatory advances in this direction, not to speak of creating means of remedy if they do not create such due diligence mechanisms. The Dutch NAP, for instance, largely confines itself to listing supportive government actions (such as awareness raising and capacity building)[47] and does not provide for legislative and enforcement measures. The Irish NAP follows a similar approach, by focussing on encouragement and awareness raising measures, while the remedy pillar is addressed merely by initiating discussions to strengthen mediation, introducing potential remedies as a standing agenda item and reviewing remedies for potential overseas victims of Irish companies operating abroad.[48]

The nature of the proscribed actions in NAPs is thus too often voluntary, almost never mandatory. This focus on voluntary instruments over regulatory measures across the EU not only hinders the effective implementation of the UNGPs in Europe, but, given the very different preparedness of businesses to engage in voluntary self-regulation, such a lack of regulatory means undermines establishing even a minimum European standard to business and human rights.[49]

IV. The Open Method of Coordination

If we have now identified these three significant shortcomings in European States' NAPs – both in terms of process and substance – the next question is whether this problem can be addressed, potentially at the European level.

A well-known example of a coordination mechanism in Europe is the OMC – a policy tool developed originally to ensure multi-lateral surveillance in the field of EU social policies.[50] While the OMC was first engaged in the late 1990s, it has

[44] See ICAR and ECCJ (n 24) 4.

[45] See Danish Government (n 34) 10–16, 19–21.

[46] See ICAR and ECCJ (n 24) 14–16.

[47] See Dutch Ministry of Foreign Affairs (34) 22–24, 34–39.

[48] See Irish Government (34) 16–19.

[49] M Neglia, 'The UNGPs – Five Years On: From Consensus to Divergence in Public Regulation on Business and Human Rights' (2016) 34:4 *Netherlands Quarterly of Human Rights* 289.

[50] For a summary of the historical development, see M Dawson, *New Governance and the Transformation of European Law* (Cambridge, Cambridge University Press, 2011) 24–68. Furthermore,

over the following two decades also been employed in other policy areas (like culture, health and education). While there is not a 'one-size-fits-all' method of coordination, but rather different processes for the different policy fields (which also have varied significantly in terms of perceived success associated with them), the Lisbon European Council in 2000 identified four key principles of any OMC process, namely guideline-setting on the European level (including timetables), the use of qualitative and quantitative indicators and benchmarks (to encourage the comparison of good practices), the setting of specific targets as well as monitoring, and finally evaluation and peer-review to realise mutual learning potential.[51]

Before considering applying the OMC to yet another policy field, one should recap on the reasons behind the OMC's original development. At its very heart the OMC tried to reconcile two competing values that lie at the core of European integration: diversity and interdependence. On the one hand, when the OMC was developed the conviction had been formed that in an ever closer Union, national (economic and other) policies would necessarily create (wanted and unwanted) spill-over effects to other Member States ('inter-dependence'). However, it was clear at the same time that uniformity could not, and maybe can never, be achieved in many policy fields in the EU;[52] first, the EU faces insufficient or unclear EU competences in a variety of fields under the European Treaties,[53] and second, Member States were and are not willing to transfer further competences to the European level. Harmonising national rules is not an option in many policy fields given the huge differences in the social and fiscal regimes of EU Member States. The OMC thus seemed the best possible compromise at the time:[54] it enabled EU coordination, led by joint principles and common goals, but it left diversity in the set-up of Member States' own policies untouched.[55] In this way the OMC has been perceived as a flexible and less rigid form of policy-making, more easily adaptable to political or legal changes, that encourages the exchange of good

on its future potential, see E Barcevičius, JT Weishaupt and J Zeitlin, 'Tracing the Social OMC from its Origins to Europe 2020' in E Barcevičius, JT Weishaupt and J Zeitlin (eds), *Assessing the Open Method of Coordination: Institutional Design and National Influence of EU Social Policy Coordination* (Houndmills, Basingstoke, Hampshire, Palgrave MacMillan, 2014) 16.

[51] European Council, 'Lisbon European Council 23 and 24 March 2000: Presidency Conclusions' (2000) para 37, www.europarl.europa.eu/summits/lis1_en.htm (last accessed 24 September 2018).

[52] See FW Scharpf, 'The European Social Model: Coping with the Challenges of Diversity' (2002) 40 *Journal of Common Market Studies* 4.

[53] See the limits on social policy measures contained in Consolidated Version of the Treaty on the Functioning of the European Union [2012] OJ C326/47 (adopted on 13 December 2007, entered into force on 1 December 2009) Art 153.

[54] J Zeitlin, 'Social Europe and Experimentalist Governance: Towards a New Constitutional Compromise?' in G de Búrca (ed), *EU Law and the Welfare State: In Search of Solidarity* (Oxford, Oxford University Press, 2005) 213; G de Búrca, 'The Constitutional Challenge of New Governance in the European Union' (2003) 28 *European Law Review* 6.

[55] FW Scharpf, 'Legitimate Diversity: The New Challenge of European Integration' in TA Borzel and RA Cichowski (eds), *The State of the European Union, Vol 6: Law, Politics and Society* (Oxford, Oxford University Press, 2003) 79.

practices and allows for States to avoid the same mistakes as their neighbours, thereby enabling mutual learning.[56] Thus, the OMC was perceived (at least in the beginning) as the long-desired compromise between the two seemingly irreconcilable values of inter-dependence and diversity that characterise the European integration project.

V. Conceptual Suitability of an OMC for the UNGP NAP Process

This rationale behind the OMC's creation emphasises the method's potential suitability also for the field of business and human rights. The UNGPs are, inter alia, supposed to close governance gaps in an economy that is globalised and inter-dependent at the same time:[57] to enforce human rights vis-à-vis businesses 'at home' would not be an incomplete solution to the problem. In a globalised economy, addressing business' activities 'abroad' is equally important. The ability of states to enforce human rights in relation to businesses holistically thus increasingly depends on cooperation with other States given that businesses may produce their products in one State, process in a second one, and sell it mainly in a third. In order to avoid large inconsistencies between national economies – and so as not to create incentives for a race to the bottom of labour and production standards – internationally-agreed norms were urgently needed for businesses wherever they operated. At the same time, differences in national markets as well as in national political and legal systems make clear that a 'one-size-fits-all' solution is impossible to find. In the past, attempts along these lines failed rather poorly, in particular in the early 2000s Draft Norms on the Responsibilities of Transnational Corporations and Other Business Enterprises with Regard to Human Rights.[58] A recent approach within the UN Human Rights Council to establish a new treaty regime[59] to proscribe rather strict global standards has gained some momentum over the last years, but is still far from realising such a treaty, in particular given that some of the key players oppose such a treaty

[56] O De Schutter and S Deakin, 'Reflexive Governance and the Dilemmas of Social Regulation' in O De Schutter and S Deakin (eds), *Social Rights and Market Forces: Is the Open Coordination of Employment and Social Policies the Future of Social Europe?* (Brussels, Brulyant, 2005) 3; CF Sabel and J Zeitlin, 'Learning from Difference: The New Architecture of Experimentalist Governance in the European Union' in CF Sabel and J Zeitlin (eds), *Experimentalist Governance in the European Union* (Oxford, Oxford University Press, 2010) 1.

[57] Human Rights Council, 'Protect, Respect and Remedy: A Framework for Business and Human Rights' A/HRC/8/5, 7 April 2008, para 3.

[58] See most notably, UN Economic and Social Council, 'Draft Norms on the Responsibilities of Transnational Corporations and Other Business Enterprises with Regard to Human Rights', E/CN.4/Sub.2/2003/12, 26 August 2003.

[59] Human Rights Council, 'Elaboration of an International Legally Binding Instrument on Transnational Corporations and other Business Enterprises with Respect to Human Rights', A/HRC/RES/26/9, 14 July 2014.

on business and human rights strictly.[60] This resistance is only to become more pronounced, given in particular that the Human Rights Council as a whole has lost the support of some key players within the UN recently, most notably the United States (US).[61]

While the approach of implementation through NAPs already rather explicitly reflects the need for diversity in the field of business and human rights,[62] what is currently missing is a complementing tool that ensures that this diversity is also matched with a certain coherence which reflects the described inter-dependence. The OMC could be this tool: it provides valuable lessons on how to balance these two at first sight conflicting values of inter-dependence and diversity in various other policy fields.

Critics might question the proposal to extend the use of the OMC – a method that has not only convinced observers, but also disappointed in some areas. The OMC has been accused, for instance, of being non-effective and too voluntary, incentivising rather the listing of existing programmes or over-emphasising achievements rather than promoting real progress.[63] States have at times picked and chosen which EU established principles to follow, and which to disregard, depending on political opportunity: exactly the same development we have already observed with the early NAPs.[64] The current NAP process is very nationally-dominated, with no established possibilities for international comparison and with no incentives to meet international standards.

However, the strengths of the OMC should have become equally clear. Additionally, the OMC has been observed to create 'second order' effects,[65] thus making policy-making overall more responsive to substantive goals, to increase cooperation between different governmental units and to raise awareness for the connectedness of causes and effects of policy change. As can be seen in the two NAP Guiding documents, all of these advantages that the OMC carries would also be important elements for the successful implementation of the UNGPs through NAPs.

[60] P Thielbörger and T Ackermann, 'A Treaty on Enforcing Human Rights Against Business: Closing the Loophole or Getting Stuck in a Loop?' (2017) 24 *Indiana Journal of Global Legal Studies* 68–72.

[61] P Thielbörger and L Dawson, 'America (and its Allies) First – Human Rights Second: On the US' Decision to leave the UN Human Rights Council' (2018) Bofax 509E 29 June 2018.

[62] See UNWG Guidance (n 13) 4.

[63] See, eg, M Eckhardt, 'The Open Method of Coordination on Pensions: an Economic Analysis of its Effects on Pension Reforms' (2005) 15 *Journal of European Social Policy* 247; M Lodge, 'Comparing Non-Hierarchical Governance in Action: The Open Method of Coordination in Pensions and Information Society' (2007) 45 *Journal of Common Market Studies* 2.

[64] See ICAR and ECCJ (n 24).

[65] On the OMC's national effects, see Dawson (n 50) 164–234; M Heidenreich and J Zeitlin, *Changing European Employment and Welfare Regimes: The Influence of the OMC on National Reforms* (London, Routledge, 2009).

VI. Conditions for Extending the OMC to the UNGPs' Implementation

To successfully import the OMC to the field of business and human rights, certain elements would need to be ensured. Three particularly important ones are peer-review, indicators and benchmarks, as well as the inclusion of a wide range of actors during the drafting process.

First, supervision through specialised committees of EU and national representatives to assess national plans according to agreed EU objectives and indicators is crucial. This form of peer review serves a double purpose: it allows states to critically assess the performance of other states, in particular where such negative performance also affects them in the form of spill-over effects,[66] which in the case of conducting business in Europe is in many ways almost inevitable. The positive effects of peer-review, however, are maybe even more important[67] (and should be the focus of the discussion with regard to peer-review): peer-review also holds the potential of deepening relations with other States, understanding better their political and economic systems and enabling mutual learning through the exchange of bad experiences and, even more importantly, good practices.[68]

Second, indicators played a key role in the OMC's success. They create a solid basis for informed decision-making by national policy-makers. In the field of social policy, for instance, the Social Protection Performance Monitor (SPPM) tracks the performance of EU Member States according to different metrics of social performance,[69] and has been considered to be one of the OMC success stories. The development of indicators is not only crucial in order to allow for international comparison, but also for policy-makers to understand the causal relationships between different forms of regulation and policy outcomes: which tools have proven effective for delivering the desired outcomes, and which have been non-effective (or even produced undesired side effects). The goal of the use

[66] This is also a key rationale behind the coordination of national budgets – significant economic imbalances could de-stabilise the Eurozone, jeopardising the financial stability of others; see explanations in European Commission, 'European Semester: A New Architecture for the New EU Economic Governance – Q&A', MEMO/11/14 (12 January 2011).

[67] J Visser, 'The OMC as Selective Amplifier for National Strategies for Reform' in J Zeitlin and P Pochet (eds), *The Open Method of Coordination in Action: The European Employment and Social Inclusion Strategies* (Brussels, Peter Lang, 2005) 173; S Kroger, *Soft Governance in Hard Politics: European Coordination of Anti-Poverty Policies in France and Germany* (Wiesbaden, VS Verlag, 2008) 44–46.

[68] On learning under the OMC, see also CM Radaelli, 'Europeanization, Policy Learning and New Modes of Governance' (2008) 10 *Journal of Comparative Policy Analysis: Research and Practice* 3.

[69] European Commission, Social Protection Committee, 'Social Protection Performance Monitor (SPPM) – Methodological Report by the Indicators Sub-group of the Social Protection Committee' (17 October 2012), http://ec.europa.eu/social/BlobServlet?docId=9235& (last accessed 24 September 2018).

of indicators is then not so much a convergence of rules between the States, but gaining a better understanding of the capacities and limitations of the different policy choices that each State has to make. As highlighted before, the use of indicators and benchmarks has been particularly neglected in the NAPs States have produced so far: an OMC procedure could prove to be particularly helpful in creating a culture of using indicators and benchmarks in NAPs on business and human rights.

Third, the OMC has disappointed some observers in particular with regard to participation and transparency.[70] National parliaments and regional bodies of the executive were often found to be omitted (or at least not sufficiently involved) when drafting national plans within the OMC. This was met with a lack of national and regional ownership of said plans; as a consequence, 'Brussels'-set targets were often not sufficiently respected when transformed into national action.[71] This problem is particularly pertinent where this transformation crucially depends on either the involvement of different levels of government (eg in Germany where the 'Länder' hold particularly extensive competences in the executive and also in the legislation under the German Constitution) or where the transformation depends on the strong control through national parliaments (eg in most Scandinavian countries with their tradition of strong parliaments). The lesson then for a potential OMC in the case of UNGP NAPs is to allow for wide input from the different State institutions at the different State levels in order to maximise the OMC's potential and to create the widest possible acceptance within the different State institutions. These three criteria – the establishment of a peer-review procedure, the use of indicators and benchmarks, as well as employing a very inclusive drafting and reviewing process – would provide an appropriate institutional and procedural infrastructure for the OMC. The UNGP NAP process and the OMC have many features in common, both in terms of goals as well as political background, so that the lessons, both positive and negative, learnt from OMC's history of the last decades can be of significant value to the UN and EU's business and human rights strategies.

VII. Integrating an OMC for Business and Human Rights in Existing EU Governance Structures

The vast majority of currently existing NAPs stem from EU Member States (with the exception of Columbia, Switzerland, the US and Chile).[72] This creates an

[70] M Büchs, 'How Legitimate is the Open Method of Coordination?' (2008) 46 *Journal of Common Market Studies* 4; S Kröger, 'The End of Democracy as we know it? The Legitimacy Deficits of Bureaucratic Social Policy Governance' (2007) 29 *Journal of European Integration* 5.

[71] Dawson (n 50) 199–206.

[72] See n 12.

opportunity, if not an expectation for European coordination. Indeed the EU has been very active in the field of business and human rights, as evidenced by frequent references of NAPs to existing EU programmes, be they strategies on CSR or even direct EU legislative measures on the subject of business and human rights.[73] The situation is complicated, however, by the fact that the competence to implement a comprehensive business and human rights strategy is shared between Member States and the Union: EU legislation exists in some areas but not in others, raising issues concerning the coherence of EU and national measures and potentially limiting Member States' own powers to set binding standards where EU legislation exists.[74] This protracted situation emphasises another facet of the added value of developing a European OMC process for business and human rights.

While the proposal to apply an OMC to EU fundamental rights more generally has been around for a while,[75] the idea to develop an OMC specifically to the field of business and human rights is new. To apply the OMC to the field of European fundamental rights more generally has, however, been confronted with two major criticisms in the past.

First, the Union's competence to develop policies in the field of business and human rights has often been contested and cannot be considered a clear case.[76] Second, open coordination processes have sometimes been perceived as a bureaucratic and financial burden,[77] and the available resources for the promotion of fundamental rights might be better invested in substantive then coordinative programmes, so the argument goes. These two criticisms do however not apply equally to the specific sub-field of *business and* human rights.

Regarding the competence-based obstacle, many issues within the NAPs fall, as mentioned above, under shared competences. The OMC for business and human rights could at the same time be used to monitor national implementation of already existing EU laws that hold a business and human rights dimension. This would ensure and strengthen consistency and coherence of these laws in the different Member States. Some EU directives already even establish a duty for the

[73] See, eg, Government Offices of Sweden, 'Action Plan for Business and Human Rights', August 2015, 27 www.government.se/4a84f5/contentassets/822dc47952124734b60daf1865e39343/action-plan-for-business-and-human-rights.pdf (last accessed 24 September 2018); Finnish Ministry of Employment and the Economy (n 38) 16–19.

[74] See European Commission, 'Commission Staff Working Document on Implementing the UN Guiding Principles on Business and Human Rights – State of Play', SWD(2015) 144 final (14 July 2015).

[75] See O De Schutter, 'The Implementation of the Charter of Fundamental Rights through the Open Method of Coordination', NYU School of Law, Jean Monnet Working Paper 07/04 (2007) 4, www.jeanmonnetprogram.org/archive/papers/04/040701.rtf (last accessed 24 September 2018); S Smismans, 'How to be Fundamental with Soft Procedures? The OMC and Fundamental Social Rights' in G de Búrca and B de Witte (eds), *Social Rights in Europe* (Oxford, Oxford University Press, 2005) 217.

[76] For a historical overview of this problem, see P Alston and JHH Weiler, 'An "Ever Closer Union" in Need of a Human Rights Policy: The European Union and Human Rights' in P Alston (ed), *The EU and Human Rights* (Oxford, Oxford University Press, 1999) 2, 22–27.

[77] See, eg, the resistance to (and temporary abolition of) the social inclusion OMC from 2010–2012, described in M Daly and P Copeland, 'Poverty and Social Policy in Europe 2020: Ungovernable and Ungoverned' (2014) 42:3 *Policy and Politics* 351.

European Commission to monitor their national implementation,[78] so the OMC would help to fulfil this obligation. That there is no explicit legal basis for the establishment of such an OMC procedure does not hinder its employment: this was the same for the other policy areas in which an OMC had previously been employed.[79]

Second, an OMC on business and human rights would hardly be a significant additional burden, both in financial and bureaucratic terms. Most of the so-called 'burden' is already caused through the requirement to develop and update a national action plan itself; involved actors would be in a good position to also evaluate the NAPs of other EU Member States. They might also gain further expertise in this process, which might save time and financial resources when updating their own NAPs in the future. Also for the European Commission not much additional work would be created: it has already now invested resources in organising peer reviews in the field of CSR and human rights.[80] The European Council's Working Group on Human Rights (COHOM) already monitors the implementation of the UNGPs in the Member States as part of its work on the EU's Strategic Framework on Human Rights and Democracy.[81] Synergies with existing institutions and their work on related fields could thus minimise the need for investing additional resources for an OMC procedure in the field of business and human rights.

VIII. The Added Value of an OMC for Business and Human Rights and the Design Thereof

If then the EU does already so much work in the field of business and human rights, what would an OMC procedure for business and human rights add, if anything?

First, such an OMC procedure could have a coordinating function also within initiatives in the business and human rights field, thereby helping to avoid duplication or contradiction in the implementation of the different business and

[78] See the duty contained in EU accounting directives for the Commission to review national implementation prior to 2018; see Directive 2013/34/EU of the European Parliament and of the Council of 26 June 2013 on the annual financial statements, consolidated financial statements and related reports of certain types of undertakings [2013] OJ L182/19.

[79] This argument holds only, of course, if the OMC is used as mechanism to support and complement, not as a means to secretly entirely harmonise the laws of the Member States, as otherwise indeed the EU would act outside its competence.

[80] See European Commission (n 10) 12, point 4.7; see also Member States' reports of 'Peer Review on Corporate Social Responsibility' http://ec.europa.eu/social/keyDocuments.jsp?advSearchKey=CSRprreport&mode=advancedSubmit&langId=en (last accessed 24 September 2018); see also S Bijlmakers, M Footer and N Hachez, 'The EU's Engagement with the Main Business and Human Rights Instruments' 44 www.fp7-frame.eu/wp-content/uploads/2016/09/Deliverable-7.4.pdf (last accessed 24 September 2018).

[81] European Commission (n 69).

human rights programmes at the level of the Member States and the Union itself. Similarly, EU Member States are already under the international obligations they have committed to, such as the ILO Tripartite Declaration of Principles Concerning Multinational Enterprises and Social Policy[82] or the Organisation for Economic Cooperation and Development (OECD) Guidelines for Multinational Enterprises.[83] A forum for institutionalised cooperation between national and EU actors in the different areas relevant to the field of business and human rights, an OMC process could enhance policy coherence and make the approach of the Member States and the Union more consistent.

Second, an OMC process could help to identify implementation gaps and help to develop European policy proposals. This is particularly pertinent for business activity with a strong cross-border element. At the same time, Union-wide action would prevent the perception of creating incentives for corporations to re-locate their businesses to those EU Member States with the lowest standard.[84] An OMC process could help to identify potentials and limitations of future EU action on business and human rights,[85] or action within Member States.

Third, the OMC should set incentives for Member States to deliver on the promises made in their respective NAPs, or to make these commitments in the first place. Timetabling should lead states to make concrete commitments including specific deadlines (one of the shortcomings identified above in the current NAPs); in case of failure to set deadlines or adhere to them, the OMC procedure would reveal this shortcoming. Peer review in that way functions as a nudging mechanism – a mechanism by now well known to deliver policy effects.[86]

Fourth, and maybe most importantly, the OMC would create a space for mutual learning in the field of business and human rights and enable the deepened exchange of good practices between EU Member States.[87] For these reasons, a peer review procedure for business and human rights was previously considered by the Commission, but was eventually not established, although some Member States had explicitly expressed support for this policy proposal.[88] Such Member State support can still be assumed today.

[82] ILO, 'Tripartite Declaration of Principles Concerning Multinational Enterprises and Social Policy', 5th edn (March 2017) www.ilo.org/empent/Publications/WCMS_094386/lang--en/index.htm (last accessed 24 September 2018).

[83] OECD, 'OECD Guidelines for Multinational Enterprises' (2011 edn) http://mneguidelines.oecd.org/guidelines/ (last accessed 24 September 2018).

[84] On this issue, see, out of many, S Deakin, 'Regulatory Competition after Laval' (2007–08) 10 *Cambridge Yearbook of European Legal Studies* 581.

[85] On this argument in relation to a broader OMC in fundamental rights, see De Schutter (n 75).

[86] E Towfigh and C Traxler, 'Nudges Polarize!' in A Kemmerer, C Möllers, M Steinbeis and G Wagner (eds), *Choice Architecture in Democracies – Exploring the Legitimacy of Nudging* (Baden-Baden, Nomos, 2016) 321–28.

[87] This is one of the goals highlighted in the EU's 2011 CSR strategy, see European Commission (n 10).

[88] See European Commission (nn 69 and 74).

So, what should an OMC for business and human rights look like? There is no 'one-OMC-fits-all' model,[89] quite the contrary. The procedures have been very different, depending on the policy field where they were employed. A business and human rights OMC can thus be shaped rather flexibly to meet the preferences and needs of the actors and sectors involved, and it can also be adjusted over time. However, certainly, some minimum elements would need to be given in order for a coordinating procedure to be considered an OMC in the sense of the Lisbon criteria[90] to deliver the above mentioned desired effects: first, a common timetable for the production, and also revision of NAPs, should be established. Ideally, this would form part of a bi-annual or tri-annual cycle. Second, one or several specific institutions within the EU should be determined (eg a committee of national (and EU) representatives, within the Commission or Council, or as a joint institution). It should be tasked to coordinate and oversee the NAP process and to conduct or organise the state-to-state peer review. Third, the need for both qualitative and quantitative indicators has been stressed.[91] If the institution consists (at least partly) of independent experts, they would be in a good position to develop indicators to allow for benchmarking and comparing of national performance (this could build on existing indicator systems for CSR used by other international organisations[92] or developing the framework for a specific European indicator system). Fourth, civil society involvement is essential. This has become clear already in the national NAP processes on the national plane; it is equally the case on the European level (see for instance the EU's multi-stakeholder platform on CSR). Herein lies a chance for greater internationalisation / Europeanisation of civil society initiatives in the field of business and human rights. Finally, existing programmes in the field of business and human rights must be taken into account, so that duplication and contradiction is avoided. Special attention would thus need to be given within a business and human rights OMC to connect the NAP processes with the EU's ongoing and rather far-developed CSR strategy, eg by including the relevant actors in the monitoring and the peer-review process of the NAPs.

OMC procedures have had mixed success in the past, depending on the policy fields and whether the specific OMC managed to adapt sufficiently to the specifics of the given policy field. Expectations for such a new OMC should not be unrealistic, particularly not in the beginning. However, while an approach through European legislation is unrealistic and relying on national approaches to NAP

[89] See B Laffan and C Shaw, 'Classifying and Mapping OMC in Different Policy Areas', NEW-GOV Working Paper (2005) 2.

[90] European Council (n 51).

[91] See n 74.

[92] See, eg, the UN Development Programme's (UNDP's) methodology for CSR country-level assessment, see M Kostulska, 'UNDP Develops New Measurement Tools for Corporate Social Responsibility' (2011) https://business.un.org/en/documents/9472 (last accessed 24 September 2018). See also Global Reporting Initiative, 'GRI Standards' www.globalreporting.org/standards (last accessed 24 September 2018).

design and review alone has not yielded the desired effects, the OMC could be a reasonable compromise between these two extreme scenarios. The focus of the debate on business and human rights should be shifted to the question of how implementation of the UNGPs can be improved,[93] rather than focusing on how to improve or enlarge the existing framework, eg through a new treaty.[94] This is certainly a worthwhile endeavour too – it should, however, not take away attention from ensuring the implementation of the UNGPs.

IX. EU Law as Silver Bullet for International Law's Weakness of Implementation?

What can be learned from this specific issue of business and human rights for the broader issue of the relationship of international and European law?

The field of business and human rights has proven to be a prime example of a field in which international and European law are not competing (as they do in many other areas) and potentially even contradicting each other, but rather complement each other considerably. This is the case as, in the field of business and human rights, both legal levels do not claim for themselves the competence to set the rules. It is rather a field in which innovative norm creation stems clearly from the international sphere, while the implementation falls rather clearly in the domestic (and additionally, as I have suggested in this article, in the European) domain. There is thus no struggle for supremacy in this policy field – rather, both have accepted their specific roles. This is a precondition for fruitful complementation of otherwise competing legal orders. In this way, both legal levels bring to the table what they can deliver best: the international level coordinating the struggle for a global consensus for a set of rules (and in a globalised economy with trans-national corporations acting worldwide, nothing less is needed); and the national and regional level, holding stronger institutions and being in a closer position to monitor companies' human rights records in specific countries, delivering implementation.

The question is then: should this mutually beneficial relationship not be extended to many more policy fields, thus allowing European law to be employed more often to overcome international law's famous weakness of implementation? To put it more provocatively, would a European OMC procedure not be beneficial for all treaties that lack (national or international) enforcement?

The answer is no. Apart from the obvious fact that this would overburden the capacity of the EU, it is rather the specifics of the field of business and human

[93] See Thielbörger and Ackermann (n 6).

[94] S Deva and D Bilchitz, *Building a Treaty on Business and Human Rights* (Cambridge, Cambridge University Press, 2017).

rights that create greater potential for a European OMC procedure. These specific attributes are both historical and legal.

First, it is undeniable that the EU in its infancy was an institution to (almost exclusively) foster economic exchange (and through economic prosperity ensure peace and security in Europe). The internal market – until today the heart of the European project – was mainly designed as a single market to guarantee the free movement of goods, capital, services and labour. Only later in the late 1960s and early 1970s – significantly pushed through by the European Court of Justice inter alia in *Stauder*[95] and *Internationale Handelsgesellschaft*[96] – was the idea of complementing fundamental rights, as part of unwritten principles, added to the body of European law. Until today, while the area of fundamental rights gains more and more importance,[97] the European Union remains an organisation with its greatest powers and competences in the economic field, given, for instance, its exclusive competences in this area (including in regards to the external economic relations of its Member States).

On the other hand, the UN is an international organisation that was, apart from its mission to promote international peace and security, explicitly founded for the promotion of human rights (Article 1(3) UN Charter). While the UN has often failed to deliver on its ambitious promises, it is clear that the promotion of human rights lies at the heart of the organisation. There is no other international governmental organisation to promote human rights on a global scale to the same extent; the most relevant actors have rather formed within the UN (eg the Human Rights Council or the High Commission for Human Rights) than as self-standing institutions. To join forces in the field of business and human rights, is just the logical consequence of the two original mandates of the two organisations. Not tackling the issue would be neglecting a significant part of their mandate; tackling it alone would be to neglect the expertise and core mandate of the respective other organisation.

Second, the idea of applying human or fundamental rights to non-state actors is less new to the European plane than it is to the international one. The European Court of Justice has established in a rather long standing line of judgments – *Defrenne v Sabena No 2*,[98] *Mangold*,[99] *Kücükdeveci*,[100] just to name a few

[95] Judgment of the Court of 12 November 1969 Case 29-69 *Erich Stauder v City of Ulm – Sozialamt*, Judgment of the Court of 12 November 1969.

[96] Case 11-70 *Internationale Handelsgesellschaft mbH v Einfuhr- und Vorratsstelle für Getreide und Futtermittel* Judgment of the Court of 17 December 1970, Grounds of Judgment, para 3.

[97] See more extensively on the topic, M Dawson, *Governance of EU Fundamental Rights* (Cambridge, Cambridge University Press, 2017).

[98] Case 43-75 *Gabrielle Defrenne v Société anonyme belge de navigation aérienne Sabena*, Judgment of the Court of 8 April 1976, Law, paras 4–25.

[99] C-144/04 *Werner Mangold v Rüdiger Helm* Case, Judgment of the Court (Grand Chamber) of 22 November 2005, paras 74–79.

[100] Case C-555/07 *Seda Kücükdeveci v Swedex GmbH & Co KG*, Judgment of the Court (Grand Chamber) of 19 January 2010, paras 50–56.

significant ones – the notion of horizontal direct effect, thus the idea that individuals can invoke European provisions not only in relation to a Member State, but (under certain conditions and depending on the act involved) also in relation to individuals. European law is less estranged by the idea that its provisions can also apply directly to private actors as duty holders, while in international law this is, until today, considered by many as a doctrinal impossibility. European law has thus experimented with the idea of horizontality (unsurprising, given that the EU carries certain State-like features and powers not found otherwise on the international plane and certainly not in the UN). Supporting the enforcement of international norms also against private actors is thus not only consistent with the EU's own legal system – it is promoting a distinct feature of European law also when implementing international norms stemming from the UN system.

The two reasons for the great potential of a European OMC for business and human rights then stem on the one hand from the two missions of the EU and the UN, and are supported on the other hand by the fact that EU law (as the level of enforcement and implementation) has already successfully experimented with an idea that is rather new for the international plane. Complementing institutional mission as well as promoting legal coherence between the norm-creating and implementing levels can serve as catalysts for the complementing effect of international and European law in the field of business and human rights.

X. Conclusion

Implementing the UNGPs on business and human rights will be a difficult and lengthy process. The UNGPs are certainly not the most ambitious approach to the issue of business and human rights. A treaty that is directly binding on corporations – a proposal ('zero draft') for which has very recently been published by the Government of Ecuador[101] – would be the more innovative and far-reaching approach. However, the UNGPs remain until today the one approach that has united different stakeholders – stakeholders that have bitterly opposed each other on the issue for decades – and the one approach that most States now support. Thus, even when arguing for a treaty on business and human rights, attention should not be shifted away from the implementation of the norms we have already – as dissatisfying and incomplete one might, rightly or wrongly, find them to be. In this way, the national NAP process and hard law approaches in the field of business and human rights should not be seen in oppositional terms. To the contrary, both approaches should be followed through simultaneously. Coordination mechanisms like the OMC do not frustrate the achievement of 'hard' law; they rather build the trust and cooperation that is ultimately needed for approaches

[101] Zero Draft, Government of Ecuador, 16 July 2018, available at www.business-humanrights.org/sites/default/files/documents/DraftLBI.pdf (last accessed 24 September 2018).

with stronger legal force in the future. Mutual learning, joint trust and creating infra-structure are the first steps for realising ambitious binding standards later.

On the more abstract level, the field of business and human rights has all too often focused on the debate of the international versus the national plane. Should rules be established internationally, or should this be achieved in a decentralised manner through national legislation? Too little attention has been paid to possible solutions in the middle ground, eg the regional level. The OMC for business and human rights is exactly this: a combining link between the internationally accepted standards (the UNGPs) and national implementation (the NAPs). One might explore whether the OMC might also be suitable for other policy fields; for the field of business and human rights the suitability stems from two specific notions: first, because business and human rights lies at the intersection of the two respective mandates of the EU and the UN, and second, applying international human rights standards to corporations is not alien to the EU's legal order, it is rather the logical extension of 'horizontality' – one of the distinct features of EU law.

The publication by the EU Fundamental Rights Agency of an opinion recommending exactly such establishment of an EU OMC for business and human rights[102] emphasises that the proposal is not naïve wishful thinking, but could become a political reality. For an OMC in the field of business and human rights to be successful, however, the lessons of the OMC's past (both positive and negative) in other policy fields have to be taken into account. A balanced OMC could become a meaningful incentive to encourage Member States to take NAPs more seriously and act more ambitiously when setting national goals. The establishment of such an experimental process for comparing national efforts in the business and human rights field could also be a positive example for other States in other regions and encourage them not to act in isolation with regard to their NAPs, but rather to coordinate and compare their efforts with their neighbours.

[102] EU Fundamental Rights Agency (n 4).

PART III

The EU and 'Third' Countries

8

On the Cusp: Brexit and Public International Law

KIERAN BRADLEY*

I. Introduction

The management of the withdrawal of the United Kingdom from the European Union, universally dubbed 'Brexit', throws up a myriad of legal issues, including many with an international law aspect. These include the possibility of the United Kingdom's withdrawing from the Union without resorting to the procedure of Article 50 of the Treaty on European Union (TEU), the legal character of the Withdrawal Agreement, and the basis for any financial obligations of the United Kingdom towards the Union after Brexit. Other issues include the possibility for the United Kingdom to take trade initiatives before Brexit occurs, and the revocability of the United Kingdom's notification of intention to withdraw. These are briefly examined in turn below and are followed by even briefer conclusions.

II. 'Don't Trigger Article 50 – Just Leave'

In the aftermath of the Brexit referendum, the question was raised as to whether the United Kingdom could withdraw from the European Union simply by repealing the European Communities Act 1972. The case for doing so was put forcefully by Detter de Frankopan thus:

> [s]econd rate lawyers are misleading everyone in the country by insisting that, in order to leave the European Union it is essential to 'trigger' Article 50 in its entirety.

* Kieran Bradley is Special Adviser at CJEU, writing in an exclusively private capacity; the views expressed are purely personal and may not be attributed in any way to the Court or any member or department thereof. My best thanks are due to Vicky Hanley, Stanislas Adam and Paschalis Paschalidis for their comments on an earlier version of the text; responsibility for any errors is that of the author alone.

> This line has been swallowed whole by the government, the media and commentators. It is, however, absolute nonsense. Under international law and under Article 50(1) itself, only notice to leave is necessary.[1]

While this thesis does not resist serious examination under either Article 50 TEU or international law as expressed in the Vienna Convention on the Law of Treaties 1969 ('Convention' or 'VCLT'), it puts the spotlight on the somewhat obscure wording of Article 50(1) TEU, and the inadequacy of Article 50 TEU as a whole in the light of the relevant provisions of the Convention.

Where a multilateral treaty provides for an exit clause,[2] the general rule is that 'withdrawal of a party may take place only as a result of the application of the provisions of the treaty', under Article 42(2) VCLT.[3] It is fairly clear from the ordinary meaning of Article 50 TEU, whether read according to the canons of interpretation of international or European Union law, that the decision of a Member State under paragraph 1, which provides that '[a]ny Member State may decide to withdraw from the Union in accordance with its own constitutional requirements', does not itself bring about that State's withdrawal. In particular, a State which decides to withdraw is obliged under Article 50(2) TEU to 'notify the European Council of its intention'; the withdrawal will only become effective either in accordance with an agreement between the State and the Union or automatically two years after the notification (or an agreed later date). Immediate unilateral withdrawal such as Detter de Frankopan and others have suggested is not an option in Union or international law, and indeed the United Kingdom Government has itself acknowledged that such an act 'would be a breach of international and EU law [which would] create a hostile environment in which to negotiate either a new relationship with the remaining EU Member States, or new trade agreements with non-EU countries'.[4]

So what is the point of Article 50(1) TEU? In the first place, it declares the right of a Member State, as a matter of Union law, to take such a decision, whereas before the Treaty of Lisbon the very existence of a right to withdraw was open to doubt.[5] However, the Treaty rules regarding withdrawal, and a possible re-accession, are set out in Article 50(2) to (5) TEU; Article 50(1) thus only refers to the taking of a decision to withdraw at the national level, the means of adoption of which should in principle be a matter of complete indifference to the Union. In fact, the procedure of Article 50 TEU could operate just as well, from the perspective of the European Union, if Article 50(1) TEU were to be deleted; the notification

[1] *Money Week*, 21 November 2016, https://moneyweek.com/dont-trigger-article-50-just-leave/.

[2] See generally L Helfer, 'Exiting Treaties' (2005) 91 *Virginia Law Review* 1579.

[3] See also Art 54(a) VCLT and section VI. B.

[4] HM Government, *The Process for Withdrawing from the European Union* (February 2016) www.gov.uk/government/uploads/system/uploads/attachment_data/file/503908/54538_EU_Series_No2_Accessible.pdf.

[5] J Weiler, 'Alternatives to Withdrawal from an International Organisation: The Case of the European Economic Community' (1985) 20 *Israel Law Review* 282; see also section VI. C.

presupposes that the necessary decision has been taken at the national level and in accordance with the Member State's own constitutional requirements.

But Article 50(1) TEU does not stop at declaring that a Member State may take such a decision; it goes on to stipulate that, as a matter of *Union* law, the State must comply with 'its own constitutional requirements'. The matter is fraught with difficulty; though some Member States have explicit constitutional provisions on accession to the European Union, it seems improbable that many will have equivalent such provisions for withdrawal. In the United Kingdom itself, the Government was incapable of properly identifying the relevant constitutional requirements, and went down to a spectacular defeat on the question before the Supreme Court.[6] The inclusion of this phrase in Article 50(1) TEU could, on one reading, also be taken to mean that compliance with such requirements falls in principle within the jurisdiction of the political institutions of the European Union, and in the last resort that of the Court of Justice of the European Union (CJEU).[7] On the other hand, the German *Bundesverfassungsgericht* has taken the view that '[w]hether these requirements have been complied with in the individual case can … only be verified by the Member State itself, not by the European Union or the other Member States'.[8] This certainly makes good sense, as the CJEU's institutional competence is in the area of European Union, not national, law.

The most-widely accepted explanation for the reference to national requirements is that the authors of Article 50 TEU, of whom there were a surprising number,[9] intended to exclude the imposition of any requirements of Union law to the Member State's decision to withdraw. If that was the case, then this proviso was at best superfluous, as the same effect could have been achieved more neatly by omitting it entirely. Another possible explanation is that the authors simply took over the equivalent rule from Article 49(2) TEU, which requires ratification of an accession agreement by the Member States and the acceding State(s). If so, the analogy is inapposite; unlike a decision to withdraw from the Union, an accession agreement is not an act adopted by a single State under its national legal arrangements, but a multilateral agreement which takes effect on the international and European levels, between the Member States of the Union and one or more third States. The proviso that an accession agreement be ratified in accordance with the constitutional requirements of the Member States therefore serves a number of purposes of Union law. In the first place, it establishes that the Member States may

[6] *R (Miller and others) v Secretary of State for Exiting the European Union* [2017] UKSC 5.

[7] For simplicity, the term 'Court [of Justice]' will be used indifferently to denote the institution, the Court of Justice of the European Union, as well as its composite parts, the Court of Justice and the General Court, except where it is necessary to distinguish between these.

[8] 2 BvE 2/08 et al, judgment of the Second Senate of 30 June 2009, para 330 http://www.bundesverfassungsgericht.de/SharedDocs/Entscheidungen/EN/2009/06/es20090630_2bve000208en.html.

[9] Of these, Lord Kerr of Kinlochard, in his capacity as former Secretary General of the European Convention (2002–2003) is the most vociferous, though claims have been made for different members of the Presidium of the Convention.

not indicate their approval of the accession agreement by any less formal means than that which applies for an international agreement which they conclude under their own initiative. Moreover, it allows the Union to determine on what precise date the conclusion procedure is terminated, and hence when the accession agreement comes into force.

In December 2017, proceedings were launched before the High Court of England and Wales seeking to establish that, while the Government had been authorised to notify the United Kingdom's intention to withdraw, no logically prior 'constitutionally valid withdrawal decision' had in fact ever been taken. The application for judicial review was finally rejected on 12 June 2018 as being out of time and 'Totally without Merit'.[10]

III. Nature of the Withdrawal Agreement

If ever there was an agreement which was situated on the cusp of European Union and public international law, it is the Withdrawal Agreement foreseen by Article 50(2) TEU. This provides that the agreement, which should 'set[] out the arrangements for [the] withdrawal' of the State concerned, is to be negotiated between the Union and the withdrawing Member State. A priori, at the time it is being negotiated and is concluded, the agreement is not an 'international agreement' as defined in Article 216(1) of the Treaty on the Functioning of the European Union (TFEU), that is, an agreement '[t]he Union may conclude with one or more third countries or international organisations', as the United Kingdom is neither of these. Moreover, if it were considered to be an international agreement, the procedural provisions of Article 218 TFEU would in principle apply unless they are expressly excluded; by this token, Article 218(1) TFEU should have indicated that the procedure it established was 'without prejudice' to Article 50 TEU, as it does with regard to commercial policy agreements concluded under the 'specific provisions' laid down in Article 207 TFEU. As the Court of Justice has repeatedly emphasised,

> following the entry into force of the Treaty of Lisbon … [Article 218 TFEU] now lays down a single procedure of general application concerning the negotiation and conclusion of international agreements which the European Union is competent to conclude in the fields of its activity, including the CFSP, except where the Treaties lay down special procedures.[11]

Instead Article 50(2) TEU explicitly applies Article 218(3) TFEU to the Withdrawal Agreement, and lays down all the other procedural steps for the negotiation

[10] *R (on the application of Elizabeth Webster v Secretary of State for Exiting the European Union* [2018] EWHC 1543 (Admin).

[11] Case C-658/11 *Parliament v Council (Pirates of Mauritius)* ECLI:EU:C:2014:2025, para 52.

and conclusion of this agreement, including regarding the participation of the European Parliament, the voting rule in the Council and, implicitly, the absence of Member State ratification. The most natural reading of this provision is that the remainder of Article 218 TFEU would not apply in this context, and that the Court has therefore not been granted jurisdiction to provide an opinion, in accordance with Article 218(11) TFEU, on the compatibility of this agreement with the Treaties and with Union law in general.

It is, however, true that at the time it comes into force, and by virtue of its coming into force, the agreement will also become an act of international law, regulating the relationship between the Union and a third State. It will be binding on the Union and the remaining Member States by virtue of Article 216(2) TFEU,[12] but on the United Kingdom after Brexit only as a matter of international, not Union, law. Even if the procedure for its negotiation and conclusion necessarily differs from that of other international agreements, the legal character of the Withdrawal Agreement is strictly comparable, albeit that it is limited in content to withdrawal arrangements. Moreover, the procedure laid down by Article 50 TEU was clearly inspired by the equivalent provisions of the VCLT, even if only some of these provisions were taken over, and that in an incomplete fashion.[13]

It could also be argued that such an agreement, the first (and, most would hope, only) one of its kind, is crying out for the possibility of an ex ante review by the Court, given its novelty and impact on the activities of the Union. As the Court noted in its Opinion on the *Agreement on Bananas*, 'the purpose of the [Opinion] procedure is to forestall complications which would result from legal disputes concerning the compatibility with the Treaty of international agreements binding on the [Union]'.[14] The Court went on to opine that a negative ruling ex post 'could not fail to provoke, not only in the [Union] context but also in international relations, serious difficulties and might give rise to adverse consequences for all interested parties'.[15] In the context of the Brexit agreement, one need only think, for example, of the likely difficulties of designing a dispute settlement system which reconciles the United Kingdom's red line against allocating jurisdiction to the Court of Justice with that Court's case law on the autonomy of the Union's legal order,[16] or the risk that one or other of the provisions on citizens' rights falls foul of a general principle of Union law, such as those on the protection of fundamental rights under the Charter.[17] In a different context,

[12] Joint Report from the negotiators of the European Union and the United Kingdom Government on progress during phase 1 of the negotiations, TF50 (2017) 19, Brussels, 8 December 2017 (the 'joint Report of 8 December 2017') para 57.

[13] See section VI. B.

[14] Opinion 3/94 *Agreement on Bananas* ECLI:EU:C:1995:436, para 3.

[15] ibid para 17.

[16] See in particular Opinion 1/91 *First EEA Agreement* ECLI:EU:C:1991:490, Opinion 1/09 *Unified Patent Court Agreement* ECLI:EU:C:2011:123, and Opinion 2/13 *Accession to the European Convention on Human Rights II* ECLI:EU:C:2014:2454.

[17] See, eg, Case C-540/03 *Parliament v Council* ('family reunification') ECLI:EU:C:2006:429.

the Court relied on the manifest 'interest of the [Union] legal order' to forestall differences of interpretation of secondary legislation in order to justify assuming jurisdiction which was not evidently conferred on it by the Treaty.[18] Equally, the Court claims exclusive jurisdiction, which is not conferred on it in explicit terms by the relevant Treaty provisions, to rule that a measure of Union secondary law is invalid.[19] The Court has also been known to adopt extraordinary decisions to cope with extraordinary situations,[20] in carrying out its general duty under Article 19(1) TEU to 'ensure that in the interpretation and application of the Treaties the law is observed'.

It follows from the same Opinion on the *Agreement on Bananas* that the interest of the Union in obtaining a ruling from the Court is not necessarily sufficient in itself to overcome a procedural hurdle to the Court's jurisdiction to providing such an Opinion. However, in the *Bananas* Opinion procedure, the request had in effect become moot, as the Agreement in question had already been concluded by the time the Court was in a position to provide the Opinion, and the Opinion could not therefore have forestalled any legal difficulty. This would not be the case were the Court to be requested to provide an Opinion on the envisaged Withdrawal Agreement; provided the Court were given sufficient time to draft the Opinion, such a request could therefore achieve the objectives of the Article 218(11) TFEU procedure.[21]

IV. 'Can't Pay? Won't Pay!'

One of the most striking, and perhaps effective, arguments for the 'Beleavers' in the Brexit referendum campaign was the claim, splashed in letters a metre high on a red double-decker bus, that the United Kingdom 'send[s] the EU £350 million a week' and the implication that following Brexit the money would be spent on the National Health Service (NHS) instead. The man standing beside the bus in the iconic photograph, Boris Johnson, in his capacity as Foreign Secretary, subsequently agreed with a fellow MP in the House of Commons that the Union could 'go whistle' if it expected the United Kingdom to make any budgetary contribution as part of a withdrawal agreement. During the course of the negotiations, the Government adopted a more emollient tone, and it may be that it is the citizens of the United Kingdom who expected Brexit to lead to a bonanza of extra funding for the NHS who will have a lot of whistling to do.

[18] Joined Cases C-297/88 and 197/89 *Dzodzi* ECLI:EU:C:1990:360, para 37.

[19] Case 314/85 *Foto-Frost* ECLI:EU:C:1987:452.

[20] Case 294/83 *Les Verts v Parliament* ECLI:EU:C:1986:166.

[21] See also S Adam, *La procédure d'avis devant la Cour de justice de l'Union européenne* (Brussels, Bruylant, 2011) para 480 to 489.

Despite having access to its 'own resources', the Union budget depends directly for its revenue on monies collected or contributed by the Member States; the departure of a Member State inevitably leads to a shortfall in revenue, which is quite significant in the case of Brexit, of the order of 12 per cent before the application of the United Kingdom rebate. The European Union has always taken for granted that the United Kingdom would honour the financial commitments, which are often spread over several spending years, undertaken by the Union relying on transfers from the 28 Member States. Thus the European Council guidelines of 29 April 2017 stated rather blandly that

> [a] single financial settlement – including issues resulting from the MFF as well as those related to the European Investment Bank (EIB), the European Development Fund (EDF) and the European Central Bank (ECB) – should ensure that the Union and the United Kingdom both respect the obligations resulting from the whole period of the UK membership in the Union. The settlement should cover all commitments as well as liabilities, including contingent liabilities.[22]

Given the sensitivity of the financial question, which regularly threatened to derail the negotiation process, at least in the early days, it is regrettable that Article 50 TEU omits to resolve, or even evoke, the question of whether the United Kingdom is under any legal obligation to make a budgetary contribution to the Union on withdrawal. At the very least, it would have been possible to make withdrawal conditional on the satisfaction by the withdrawing State of all the financial obligations it had contracted as a result of its membership, as is the case, to take a random example, of withdrawal from the International Labour Organisation.[23] That said, the obligation under international law of the United Kingdom to settle its debts is, in fact, tolerably clear. This may go some way to explaining why, notwithstanding the intemperate claims of its then Foreign Secretary, the United Kingdom Government has accepted for the purposes of the Withdrawal Agreement the principle of a financial settlement, as well as a methodology defining its components, the principles for calculating the value and means of payment, and a number of ancillary matters.[24] The question could still arise, however, should the Withdrawal Agreement not be concluded for one reason or another; after all, one matter on which the parties have always been *ad idem* is that 'nothing is agreed until everything is agreed'.[25]

The obligation of the Member States to honour their financial commitments towards the Union is uncontested as a matter of Union law, and in particular the Council decision on the system of own resources of the European Union, which

[22] European Council, EUCO XT 20004/17, Brussels, 29 April 2017, para 10.

[23] Constitution of the International Labour Organisation, 1919 (as amended), Art 1(5).

[24] Joint Report of 8 December 2017 (n 12) para 57 to 86; draft Withdrawal Agreement of 14 November 2018, Part Five, https://www.consilium.europa.eu/media/37095/draft_withdrawal_agreement_incl_art132.pdf (the 'draft Withdrawal Agreement of 14 November 2018').

[25] Joint Report of 8 December 2017 (n 12) para 5.

explicitly requires the Member States to 'make the resources [so defined] available to the Commission in accordance with' the Union's financial regulation.[26] It has also been argued that 'Member States undertake a concrete obligation to finance the EU within the limits of the financial cycle provided within the Multiannual Financial Framework' (MFF).[27] The problem arises, however, because of the unqualified character of a Member State's right to withdraw from the Union, manifested by the 'guillotine' clause of Article 50(3) TEU, which provides that '[t]he Treaties shall cease to apply to the State in question from the date of entry into force of the withdrawal agreement or, failing that, two years after the notification of' that State's intention to withdraw from the Union. Under one view, the absence of an agreement would create a legal void, meaning that the United Kingdom would be under no obligation to make payments to the Union:

> [i]f the Treaties collapse for the UK, the whole legal building – all the legal documents hanging from the Treaties – will collapse. That includes the MFF, the annual budget, the programmes and the individual funding decisions for beneficiaries.[28]

Once the United Kingdom has left the Union, it becomes a third State, and its relations with the Union are governed by international law, particularly any relevant principles or rules of customary law. Of particular potential pertinence is Article 70(1) VCLT, which provides in relevant part:

> '[u]nless the treaty otherwise provides or the parties otherwise agree, the termination of a treaty under its provisions …
>
> (a) Releases the parties from any obligation further to perform the treaty:
>
> (b) Does not affect any right, obligation or legal situation of the parties created through the execution of the treaty prior to its denunciation.

It has plausibly been argued that this provision represents the state of customary international law, in the light of its legislative history and unanimous adoption at the Vienna Conference, the prevailing academic opinion, the 'logic inherent in Article 70', and the rather scant instances of its application in practice.[29]

In its report on *Brexit and the EU Budget*, the House of Lords European Union Committee started from the premise that Article 50 TEU should be interpreted in the light of Article 70 VCLT. Influenced in part by the 'collapsed building' thesis of Sánchez-Barrueco, the Committee concluded that the

> rule in Article 70(1)(b) … only applies to withdrawal from a treaty which does not have its own withdrawal procedures ('unless the treaty otherwise provides').

[26] Council Decision 2014/335/EU, Euratom of 26 May 2014 [2014] OJ L168/105, Art 8(2).

[27] T Tridimas in House of Lords European Union Committee, *Brexit and the EU Budget*, HL Paper 125, London, 4 March 2017, para 116 (hereinafter 'HoL on Brexit Budget'); Council Regulation (EU, Euratom) No 1311/2013 laying down the multiannual financial framework for the years 2014–2020 [2013] OJ L 347/884.

[28] M-L Sánchez-Barrueco, HoL on Brexit Budget (n 27) para 123.

[29] O Dörr and K Schmalenbach (eds), *Vienna Convention on the Law of Treaties – A Commentary* (Heidelberg, Springer, 2012) para 38, 1210.

> Manifestly, the TEU does, in the form of Article 50 [which] therefore takes precedence over Article 70(1)(b) of the Vienna Convention.

As Article 50 TEU does not provide to the contrary, it 'allows the UK to leave the EU without being liable for outstanding financial obligations under the EU budget or other financial instruments, unless a withdrawal agreement is concluded which resolves this issue'.[30]

In the first place, given the United Kingdom's status as a third State at the time the question would arise, the correct exercise in this context would be to interpret Article 70 VCLT in the light of Article 50 TEU and any other relevant provisions of Union law, rather than vice versa, as the United Kingdom would no longer be bound by Article 50. Second, the Committee's conclusion that Article 50 TEU is a *lex specialis* which ousts the obligations which would otherwise arise for the United Kingdom under Article 70(1)(b) of the Vienna Convention a priori contradicts the very wording of this latter provision, which applies to 'the termination of a treaty *under its provisions*' (emphasis added), as well as the termination of a treaty in accordance with Articles 65 to 68 VCLT.[31] As the United Kingdom is indubitably withdrawing from the Union in accordance with the provisions of the TEU,[32] then it follows that Article 70 VCLT is in principle applicable to the 'right[s], obligation[s] and legal situation[s]' of the United Kingdom 'created through the execution of the treaty prior to its termination'.

The Committee's misguided but convenient thesis turns on the phrase '[u]nless the treaty otherwise provides'; in its view, the fact that Article 50 TEU lays down a procedure for exiting the Union without providing that the withdrawing State is under any financial obligation means that, as one Member of the European Parliament put it, that '[y]ou can leave the Union without looking behind you'.[33] Article 70 VCLT, however, establishes exactly the contrary presumption to that on which their Lordships based their conclusion; unless the treaty from which the State is withdrawing explicitly provides that the withdrawing Member State is suddenly free of all obligations arising from membership of the Union, then Article 70(1)(b) VCLT requires it to respect those obligations. The rule in Article 50(3) TEU that '[t]he Treaties shall cease to apply to the State in question' from a given date clearly corresponds to that in Article 70(1)(a) VCLT, but it is a very large step to conclude that it also covers Article 70(1)(b) VCLT; Article 50 TEU 'says nothing as to the discontinuation of obligations already incurred in the past'.[34] If Article 50 TEU were to be interpreted 'in good faith in accordance with the ordinary meaning to be given to the terms of the treaty

[30] HoL on Brexit Budget (n 27) para 133, 37 and 38.
[31] On this distinction, see section VI.B in the present chapter.
[32] See section II.
[33] I Grässle, HoL on Brexit Budget (n 27) para 107, 31.
[34] P Craig, 'Brexit, A Drama: The Interregnum' (2017) 36 *Yearbook of European Law* 3, 38.

in their context and in the light of its object and purpose', as Article 31 of the VCLT disposes, it would be next to impossible to maintain that its essentially procedural provisions[35] liberate a withdrawing State from such an important set of substantive obligations as its share of the financial commitments the Union entered into while it was still a Member State.

The implausibility of their Lordships' thesis is further illustrated by Article 71 VCLT, which appears to have been overlooked in the Committee debate. This applies the rule of Article 70(1) VCLT to the situation where a treaty has become void and terminates because of its incompatibility with a new peremptory norm of general international law; except where they are themselves in conflict with this norm, the pre-existing rights, obligations and legal situations of the parties are maintained. If such rights, obligations and legal situations are maintained where a treaty becomes void as a matter of international law, and hence against the will of the parties when concluding the original treaty, it would be rather extraordinary indeed if a State which voluntarily withdrew from a treaty could thereby escape all such legal consequences.

V. UK Pre-Brexit External Relations Initiatives: Wessel State or Global Britain?

A. The Trade Policy Cliff Edge

A recurrent question in the legal debate is whether the United Kingdom might be entitled to commence the long process of negotiating international agreements, particularly those on trade which fall within the Union's exclusive competence, or otherwise conduct an autonomous trade policy,[36] in the period between the notification of its intention to withdraw from the Union and the date on which Brexit becomes effective. It has been suggested, for example, that

> [s]etting the legal parameters aside, it would make perfect sense to allow the United Kingdom to proceed with negotiations of trade agreements with third countries from the date of notification, providing that none of the deals would enter into force before actual Brexit.[37]

The alternative would be a so-called 'cliff edge', whereby from one day to the next the United Kingdom would find itself deprived of the benefits of the vast network

[35] M Waibel, 'The Brexit Bill and the Law of Treaties', www.ejiltalk.org/the-brexit-bill-and-the-law-of-treaties, 4 May 2017.

[36] It was reported, for example, that Trade Secretary Liam Fox would be seeking an exemption for the United Kingdom from steel tariffs announced by the Trump administration in early March 2018.

[37] A Łazowski and R Wessel, 'The External Dimension of Withdrawal from the European Union' (2017) 2016/4 *Revue des Affaires Européennes* 623–38.

of international agreements which it currently enjoys as a Member State of the European Union. At first blush, it is far from clear that, whatever its effects on the United Kingdom, such a drastic situation would be compatible with the interests of the Union or the third States concerned, particularly those which have already concluded agreements with a Union which includes the United Kingdom, its second-largest economy.

Whatever its possible economic advantages, this suggestion has been seen as legally problematic.[38] In the first place, Article 50(3) TEU clearly provides that the EU Treaties remain in force for a withdrawing State until the day of actual exit from the European Union. The United Kingdom must therefore respect the division of competences laid down by the Treaty and refrain from concluding international agreements within the sphere of the Union's exclusive competences as defined by Article 2(1) TFEU. It is, furthermore, bound throughout this period by 'the principle of sincere cooperation'. While the United Kingdom might rely on this same principle to argue for 'a fair degree of leverage and cooperation' from the Union, the case law of the Court, and in particular the *Greek IMO* and *Swedish POPs* cases[39] show that 'a breach by the Commission of the duty of cooperation (still) does not entitle a Member State to undertake actions which affect rules adopted at Union level'. At most, 'authorising the UK to start trade negotiations would be a possibility, especially for the period after triggering Article 50 TEU, but [it] depends entirely on the goodwill of the EU institutions and remaining Member States'.[40] Under this view, which may be dubbed the 'Wessel State thesis', Union law as it currently stands 'will seriously hamper the UK in preparing itself for the post-Brexit period'.

Although many of the considerations adumbrated by Wessel are in themselves unexceptionable, the conclusions drawn from them appear to extrapolate to the situation of a Member State which is withdrawing from the European Union the panoply of obligations which apply in respect of the Member States which will remain in the Union. It could be argued, however, that the possibility for the United Kingdom to take external relations initiatives in the interim period before Brexit[41] is not exclusively a matter of Union 'goodwill', but is governed by a series of legal provisions which establish obligations and rights on both sides. Thus, while it is not suggested that the United Kingdom could unilaterally initiate negotiations on trade agreements without restriction, the United Kingdom's position is significantly different to that described by Wessel.

[38] R Wessel, 'Consequences of Brexit for International Agreements Concluded by the EU and its Member States' (2018) 55 *CMLR* 101.

[39] Case C-45/07 *Commission v Hellenic Republic* EU:C:2009:81; and Case 246/07 *Commission v Sweden* EU:C:2010:203.

[40] J Larik, 'Sincere Cooperation in the Common Commercial Policy: Lisbon, a "Joined-Up" Union and "Brexit"' in M Bungenburg et al (eds), *European Yearbook of International Economic Law* (Berlin/Heidelberg, Springer, 2017) 83, 102.

[41] Or the end of the transitional period, as the case may be; see last paragraph of this section, below.

B. The Relative Character of the Union's Exclusive Competences[42]

The Ur-criterion delimiting the respective competences of the Union and the Member States to conclude international agreements, as laid down in the *ERTA* judgment and now reflected in Article 3(2) TFEU, is whether the obligations the Member State would undertake with third countries 'affect common [Union] rules or alter their scope'.[43] Wessel's view that 'the UK simply does not have the competence to *conclude* international agreements … in any … area of exclusive EU competence until it formally leaves the European Union' and that it will 'simply be pre-empted from negotiating (let alone concluding) an international agreement'[44] would be correct if, at the time the 'obligations with third countries' come into force, the Member State in question were still a Member State of the European Union. Following a withdrawal from the Union in accordance with Article 50 TEU, however, the Union's 'common rules' would no longer apply to the withdrawing State and, unless the assumption by the withdrawing State of international obligations would 'affect those rules or alter their scope', these exclusive competences of the Union would not prevent that State negotiating and concluding the agreements in question. Given the presumption in favour of Member State competence over that of the Union established by Article 4(1) TEU, in order to prohibit unilateral action by the United Kingdom, it would arguably be incumbent on the Union to demonstrate at least that such action would somehow affect what the Court described in its Opinion on the *New Lugano Convention* 'the full effectiveness of [Union] law'.[45] Thus, while it is true that where the Union exercises its exclusive competence 'it takes the place of its Member States',[46] the substitution of the Union for the Member States ceases to apply, in accordance with Article 50(3) TEU, from the moment a Member State withdraws from the Union, and by this token neither Article 50 TEU nor the nature of the Union's exclusive competence constitutes an absolute impediment to a withdrawing Member State's preparing for the post-withdrawal legal situation.

Moreover, even where the Treaty defines the Union's competences as 'exclusive' in a more absolute manner, as in Article 3(1) TFEU, the Union may nonetheless authorise a Member State to 'legislate and adopt legally binding acts' in those areas, using its powers under Article 2(1) TFEU. There is no question here of

[42] See the chapters by M Cremona and K Bradley respectively in S Garben and I Govaere, *The Division of Competences Between the EU and the Member States* (Oxford/Portland, Hart Publishing, 2017) 133 and 173.

[43] Case 22/70 *Commission v Council* ECLI:EU:C:1971:32, para 22; see also Case C-266/03 *Commission v Luxembourg* ECLI:EU:C:2005:341 para 40, cited by Wessel, and more recently Opinion 2/15 *Singapore Free Trade Agreement* ECLI:EU:C:2017:376 para 170 to 172, 180 and 181.

[44] Wessel (n 38) 107, emphasis in original.

[45] Opinion 1/03 *New Lugano Convention* ELCI:EU:C:2006:81 para 128.

[46] Opinion 2/15 (n 43) para 248.

authorising the United Kingdom to violate Union law; if it obtains such an authorisation and respects its terms, then it is acting in full conformity with Union law. Nor is this provision limited to situations where the Union is not, for one reason or another, unable to exercise its exclusive competence, for example in international fora which do not admit international organisations as members. For its part, the Union legislature appears to have taken the view that such a power pre-existed Article 2(1) TFEU, and in July 2009, for example, created a number of procedures whereby Member States could be authorised to conclude international agreements with third countries in areas of exclusive Union competence, *in casu* in family law matters.[47] As well as facilitating the respect by the Member States of their obligations towards third States under what is now Article 351 TFEU in respect of existing agreements, these procedures sought to 'provide an adequate legal framework to meet specific needs of a given Member State in its relations with a third country' by allowing them to negotiate and conclude new international agreements.[48] It can hardly be denied that in the interim period before Brexit the United Kingdom has certain 'specific needs'.

In any case, the case law on which Wessel relies falls somewhat short of a smoking gun in favour of a blanket ban on Member State action on the external stage. Thus the *Greek IMO*[49] case is good authority for the playground wisdom that two wrongs do not make a right, but does not speak to the issue of whether the United Kingdom might be entitled, as a matter of Union law, to initiate discussions on trade arrangements with third parties. There the Court held that the submission by Greece of a proposal to the International Maritime Organisation was 'likely to affect the provisions of the [existing Union] Regulation', and therefore encroached on the Union's exclusive competence. *A contrario*, it may be argued that where no relevant Union rules have been promulgated, or where Member State action would not affect any such rules or alter their scope, then the Member State would not be precluded from acting. Though recognising that the criterion is one of the effects of United Kingdom action on EU competences, Wessel's suggestion that 'there would be some room for the EU and the UK to *jointly* seek for possibilities to allow the UK to explore options for future trade'[50] is itself problematic. In particular, Article 2(1) TFEU clearly indicates that an authorisation would allow the Member

[47] Council Regulation (EC) No 664/2009 of 7 July 2009 establishing a procedure for the negotiation and conclusion of agreements between Member States and third countries concerning jurisdiction, recognition and enforcement of judgments and decisions in matrimonial matters, matters of parental responsibility and matters relating to maintenance obligations, and the law applicable to matters relating to maintenance obligations [2009] OJ L 200/25; and Regulation (EC) No 662/2009 of the European Parliament and the Council of 13 July 2009 establishing a procedure for the negotiation and conclusion of agreements between Member States and third countries on particular matters concerning the law applicable to contractual and non-contractual obligations [2009] OJ L200/46.

[48] Recital 4 in the preamble to Regulation (EC) No 664/2009 and recital 4 in the preamble to Regulation (EC) No 662/2009.

[49] Case C-45/07 *Commission v Hellenic Republic* (n 39).

[50] Wessel (n 38) 109, emphasis in original.

State to 'legislate and adopt legally binding acts' on its own, not merely explore possible solutions jointly with the Union.

C. The Principle of Sincere Cooperation Cuts Both Ways

Second, while obviously of especial relevance, the 'principle of sincere cooperation' is not merely a brake on the action of the United Kingdom but can also create obligations in this context for the Union. Before it was set out in Article 4(3) TEU, the relevant principle was identified in the case law of the Court as the legal foundation of '*mutual* duties of sincere cooperation' (emphasis added), most notably in the Order of 13 July 1990 in *Zwartveld*, where the Court lambasted the Commission's embarrassingly obdurate refusal to help a national judge ensure the proper application of Union law.[51] Indeed, it was the Court *ex proprio motu* which added the element of mutuality to an obligation which at the time the Treaty imposed solely on the Member States in what was first Article 5 EEC and subsequently Article 10 EC. It was therefore the Court, rather than Article 4(3) TEU, which 'turn[ed] this duty into a two-way street'[52] by requiring 'full mutual respect' between the Union and its Member States; the fact that this provision imposes obligations on the Union in this context is regularly downplayed, if not quite overlooked, in the literature.[53]

In accordance with Article 4(3) TEU, the 'Union and the Member States' are obliged, inter alia, 'in full mutual respect, to assist each other in carrying out the tasks which flow from the Treaties'. Amongst the tasks of the Union in the withdrawal context is that of negotiating 'an agreement with [the withdrawing] State, setting out the arrangements for its withdrawal, taking account of the framework for its future relationship with the Union'. Article 50(2) TEU only imposes this duty expressly on the Union, while the corresponding duty of the withdrawing State is part of its general obligation under Article 4(3) TEU. In the *Inland Waterways* cases, the Court held that the objective of the duty of cooperation in the external relations field is to 'facilitate the achievement of the [Union's] tasks and to ensure the coherence and consistency of [such] action and its international representation'.[54] Such a general duty does not, of course, require the European Union to accept the negotiating demands of the United Kingdom if these are not in the Union's interest; it does mean that, for example, should

[51] Case C-2/88 IMM *Zwartveld and Others* ECLI:EU:C:1990:315 para 17 and 18.

[52] A Delgado Casteleiro and J Larik, 'The Duty to Remain Silent: Limitless Loyalty in EU External Relations?' (2011) 36 *European Law Review* 522, 524.

[53] See, eg, E Neframi, who provides a very comprehensive overview of the legal situation as regards the duties of the Member States, but dismisses the corresponding duty of the institutions in a single subordinate clause in a 36-page article: 'The Duty of Loyalty: Rethinking its Scope Through its Application in the Field of EU External Relations' (2010) 47 *Common Market Law Review* 323, 325.

[54] Case C-266/03 *Commission v Luxembourg* ECLI:EU:C:2005:341 para 60; Case C-433/03 *Commission v Germany* ECLI:EU:C:2005:462 para 66.

an authorisation for the United Kingdom to commence trade negotiations contribute to the successful conclusion of a withdrawal agreement, the Union's response should be guided by its duty of sincere cooperation, rather than merely considerations of 'goodwill'.

Since this suggestion was made, the debate has moved on somewhat, in that the Commission has proposed, and the United Kingdom has accepted in principle, a set of 'specific arrangements relating to the Union's external action' which would apply during the transition period, that is, from the entry into force of the Withdrawal Agreement until at least 31 December 2020.[55] Under these arrangements, 'Union law', including that on the exclusive character of the Union's external competences and the mutual duties of sincere cooperation, would apply to the United Kingdom in its entirety, subject to certain exceptions which are not relevant in the present context. In particular, the United Kingdom would continue to benefit from the Union's international agreements, but would be prohibited, acting on its own, from taking on the international plane 'any action or initiative which is likely to be prejudicial to the Union's interests', and from concluding (but not negotiating) 'international agreements entered into in its own capacity in the areas of exclusive competence of the Union, unless authorised to do so by the Union'.[56]

VI. Revocability of the Notification of Intention to Withdraw

A. 'The One Brexit Question that Matters'

In the mass of commentary on the legal aspects of Brexit, few topics have attracted, or indeed merit, so much close scrutiny and erudite analysis as the possibility for the United Kingdom to revoke[57] its notification of intention to withdraw from the European Union (hereinafter 'notification'). In the words of one very active campaigner, it is '[t]he one Brexit question that matters'.[58] Both the High Court of England and Wales and the United Kingdom Supreme Court studiously avoided taking a position on the matter in the *Miller* proceedings, on the grounds that the parties in the cases before them had agreed that notification was not revocable;[59] on one view, however, the revocability or otherwise of the (then future) notification could have been highly relevant to the question of whether the applicants had

[55] Draft Withdrawal Agreement of 14 November 2018 (n 24) Art 129.

[56] Draft Withdrawal Agreement of 14 November 2018 (n 24) Arts 127(1) and 129(1) and (3).

[57] The term 'revoke' is used almost invariably to avoid confusion with 'withdraw' which is reserved for withdrawal from the Union, though 'rescind' has also been spotted.

[58] J Maugham, *Prospect* (24 January 2017),www.prospectmagazine.co.uk/politics/supreme-court-government-brexit-appeal-article-50-revocable.

[59] *R (Miller and others)* (n 6).

an interest in challenging the means by which the Government intended to submit the United Kingdom's notification, rather than the withdrawal itself.

A number of attempts have been made to raise the revocability issue in national courts with a view to obtaining a ruling from the Court of Justice in good time before Brexit kicks in or, better still, before the negotiations on the various agreements have been concluded.[60] The question, which may raise issues of both European Union and public international law, might also arise incidentally in proceedings which were, at the time of writing, pending before the Court of Justice or the General Court, where different possible ramifications of Brexit on the legal situation of Union citizens were at issue.[61] The Court did not, however, need to examine this question in ruling on whether the United Kingdom's notification of intention to withdraw affected the application of the European Arrest Warrant scheme in *RO*.[62] The Inner House of the Scottish Court of Session however put the question very directly in the *Wightman* reference which was lodged at the Court of Justice on 3 October 2018 with a request for expedited consideration.[63]

The political interest of the question is obvious too. If the notification were irrevocable, both parties would be faced with the stark choice between a deal and no deal; in the latter case, the entire structure of relations between the Union and the United Kingdom built up over the previous 46 years would come tumbling down, like a derelict office block, at midnight on 29 March 2019, and the parties would have to tailor their negotiating positions accordingly. The possibility of a unilateral revocation would significantly strengthen the United Kingdom's hand in the negotiations, in that rejecting an agreement proposed by the Union would not necessarily entail shutdown at B-hour. Ironically, the United Kingdom Government has indicated that the notification submitted on 29 March 2017 will not be revoked, a position which has been described by a judge of another jurisdiction as 'clearly a tactical concession without any basis in law',[64] while for their part the Presidents of both the European Council and the Commission have signalled that the Union would be glad to halt the exit process should the United Kingdom change its mind. If it could be established that as a matter of law that the notification is irrevocable, then at least the question of whether Brexit will happen or not would be settled. It would become one fixed point in a sea of legal and political uncertainty.

[60] See notably *Maugham et al v Ireland and the Attorney General*, High Court of Ireland, 2017/781 P (withdrawn).

[61] Case C-191/18 *KN v Minister for Justice and Equality* EU:C:2018:884 and Case T-458/17 *Shindler et al v Council* EU:T:2018:838. In its judgment of 7 February 2018 in *Williams et al v Staat der Nederlanden en Gemeente Amsterdam*, the Rechtbank, Amsterdam, decided to refer certain Brexit-related questions to the Court of Justice, though no such reference had yet been lodged at the time of writing.

[62] Case C-327/18 PPU *RO* EU:C:2018:733.

[63] Case C-621/18, *Wightman and Others v Secretary of State for Exiting the European Union*, pending; see also [2018] CSOH 62.

[64] Humpheys J of the Irish High Court, Judgment of 8 November 2017 para 12; see Case C-661/17 *MA and Others v International Protection Appeals Tribunal* (pending).

B. Is Article 68 VCLT Relevant?

A significant part of the legal debate has concerned the possible relevance for the interpretation of Article 50 TEU of international law, and particularly Articles 65 to 68 VCLT on the procedure for, and conditions of, a unilateral withdrawal from a treaty. Though the termination, denunciation or withdrawal from a treaty is considered to run counter to the principle *pacta sunt servanda*, the Convention recognises that such a decision by a sovereign State must be accommodated, and seeks instead to regulate the matter in a way which damages international relations least. Article 42(2) VCLT thus provides that withdrawal 'may take place only as a result of the application of the provisions of the treaty or of the … Convention' itself, while Article 65 VCLT lays down the procedure for withdrawal under the Convention. Article 65(1) VCLT presupposes that the State concerned has identified some 'ground for … withdrawing', and the State is therefore obliged not only to 'indicate the measure proposed to be taken with respect to the treaty' (which may fall short of withdrawal, such as the suspension of the operation of the treaty) but also 'the reasons therefor' in its notification of intention to withdraw. Other than in cases of 'special urgency', withdrawal does not take immediate effect on notification; a minimum three-month period allows the notifying State to change its mind and the other parties to the treaty to raise objections to the proposed withdrawal, as well as taking such measures as are necessary at the national level to take account of the withdrawal. Notification must be made in writing to the other parties and, according to Article 68 VCLT, 'may be revoked at any time before it takes effect'.

Whether by accident or design – the drafting of Article 50 TEU leaves much to be desired – the Union procedure for withdrawal incorporates some of the features of the Convention procedure, such as the requirement for formal notification and an obligatory waiting period before the withdrawal takes effect. One might regret that Article 50 TEU failed to require the withdrawing State to identify and communicate to its partners any reason for its drastic action. Worse still, in the case of the United Kingdom, the Union went out of its way to accommodate the reasons identified, before the (consultative) referendum was held, by the then Prime Minister David Cameron by offering a 'new settlement for the United Kingdom within the European Union',[65] only to find that the Government's subsequent decision to withdraw from the Union was motivated at least in part by concerns which had not been raised in the discussions on the new settlement, such as the funding of the United Kingdom's NHS and the role of the judgments of the Court of Justice in the legal order of the United Kingdom.

If it has any application, Article 68 VCLT is generally considered as comforting the revocability thesis. Much attention has been focused, therefore, on the question of whether this provision can, or should, be relied upon in the interpretation

[65] European Council conclusions of 19 February 2016, EUCO 1/16, Section I and Annex I.

of Article 50 TEU. A preliminary issue which does not appear to have inspired much interest or curiosity amongst the commentariat is whether on its terms Article 68 VCLT provides any succour to the proponents of the revocability thesis. A positive answer to this question is far from obvious.

The Vienna Convention system countenances two main ways for a State to withdraw from a treaty: 'as a result of the application of the provisions of the treaty or of the present Convention'.[66] The two possibilities are then reproduced as distinct options in Article 54(a) and 54(b) VCLT respectively. The latter option, where the treaty does not contain a withdrawal clause, may only be exercised either if 'the parties intended to admit the possibility of … withdrawal' or if a 'right of … withdrawal may be implied by the nature of the treaty'.[67] Article 68 VCLT in turn governs two separate matters: the revocation of a *notification* of withdrawal and the revocation of an *instrument* of withdrawal under Articles 65 and 67 VCLT. Notification under Article 67, paragraph 1, only concerns a 'notification provided for under Article 65, paragraph 1,' that is, withdrawal (etc) from a treaty on the grounds of a defect in its consent or invalidity of the treaty. It follows that prima facie Article 68 does not apply to other forms of withdrawal, and in particular, withdrawal in accordance with the terms of the treaty. There is a certain logic to this state of affairs; if the parties to a treaty have agreed in advance on provisions on a procedure and/or conditions for withdrawal from the treaty, these provisions must be respected in good faith, and there is no need to apply, or even justification for applying, the provisions of the VCLT on the revocation of a notification. Under this view, Article 68 VCLT would in any case be irrelevant for the interpretation of Article 50 TEU.

Should the latter view not be accepted, the second important issue is whether the Court should or could have regard to the terms of Article 68 VCLT if called upon to rule on whether the United Kingdom may unilaterally revoke its notification of intention to withdraw from the Union. Unsurprisingly, many commentators who favour a right of revocation tend also to argue in favour of the relevance of Article 68 VCLT. Thus Craig, for example, contends that

> the very architecture of Article 50 TEU is informed by the VCLT principles concerning the giving of the notification and the like. The foundational starting point of legal principle, which is reaffirmed by the VCLT, is therefore that a state can revoke prior to the two-year period running out. In doing so it is not acting illegitimately or seeking some unwarranted advantage.[68]

In a similar vein, while of the opinion that Article 68 VCLT may not reflect customary international law, Sari cites approvingly the view of the International Law Commission to the effect that 'the right to revoke the notification is really

[66] Art 42(2) VCLT.
[67] Art 56(1) VCLT.
[68] P Craig, 'Brexit: Foundational Constitutional and Interpretive Principles' (Oxford Human Rights Hub, 28 October 2016) http://ohrh.law.ox.ac.uk/brexit-foundational-constitutional-and-interpretive-principles-ii/.

implicit in the fact that it is not to become effective until a certain date'; as noted above, a notification of withdrawal in accordance with the Convention only comes into effect after a cooling off period of a minimum of three months (Article 65(1) VCLT).[69] He concludes that '[t]his point applies with full force to Article 50 TEU'. Slightly more cautiously, the 'Three Knights' 'consider that the position under the Vienna Convention may be taken into account in interpreting Article 50, although it is undoubtedly true that the rules applicable to withdrawal from the European Union are those laid down in Article 50 itself'.[70] For their part, Eeckhout and Franziou argue that Article 50 TEU subjects withdrawal from the Union to far fewer constraints than the VCLT scheme, and as a result 'cannot be construed as prohibiting revocability where international law does not; that would completely contradict the respect for a domestic constitutional decision which lies at the heart of the rationale and structure of this provision'.[71]

There is no obvious answer to the question of whether the Court would take account of Article 68 VCLT in interpreting Article 50 TEU. On the one hand, given that the 'founding treaties of the EU, unlike ordinary international treaties, established a new legal order … the nature of which is peculiar to the EU',[72] the Court might be reluctant in principle to rely on provisions of the Vienna Convention to interpret a provision of primary Union law, when, as a matter of international law, Article 50 TEU clearly constitutes a *lex specialis* compared to the Articles 65 to 68 VCLT. The Union has not acceded to the Vienna Convention, and could not do so under Article 81 thereof, which limits accession to States; moreover, a number of Member States have not acceded to it either. While the Court has applied certain provisions of the Convention as constituting customary international law,[73] notably the rules of interpretation of treaties laid down in Article 31 VCLT,[74] this is not (yet) the case with regard to Article 68 VCLT. In *Racke*, the Court held that 'the specific procedural requirements … laid down [in Article 65 VCLT] do not form part of customary international law'.[75] As Article 68 VCLT merely supplements the procedural provisions laid down in Article 65 VCLT, and indeed depends for its useful effect on this provision (and Article 67 VCLT), it could be argued that Article 68 VCLT should be treated in the same manner as Article 65 VCLT.

[69] A Sari, 'Biting the Bullet: Why the UK is Free to Revoke Its Withdrawal Notification under Article 50 TEU' (The Exeter Blog, October 2016) https://blogs.exeter.ac.uk/exeterblog/blog/2016/10/22/aurel-sari-biting-the-bullet-why-the-uk-is-free-to-revoke-its-withdrawal-notification-under-article-50-teu/.

[70] D Edward et al, 'In the Matter of Article 50 of the Treaty on European Union' (10 February 2017) www.bindmans.com/uploads/files/documents/Final_Article_50_Opinion_10.2.17.pdf (hereinafter the 'Three Knights' Opinion').

[71] P Eeckhout and E Franziou, 'Brexit and Article 50 TEU: A Constitutionalist Reading' (2017) 54 *Common Market Law Review* 695, 714.

[72] Opinion 2/13 (n 16) para 157 and 158.

[73] Case C-386/08 *Brita GmbH v Hauptzollamt Hamburg-Hafen* ECLI:EU:C:2010:91 para 42.

[74] Opinion 2/00 *Cartagena Protocol on Biosafety* ECLI:EU:C:2001:664 para 24.

[75] Case C-162/96 *Racke v Hauptzollamt Mainz* ECLI:EU:C:1998:293 para 59.

On the other hand, the Union is obliged to 'contribute to … the strict observance and the development of international law' under Article 3(5) TEU. The Court has thus held that

> the European Union is bound … when exercising its powers, to observe international law in its entirety, including not only the rules and principles of general and customary international law, but also the provisions of international conventions that are binding on it.[76]

In proposing the equivalent provision, also Article 68, of what became the 1986 Vienna Convention on the Law of Treaties between States and International Organisations, the International Law Commission noted that Article 68 VCLT 'did not raise any difficulties' and opined that '[t]here is no reason such a natural provision should not be extended' to the later Convention. In *Racke* the Court did not take a position on whether the principle on which Article 65 VCLT is based, that is, that a party which seeks to withdraw from a treaty must notify the other parties and observe a minimum period before effecting withdrawal, could be seen as reflecting either general or customary international law. Even when finding that it was not bound by Article 65 VCLT (and by extension Article 68 VCLT), however, the Court cited approvingly in its judgment the dictum of the International Court of Justice in *Gabcíkovo-Nagymaros Project* (*Hungary v Slovakia*) on the importance of 'the stability of treaties',[77] which reasoning might possibly be applied by analogy to the interpretation of Article 50 TEU, in favour of a right of revocation. Article 50 TEU is in any case a rather particular Treaty provision, governing the transition of the relations between the Union and a Member State from the sphere of Union law to that of international law, whose drafting seems to have been largely, if rather imperfectly, based on the relevant provisions of the VCLT.

C. Does Union Law Allow a Right of Revocation?

By common consent, the main battleground on which the dispute on revocability will take place is Union law and the interpretation of Article 50 TEU, whether or not the Court is minded to take account of Article 68 VCLT. There are three main schools of thought: that the United Kingdom may revoke its notification unilaterally, that it may do so with the consent of the other Member States, and that it may not do so at all.

The proponents of the 'unilateral revocability' thesis rely in the first place on the wording of Article 50 TEU. This provides that, though it takes a 'decision' to withdraw under paragraph 1 in accordance with its own constitutional requirements, the withdrawing State only notifies the European Council of its 'intention' to withdraw under paragraph 2, as if the initial decision were in some sense provisional or

[76] Case C-266/16 *Western Sahara Campaign UK* ECLI:EU:C:2018:118 para 47.
[77] 1997 ICJ 7, para 104, cited in *Racke* (n 75) para 50.

open to reversal: '[a]n "intention" is not a binding commitment; it can be changed or withdrawn. This is a matter of ordinary language'.[78] A more sophisticated version of the same argument contends that, where justified by the constitutional requirements of the withdrawing State, the notification may be given

> in a conditional form … that would allow a Member State unilaterally to withdraw a notification … for example if its constitutional requirements for leaving have not been satisfied [or] … if it is unable to negotiate acceptable terms for withdrawal and wishes to remain.[79]

Considered in isolation, the use of the term 'intention' as opposed to 'decision' in Article 50(2) TEU might be seen as lending some support to the unilateral revocability thesis. This reading is predicated on the idea that the taking of the decision at the level of the withdrawing State is an integral part of the Union procedure for withdrawal, which conditions the remainder of the procedure. Under an alternative reading of Article 50(1) TEU, however, this provision merely declares that, as a matter of Union law, a Member State has a right to withdraw from the Union and that the exercise of this right is not subject to any conditions imposed by the Treaty, or indeed under the VCLT. Prior to the Treaty of Lisbon, the very existence of such a right was contested. Article 240 EEC then provided that the Treaty of Rome was 'concluded for an unlimited period', while the first paragraph of the preamble to the Treaty declared that it was 'lay[ing] the foundations of an ever closer union among the peoples of Europe'. The prevailing, though far from unanimous, view at the time was that these features of the Treaties stood in the way of any right of unilateral withdrawal from the then European Community; it would have been somewhat difficult plausibly to maintain either that the parties to the Community Treaties 'intended to admit the possibility of … withdrawal' or that '[a] right of … withdrawal [could] be implied by the nature of the treaty', as specified in Article 56(1) VCLT.

Be that as it may, Article 50(1) TEU established once and for all, in a Treaty which abolished the 'Communities', that, as a matter of law, Member States are not locked into the Union which replaced them without any means of egress. This reading of Article 50(1) TEU as being essentially declaratory is comforted by the fact that the withdrawal procedure, which is governed exclusively by Union law, commences not with the national decision but with the notification, as witness the nine months' delay between the United Kingdom referendum and the lodging of the notification. As noted above, the procedure would not function any differently if Article 50(1) TEU were to be deleted. The use of the term 'intention' would, under this reading, merely indicate that the Member State's 'decision' to withdraw

[78] M Demetriou et al, 'In the Matter of the Unilateral Revocability of Article 50 of the Treaty on European Union' (sic) (23 November 2017) para 6 https://static1.squarespace.com/static/592d751786e6c0040d65d9c1/t/5a57a67c24a694f00f5b43c9/1515693694200/Opinion+on+Article+50.pdf.

[79] Three Knights' Opinion (n 70) para 48 and 49.

is not immediately effective, and reflects the obligation on the parties to at least attempt to come to an agreement within the two years of the date of notification, as stipulated in Article 50(2) TEU.

It is fairly clear from Article 50(2) TEU that the Member State in question must take its decision before notification; it is only '[a] Member State *which decides to withdraw*' that may lodge such a notification. The use of the present indicative 'decides', rather than the present perfect 'has decided', is hardly determinative of the existence of a right of unilateral revocation,[80] which would in any case chime ill with the remainder of the text; it would be quite irresponsible for a Member State to notify an intention which is in some sense not fully formed. Under this reading, the notification may not, as a matter of Union law, either be conditional on the respect for the Member State's constitutional requirements, or withdrawn at that State's subsequent sole convenience.

Much is made of the unilateral character of the decision to withdraw reflected in Article 50(1) TEU. This much is undeniable, but inevitable given the clear intention of the Treaty authors to give the Member States an unconditional right to withdraw from the Union, albeit deferred in time. The Member States' explicit unfettered right to initiate the procedure does not necessarily carry with it an implicit unconditional right to revoke a notification which has been given; once initiated, the procedure is no longer in the hands of the Member State which has started it, whose only role in the remainder of the procedure is to negotiate, and possibly conclude, a withdrawal agreement and, if invited, to take a position on whether the two-year period of Article 50(3) TEU should be extended. The unilateral character of the decision to withdraw does not therefore necessarily entail a right unilaterally to bring that procedure to a halt.

The Article 50 TEU procedure has correctly been described as being designed primarily to contain the adverse effects on the Union's interests, in accordance with '*une procédure quasi-communautaire*',[81] of a potentially damaging situation not of the Union's making. Article 50(3) TEU expressly defines the legal consequences of a failure of the parties to come to such an agreement: '[t]he Treaties shall cease to apply to the State in question … two years after the notification' under Article 50(2) TEU. This provision is a further indication, if one were needed, that the decision of the withdrawing State must be taken before notification; the notification starts a clearly defined time limit running, the effects of which can hardly be made to depend on the firmness or otherwise of the notifying State's intention. The suggestion that the notification could unilaterally be revoked if the withdrawing State 'is unable to negotiate acceptable terms for withdrawal and wishes to remain'[82] would not only mean that the notification is not worth the paper it is written on, but would arguably contravene the very wording

[80] Three Knights' Opinion (n 70) para 49(ii).

[81] C Hillion, 'Article 50 TEU: compétence exceptionnelle pour un retrait ordonné' (January 2018) on file with the author.

[82] Three Knights' Opinion (n 70) para 48.

of Article 50(3) TEU. As against this, however, it could be argued that the guillotine of Article 50(3) TEU does not stand in the way of a right of unilateral revocation, as this provision would no longer be applicable where the notification has ceased to exist.

As a last resort, an appeal is sometimes made what is alleged to be common sense. Article 50(5) TEU provides that 'a Member State which has withdrawn from the Union asks to rejoin, its request shall be subject to' the standard accession procedure of Article 49 TEU. It has been argued that, where 'a decision to trigger Article 50 provokes turmoil in a Member State' leading it to change its mind, for example, following a general election,

> it seems ludicrous to hold the State to the commitment to negotiate a withdrawal agreement from the EU and then afford it the opportunity to apply for readmission under Article 49. It is clearly far simpler to allow the withdrawal process to be stopped.[83]

It has also been contended that, while Article 50(5) governs the situation of a Member State which has withdrawn, 'the fact that there is no comparable provision for a Member State that changes its mind prior to withdrawing tends to indicate that no particular formalities apply: such a Member State simply remains within the Union'.[84]

In the first place, the indication that a Member State decides in accordance with its own constitutional requirements before submitting a notification of intention to withdraw presupposes that the consequences of the planned withdrawal, including any possible 'turmoil', have been comprehensively examined, and that the consultation of the electorate on the withdrawal decision, whether by referendum or a general election, has been carried out by the Member State in question in a responsible manner before notification, rather than afterwards. Moreover, the reference to 'constitutional requirements', rather than, say, mere legal requirements or other formalities, a priori betokens a degree of solemnity and decisiveness which would be inconsistent with a provisional or conditional decision.

Second, the message of Article 50 TEU considered as a whole seems to be that actions have consequences; 'decision + notification = withdrawal'. The absence of any provision regulating the possibility of a revocation or defining a procedure for dealing with one could therefore be taken as indicating that no such revocation is possible. Far from being 'ludicrous', the ineluctable character of withdrawal, once the procedure has been triggered, could be seen as a hedge against capricious decision-making by the notifying Member State. It might indeed be 'simpler' for a Member State to be entitled to notify and revoke at will, but there is nothing simple for the Union in the activation and conduct of the withdrawal procedure, which necessarily requires the mobilisation of large amounts of attention and human resources at a time when the Union and its Member States may have other calls on their time and energy. Moreover, the 'ludicrous' view seems to assume that the

[83] P Syrpis, 'What Next? An Analysis of the EU Law Questions Surrounding Article 50 TEU' (University of Bristol, 2016).

[84] Three Knights' Opinion (n 70) para 49(iv).

Member States would in some sense be obliged to welcome the notifying Member State back into the fold should it change its mind, whereas Article 50(5) TEU could be said to be designed expressly to enable the remaining Member States to say 'no' to readmission.

It has further been argued that Article 50 TEU seeks to regulate a voluntary withdrawal and that the Union's holding a Member State which had changed its mind to its original notification 'would be to afford Member States a power of expulsion in respect of an existing Member State as soon as that Member State notified an intention to withdraw'.[85] This does not necessarily follow; expulsion would entail the termination of the membership of the Union of a State which has not expressed any wish to leave the Union, which is not the same as giving effect to the expressed intention of a State voluntarily to withdraw from the Union. In the first case, it is the other Member States which took the initiative to terminate membership; in the latter case, it is the Member State concerned which took the initiative and the Union which took it seriously.

In the same vein, it has been suggested that forcing out a Member State which has had second thoughts would be 'inconsistent with the fundamental principles and aims of the European Union' including the principle of solidarity and the citizenship rights of the withdrawing Member State. Certainly, the Union's action in the framework of the operation of Article 50 TEU must take account of these and other general principles of Union law. It should be recalled, however, that deciding to withdraw from the Union could hardly be more inconsistent with its fundamental principles and aims, and an appeal to such general considerations would not of itself justify allowing the Member State to escape the consequences of its actions.

An intermediate view between the possibility of unilateral revocation and no revocation at all would be revocation with the agreement of the Union and all the Member States. Such a revocation by consensus would have to overcome the terms of Article 50(3) TEU, which appears to provide for only two outcomes to the procedure of Article 50(2) TEU, that is, withdrawal by agreement or withdrawal without an agreement. In this context, it could be argued that if revocation by consent of the other Member States were intended, then Article 50(3) TEU would have provided a procedure and voting rule for such a course, as it did for the possible postponement of the date of withdrawal. Moreover, it could be contended that the acceptance of a revocation by the European Council *à 27* would be tantamount to bypassing these provisions, whereas the Court has long held that 'the Treaty can only be modified by means of the amendment procedure' (now 'procedures') provided therein.[86]

That said, if Article 50 TEU is intended to limit the damage to the interests of the Union which would result from the withdrawal of a Member State, refusing

[85] Demetriou et al (n 78) para 17.
[86] Case 43/75 *Defrenne v SABENA* ECLI:EU:C:1976:56 para 53.

any possibility of revocation even by consensus would run counter to that aim; moreover, if maintaining the stability of international agreements in general is accepted as a valid Union objective,[87] *a fortiori* it should be relevant in the context of Article 50 TEU. Moreover, as noted above, Article 50(3) TEU, which is the main textual support for the view that the United Kingdom may not revoke its notification under any conditions, does not in fact constitute an insuperable legal barrier to revocation, as the application of this provision depends on there being a pending notification Article 50(1) TEU from a withdrawing State, which would no longer be the case.

VII. Conclusions

The outstanding characteristic of the Brexit process is the uncertainty it generates at every level and in every sphere of activity which it touches;[88] it would therefore be premature, if not positively misleading, to come to too definite conclusions on most of the legal issues examined above. Certain matters, such as the duty of the United Kingdom to make financial contributions to the Union budget after and as a result of Brexit, may be resolved at the political level; this postpones rather than resolves the question, particularly should any other Member State decide to quit the Union in the future, or should the terms of Article 50 TEU be reviewed in a later Treaty revision exercise. On other matters, the Court of Justice is already being invited to provide guidance, for example, on the impact of the scheduled withdrawal on the legal situation of citizens and on the revocability of a notification of intention to withdraw. In so doing, the Court will not only have to tackle the deficiencies of Article 50 TEU, but may have to revisit the role of international law in the Union's legal order and indeed, for the greater good of the wider community, interpret certain provisions of international law, including the Vienna Convention on the Law of Treaties.

In due course, barring an improbable revocation of the United Kingdom notification, the Withdrawal Agreement itself will require interpreting, as will any agreement or agreements governing the future relations between the Union and the United Kingdom. Alternatively, should no such agreement(s) be reached, the resulting legal chaos is likely to keep courts in both territories occupied for years to come, wrestling with questions of Union and public international law, as well as large doses of national law. Whatever happens, the European Union and its legal order will never be the same again.

[87] See text to n 77 above.

[88] See also D Phelan, 'Brexit and British Europe, Fexit and Ireland – Complexity and the Nature of Law, Democracy and the Division of Powers, and the Rule of Law' in A Kellerhals and T Baumgartner (eds), *New Dynamics in the European Integration Project – Europe post Brexit* (Zurich, Schulthess, 2018) 19.

9

EU Enlargement, Extra-Territorial Application of EU Law and the International Dimension

CHRISTOPHE HILLION AND VINCENT DELHOMME

I. Introduction

The EU enlargement policy entails several forms of 'extra-territorial application' of EU law – understood here as the application of EU norms beyond the Union's territory[1] – involving distinct interplays between Union law and international law. Thus the *acquis* which candidates for membership must adopt and apply prior to their integration into the Union's legal order does not only comprise EU law *stricto sensu*, it also includes several norms of international law whose compliance the EU requires prior to accession.[2] The specific combination of EU and international norms that the Union thereby projects in the pre-accession context, contrasts with the way in which EU and international norms traditionally interact in EU law, given the entrenched principle of autonomy of the EU legal order.[3] In effect, the EU enlargement policy is deeply embedded in, and potentially contributes to strengthening substantive international law.

[1] On the more general notion of extra-territoriality of EU Law, see eg, J Scott, 'Extraterritoriality and Territorial Extension in EU Law' (2014) 62 *American Journal of Comparative Law* 1, 87; J Scott, 'The New EU "Extraterritoriality"' (2014) 51 *Common Market Law Review* 5, 1343.

[2] Further, see eg, R Petrov, *Exporting the Acquis Communautaire through European Union External Agreements* (Baden-Baden, Nomos, 2011).

[3] See the seminal decision Case 6/64 *Costa v ENEL* ECLI:EU:C:1964:66 and, more recently, Case C-402/05 *Kadi and Al Barakaat International Foundation* ECLI:EU:C:2008:461. Further on the principle of autonomy, see M Klammert, 'The Autonomy of the EU (and of EU Law): Through the Kaleidoscope' (2017) 42 *European Law Review* 6, 815; B de Witte, 'A Selfish Court? The Court of Justice and the Design of International Dispute Settlement beyond the European Union' in M Cremona and A Thies (eds), *The European Court of Justice and External Relations Law: Constitutional Challenges* (Oxford, Hart Publishing, 2014) 33; D Kochenov, 'EU Law without the Rule of Law: Is the Veneration of Autonomy Worth It?' (2015) 34 *Yearbook of European Law* 74; N Nic Shuibhne, 'What is the Autonomy of EU Law and Why Does that Matter?' (2018) *Nordic Journal of International Law* (forthcoming).

That the EU should project its norms, including international law elements, towards a candidate for membership is legally unsurprising. EU law requires it, at least to a certain extent. Yet, this chapter also suggests that several shortcomings impede the effectiveness of this legal mandate, which lay bare inconsistencies in the way the EU relates to international norms.

The chapter is structured as follows: the first part maps out the various expressions of the specific extra-territorial application of EU law in the context of the Union's enlargement. The second part discusses its possible legal and normative underpinnings. In its final part, the chapter points to some of the shortcomings hampering the *raison d'être* of that legal phenomenon.

II. Forms of 'Extra-Territorial Application' of EU Law in the Enlargement Context

The EU enlargement context displays various forms of extra-territorial application of EU law, which this first section outlines. For the purpose of this discussion, the notion of *extra-territorial application* is understood broadly to signify that the EU acquis which candidates have to apply to accede is substantively and normatively more significant than the acquis applicable to the Member States.

A. Projection of EU Acquis beyond EU Territory

The first expression of extra-territorial application of EU law is rather unexceptional and unsurprising. The conditions for accession to the EU, as broadly defined in the so-called Copenhagen criteria, comprise 'the candidate's ability to take on the obligations of membership including adherence to the aims of political, economic and monetary union'.[4] Moreover, the *negotiating frameworks* which the Member States set out at the start of accession negotiations typically underline that 'accession implies the timely and effective implementation of the acquis'.[5] The candidate thus progressively adapts its own norms to EU legal requirements to be able to operate in the Union legal order from the moment of

[4] See European Council, Copenhagen, Conclusions of the Presidency (1993) 13: 'Membership requires that the candidate country has achieved stability of institutions guaranteeing democracy, the rule of law, human rights and respect for and protection of minorities, the existence of a functioning market economy as well as the capacity to cope with competitive pressure and market forces within the Union. Membership presupposes the candidate's ability to take on the obligations of membership including adherence to the aims of political, economic and monetary union.'

[5] See, eg, *Negotiating Framework for Serbia*, 2013 Ministerial meeting opening the Intergovernmental Conference on the Accession of Serbia to the European Union (Brussels, 21 January 2014) CONF-RS 1/14, para 31.

its accession. States aspiring to EU membership must therefore adopt and apply EU law before entry.[6]

Two out of the 35 chapters of the accession negotiations[7] deal specifically with the EU external action acquis: namely, Chapter 30 on external relations and Chapter 31 on foreign, security and defence policy. Both chapters require the candidates' compliance with the relevant binding EU legislation, international agreements and political documents. Any candidate country must commit itself to denounce its own international agreements in areas of EU competence and in turn accept the international commitments of the EU, covering both 'international agreements concluded by the Union, by the Union jointly with its Member States, and those concluded by the MS among themselves with regard to Union activities'.[8]

Any applicant country is also

> required to progressively align its policies towards third countries and its positions within international organisations with the policies and positions adopted by the Union and its Member States[9] […], to progressively align with EU statements, and to apply sanctions and restrictive measures when and where required.[10]

While a potential source of friction for Member States, the obligation to conform to the EU external action acquis may pose a particular challenge for candidate countries whose priorities, prior to their accession, may differ from those of the EU, sometimes even quite significantly.

Serbia is a case in point. Although firmly engaged on the path of EU integration, this country still enjoys a close relationship with the Russian Federation,[11] and does not appear ready to renounce such ties against the promise of EU membership, for instance by joining the current regime of EU sanctions against Russia.[12] 'Clearly, neither the acceleration of EU accession talks, nor the escalating crisis in Ukraine (including Crimea) or the failure of the proposed South Stream pipeline has succeeded in derailing relations between Serbia and Russia.'[13] This political standpoint has been strongly reiterated by Serbia's President since.[14]

[6] This particular form of extra-territorial application of the EU acquis is in principle transitional: it is no longer extra-territorial the moment the candidate becomes a Member State.

[7] To be found at https://ec.europa.eu/neighbourhood-enlargement/policy/conditions-membership/chapters-of-the-acquis_en.

[8] Negotiating Framework for Serbia (n 5) para 31.

[9] Chapter 30 of the acquis.

[10] Chapter 31 of the acquis.

[11] 'Perhaps most importantly from the point of view of Belgrade, Russia has offered political support for Serbia to take a hard position on Kosovo, a stance which Serbia has reciprocated somewhat by refusing to join in with EU sanctions against the Kremlin as a reaction to Russian interference in Ukraine.' European Parliament, *Serbia's Cooperation with China, the European Union, Russia and the United States of America* (Directorate-General for External Policies, 2017) 6.

[12] See Regulation (EU) No 833/2014 of 31 July 2014 concerning restrictive measures in view of Russia's actions destabilising the situation in Ukraine [2014] OJ L229/1–11.

[13] European Parliament (n 11) 6.

[14] G Filipovic and M Savic, 'EU Membership Won't Change Serbian-Russian Ties, Vucic Says' (Bloomberg, 2018), accessed at www.bloomberg.com/news/articles/2018-02-21/eu-membership-won-t-change-serbia-s-ties-with-russia-vucic-says.

The extra-territorial application of EU law in the enlargement context has also taken place on the basis of association agreements such as the Stabilisation and Association Agreements,[15] and the earlier Europe Agreements.[16] These contractual arrangements serve as vehicles to foster the associate state's alignment with the EU acquis, for instance in the field of competition and state aid rules. In the same vein, the Energy Community Treaty and the Transport Community Treaty, negotiated between the EU and the candidates from South-East Europe, envisage the latter's adoption and application of some aspects of the related acquis, prior to accession.[17]

B. Projection of the Acquis beyond the Scope of Application of EU Law

Outside the standard adoption of the acquis by the applicants for membership, enlargement involves a second form of extra-territorial application of EU law, namely the application of EU norms to the candidates *beyond* their scope of application to the Member States, and/or *beyond* their intended normative effects. Two particular examples typify the phenomenon.

First, EU fundamental rights appear to have a broader legal force in the enlargement context than internally vis-à-vis the Member States. Respect for fundamental rights is both an eligibility condition for membership, as expressed by the first Copenhagen criterion[18] and Article 49(1) of the Treaty on European Union (TEU),[19] and an integral part of the EU acquis, contained in a specific chapter on 'judiciary and fundamental rights'[20] which the candidate country

[15] See for instance Title VI of the Stabilisation and Association Agreement between the EU and Serbia: *Stabilisation and Association Agreement between the European Communities and their Member States of the one and the Republic of Serbia*.

[16] See for instance Title V of the Europe Agreement between the then Community and Poland: *Europe Agreement Establishing an Association between the European Communities and their Member States and the Republic of Poland*, and the analysis in M Maresceau and E Lannon (eds), *The EUs Enlargement and Mediterranean Strategies A Comparative Analysis* (New York, Palgrave in association with European Institute, University of Ghent, 2001).

[17] Treaty establishing the Energy Community and Treaty establishing the Transport Community.

[18] 'Membership requires that the candidate country has achieved stability of institutions guaranteeing democracy, the rule of law, human rights and respect for and protection of minorities', European Council (n 4).

[19] Article 49(1) TEU stipulates that 'Any European State which respects the values referred to in Article 2 and is committed to promoting them may apply to become a member of the Union.' Article 2 TEU provides: 'The Union is founded on the values of respect for human dignity, freedom, democracy, equality, the rule of law and respect for human rights, including the rights of persons belonging to minorities. These values are common to the Member States in a society in which pluralism, non-discrimination, tolerance, justice, solidarity and equality between women and men prevail.'

[20] Chapter 23 of the acquis.

must embrace, as a matter of priority.[21] In assessing whether candidates respect the values of Article 2 TEU, including human rights, the Charter of Fundamental Rights of the European Union (CFR) constitutes both a source and yardstick to assess *all* conduct of the candidate. In other words, the Charter is given a wider application in the enlargement context than inside the EU where its applicability to the Member States is limited to situations where the latter implement Union law, in line with Article 51 CFR.[22] While the Court has understood the scope of application of the Charter broadly,[23] this however does not amount to an application extended to all Member States' conduct as in the case of candidate countries.[24]

Second, EU foreign policy appears more developed in the context of enlargement, and more constraining as a result for candidates than for Member States. For example, the EU and its Member States expect Serbia to 'normalise' its relations with Kosovo as a prerequisite for a successful accession negotiation, in a way that comes close, albeit implicitly, to a de facto recognition,[25] even if several Member States have specifically refrained from such a recognition.[26] Thus Serbia's progress towards accession is measured against its

> continued engagement […] towards a visible and sustainable improvement in relations with Kosovo [emphasising that] [t]his process shall ensure that *both can continue on their respective European paths*, while avoiding that either can block the other in these efforts and should gradually lead to the comprehensive normalisation of relations between Serbia and Kosovo, in the form of a legally binding agreement by the end of Serbia's accession negotiations, *with the prospect of both being able to fully exercise their rights and fulfil their responsibilities*.[27]

Not only is the scope of application of EU projected norms broader than internally, related enforcement mechanisms may also be activated more swiftly in the accession process than inside the Union. Hence a candidate's serious and persistent breach of the values contained in Article 2 TEU may lead to the suspension

[21] C Hillion, 'Enlarging the European Union and its Fundamental Rights Protection' in I Govaere et al (eds), *The European Union in the World: Essays in Honour of Professor Marc Maresceau* (Leiden, Martinus Nijhoff, 2014) 562.

[22] According to Article 51(1) of the Charter of Fundamental Rights of the European Union: 'The provisions of this Charter are addressed to the institutions and bodies of the Union with due regard for the principle of subsidiarity and to the Member States only when they are implementing Union law. They shall therefore respect the rights, observe the principles and promote the application thereof in accordance with their respective powers.'

[23] See, eg, Case C-617/10 *Åkerberg Fransson* ECLI:EU:C:2013:105.

[24] On the application of the Charter of Fundamental Rights to candidate states, see E Tanchev, 'Impact of the EU Charter of Fundamental Rights on the Candidate Countries' in A Kellermann, JW de Zwaan and J Czuczai (eds), *EU Enlargement: The Constitutional Impact at EU and National Level* (The Hague, TMC Asser Press, 2001).

[25] C Hillion, 'Adaptation for Autonomy? Candidates for EU Membership and the CFSP' (2017) *Global Affairs* 5.

[26] Namely Romania, Greece, Slovakia, Cyprus and Spain.

[27] Negotiating Framework for Serbia (n 5) para 5 (emphasis added).

of the accession process on a proposal of the Commission and a decision of the Council using qualified majority voting.[28] This procedural arrangement strikingly contrasts with the taxing procedure applicable to Member States pursuant to Article 7(2) TEU, according to which 'the existence of a serious and persistent breach by a Member State of the values referred to in Article 2 [TEU]' has to be determined by the European Council acting by unanimity.[29]

C. Projection of the Acquis beyond EU Law *stricto sensu*

Enlargement entails a third type of extra-territorial application of EU law, involving original interplays with international norms. Thus, the EU invokes and promotes rules that do not pertain to Union law *stricto sensu*, though presented as acquis for the purpose of the pre-accession process. EU accession conditionality typically requires that candidates comply with, and or accede to international conventions to which the EU itself, or even some of its Member States, are not a party.

A case in point is the area of minority protection. The accession conditions enshrined in the Copenhagen criteria, and partly in Article 2 TEU since the Treaty of Lisbon, require that any candidate respect and protect minorities.[30] This has been particularly important in the accession process of Central and Eastern European countries and is still a salient issue for the region of the Western Balkans.[31] Given the limited EU competence in the field, and consequently its limited acquis,[32] the Union has assessed the candidate's fulfilment of the 'minority' criterion by reference to international norms, such as the Framework Convention for the Protection of National Minorities.[33] The candidates' accession to, and compliance with this Convention would thus play a part in fulfilling the condition,[34] although the Convention does not formally belong to

[28] Para 4 of the Negotiation Framework for Serbia (n 5) stipulates: 'In the case of a serious and persistent breach by Serbia of the values on which the Union is founded, the Commission will, on its own initiative or on the request of one third of the Member States, recommend the suspension of negotiations and propose the conditions for eventual resumption. The Council will decide by qualified majority on such a recommendation, after having heard Serbia, whether to suspend the negotiations and on the conditions for their resumption.'

[29] Hungary has thus repeatedly expressed its intention to veto any use of Article 7(2) TEU against Poland in the present row over the latter's alleged breach of the rule of law.

[30] The Copenhagen criteria talks about 'respect for and protection of minorities', while Article 2 TEU sets as a value of the Union the 'respect for human rights, including the rights of persons belonging to minorities'.

[31] See Ministerial meeting opening the Intergovernmental Conference on the Accession, 'EU Opening Statement for Accession Negotiations' (2014) para 14.

[32] See, eg, C Hillion, 'Enlargement of the European Union – The Discrepancy between Membership Obligations and Accession Conditions as Regards the Protection of Minorities' (2004) 27 *Fordham International Law Journal* 726–31.

[33] This Convention is a multilateral treaty of the Council of Europe and counts 39 Member States to date: *Framework Convention for the Protection of National Minorities*.

[34] Further, see eg, C Hillion, 'The Framework Convention for the Protection of National Minorities and the European Union', Conference enhancing the impact of the Framework Convention, 2008, Strasbourg, 4.

EU law: the Union is not a signatory, while some Member States are not even party to it.[35] In other words, the EU accession acquis in this field is broader than what is applicable to Member States: it consists of a body of international norms instrumentalised for the purpose of determining whether a state is fulfilling accession conditions.

The rule of law, and more generally the values of Article 2 TEU and the 'political' Copenhagen criteria, offer other illustrations of the same phenomenon. As was previously mentioned, the relevant part of the acquis is now contained in a specific Chapter 23 on 'judiciary and fundamental rights'. When examining the substance of what is negotiated in the context of that chapter, one finds international conventions and various instruments, eg of the Council of Europe, including non-binding documents which the candidate must nevertheless incorporate in its laws, or at the very least in its practices, for the purpose of meeting the EU accession conditions.

In the case of Serbia, the Commission's screening report on Chapter 23 assesses its situation regarding fundamental rights against several instruments of international law.[36] The instruments mentioned include the European Convention against Torture and Other Cruel, Inhuman or Degrading Treatment or Punishment, as well as the UN Convention against Torture and Other Cruel, Inhuman or Degrading Treatment or Punishment,[37] or the recommendations of the UN Committee on the Elimination of all Forms of Racial Discrimination.[38] In the same vein, the 2013 Commission's Explanatory Screening for Serbia[39] refers as 'legal instruments for reference' regarding the judiciary to recommendations of the Council of Europe[40] or of the UN Human Rights Commission.[41] In doing so, the EU not only broadens the acquis with which candidates are supposed to comply in order to become a Member State, but arguably gives these instruments a stronger normative effect than they normally would have, commensurate to the reward of acceding the EU.

Similarly, association agreements concluded with candidates often 'legalise' extra-EU documents, which then become part of the legal underpinnings of the relation, and thus a condition to accede even though they are not legally binding on the Member States as a matter of EU law.[42]

[35] Belgium, Greece and Luxembourg are signatory states, France has neither signed nor ratified the Convention.

[36] European Commission, 'Screening Report Serbia Chapter 23 – Judiciary and Fundamental Rights' (2014).

[37] ibid 11.

[38] ibid 19.

[39] European Commission, Negotiating Accession to EU, MD 177/13; 24 September 2013.

[40] See, eg, Recommendation CM/Rec(2010)12 of the Committee of Ministers to Member States on Judges: Independence, Efficiency and Responsibilities.

[41] See, eg, 'Bangalore Principles of Judicial Conduct', UN Human Rights Commission, 23 April 2005.

[42] Reference can be made here to Article 2 of the Association Agreements between the EU and Serbia, and with Montenegro, respectively. Similarly drafted, the provision foresees that: 'Respect for democratic principles and human rights as proclaimed in the Universal Declaration of Human Rights and as defined in the Convention for the Protection of Human Rights and Fundamental Freedoms, in the

III. Foundations of Extra-Territorial Application of EU Law in the Enlargement Context

Having identified expressions of the extra-territorial application of EU law in the enlargement context, involving specific interactions between the acquis and international law, the discussion now turns to possible legal explanations underpinning such practices. A glance at the EU Treaties suggests at least three such explanations: first, the EU accession procedure itself (Article 49 TEU), second, the EU foreign and neighbourhood policy objectives (Articles 3(5), 8 and 21 TEU), and third, and more generally, the constitutional mandate of the Union (Articles 3(1) and 13 TEU). Arguably, these are solid, if incomplete, grounds for the active extra-territorial application of EU rules in the context of enlargement.

A. The Accession Rationale

Article 49 TEU requires that the applicant respect and promote the founding values of the EU, as enshrined in Article 2 TEU. Preliminary compliance and commitment to promote these values amounts to an admissibility condition. In addition, the EU accession clause foresees that '[t]he conditions of eligibility agreed upon by the European Council shall be taken into account',[43] thus underscoring the significance of the Copenhagen criteria which, as mentioned earlier, refer to the candidate's ability to take on the EU acquis as a whole. This very notion is a consolidation of a founding principle of EU enlargement: ever since they decided to accept new members in 1969,[44] the founding Member States' position has consistently been that accession presupposes the full acceptance of the acquis.

Seen in this light, a candidate's gradual adoption of the EU acquis *prior* to its accession is uncontroversial. It is fully in line with the Treaty-based procedure, codifying long practice, and which stems from a functional argument: namely to ascertain that the new Member State fully operates in the EU legal order *upon* accession. EU norms are not imposed on those states; their far-reaching normative effect stems from a state's intention to become a member of the EU, and thus to comply with its rules.

Helsinki Final Act and the Charter of Paris for a New Europe, respect for principles of international law, including full cooperation with the International Criminal Tribunal for the former Yugoslavia (ICTY), and the rule of law as well as the principles of market economy as reflected in the Document of the CSCE Bonn Conference on Economic Cooperation, *shall form the basis of the domestic and external policies of the Parties and constitute essential elements of this Agreement*' (emphasis added).

[43] Article 49(1) TEU.

[44] At the Hague Summit of 1969, the Heads of State or Government of the Member States decided to open negotiations with four applicant countries: Denmark, Ireland, Norway and the United Kingdom.

B. The EU External Action Mandate

The extra-territorial application of EU law towards candidates also corresponds to the mandate with which the EU has been endowed vis-à-vis the rest of the world in general, and in relation to neighbouring states, in particular. There is a EU foreign policy rationale behind the extra-territorial application of EU law vis-à-vis candidates for membership, as third states and as neighbours of the EU.

Not only does Article 3(5) TEU require that '[i]n its relations with the wider world, the Union *shall uphold and promote its values and interests*',[45] Article 21 TEU goes further when providing that

> The Union's action on the international scene shall be guided by the principles which have inspired its own creation, development and enlargement, and which it seeks to advance in the wider world: democracy, the rule of law, the universality and indivisibility of human rights and fundamental freedoms, respect for human dignity, the principles of equality and solidarity, and respect for the principles of the United Nations Charter and international law.[46]

It also states that

> The Union shall define and pursue common policies and actions, and shall work for a high degree of cooperation in all fields of international relations, in order to: [...] (b) *consolidate and support democracy, the rule of law, human rights and the principles of international law.*[47]

Both provisions thereby provide a basis for the Union to *project* its values and principles, and those of international law in relation to applicants for membership. Doing otherwise would be surprising, as candidates aspire to be part of the EU and thus to become themselves active promoters of those principles as a member, in accordance with Article 21 TEU, and in line with their duty of sincere cooperation. The projection of norms through EU external action transcends the scope of EU law to encompass international standards to which the EU subscribes, or is committed to promote.

In relation to the neighbouring states more particularly, Article 8 TEU foresees that the EU is to engage with neighbouring states, thus including those European states that could become members, with a view to establishing an area founded on EU values. Here again, the EU finds mandate to project its values and the international norms associated to it beyond its geographical borders.

In sum, reference to international norms in the context of enlargement does find a legal basis too. Enlargement is not only geared towards preparing a candidate to respect the acquis *stricto sensu*, it transforms third European states into

[45] Article 3(5) TEU (emphasis added).
[46] Article 21(1) TEU (emphasis added).
[47] Article 21(2) TEU (emphasis added).

functioning Member States, able to contribute to fulfil the objectives of the EU on the international stage. Enlargement is an EU foreign policy, underpinned by the particular objectives that the Union pursues on the European and world stages.

C. The Constitutional Mandate

The third, and complementary basis for the extra-territorial application of EU law in the context of enlargement can be located in the *general* mandate of the EU, and of its institutions. Under Article 3(1) TEU, 'The Union's aim is to promote peace, its values and the well-being of its people', while Article 13(1) TEU provides that the Union's institutional framework 'shall aim to promote [the] values [of the Union], advance its objectives, serve its interest those of its citizens and those of the Member States, and ensure the consistency, effectiveness and continuity of its policies and actions'. The EU and its institutions are thereby mandated to project the Union's fundamental norms. Article 13(2) TEU bolsters this mandate by establishing an obligation of cooperation among EU institutions, and in turn an obligation to act in conformity with the objectives contained in the Treaties.

Hence EU primary law provides, if only partially, various legal foundations for the different forms of extra-territorial application of EU law. The EU is notably instructed to project its norms and promote international standards vis-à-vis candidates that are destined to become part, as Member States, of that collective promotion effort.

IV. Shortcomings in the Extra-Territorial Application of EU Law Characterising the Enlargement Policy

The extra-territorial application of the EU acquis, as presented earlier, potentially helps the promotion of, and compliance with international norms, in line with EU objectives. Yet such a contribution to hardening international law may be genuine only if the application of EU norms by the candidates is matched by EU backing, and equivalent obligations at the domestic level. In this last part, the chapter briefly sheds light on various deficiencies in these respects.

A. Deficient Interaction between Compliance and Conditionality

Conditionality in the enlargement policy context entails the expectation that once it has adopted and applied the projected EU norms, the candidate may progress on its path to membership.[48] Negotiating frameworks thus typically provide that '[t]he negotiations will be based on [the candidate]'s own merits and the pace will depend on [its] progress in meeting the requirements for membership'.[49]

On this basis, any EU failure to deliver, in the sense of not appropriately rewarding a candidate's genuine progress in its adoption of the EU acquis, potentially damages the effectiveness and acceptance of the extra-territorial application of Union norms. The incentive for candidates to apply EU law prior to accession will diminish if progress in this regard is not matched with similar progress in the accession process. The situation of Macedonia is a case in point.[50]

Conversely, failure to take actions in the face of plain non-compliance with the EU acquis equally undermines the effectiveness of conditionality and of the extra-territorial application of EU norms which it involves. The current EU approach towards Turkey typifies the tension for the EU between the defence of its values and norms in the context of enlargement, and the pursuit of its strategic interests.[51] Violations of fundamental rights and attacks on the rule of law in the country should justify a reaction of the EU Member States, possibly in the form of a suspension of accession talks, a path which the EU has nevertheless refrained from taking – so far. Turkey remains a key partner in the region, particularly in addressing migration.

Such a *realpolitik*-inspired approach considerably hampers the value of the EU's projected norms and undermines the EU enlargement methodology in the eyes of other candidates. This situation is even more paradoxical and damaging, if one considers that all recent adjustments and developments of the enlargement policy point towards stronger conditionality, and in turn additional Member States' opportunities to hold up or stop the process in consideration of non-compliance with accession conditions.[52]

B. Inconsistencies

The second noticeable, and related, shortcoming in the extra-territorial application of EU law is the gap between EU norms as applied to and by candidates on the

[48] Further on conditionality, see, eg, M Maresceau, 'Pre-Accession' in M Cremona, *The Enlargement of the European Union* (Oxford, Oxford University Press, 2003).

[49] Negotiating Framework for Serbia (n 5) para 2.

[50] Macedonia, or the Former Yugoslav Republic of Macedonia (FYROM), was granted candidate status by the Council in 2005. Since then, the Commission has repeatedly recommended opening the negotiations with the country, an initiative vetoed by Greece due to the enduring conflict over the use of the term 'Macedonia'. Further, see, eg, E Fouéré, 'Maintaining Momentum in Enlargement' (CEPS Commentary, 26 April 2018).

[51] See in this regard, Article 3(5) TEU: 'In its relations with the wider world, the Union shall uphold and promote *its values and interests* and contribute to the protection of its citizens', and Article 22 TEU: '*On the basis of the principles and objectives set out in Article 21*, the European Council shall identify *the strategic interests* and objectives of the Union' (emphasis added).

[52] See, eg, C Hillion, 'The Creeping Nationalisation of the EU Enlargement Policy' (2010) *SIEPS Report* 6.

one hand, and norms as applicable and enforceable within the EU, on the other. As suggested above, the EU acquis for the purpose of accession is broader, and subject to swifter enforcement and sanction mechanisms, compared to the applicable EU internal regime.

This differentiation partly rests on the premise that extra-territorial application of EU norms in the pre-accession phase entails irreversible legal adaptation to the requirements of membership. Once admitted to the Union, based on their fulfilment of accession conditions, new Member States thus benefit from the presumption that they respect the values and norms of the Union, as values common to the Member States. On that basis, the broader acquis and the pre-accession enforcement/sanction mechanisms are deemed no longer relevant.

This premise is quite obviously flawed. The disconnection between the EU acquis as applicable to the Member States and the accession acquis is therefore problematic. Not only because of the well-established *double standard* critic that undermines the effectiveness of the whole projection of EU norms,[53] but also because *backsliding* does happen.[54] As the situation in Hungary and Poland epitomises, pre-accession respect for fundamental EU norms may diminish post-accession. Extra-territorial application (ie prior preparation for membership) and compliance with EU norms by the time of accession does not guarantee irreversibility of adaptation, justifying as a more consistent pre and post enforcement approach.[55]

EU internal norms, enforcement mechanisms and ambitions therefore ought to match EU accession norms and enforcement. This would be in line with the requirements of Article 21(1) TEU and its reference to the EU foreign policy as being guided by the principles that have underpinned the Union's creation and enlargement, among which the respect for international law, as well as consistent with the imperative of coherence established by Article 21(3) TEU. It would indeed remedy the paradoxical situation whereby some international norms are less well-enforced within the EU than in the context of accession. While enlargement boosts the effects of international norms, it may also damage their authority if backsliding occurs post-accession.

V. Conclusion

The extra-territorial application of EU law as defined in the first part of the chapter is an essential element of the EU enlargement process. It aims at ensuring the candidates' capacity to function as fully-fledged Member States upon accession,

[53] See, eg, Editorial Comments, 'Fundamental Rights and EU Membership: Do As I Say Not As I Do!' (2012) 49 *Common Market Law Review* 2, 481.

[54] See, eg, the various contributions in C Closa and D Kochenov (eds), *Reinforcing Rule of Law Oversight in the European Union* (Cambridge, Cambridge University Press, 2016).

[55] Hillion (n 21) 569.

and loyal supporters of the EU's aims and action, including on the international stage. As it has been seen, the acquis that candidates must adopt and apply transcends the strict perimeters of EU law as applied internally. This differentiation reflects a holistic notion of EU membership that requires not only compliance with the EU acquis *stricto sensu* as Member, but also the preliminary respect for a broader array of rules and principles that underpin coexistence and mutual trust among Member States.

The inclusion in this exported acquis of international norms that are not applicable to Member States as a matter of EU law can indeed serve a dual purpose: first, it strengthens the values and principles on which the EU is founded and that all aspirant members must respect and second, it supports the EU's commitment towards international law and multilateralism. While the EU has borrowed and instrumentalised international norms for its own purposes, it has also strengthened their normative effect.

Yet, the recurring inconsistencies between the pre-accession conditions and membership obligations impede the very rationale of extra-territoriality. In effect, the extra-territorial application of EU norms serves its purposes only in so far as substantive and institutional coherence between the internal and the external is secured.

10

Law and Practice of the EU's Trade Agreements with 'Disputed' Territories: A Consistent Approach?

GUILLAUME VAN DER LOO

I. Introduction

A specific area where EU law and international law meet is the territorial application of international (trade) agreements concluded by the EU with third countries involving a territory over which the third country does not exercise effective control, or a territory without the sovereignty of the third State in question over that territory being recognised by the EU (hereinafter referred to as 'disputed territories'). This is not a new phenomenon as, for example, the Court of Justice of the European Union (CJEU) had to interpret in the 1990s the territorial application of the Association Agreement (AA) with Cyprus[1] to goods originating from the areas not under the effective control of the Government of the Republic of Cyprus (ie the so-called 'Turkish Republic of Northern Cyprus').[2] However, more recently the territorial application of several international agreements concluded by the EU involving 'disputed' territories has led to legal proceedings before the CJEU, diplomatic tensions with third countries or the adoption of specific EU trade policies or instruments towards these territories. These situations include the application of the EU-Israel AA to the occupied territories of the West Bank and the Gaza Strip, the EU-Morocco AA to the Western Sahara, the EU-Moldova and Georgia AAs to their respective 'frozen conflict' areas and the EU-Ukraine AA to Crimea and Sevastopol.[3] It has to be stressed that the legal status of these different territories is in most

[1] Pre-Treaty of Lisbon agreements concluded by the Community are referred to in this text as agreements concluded by the EU.

[2] Case C-432/92 *Anastasiou and Others* ECLI:EU:C:1994:277.

[3] In this contribution the concept of 'disputed territories' refers only to disputes of a territorial nature concerning non-EU Member States. Therefore, disputes between Member States, for example concerning Gibraltar or the delimitation of Croatian-Slovenian waters, are not covered here.

cases very different under international law, as it will be demonstrated in this contribution.[4] Be that as it may, it remains relevant to analyse and compare the EU's international agreements and trade policies involving these territories. In particular, in the light of the general framework of this volume, this contribution will analyse these cases by focussing on the interaction between EU law and international law. In the case of the EU-Israel AA and the EU-Morocco AA especially, the relation between EU law and international law emerged as the General Court and the Court of Justice (hereinafter: 'the Court') interpreted the territorial application of these EU international agreements through the interpretation and application of international treaty law. The CJEU has employed in many cases the international law of treaties in its judicial reasoning, including references to the provisions of the 1969 Vienna Convention on the Law of Treaties (VCLT). Whereas the CJEU has rejected the application of the VCLT to the Union Treaties,[5] it has applied the provisions of the VCLT to international agreements concluded by the EU, to the extent that these provisions represent customary international law. For instance, the CJEU has relied on the VCLT with regard to general rules of treaty interpretation when defining 'an international agreement' (Article 2(1)(a) VCLT),[6] when examining the scope of the international law obligations that exist during the period before an international agreement enters into force (Article 18 VCLT),[7] or even when terminating an international agreement.[8] However, most cases in which the CJEU applied the law of the treaties concerned the application of general rules of treaty interpretation, codified in Article 31 VCLT. The CJEU has invoked Article 31(1) VCLT numerous times to examine the 'object and purpose' of the agreement,[9] in particular to determine whether to interpret a provision of an agreement in the same manner as a rule under EU law,[10] or even when determining the appropriate legal basis for the conclusion of an agreement under EU law.[11] The CJEU's recent case law on international agreements concluded with third countries involving 'disputed' areas is relevant in this context because in these cases the CJEU has also relied

[4] For an excellent comparative analysis of the EU's trade agreements involving 'occupied' territories, focusing on the legality under international law, see E Kassoti, 'The Legality under International Law of the EU's Trade Agreements Covering Occupied Territories: A Comparative Study of Palestine and Western Sahara' *CLEER Papers* 2017/3.

[5] Joined Cases T-27/03, T-46/03, T-58/03, T-79/03, T-80/03 and T-98/03 *SP SpA et al v Commission* ECLI:EU:T:2007:317 para 58.

[6] Opinion 1/13 (Hague Convention) ECLI:EU:C:2014:2303 para 37.

[7] Case T-115/94 *Opel Austria v Council* ECLI:EU:T:1997:3 para 78; Case T-231/04 *Greece v Commission* ECLI:EU:T:2007:9 para 86.

[8] Case C-162/96 *Racke v Hauptzollamt Mainz* ECLI:EU:C:1998:293.

[9] See for instance C-344/04 *IATA and ELFAA* ECLI:EU:C:2006:10.

[10] For an explicit reference to Art 31 VCLT, see for example Case C-416/96 *Eddline EL-Yassini* ECLI:EU:C:1999:107 para 47. For a reference to this international treaty law principle, but without explicitly referring to the VCLT, see for instance Opinion 1/91 (EEA) and Case C-270/80 *Polydor and Others v Harlequin and Others* ECLI:EU:C:1982:43.

[11] Opinion 2/00 (Cartagena Protocol) ECLI:EU:C:2001:664.

on other elements of treaty interpretation, included in Article 31 VCLT, which are rarely invoked by the CJEU,[12] ie subsequent agreement between the parties regarding the interpretation of the agreement (Article 31(3)(a) VCLT), subsequent practice in the application of the agreement (Article 31(3)(b) VCLT) or any relevant rules of international law applicable in relations between the parties (Article 31(3)(C) VCLT). Moreover, in these cases the CJEU had for the first time recourse to the principle of *pacta tertiis nec nocent nec prosunt* (hereinafter '*pacta tartiis*'), enshrined in Article 34 VCLT, under which a treaty does not create either obligations or rights for a third State without its consent.

By applying the VCLT, the CJEU contributes to the 'strict observance and development of international law' (Article 3(5) TEU). This attributes to the image of the CJEU as an international law friendly, or *völkerrechtsfreundlich*, court.[13] However, since recent landmark cases such as *Kadi* or *Intertanko*, it has been argued that the Court's approach to international law appears to be more 'dualist' in that it restricts the effect of international law within the EU legal order.[14] Moreover, with regard to international treaty law, it has been argued that the Court often deviates from the way in which other courts and bodies have applied the same principles of international treaty law and that the CJEU uses the VCLT in a 'selfish' manner, undermining the development of international law.[15] This contribution therefore aims to analyse and compare the CJEU's 'international treaty law approach' in the recent cases relating to the territorial application of international agreements involving 'disputed' territories. In addition, the specific EU trade policies and instruments adopted by the Union towards these territories will also be analysed and compared.

This contribution will first analyse the international agreements which remain silent with regard to their application in the respective 'disputed' territories, ie the EU-Israel AA and the EU-Morocco AA and its Agricultural Protocol. Only these two agreements have been interpreted by the CJEU. In the case of the latter, both the judgment of the General Court and the Court of Justice will be explored. In addition, the broader policy implications of these cases for the EU-Morocco trade relations are discussed. Finally, the territorial application of the recent AAs concluded with several Eastern Partnership countries are analysed, focussing on the application of the EU-Georgia and EU-Moldova AAs in their respective 'frozen' conflict areas and the EU-Ukraine AA in Crimea and Sevastopol.

[12] PJ Kuijper, 'The Court and the Tribunal of the EC and the Vienna Convention on the Law of Treaties 1969' (1998) 25 *Legal Issues of Economic Integration* 1–23.

[13] For a discussion on this point, see the different contributions in E Cannizzaro, P Palchetti and RA Wessel (eds), *International Law as Law of the European Union* (Leiden/Boston, Martinus Nijhoff Publishers, 2012). On this issue, see also A Rosas, 'With a Little Help from My Friends: International Case-Law as a Source of Reference for EU Courts' (2005) *The Global Community Yearbook of International Law & Jurisprudence* 217–29.

[14] C Eckes, 'International Law as Law of the EU: the Role of the European Court of Justice' in Cannizzaro, Palchetti and Wessel (n 13) 353–78.

[15] J Odermatt, 'The Use of International Treaty Law by the Court of Justice of the European Union' (2015) 17 *Cambridge Yearbook of European Legal Studies* 121–44.

II. The EU-Israel Association Agreement and the Occupied Territories

The territorial application of the EU-Israel AA, and in particular the application of its rules of origin in relation to Israel's occupied territories, has been the subject of disagreement between the EU and Israel for more than a decade.[16] The EU does not recognise Israel's sovereignty over the territories it has occupied since June 1967, namely the Golan Heights, the Gaza Strip and the West Bank and does not consider them to be part of Israel's territory.[17] However, the EU did not insist during the negotiations on its AA with Israel on addressing the non-application of this agreement to these occupied territories in the agreement's territorial application clause. Article 83 of the EU-Israel AA only states that the agreement will apply to the territories in which the Treaties establishing the European Community and the European Coal and Steel Community are applied and 'to the territory of the State of Israel'. Nevertheless, from the very start of the EU-Israel AA, the EU has consistently held that the occupied territories are not covered by the agreement and that products originating in these territories cannot benefit from preferential access to the EU on the basis of the EU-Israel AA.[18] The Commission adopted over the years several notices to inform Member States, economic operators and consumers on this legal situation and to complain about the inadequate cooperation of the Israeli authorities in the framework of the Protocol on Origin to the EU-Israel AA.[19] Moreover, the EU raised this issue during several EU-Israel Association Councils.[20]

In the *Brita* case,[21] the Court finally had the opportunity to clarify the territorial application of the EU-Israel AA. Brita, a German company, imported drink-makers from an Israeli supplier. The German customs authorities refused to give preferential treatment to Brita on the basis of the EU-Israel AA because the Israeli customs authorities failed to conclusively specify the origin of the goods, notably whether or not the goods came from Israeli settlements in the occupied territories.

[16] Euro-Mediterranean Association Agreement establishing an association between the European Communities and their Member States, of the one part, and the State of Israel, of the other part [2000] OJ L147/3.

[17] See for instance Foreign Affairs Council conclusions on the Middle East Peace Process adopted on 12 May 2012, 10 December 2012, 17 November 2014 and 18 January 2016.

[18] See, eg, European Commission, 'Implementation of the Interim Agreement on Trade and Trade-Related matters between the European Community and Israel' SEC(1998) 695 final, 12 December 1998.

[19] Notice to importers – Importations from Israel into the Community, 8 November 1997 [1997] OJ C 388/13; Notice of 23 November 2001 to importers – Imports from Israel into the Community [2001] OJ C 328/6 and Revised Notice to Importers on Imports from Israel into the Community [2005] OJ C20/2.

[20] See, eg, Declaration of the European Union, Second Meeting of the EU-Israel Association Council, 20 November 2001.

[21] Case C-386/08 *Brita GmbH v Hauptzollamt Hamburg-Hafen* ECLI:EU:C:2010:91. For comments on this case, see M Maresceau, 'The Brita Ruling of the European Court of Justice: A Few Comments' in I Govaere, R Quick, M Bronckers (eds), *Trade and Competition Law in the EU and Beyond* (Cheltenham, Edward Elgar Publishing, 2011) 276–89.

In response, Brita brought an action against this decision, and the *Finanzgericht* Hamburg decided to put four preliminary questions to the Court. While in the first and last question the *Finanzgericht* essentially wanted to know whether the customs authorities of the importing Member State may refuse to grant the preferential treatment provided for under the EU-Israel AA if the goods in question originate in the West Bank, the two middle questions related to the verification procedure included in the Protocol to the EU-Israel AA on rules of origin.

The Court confirmed in *Brita* the consistent view of the EU institutions that goods produced in the occupied territories of the West Bank are not covered by the territorial scope of the EU-Israel AA and, therefore, cannot benefit from preferential tariff treatment under this agreement. In order to define the territorial scope of the agreement, the Court relied on international treaty law. In particular, the Court interpreted the territorial application clause of the agreement (ie Article 83) in accordance with the rules of the VCLT. As noted in the introduction, the CJEU has in many cases invoked VCLT rules concerning treaty interpretation, in particular Article 31(1) VCLT concerning the 'object and purpose' of an agreement. However, the Court's approach with regard to Article 31 VCLT in *Brita* was in several ways unprecedented.

First, in *Brita* the Court tried for the first time to clarify why it feels bound to have recourse to these rules. Initially the Court simply argued that these rules were applied as rules of customary international law. But in Brita the Court tries for the first time to explain why these rules are applicable to the EU-Israel AA by focusing on Article 3(b) of the Convention. The Court recognised that the VCLT applies to treaties between States. However, presumably because not only was the EU involved in this case but also another international person that is not a State, ie the Palestinian Authority,[22] the Court underlined Article 3(b) of the VCLT: the fact that the Convention does not apply to international agreements concluded between States and other subjects of international law is not to affect the application to them of any of the rules set forth in that Convention to which they would be subject under international law independently of the Convention. Therefore, the Court concluded that the rules laid down in the VCLT apply to the EU-Israel AA, in so far as they are an expression of general international customary law.[23] Moreover, the Court recalled its settled case law stating that a series of provisions in the VCLT reflect the rules of customary international law which, as such, are binding upon the Community (now Union) institutions and form part of the Community (now Union) legal order.[24]

[22] On this point, see PJ Kuijper, 'Case C-386/08, Brita GmbH v Hauptzollamt Hamburg-Hafen Judgement of the European Court of Justice of 25 February 2010' (2010) 37 *Legal Issues of Economic Integration* 246.

[23] The CJEU confirmed this approach in C-464/13 and C-565/13 *Oberto and O'Leary* ECLI:EU:C:2015:163.

[24] *Brita* (n 21) para 42; *Racke v Hauptzollamt Mainz* (n 8) paras 24, 45 and 46. For references to the VCLT for the purposes of the interpretation of association agreements concluded by the EU, see also *El-Yassini* (n 10) para 47 and Case C-268/99 *Jany and Others* ECLI:EU:C:2001:616 para 35.

The *second* innovative element is that the Court relied on one of the other elements of treaty interpretation included in Article 31 VCLT, ie paragraph (3)(c) of that Article which states that when interpreting an agreement account is to be taken, together with the context, of any relevant rule of international law applicable in the relations between the parties, together with Article 34 VCLT which codifies the *pacta tertiis* principle. The Court argued that the *pacta tertiis* principle is one of the relevant rules of international law applicable to the EU-Israel AA within the meaning of Article 31(3)(c) VCLT.[25] In view of this, the Court concluded that to interpret Article 83 of the EU-Israel AA as meaning that the Israeli customs authorities enjoy competence in respect of products originating in the West Bank would be contrary to the *pacta tertiis* principle, as consolidated in Article 34 of the VCLT, because this would impose an obligation on the Palestinian customs authorities (ie the third party) to refrain from exercising their competences conferred upon them by the EU-PLO AA.[26] Therefore, the Court held that Article 83 of the EU-Israel AA must be interpreted as meaning that products originating in the West Bank do not fall within the territorial scope of the agreement and, as a result, do not qualify for preferential treatment under that agreement. In addition, the Court also made an analogy to *Anastasiou* in which it ruled that the validity of certificates on the proof of origin issued by authorities other than those designated by name in the relevant agreement cannot be accepted.[27]

Thus, in order to determine the territorial scope of the EU-Israel AA (ie Article 83) and to rely on the *pacta tertiis* principle, the Court juxtaposed this agreement to the territorial application of another international agreement to which Israel is not a party, ie the EU-PLO AA. This approach was strongly criticised by international lawyers because the Court used Article 31 VCLT, a rule of treaty interpretation, to have recourse to Article 34 VCLT, a rule about the relative effect of treaties.[28] Moreover, Cannizzaro argued that 'one fails to see how the agreement between the EC and the Palestinian authority can be taken into account in the interpretation of another unrelated agreement between the EC and Israel'.[29]

[25] *Brita* (n 21) paras 43–44.

[26] An Interim Association Agreement on Trade and Cooperation was concluded between the EU and the Palestine Liberation Organisation (PLO) on behalf of the Palestinian Authority in 1997 (for text, see Euro-Mediterranean Interim Association Agreement on trade and cooperation between the European Community, of the one part, and the Palestine Liberation Organization (PLO) for the benefit of the Palestinian Authority of the West Bank and the Gaza Strip, of the other part, [1997] OJ L187, 16 July 1997).

[27] *Anastasiou* (n 2) paras 37–41. In this respect, the Court argued, just like the Advocate General, that the customs authorities of the importing Member State may not make an elective determination, leaving open the question of which agreement should be taken into account, ie the EU-Israel AA or the EU-PLO AA (para 58).

[28] On this point, see Odermatt (n 15) 140.

[29] E Cannizzario, 'A Higher Law for Treaties?' in E Cannizzaro (ed), *The law of Treaties Beyond the Vienna Convention* (Oxford, Oxford University Press, 2011) 432.

It is obvious that the Court relied on another agreement concluded by the EU (ie the EU-PLO Interim AA), and not on the body of international law on Israel's borders (eg the 2004 Advisory Opinion of the International Court of Justice (ICJ) concerning the construction of a wall, the 1995 Israeli-Palestinian Interim Agreement; the Plan for the Partition of Palestine, drawn up by United Nations Special Committee on Palestine (UNSCOP); or relevant UN Security Council Resolutions 242 (1967) and 338 (1973)) in order to avoid dealing with the thorny issue of the Israel-Palestine conflict.[30] It has even been observed that the Court simply relied on the *pacta tertiis* principle (and its *Anastasiou* case law) to touch 'as little as possible on fundamental questions of foreign policy and law' and to avoid discussing one of the most sensitive and debated issues of international law and politics, ie the Israeli-Palestine borders and the legal consequences of the Israeli settlements.[31] This approach is difficult to reconcile with the image of the Court's open attitude towards rules of international law. Only Advocate General Bot relied on the aforementioned body of international law in order to conclude that the West Bank and the Gaza Strip are not covered by the EU-Israel AA.[32]

Despite the Court's ruling, a large number of goods originating in the occupied territories were still labelled as 'made in Israel' and received preferential treatment on the grounds of the EU-Israel AA.[33] In view of this, the Commission adopted in November 2015 a new interpretative Notice. The Commission recalled that when under EU law the indication of origin is mandatory, it must be correct and not misleading (and that enforcement of the relevant rules remains the primary responsibility of Member States). The Notice specifies that 'Made in Israel' used for the products coming from Israeli settlements would mislead the consumers and is inconsistent with existing EU legislation. The Commission provides for some suggestions which could be used instead, such as 'product from the West Bank (Israeli settlement)'.[34] This approach was criticised because it illustrates that

[30] Álvaro de Elera even argued that by following this line of reasoning the Court 'decided to consider that the origin of the competence of Palestinian authorities was neither any kind of sovereignty or jurisdiction exercised by the Palestinian authorities over the Gaza and West bank territories, nor very simply the territorial scope of the EC-PLO agreement, but rather the fact that that agreement conferred certain competences on the PLO authorities' (A de Elera, 'The Frente Polisario Judgments: An Assessment in the Light of the Court of Justice's Case Law on Territorial Disputes' in J Czuczai, F Naert (eds), *The EU as a Global Actor – Bridging Legal Theory and Practice* (Leiden/Boston, Brill/Nijhoff, 2017) 273).

[31] R Holdgaard and O Spiermann, 'Case C-386/08, Brita GmbH v. Hauptzollamt Hamburg-Hafen, Judgment of the Court of Justice (Fourth Chamber) of 25 February 2010' (2011) 48 *Common Market Law Review* 5, 1667–85.

[32] Opinion of Advocate General Bot delivered on 29 October 2009, Case C-386/08 *Brita GmbH v Hauptzollamt Hamburg-Hafen*, paras 109–112.

[33] This practice was also criticised by the European Parliament (European Parliament Resolution of 16 February 2012 on the proposal for a Council decision on the conclusion of the regional Convention on pan-Euro-Mediterranean preferential rules of origin, 2012/2519).

[34] Interpretative Notice on indication of origin of goods from the territories occupied by Israel since June 1967, C(2015) 7834 final, 11 November 2015.

the EU has largely addressed the question of importation of these products as a question of correct labelling for the purpose of ascertaining whether they benefit from preferential treatment under the AA, and not as a question of compliance with international law.[35] This Notice was also strongly condemned by Israel to the point of chilling down diplomatic contacts with the EU.[36]

III. The EU-Morocco Association Agreement and the Western Sahara

A. The General Court's Judgment (Case T-512/12)

The territorial application of the EU-Morocco AA, including the 2010 agreement on agricultural, processed agricultural and fisheries products (hereinafter: 'the Agricultural Protocol'), was also the subject of judicial proceedings before the CJEU and led to diplomatic tensions between the EU and Morocco.[37] In particular, the application of these agreements to the Western Sahara has been a controversial issue. The Western Sahara is recognised as a Non-Self-Governing Territory in accordance with Article 73 of the UN Charter and the right to self-determination for Non-Self-Governing Territories, the Western Sahara in particular, has been

[35] Kassoti argues that short of a total ban on the import of settlement products, the EU's approach to settlement goods is in breach of its international obligation of non-recognition and non-assistance in maintaining a situation created by a serious breach of a peremptory norm of international law within the meaning of Art 42 of the Draft Articles on the Responsibility of International Organisations. In addition, the author holds that, considering the Namibia Advisory Opinion, no economic relations can be maintained with Israel that would contribute to the development of the settlements in the occupied Palestinian territories (see Kassoti (n 4) 28).

[36] Prime Minister Benjamin Netanyahu stated in a press release that 'the EU decision [regarding labelling] is hypocritical and constitutes a double standard; it singles out Israel and not the 200 other conflicts around the world. The EU has decided to label only Israel, and we are not prepared to accept the fact that Europe is labelling the side that is being attacked by terrorism' (Israel Ministry of Foreign Affairs, 'PM Netanyahu's Response to EU Decision Regarding Product Labelling' (11 November 2015)). The Notice was eventually discussed by the High Representative (HR) Mogherini and Prime Minister Netanyahu in February 2016. The HR stressed that 'indication of origin does not constitute a boycott and should in no way be interpreted as such'. The EU and Israel agreed to convene an EU-Israel Association Council at the earliest possible opportunity, however this meeting has still not taken place (EEAS, High Representative/Vice-President Federica Mogherini speaks with Prime Minister of Israel, Benjamin Netanyahu, press release, 12 February 2016).

[37] For the text of these agreements, see respectively Euro-Mediterranean Agreement establishing an association between the European Communities and their Member States, of the one part, and the Kingdom of Morocco, of the other part, [2000] OJ L70/2, 18 March 2000; and Agreement in the form of an Exchange of Letters between the European Union and the Kingdom of Morocco concerning reciprocal liberalisation measures on agricultural products, processed agricultural products, fish and fishery products, the replacement of Protocols 1, 2 and 3 and their Annexes and amendments to the Euro-Mediterranean Agreement establishing an association between the European Communities and their Member States, of the one part, and the Kingdom of Morocco, of the other part [2012] OJ L241, 8 March 2012.

stressed several times by the UN and the International Court of Justice.[38] The largest part of the Western Sahara is still controlled by Morocco, while the Front Polisario (the movement which seeks independence for the Western Sahara) controls the remainder. The EU and its Member States have never recognised, *de facto* or *de jure*, Moroccan sovereignty over Western Sahara. Similar to the EU-Israel AA, this issue is not addressed in the EU-Morocco AA or its subsequent protocols. Article 94 of the AA merely states that the agreement applies to the Kingdom of Morocco, without specifically precluding the application of the agreement to the Western Sahara. However, the key difference with the application of the EU-Israeli AA, described above, is that the EU *de facto* applies the EU-Morocco AA to the Western Sahara.[39] For example, the Commission's Food and Veterinary Office made a number of inspection visits to the Western Sahara; 140 approved exporters under the AA were located in the Western Sahara and the Commission and the Council have reluctantly admitted in proceedings before the CJEU that the agreement is *de facto* applied to the Western Sahara.[40] The Commission also stated that the 2006 EU-Morocco Fisheries Partnership Agreement (FPA) and its Protocol from 2013 apply to the Western Sahara waters.[41] However, the Council

[38] See, eg, UN General Assembly Resolution 34/37 of 21 November 1979 on the Question of the Western Sahara and the Advisory Opinion of the International Court of Justice of 16 October 1975 on the Western Sahara.

[39] It has to be noted that, contrary to the EU, Norway has stated that the EFTA-Morocco FTA is not applicable to the Western Sahara since the Western Sahara is not part of Morocco's territory (see reply given by the Norwegian Minister for Foreign Affairs to a parliamentary question (11/05/2010)). Also the US does interpret its FTA with Morocco as not including the Western Sahara because 'the United States and many other countries do not recognise Moroccan sovereignty over Western Sahara' (see the letter from the US Trade Representative R Zoellick to Rep J Pitts, 22/07/2004, 150 Cong Rec H667).

[40] On these points, see the Opinion of AG Wathelet delivered in Case C-104/16 *Council v Front Polisario* ECLI:EU:C:2016:667 paras 63–100 and Case T-512/12 *Front Polisario v Council* ECLI:EU:T:2015:953, paras 74–82.

[41] The 2006 EU-Morocco FPA applied to 'waters falling within the sovereignty or jurisdiction of Morocco' (Art 2(a) of the FPA ([2006] OJ L141/9)). However, the Commission acknowledged that fishing by EU vessel has taken place in the Waters of Western Sahara (Reply from European Commissioner Ferrero-Waldner to Written question E-4425/08, 12 September 2008). The European Parliament refused to renew the protocol in 2011 because of, inter alia, doubts regarding its compatibility with international law since it was not clear whether the agreement benefited the population of the Western Sahara (European Parliament Resolution of 14 December 2011 (2011/2949)). The European Parliament eventually approved the new Fisheries Protocol negotiated and signed in 2013 (for text, see Protocol between the European Union and the Kingdom of Morocco setting out the fishing opportunities and financial contribution provided for in the Fisheries Partnership Agreement between the European Union and the Kingdom of Morocco [2013] OJ L328/1, 7 December 2013). Also this agreement applies 'to waters falling within the sovereignty or jurisdiction of Morocco' and the Commission has clarified that the Western Sahara waters are included in the new Protocol and that this is compatible with international law (Answer given by Ms Damanaki on behalf of the Commission to Written Question E-007185/2013, 17 September 2013). The Parliament's legal service argued, mainly on the basis of the 2002 Opinion issued by the UN Under-Secretary General for Legal Affairs and Legal Counsel (the Corell Opinion), that Morocco, as a 'de facto administering power', is responsible for the economic development of the Western Sahara and that the Protocol is compatible with international law as long as 'a certain amount of the financial contribution [granted by the EU] is allocated by Morocco to the benefit of Western Sahara population' (Legal Service of the European Parliament,

added that this *de facto* application should not be seen as recognition of Morocco's sovereignty over the Western Sahara.[42]

In a remarkable judgment delivered on 10 December 2015, brought by the Front Polisario in an action for annulment of the Council decision concluding the Agricultural Protocol, the General Court annulled the decision at issue, in so far as it approves the application of the agricultural agreement to the Western Sahara.[43] After having attributed to the Front Polisario the status of 'legal person' in the sense of Article 263 of the Treaty on the Functioning of the European Union (TFEU), the General Court analysed whether the Front Polisario was 'directly and individually concerned' by the contested act. The General Court required for this a preliminary determination whether or not the Agricultural Protocol applied to the territory of the Western Sahara.[44] The General Court's judicial reasoning with regard to the territorial scope of the agreement and international treaty law was different from the Court's reasoning in *Brita*.

In order to define the territorial scope of the agreement, the General Court repeated the Court's reasoning in *Brita* and previous cases that the rules laid down in the VCLT apply to agreements concluded by the EU in so far as they are an expression of customary international law.[45] Therefore, the General Court argued that the Agricultural Protocol needs to be interpreted in accordance with Article 31 VCLT. However, by contrast, the General Court essentially held that the general principle of international law of the relative effect of treaties, of which Article 34 VCLT is a particular expression, was not relevant for the interpretation of the Agricultural Protocol with Morocco because the particular circumstances in this case are different from those in the *Brita* case. The General Court held that the *pacta tertiis* principle was not relevant in this context because the EU has not concluded a comparable agreement covering products originating in the Western Sahara with the Front Polisario, or with any State or other

Legal Opinion: Protocol between the European Union and the Kingdom of Morocco setting out the fishing opportunities and financial contribution provided for in the fisheries Partnership Agreement in force between the two parties, SJ-0665/13, D(2013)50041, 04 November 2013, para 29). For a more detailed analysis on this issue, see Kassoti (n 4) 38.

[42] For, eg, during the hearings of Case T-512/12, the Council stated that the EU and Morocco 'agree to disagree[:] they have a mutual understanding that the European Union accepts the application of the agreement to the territory of Western Sahara and Morocco does not use this as an argument in support of its claim to sovereignty […]' (quoted in the Opinion of AG Wathelet (n 40)).

[43] *Front Polisario v Council* (n 40). It has to be noted that this 'partial annulment' seems to be at odds with the case law of the CJEU which states that the partial annulment of an EU act is possible 'only in so far as the elements whose annulment is sought may be severed from the remainder of the act' (Case C-425/13 *Commission v Council* ECLI:EU:C:2015:483 para 94). Considering that neither the Council decision nor the agreement itself refer to the territorial application to the Western Sahara, it remains unclear how this decision could be partially annulled.

[44] For a critique on the General Court's conclusion that the Front Polisario should be considered a legal person within the meaning of Art 263 TFEU and the General Court's assumption that the Front Polisario is 'directly and individually concerned' only in the case where the agreements itself is applied to the territory of the Western Sahara, see De Elera (n 30) 275–78.

[45] *Front Polisario v Council* (n 40) paras 90–93.

entity (analogous to the EU-PLO Agreement in the *Brita* case).[46] Thus, similar to the Court's reasoning in *Brita*, the General Court actually also aimed to rely on another international agreement concluded by the EU (and not the body of international law with regard to the status of the Western Sahara) to invoke the *pacta tertiis* principle.

But next, the General Court recalled that the agreement needs to be interpreted in accordance with Article 31 VCLT. In particular, the General Court held that 'in accordance with that article, account must be taken in particular of the context in which an international treaty appears' and that the elements of the *de facto* application of the agreement in the Western Sahara (described above), are part of that context.[47] According to the General Court, the EU was well aware that Morocco considers the Western Sahara as an integral part of its territory and that the Council and the Commission accepted that Morocco *de facto* applies the AA in that territory. Because the EU did not oppose this application, for example in Article 94 of the AA or in the Agricultural Protocol, the General Court argued that the EU accepted, at least implicitly, that the AA and the Agricultural Protocol encompass the Western Sahara. Taking into account this specific 'context', the General Court concluded that the agreement also applies to the territory of the Western Sahara and, therefore, granted Front Polisario legal standing. The General Court did not however specify which paragraph or which specific element of treaty interpretation of Article 31 VCLT it was relying on. Because the General Court referred several times to the 'context' of the agreement, it was most likely referring to Article 31(2) VCLT. However, if this was the case, the Court failed to clearly identify, pursuant to Article 31(2)(a) and (b) VCLT, an agreement or an instrument that was accepted by both parties in which they confirm that the AA applies to the Western Sahara.[48] Because the General Court stressed that the *de facto* application of the agreement in the Western Sahara is a part of that context, it could also be, as observed by the Court in the appeal judgment and Advocate General Whathelet, that it was relying on the 'subsequent practice' rule enshrined in Article 31(3)(b) VCLT. However, this would also constitute an incorrect reading of Article 31 VCLT as a 'subsequent practice' is something which needs to be taken into account 'together with the context' of an agreement, but which is not an element of this context. Moreover, the General Court also did not analyse whether the *de facto* application constitutes the existence of an agreement between the parties to amend the interpretation of Article 94 of the AA, although this is required by Article 31(3)(b) VCLT.[49] Moreover, the CJEU has been reluctant to take into account 'subsequent practice' when interpreting

[46] *Front Polisario v Council* (n 40) para 96.

[47] *Front Polisario v Council* (n 40) para 99.

[48] It is unlikely that the Agricultural Protocol can be considered as a relevant agreement in the meaning of Art 31(2)(a) VCLT because this Protocol only replaced a selected list of trade-related provisions of the AA and did not cover institutional provisions such as Art 94 of the AA.

[49] This was also noted by the CJEU in the appeal judgment (para 122).

international agreements.[50] In *Anastasiou* the Court considered, but rejected, this treaty law principle. The Court held in this case that the *de facto* acceptance of certificates issued by the Turkish Republic of Northern Cyprus did not amount to such subsequent practice as this did not warrant a departure from the clear, precise and unconditional provisions of the 1977 Protocol.[51] However, in a more recent case concerning the interpretation of the Convention defining the Statute of the European Schools, the Court accepted that the case law of the Complaints Board of the European Schools should be considered to be a subsequent practice in the application of that Convention in the meaning of Article 31(3)(b) VCLT.[52] Kuijper also noted a specific problem relating to the 'subsequent practice' rule, ie that only open and official practice can be recognised; 'hidden practice which cannot stand the light of day is not good enough to contribute to subsequent practice'.[53] This consideration is relevant in the context of the EU-Morocco AA. Although the Commission and Council did not actively hide the application of the AA to the Western Sahara, it is clear that they were not very enthusiastic to acknowledge and communicate about this practice.

With regard to the substance of the case, the General Court dismissed all 11 pleas of Front Polisario. In reality, all the pleas in law in the application concerned the question as to whether there is an absolute prohibition against concluding an international agreement on behalf of the EU which may be applied to a territory in fact controlled by a non-member State, without the sovereignty of that State over that territory being recognised by the EU or, more generally, by all other States.[54] Recognising that the EU institutions enjoy a wide discretion in the field of economic relations,[55] the General Court rejected each of the pleas as none of them made it possible to establish, under EU law or international law, the existence of an absolute prohibition for the EU to conclude an agreement with a third State capable of being applied to a disputed territory.[56] According to the General Court, the EU institutions enjoy a wide discretion as regards whether it is appropriate to conclude an agreement with a third country which will be applied to a disputed territory. However, because the EU institutions enjoy a wide discretion in such a situation, the General Court held that it must verify whether the institutions have examined 'carefully and impartially' all the relevant facts of the individual case, facts which support the conclusions reached.[57] The General Court

[50] The Court has also rejected the notion that 'subsequent practice' is of relevance when interpreting EU primary law (*France v Commission* ECLI:EU:C:1994:305 para 36).

[51] *Anastasiou* (n 2).

[52] *Oberto and O'Leary* (n 23).

[53] Kuijper (n 12) 9.

[54] *Front Polisario v Council* (n 40) para 117.

[55] See, eg, T-572/93 *Odigitria v Council and Commission* ECLI:EU:T:1995:131 para 38.

[56] *Front Polisario v Council* (n 40) paras 214–16 and 220. The fact that the General Court rejected the 11 pleas in law to then transform a plea of lack of motivation into an additional plea of manifest error of assessment was critised by De Elera (n 30) 282.

[57] C-269/90 *Technische Universität München* ECLI:EU:C:1991:438 para 14; C-77/09 *Comércio Internacional e Servios* ECLI:EU:C:2010:803 para 57.

concluded in this case that the Council failed to examine, carefully and impartially, all the relevant facts in order to ensure that the production of goods for export is not conducted to the detriment of the population of the Western Sahara, or entails infringements of fundamental rights.[58] Thus, the General Court ruled that the EU is under an obligation to ensure that its (trade) agreements do not 'indirectly encourage' an infringement of fundamental rights of non-EU nationals in a non-EU territory, or that the EU 'benefits from them'.[59] Therefore, the General Court concluded that the Council decision concluding the Agricultural Protocol had to be annulled in so far as it approves the application of the agreement to the Western Sahara.

The judgment of the General Court irritated the Moroccan Government and four days after this judgment, during the EU-Morocco Association Council, the EU and Morocco discussed the consequences of the case.[60] On the same day of this meeting, the Council decided to lodge an appeal against this judgment. Despite this legal reaction of the Council, the Moroccan Government issued a press release in February 2016 in which it 'rejected totally the judgment' and 'denounced its political character its unfounded arguments, its biased reasoning and its conclusion contrary to international law' and suspended all contact with the EU institutions.[61]

B. The Court's Judgment (Case C-104/16)

In its appeal judgment, the Court (Grand Chamber) quashed the judgment of the General Court and ruled that the Agricultural Protocol and the AA do not apply to the territory of the Western Sahara.[62] Similar to the General Court, the Court interpreted the territorial application of the EU-Morocco AA and the Agricultural Protocol by relying on Article 31 VCLT. However, the Court argued that the General Court was not only bound by Article 31(1) VCLT, but also by the rules laid down in Article 31(3)(c) pursuant to which the interpretation of a treaty must be carried out by taking account of any relevant rules of international law applicable in the relations between the parties.[63] The Court identified three relevant rules of international law applicable to the EU-Morocco AA that determine how the territorial scope of this agreement needs to be interpreted: the principle of self-determination, Article 29 VCLT ('Territorial Scope of Treaties') and the principle of the relative effect of treaties (ie the *pacta tertiis* principle).

[58] *Front Polisario v Council* (n 40) para 228.
[59] *Front Polisario v Council* (n 40) para 231.
[60] EU-Morocco Association Council, 14 December 2015.
[61] Déclaration de M le ministre de la Communication Porte-Parole du Gouvernement au sujet de l'évolution des relations entre le Royaume du Maroc et l'Union européenne, 25 February 2016.
[62] Case C-104/16 *Council v Front Polisario* ECLI:EU:C:2016:973.
[63] ibid para 86. To that effect, see also *Brita* (n 21) para 43; C-402/05 and C-415/05 *Kadi and Al Barakaat International Foundation v Council and Commission* ECLI:EU:C:2008:461 para 291.

For the principle of self-determination, the Court noted that this customary principle of international law is a rule of international law applicable to the EU-Morocco relations by relying on Article 1 of the UN Charter and, in particular, the relevant UN General Assembly Resolutions and the Advisory Opinion of the ICJ on the Western Sahara. The ICJ stated in this Opinion that the principle of self-determination is applicable to all non-self-governing territories and to all peoples who have not yet achieved independence. Moreover, the Court recalled that UN General Assembly Resolution 2625, referred to in the ICJ Opinion, specifies that 'the territory of a colony or other Non-Self-Governing Territory has, under the UN Charter, a […] separate and distinct [status]'.[64] In view of this 'separate and distinct status' accorded to the territory of the Western Sahara by virtue of the principle of self-determination, the Court came to the conclusion that 'the territory of the Kingdom of Morocco' set out in Article 94 of the EU-Morocco AA cannot be interpreted as including the Western Sahara. The Court also argued that the Article 29 VCLT precluded the Western Sahara from being included in within the territorial scope of the agreement and that the General Court incorrectly assumed that, in so far as the Council and the Commission were aware of the position of Morocco that the AA might apply to the Western Sahara, those institutions had tacitly accepted that position.

In relation to the international law principle of the relative effect of treaties (the *pacta tertiis* principle codified in Article 34 VCLT), the Court held, contrary to the General Court, that this principle has to be taken into account because there is a 'third party' affected by the EU-Morocco AA. The Court confirmed that due to the distinct and separate status that the ICJ and several UN Resolutions granted to the Western Sahara, based on the principle of self-determination, the people of the Western Sahara must be treated as a 'third party' within the meaning of the *pacta tertiis* principle. Because the people of the Western Sahara did not express any such consent, the Court concludes that the AA cannot be interpreted to include the Western Sahara.[65]

The Court's approach to treaty interpretation in this case deserves some comment. First, the CJEU held that the fact that the EU and Morocco *de facto* apply the agreement to the Western Sahara is no sufficient evidence of a 'subsequent practice' within the meaning of 31(3)(b) VCLT. The Court correctly held that the General Court did not analyse whether the *de facto* application of the agreement in the Western Sahara constitutes an agreement between the parties to amend the interpretation of Article 94 of the AA, as required by Article 31(3)(b) VCLT.[66] Advocate General Wathelet also argued that this *de facto* application cannot constitute a 'subsequent practice' within the meaning of Article 31(3)(b) because it is no sufficient proof of an 'indisputable concordance between the

[64] *Council v Front Polisario* (n 62) para 90.
[65] *Council v Front Polisario* (n 62) paras 104–07.
[66] *Council v Front Polisario* (n 62) para 122.

positions of the parties such as to establish the meaning of a treaty provision'.[67] Moreover, the Advocate General holds that 'subsequent practice' cannot override the clear terms of a treaty 'unless it constitutes a practice, which is known to and accepted by the parties and is sufficiently widespread and sufficiently long term to constitute a new agreement in itself'.[68] Significantly, the Court's reasoning to reject the 'subsequent practice' rule was rather vague. The Court holds that a purported intention of the EU to apply the agreement to the Western Sahara would imply that the EU intends to implement the agreements incompatible with the principles of self-determination and of the relative effect of the treaties, even though the EU repeatedly expressed the need to comply with these principles. The Court continues that this interpretation would be incompatible with the general international treaty law principle that treaty obligations must be performed in good faith (Article 31(1) VCLT).[69] Thus, the reasoning of the Court is based on the remarkable assumption that it is unthinkable that the EU would not act in good faith or contrary to international law.

The Court was also creative in interpreting and applying international treaty law by extending the *pacta tertiis* principle to non-State actors, as it had done before in *Brita*, and by assuming that the legal status of non-self-governing territories (as entities separate and distinct from the States administering them) also implies that these entities enjoy territorial sovereignty over that territory.[70] With regard to the latter, it has been argued that sovereignty remains with the administering State.[71] For example, in its Advisory Opinion on Western Sahara, the ICJ clarified that the future status of the non-self-governing territory did not relate to 'existing territorial rights or sovereignty over the territory'.

Because the Agricultural Protocol does not apply to the Western Sahara, the Court concluded that Front Polisario could not be directly and individually concerned – and had therefore no legal standing – and set aside the judgment of the General Court.

In sum, the Court's reliance on international law in *Front Polisario* was, similar to its approach in *Brita*, selective. Again, in an attempt to circumvent a politically sensitive issue, 'the Court used selectively international rules on treaty interpretation to limit the legal applicability of the EU-Morocco agreements to the latter's

[67] Advocate General Wathelet was more critical on the Council's 'application without recognition'. He criticised the Council's 'contradictory approach to de facto applying an agreement with a third country in a territory without recognising that that country has any legal competence or authority in that territory'. For the Advocate General 'applicability necessarily and inevitably implies recognition' (n 40) para 86.

[68] ibid paras 96–100. The Advocate General also criticised the Court's broad interpretation of the ICJ's reading of 'subsequent practice' in *Case concerning the Temple of Preah Vihear (Cambodia v Thailand)*, judgment of 15 June 1962, ICJ Reports 1962. In *Oberto and O'Leary* (n 23), the Court argued that the ICJ held in this case that 'the subsequent practice followed in the application of a treaty may override the clear terms of that treaty if that practice reflects the parties' agreement'.

[69] *Council v Front Polisario* (n 62) para 124.

[70] On this point see, Kassoti (n 4) 44.

[71] J Crawford, *Creation of States in International Law* (Oxford, Clarendon Press, 2006) 613.

territory, while stopping short of addressing the de facto application of the agreements to Western Sahara'.[72] One can also identify a paradox in the reasoning of the Court in relation to the *pacta tartiis* principle. On the basis of this international law principle the Court comes to the conclusion that the Agricultural Protocol cannot apply to the Western Sahara, although it is aware that the agreement is *de facto* applied in that territory. However, as a 'third party' within the meaning of Article 34 VCLT, Front Polisario, or the people of the Western Sahara, cannot rely on this international law principle before the Court in order to challenge this *de facto* application, as the Court uses the *pacta tertiis* principle to deny that third party legal standing. Thus, Front Polisario cannot challenge the *de facto* application of the agreement in the territory of the Western Sahara because *de iure* this didn't happen.

C. The Policy Implications of the 'Polisario Saga'

Because Front Polisario's action for annulment was dismissed by the Court, the reaction of the Moroccan Government was more positive compared to its suspension of diplomatic relations after the judgment of the General Court. Nevertheless, the judgment undermined Morocco's long-standing territorial claim over the Western Sahara. The High Representative Mogherini and the Moroccan Minister of Foreign Affairs adopted a joint statement which mentions that they 'took note' of the Court's judgment and that they would 'work together on any issue relating to its application in the spirit of the EU-Morocco privileged partnership'.[73] Also Front Polisario was not dissatisfied with the outcome of this judgment because the Court ruled that the Western Sahara is not covered by the agreement. This implies that the EU will need to terminate the *de facto* application of the agreement to the Western Sahara and the granting of preferential treatment to products originating in that territory on the basis of that agreement. Also the Council could not have been unhappy with this judgment as the Court upheld the appeal of the Council and set aside the ruling of the General Court. However, whereas the Court agreed with the Council that the *de facto* application of the agreement does not imply that the Western Sahara is covered by the territorial scope of the agreement, it rejected the Council's assertation that the agreement can nevertheless be *de facto* applied to the Western Sahara.

Meanwhile the Commission has provided guideliness to the customs authorities of the Member States on the implications of the ruling of the CJEU.

[72] Kassoti (n 4) 45.

[73] 'Déclaration conjointe par Federica Mogherini et le Ministre des Affaires étrangères et de la coopération du royaume du Maroc Salahddine Mezouar', 21 December 2016. In another joint statement adopted in February 2017, both the EU and Morocco reconfirmed their 'key' partnership and stated that technical working groups will convene to discuss the next steps of their important trade relationship (Déclaration conjointe de Federica Mogherini et le Ministre délégué aux Affaires étrangères du Royaume de Maroc, Nasser Bourita suite à leur rencontre, 7 February 2017).

The Commission specified in particular that, 'in case of reasonable questions regarding the origin of goods', customs authorities should make inquiries in accordance with the arrangements for administrative cooperation laid down in a protocol to the EU-Morocco AA.[74] Indeed, the termination of the *de facto* application has not the effect of a trade ban, as products originating in the Western Sahara can still be imported into the EU (but without benefitting from the preferential treatment under the Agricultural Protocol). With regard to imports prior to the date of the judgment of the CJEU, the Commission has informed the Member States' customs authorities that, 'taking into account the exceptional factual circumstances of the case as detailed in the Court ruling', it is not justified to recover the relevant amounts of duty from the importing companies.[75] As a consequence, the national customs authorities should not initiate recovery proceedings for imports of Western Sahara products which occurred before 22 December 2016.

The Commission is also working on the best way to follow up on the Court's ruling, 'taking into account the long-standing EU-Morocco partnership as well as the interests of the people of Western Sahara, and with a view to preserving trade exchanges in a context of legal certainty'.[76]

To that end, the Commission submitted on 19 April 2017 to the Council a Recommendation for a Council Decision authorising the opening of negotiations on the adaptation of protocols to the EU-Morocco AA, and draft Directives for the negotiation of an agreement between the EU and Morocco. The Council authorised the Commission on 29 May 2017 to negotiate an agreement on the adaptations of protocols to the EU-Morocco AA. Presumably the EU will try to include a territorial application clause explicitly excluding the application to the Western Sahara, although this would be difficult for Morocco to accept. In any case, in a meeting between HR Federica Mogherini and the Minister of Foreign Affairs of Morocco on 23 October 2017, both parties expressed 'their joint determination to complete the negotiations as soon as possible'.[77] Several other (pending) cases before the Union Courts concerning the Western Sahara could further complicate these negotiations. The first case is a preliminary ruling procedure submitted by the High Court of Justice of England and Wales concerning the interpretation and validity of the EU-Morocco AA and the Fisheries Partnership Agreement,[78]

[74] Answer given by Mr Moscovici on behalf of the Commission, E-002035/2017, 20 July 2017.

[75] Joint answer given by Mr Moscovici on behalf of the Commission to Written questions, E-003092/17, E-001582/17, E-003026/17, 11 September 2017.

[76] Answer given by Vice-President Mogherini on behalf of the Commission, EN E-005404/2017, 22 November 2017. See also Recommendation for a Council Decision authorising the opening of negotiations on the adaptation of protocols to the Agreement between the European Union and the Kingdom of Morocco (General Secretariat of the Council, 29 May 2017, 9094/1/17).

[77] Meeting between HR/VP Federica Mogherini and HE Mr Nasser Bourita, the Minister of Foreign Affairs of the Kingdom of Morocco, press release of the EU Delegation to Morocco, 23 October 2017.

[78] On 27 February 2018 the Court delivered its judgment in Case C-266/16 *Western Sahara Campaign UK* ECLI:EU:C:2018:118. In line with its reasoning in *Council v Front Polisario*, the Court argued that the (waters adjacent to the) territory of Western Sahara is not included within the scope of the Fisheries

the second case concerns Polisario's request for an annulment of the Council decision to conclude the EU-Morocco Fisheries Protocol.[79]

One can argue that products originating in the Western Sahara which require under EU legislation an indication of origin should, similar to products from the Israeli occupied territories, be labelled as 'product from the Western Sahara' (instead of Morocco), as advocated, for example, by several Members of the European Parliament (MEPs).[80] The EU has indeed been criticised for applying double-standards because it has introduced specific labelling requirements for products originating from the occupied Palestinian territories, but not for products originating from the Western Sahara.[81] In response to this critique, the Commission just stressed the different legal situation of these two cases, while remaining silent on the issue of labelling.[82] In its answers to several parliamentary questions, the Commission dodged this thorny issue and has argued that 'neither the Association Agreement, nor the Agriculture Agreement foresees any specific rules regarding requirements as to the labelling of products' and that 'products originating in Morocco and imported into the Union can thus not be differentiated on a territorial basis'.[83] This is a remarkable argument because the lack of such a requirement in the EU-Morocco AA or the Agricultural Protocol is irrelevant for the adoption of an Interpretative Notice on indication of origin of goods. For example, the 2015 Notice on indication of origin of goods from the occupied territories (see above) was not foreseen in the EU-Israel AA. In this Notice, the Commission merely summarised and clarified exiting EU legislation according to which the indication of the origin of a product must be correct and not misleading for the consumer (both in the case when Union legislation requires the indication of origin or when it is provided on a voluntary basis). In addition, as noted

Agreement or the associated Protocols as this would be contrary to the UN Convention on the Law of the Sea and certain rules of general international law applicable between the EU and Morocco, including the principle of self-determination and the *pacta tertiis* principle. This case could not be properly analysed in time before this publication went to print. However, for a brief analysis, including on the policy implications of these different cases, see G Van der Loo, 'The Dilemma of the EU's Future Trade Relations with Western Sahara: Caught between Strategic Interests and International Law?' (CEPS Commentary, 18 April 2018).

[79] Case T-180/14 *Front Polisario v Council* ECLI:EU:T:2018:496. In April 2018 Front Polisario also brought an action for annulment against Council Decision (EU) 2018/146 of 22 January 2018 on the conclusion, on behalf of the Union, of the Euro-Mediterranean Aviation Agreement between the European Community and its Member States, of the one part, and the Kingdom of Morocco, of the other part [2018] OJ L26/4 (Case T-275/18 *Front Polisario v Council* (pending).

[80] See, eg, Question for written answer to the Commission, P-001023/2011, 18 February 2011; Question for written answer to the Commission, B Lange (S&D), Subject: Labelling of Goods from Western Sahara, E-007130-14, 24 September 2014.

[81] See, eg, the question of MEP Fiorello Provera to the Commission, E-000235-14, 10 January 2014.

[82] See answer given by High Representative/Vice-President on behalf of the Commission to questions, E-000235/2014, 13 March 2014; E-015222/15 and E-015472/15, 4 February 2016.

[83] Answer given by Mr Cioloş on behalf of the Commission, E-003971/2013, 11 June 2013; Answer given by Vice-President Mogherini on behalf of the Commission, E-007130/2014, 27 January 2015; Joint answer given by High Representative/Vice-President Ashton on behalf of the Commission to E-001004/11, P-001023/11, E-002315/11, 14 June 2011.

above, the Commission argued that 'Made in Israel' used for the products coming from Israeli settlements would mislead the consumers and therefore provided some alternative suggestions which could be used instead, such as 'product from the West Bank (Israeli settlement)'.[84] It is hard to see why the indication 'Made in Israel' for products originating in the occupied territories would be misleading in the sense of the relevant EU legislation, and the indication 'Made in Morocco' for products originating in the Western Sahara, particularly now the Court has made it clear that the EU-Morocco AA does not cover the Western Sahara. Therefore, in order the ensure that the relevant EU legislation is correctly applied (ie not misleading for consumers), and to create clarity for consumers, economic operators and the Member States (who have to enforce these rules), the Commission should adopt an Interpretative Notice stating that the indication 'product from Morocco' for products originating in the Western Sahara is incorrect under EU law, and that an expression such as 'products from the Western Sahara' should be used instead.

IV. The Eastern Partnership Association Agreements and Disputed Territories

A. The Association Agreements with Moldova and Georgia and their 'Frozen Conflict Areas'

Whereas the territorial application clause of the (trade) agreements with Israel and Morocco do not explicitly exclude their application to the respective disputed territories, the EU's recent AAs and 'Deep and Comprehensive Free Trade Areas' (DCFTAs) concluded with Moldova and Georgia prevent the application of these agreements to their respective 'frozen conflict areas' or 'breakaway regions',[85] ie Transnistria (Moldova) and Abkhazia and South Ossetia (Georgia). Since these regions broke away from Moldova and Georgia in the aftermath of the dissolution of the Soviet Union, they have each established their own legal system, but their independence is not recognised by the EU and most UN Members. This is therefore a different situation compared to the Israel and Morocco cases analysed

[84] Interpretative Notice on indication of origin of goods from the territories occupied by Israel since June 1967, C(2015) 7834 final, 11 November 2015.

[85] For the text of these agreements, see Association Agreement between the European Union and the European Atomic Energy Community and their Member States, of the one part, and Georgia, of the other part [2014] OJ L261, 30 August 2014; and Association Agreement between the European Union and the European Atomic Energy Community and their Member States, of the one part, and the Republic of Moldova, of the other part [2014] OJ L260, 30 August 2014. For an analysis of these agreements, including the AA concluded with Ukraine, see G Van der Loo, 'The EU-Ukraine Association Agreement and Deep and Comprehensive Free Trade Area: A New Legal Instrument for EU Integration without Membership?' (Leiden/Boston, Brill/Nijhoff, 2016).

above, since it concerns agreements concluded by the EU with third countries involving a territory over which the third country does not exercise effective control (and not a territory without the sovereignty of the third State in question over that territory being recognised by the EU).

The territorial application clauses of both agreements state that the AAs will apply 'to the territory of [the Republic of Moldova/Georgia]', but add a specific paragraph on the territorial application in relation to those areas 'over which the Government of [Georgia/Moldova] does not exercise effective control'.[86] Without explicitly referring to Transnistria/Abkhazia and South Ossetia, it is obvious that these territories are targeted. This specific paragraph states that the application of the AA or the DCFTA (which is an integral part of the AA) in these areas will only commence 'once [Georgia/Moldova] ensures the full implementation and enforcement of this Agreement, or of [its DCFTA], respectively, on its entire territory'.[87] The application needs to be activated by a decision of the Association Council, the main joint institution established by these agreements. Because the Association Councils decide by consensus, both parties, including the EU, must agree and confirm that Georgia or Moldova ensure the implementation and enforcement of the AA or DCFTA over these territories. Conversely, if a party considers that the implementation and enforcement cannot be guaranteed in these areas, the application of the DCFTA can be suspended in relation to the areas concerned.[88]

Whereas it is unlikely that the EU-Georgia AA or DCFTA will be applied in Abkhazia and South Ossetia in the near future in the light of the (geo-)political situation in the region, the EU-Moldova Association Council decided on 18 December 2016 that the Moldovan DCFTA (thus not the entire AA) shall apply to the entire territory of Moldova from 1 January 2016, including Transnistria.[89] Transnitria benefited from the autonomous trade preferences (ATPs) that the EU applied since 2008 to Moldova. Initially these ATPs only covered industrial goods but after Russia's ban on several Moldovan agricultural products, the EU broadened the ATP in 2013 and 2014 to wine and Tariff Rate Quotas (TRQs) for some agricultural products.[90] Although the Moldovan DCFTA entered provisionally into force on 1 September 2014, the ATP continued to apply until 31 December 2015. Because Transnistria was facing the end of preferential access to the EU with the termination of the ATP regime, the EU, Moldova and Transnistria launched informal discussions on how to extend the DCFTA to Transnistria from

[86] Art 462 EU-Moldova AA and Art 426 EU-Georgia AA.

[87] Art 462(2) EU-Moldova AA and Art 426(2) EU-Georgia AA. The latter explicitly refers to Georgia's regions Abkhazia and Tskhnivali region/South Ossetia.

[88] Art 462(4) EU-Moldova AA and Art 426(4) EU-Georgia AA.

[89] Decision 1/2015 EU-Moldova Association Council of 18 December 2015. The Republic of Moldova has informed the European Commission that it will be able to ensure the full implementation and enforcement of Title V (Trade and trade-related matters) of the Agreement on its entire territory from 1 January 2016.

[90] Regulation (EU) 1383/2014 amending Council Regulation (EC) 55/2008 introducing autonomous trade preferences to the Republic of Moldova [2014] OJ L372/2.

1 January 2016, after the termination of the ATP. Economic and (geo-)political considerations nudged these three parties towards a deal. Because the EU has become the biggest export market for Transnistrian exporters, Transnitria wanted to preserve its preferential access to the EU market. The EU, on the other hand, was willing to extend the DCFTA application to Transnistria because this can contribute to the reunification of the country and, most likely, because it would make the economy of this region less dependent on Russia. Significantly, the decision of the Association Council which confirmed that the DCFTA will be applied to the entire territory of Moldova – including Transistria – was preceded by a technical 'deal' between the EU, Moldova and the leadership of Transnistria. The EU facilitated negotiations between the leadership of the breakaway region and Moldova on an agreement on the conditions that the separatist enclave has to meet in exchange for facilitated access to the EU market.[91] The exact text of the agreement was not made public, but the main parameters of the deal have been leaked and reported.[92] Whereas Moldova agreed to continue issuing export certificates to economic entities from Transnistria (as it has done for the ATP), the breakaway region agreed to fulfil certain conditions in exchange for preferential access to the EU market. In light of the Court's *Anastasiou* case law, no other option was possible as the EU can only recognise certificates issued by Moldovan authorities, and not by 'Transnistrian' authorities. The Transnistrian leadership agreed, inter alia, to lift its import duties on EU products in line with Moldova's DCFTA tariff schedules, to give access to Moldova's competent bodies in order to verify compliance with Sanitary and Phytosanitary (SPS) requirements and standards, to comply with key World Trade Organisation rules, to introduce a VAT system and to gradually approximate to EU legislations and standards in order to reduce non-tariff barriers.[93] This deal illustrates that there was a strong political will from the EU side to be as flexible as possible with regard to the DCFTA application in Transnistria. The EU did not even insist that the entire DCFTA needs to be applied in Transnistria, most likely because from an economic, legal and political point of view this is not realistic. However, this is actually incompatible with the territorial application clause of the DCFTA which states that the Association Council can only apply the entire DCFTA to Transnitria (and not only parts thereof).[94] In order to assist Moldova and Transnistria with the implementation of the DCFTA, the EU prolonged in 2015 the European Union Border Assistance Mission to Moldova and Ukraine

[91] See, eg, Answer given by Ms Malmström on behalf of the Commission, E-001168/2016, 4 April 2016. In this answer the Commission also confirms that representatives of the Transnistria region were invited to, and took part in observer capacity in, the negotiations on the DCFTA.

[92] See, eg, S Secrieru, 'Transnistria Zig-zagging towards a DCFTA', *PISM Policy Paper* No 4, January 2016. The author of this contribution also discussed this 'deal' with officials of the EEAS, the EU Delegation in Moldova and the MFA of Moldova during several meetings and interviews in Brussels and Chisinau in the summer of 2016.

[93] ibid.

[94] Art 462 EU-Moldova AA.

(EUBAM) for a further two years.[95] The renewed mandate gives EUBAM a greater role in assisting Moldova and Ukraine to fulfil the DCFTA commitments and to contribute to the settlement of the Transition conflict.

B. The EU-Ukraine Association Agreement and Crimea and Sevastopol

With regard to the EU-Ukraine AA and DCFTA, it has to also be noted that the territorial application clause of this agreement does not address the annexation of Crimea and Sevastopol by Russia because this situation occurred after the initialling (but before signature) of the agreement.[96] However, the territorial application of the AA was addressed in the Final Act between the EU and Ukraine regarding the signature of the EU-Ukraine AA on 27 June 2014.[97] In this document, the EU and Ukraine agreed that the AA – thus not only the DCFTA –:

> shall apply to the entire territory of Ukraine as recognised under international law and shall engage in consultations with a view to determine the effects of the Agreement with regard to the illegally annexed territory of the Autonomous republic of Crimea and the City of Sevastopol in which the Ukrainian Government currently does not exercise effective control.[98]

Moreover, almost immediately after Russia's annexation of Crimea the European Council stated that it does not recognise Russia's annexation of these territories.[99] Therefore, products originating in Crimea are by the EU still considered to be goods originating in Ukraine and can benefit from the preferential trade regime foreseen in the DCFTA. However, in practice, only Russian authorities are now able to issue the relevant origin certificates for products manufactured or processed in Crimea. As noted above, the CJEU confirmed that the EU cannot accept the proof of origin issued by authorities other than those designed by name in the relevant (preferential) agreement.[100] Because there are no competent 'Ukrainian' customs authorities in Crimea anymore to establish the origin of the goods as 'Ukrainian', the products can *de facto* not benefit from preferential treatment of the DCFTA. Moreover, as a part of the EU's non-recognition policy, the Council imposed

[95] Addendum of Memorandum of Understanding between the European Commission, the Republic of Moldova and the Government of Ukraine on the EUBAM Mission to the Republic of Moldova and to Ukraine of 7 October 2005.

[96] For the text of the EU-Ukraine AA, see Association Agreement between the European Union and its Member States, of the one part, and Ukraine, of the other part [2014] OJ L161/3, 29 May 2014.

[97] Final Act between the European Union and the European Atomic Energy Community and their Member States, of the one part, and Ukraine, of the other part, as regards the Association Agreement, Council of the European Union [2014] OJ L278/4.

[98] This final act can be considered as an instrument or agreement in the meaning of Art 31(2) VCLT.

[99] European Council Conclusion, Brussels, 20/21 March 2014, EUCO 7/1/14, para 29.

[100] *Anastasiou* (n 2).

substantial restrictive measures on economic relations with Crimea and Sevastopol. In June 2014 the Council adopted an import ban on goods from Crimea or Sevastopol into the EU, unless they have Ukrainian certificates.[101] In addition, the Council adopted in July 2014 further trade and investment restrictions for Crimea and Sevastopol which include a ban on new investment in several sectors in Crimea and Sevastopol, including infrastructure projects in the transport, telecommunications and energy sectors and the exploitation of oil, gas and minerals. Also key equipment for these sectors may not be exported to Crimea and Sevastopol.[102] These sanctions were further broadened in December 2014 when the Council adopted a full ban on investment in Crimea or Sevastopol, along with a prohibition to supply tourism services in Crimea. On 19 June 2017, the Council extended these measures until 23 June 2018.

Finally, it should be noted that the EU launched in February 2017 negotiations on a new comprehensive agreement with Azerbaijan to replace the current Partnership and Cooperation Agreement.[103] It remains to be seen how this agreement with tackle the 'frozen conflict' in Nagorno-Karabakh, a territory over which Azerbaijan does not exercise effective control. An option would be to include a territorial application clause similar to the one included in the Moldova and Georgia AAs. In this case, the application of the new EU-Azerbaijan agreement to the territory of Nagorono-Karabakh would only start if the highest joint institution established by that agreement decides that the Azerbaijan effectively exercises control over that territory.[104]

V. Conclusion

This contribution illustrates that both the case law of the CJEU and the policies of the Union in relation to the EU's trade relations with 'disputes territories' are rather inconsistent, even considering the important factual and legal differences of these cases.

The inconsistency in the case law relates to the CJEU's selective usage of international treaty law. The Court's shifting approach to international law has led to the belief that the CJEU is not *Völkerrechtsfreundlich* at all, but 'if and when possible it will [act]in harmony with international law, but if and when impossible to

[101] Council Decision 2014/386/CFSP of 23 June 2014 concerning restrictions on goods originating in Crimea or Sevastopol, in response to the illegal annexation of Crimea and Sevastopol [2014] OJ L183/70.

[102] The European Commission has prepared together with the EEAS an 'Information Note to EU business operating and/or investing in Crimea/Sevastopol' (SWD(2014) 300 final, 11 June 2015).

[103] EEAS, 'EU-Azerbaijan Relations', 1 November 2017.

[104] The recent EU-Armenia Comprehensive and Enhanced Partnership Agreement, signed on 24 November 2017, merely refers in the preamble to the commitment of both Parties to a peaceful and lasting settlement of the Nagorno-Karabakh conflict in line with the relevant international agreements and conventions (for the text of the agreement, see JOIN(2017) 36 final).

do so harmoniously, international law will take the backseat'.[105] However, whereas the cracks in the Court's *Völkerrechtsfreundlich* image are mainly attributed to the Court's attempts to safeguard the autonomy of the EU legal order (as for example in *Kadi*), the *Brita* and *Polisario* cases also reveal that the CJEU relies in a 'selfish' way on international treaty law in order to dodge sensitive political issues. In both cases the Court relied on Article 31 VCLT and the *pacta tertiis* principle, codified in Article 34 VCLT, to determine the territorial scope of the international agreements in question. However, in *Brita* the Court could identify an affected third party within the meaning of Article 34 VCLT (ie the Palestinian customs authorities) by simply relying on the EU's international agreement with that third party (ie the EU-PLO AA) – and thus avoiding a politically sensitive discussion on the body of international law on Israel's borders and the occupied territories. In the absence of such an agreement in the context of the Western Sahara, the Court relied on the body of international law with regard to the Western Sahara in order to conclude that the Western Sahara has a 'separate and distinct status', and is therefore a third party within the meaning of the principle of the relative effect of treaties. Although this approach can be considered as 'international law friendly', this contribution illustrated that the Court relied in a selective and creative way on international treaty law, in particular in relation to Article 31 VCLT.

Also the Union's trade policies towards these disputed areas can hardly be described as consistent. The EU recognises neither Israel's sovereignty over the occupied territories nor Morocco's sovereignty over the Western Sahara. However, whereas the EU has consistently held that the occupied territories are not covered by the EU-Israel AA and that products originating in these territories cannot benefit from preferential access to the EU on the basis of that agreement, the EU has been *de facto* applying the EU-Morocco AA and its Agricultural Protocol to the Western Sahara. Significantly, the CJEU rejected in *Polisario* the Council's position that the Union can *de facto* apply the agreement to products originating in the Western Sahara without recognising Morocco's sovereignty over that territory. This implies that the EU will need to terminate the *de facto* application of the agreement to this territory, or it will need to acquire the consent of the people of the Western Sahara to include the Western Sahara in the territorial scope of the agreement.[106] The Union has also been blamed for applying double-standards because it has introduced specific labelling requirements for products originating from the occupied Palestinian territories, but not for products originating from the Western Sahara. It is indeed surprising that the indication 'Made in Israel' for products originating in the occupied territories would be misleading in the sense of the relevant EU legislation, but the indication 'Made in Morocco' for products originating in the Western Sahara would not be, particularly now the Court has made it clear that the EU-Morocco AA does not cover the Western Sahara.

[105] J Klabbers, 'Völkerrechtsfreundlichkeit? International Law and the EU Legal Order' in P Koutrakos (ed), *European Foreign Policy* (Cheltenham, Edward Elgar Publishing, 2011) 97.
[106] On this point, see, Van der Loo (n 78).

The Union's trade relations with the 'frozen conflict areas' in Moldova and Georgia are different from the two aforementioned cases since these concern agreements concluded by the EU with third countries involving a territory over which the third country does not exercise effective control (and not a territory without the sovereignty of the third State in question over that territory being recognised by the EU). Contrary to the EU-Israel and Morocco AAs, the territorial application clauses in the AAs with Moldova and Georgia do address this situation, excluding the agreements' application to the territories over which the respective governments of Georgia and Moldova do not exercise effective control. However, for (geo-)political reasons the Union adopted a flexible stance towards Moldova and agreed that Moldova 'ensures the full implementation and enforcement' of the DCFTA in Transnistria – although in practice this is hardly the case – and applies the DCFTA to that territory. In the case of the EU-Ukraine AA, the EU's approach to goods from Crimea or Sevastopol is consistent with the Union's non-recognition policy and the settled case law of the CJEU on the certification of rules of origin as only products with Ukrainian certificates can enter the Union, although in practice this is not an option anymore.

11

We'll Always have Geneva: The Existential Crisis of the US-led Multilateral Trading System and the EU Reactions

MICHAEL HAHN

I. Introduction: 'Burning down the House'

Before the election of the 45th President of the US in November 2016, the World Trade Organisation (WTO) was viewed as an organisation in (legislative) crisis and hence sub-optimally efficient: an organisation created for like-minded free traders had become a truly global international organisation, in which every not completely insignificant economy – with the exception of Iran – was participating. Due to the fact that the leadership of the old trade powers – the US, the EU, Japan, Australia, Canada – had lost its dominance, whereas the emerging actors had only learned to derail undesirable initiatives but had failed to acquire the art of constructive deal-making, nobody expected a quick conclusion of the Doha Round. This shortcoming, however, was viewed as a long-term problem. The steady but slow decline of the WTO's function as forum for negotiations and law making was treated not unlike global warming in the last quarter of the twentieth century: the experts viewed the need to change the course as a matter of the highest urgency, whereas the decision-makers were busy with other things.

Moving from the WTO to its environment: 18 months ago, a US-centred butterfly-shaped area of two Megaregionals, the Transatlantic Trade and Investment Partnership (TTIP) and the Trans-Pacific Partnership (TPP) was seen as a likely event for 2017/2018. Opinions were divided, whether that would be the successor of the WTO or just a 'laboratory of ideas' that would constitute a welcome competition for the WTO and force it to adapt to the new realities. Albeit much of the 'legislative action' was taking place in the bilateral arena through preferential trade agreements (PTAs), these agreements, in both letter and spirit, refer to WTO law, including the jurisprudence of the WTO Appellate Body, as floor and reference point. In doing so, the relevance and legitimacy of WTO law was seen as being confirmed.

Another reason for the tentatively optimistic (or only mildly pessimistic) assessment of the future of the WTO was its Dispute Settlement Mechanism (DSM). The EU, the US, but also China were (and are) frequent users. Of course, problems existed, but were seen as deserving observation, not mandating immediate action: There was clogging of the system,[1] not least due to the overuse of the system by the epic battle between the EU and the US regarding their respective subsidisation of large civil aircraft. Also, the US regularly expressed displeasure with an allegedly overly activist stance of the Appellate Body, which manifested itself in the elimination of several American Appellate Body members after their respective first terms[2] and, in the last year of the Obama administration, the refusal to prolong the South Korean Appellate Body member's term for a second (and final) term, explained as a reaction to what the US perceived as overly aggressive questioning of counsel and biased reports.

The major bone of contention expected to come up was whether and how the DSM would be able to deal with China and its subsidy-driven creation of excess capacity, especially given that a deadline prescribed by the Protocol of Accession of China was approaching. In so far, the Appellate Body report in *Argentina – Biodiesel*[3] was seen as particularly unhelpful with regard to allowing Western (and emerging countries other than China) to prevent importation of artificially cheap imports.

Looking back, it would seem that these were the good times: The US President now describes the WTO as having been good for everyone,[4] except the US (which, of course, has been the preeminent creator of the system, going back to the fourth point of the Atlantic Charter).[5] President Trump is on record as describing the WTO as a 'disaster'; he has stated that the US would leave the WTO if he considered that it did not serve US purposes. In particular, it has been reported that if the Chinese complaint against the US' and the EU's treatment of China as Non-Market Economy (NME), currently pending at the panel phase (DS 515 and 516) would end with a win for China, the US would walk away from the system. Given that the current administration has pulled out of the TPP, these threats are not perceived as being completely implausible. Lately, the 45th US President

[1] CD Ehlermann, 'The Workload of the WTO Appellate Body: Problems and Remedies' (2017) 20 *Journal of International Economic Law* 705–34.

[2] Ms Merit Janow's tenure ran from 2003 to 2007, Ms Jennifer Hillman's tenure lasted from 2007 to 2011.

[3] Appellate Body Report, *European Union – Anti-Dumping Measures on Biodiesel from Argentina*, WT/DS473/AB/R, adopted 6 October 2016, DSR 2016:IV, para 6.37 et seq.

[4] 'The WTO, World Trade Organisation, was set up for the benefit for everybody but us. They have taken advantage of this country like you wouldn't believe': www.factcheck.org/2017/10/trump-wrong-wto-record/ (last accessed 1 October 2018).

[5] *cf* http://avalon.law.yale.edu/wwii/atlantic.asp (last accessed 1 October 2018).

expressed doubt as to the relevance of the most important function of the WTO and its DSM – to keep the peace in trade relations: a presidential tweet stated that 'trade wars are good, and easy to win'.[6]

II. The EU Reaction: An Overview

The scepticism of the Trump administration towards the multilateral liberal order, including the North Atlantic Treaty Organisation (NATO), the WTO and, more generally, the rule of law in international relations was not surprising for anyone: this is exactly what candidate Trump had offered as an alternative world view during his successful election campaign.

While the EU and its Member States, not unlike the rest of the world, has largely avoided directly contradicting the US President's views on trade and investment in principle, a clear pattern can be noted: In contrast to the tune of transactional *ad hoc* trade 'governance' popular in the Trump White House, the EU engaged in multiple efforts to strengthen the rules-based approach to international economic governance: in the WTO, it sought common ground with the US, eg suggesting together with Japan, that systemic issues emanating from China's membership in the WTO should be addressed.[7]

However, the focus of the EU lay on strengthening bilateral trade relationships: clearly for political purposes, the EU and Japan announced leaders' agreement as to the new Japan – EU Free Trade Agreement (FTA), as it was still being negotiated (and not just subject to legal scrubbing). Negotiations with Australia[8] and New Zealand[9] have started or are about to start. The Comprehensive Economic and Trade Agreement (CETA) entered into force provisionally on 21 September 2017,[10]

[6] https://twitter.com/realDonaldTrump/status/969525362580484098; https://www.washingtonpost.com/news/business/wp/2018/03/02/trump-insists-trade-wars-are-good-and-easy-to-win-after-vowing-new-tariffs/?noredirect=on&utm_term=.eaad25b325ab (last accessed 10 October 2018).

[7] 'EU, Japan and US to Ramp up Trade Pressure on China: Three Economies will Target "Severe Excess Capacity" in Sectors Like Steel' *Financial Times*, 12 December 2017, available at https://www.ft.com/content/5f0aad90-deae-11e7-a8a4-0a1e63a52f9c. See also the shared EU/US Legal Interpretation – Article VI:1 of the General Agreement on Tariffs and Trade 1994, the Second Note Ad GATT 1994 Article VI:1, the Practice of the GATT Contracting Parties in the Application of GATT 1994 Article VI:1, the Accessions of Poland, Romania, and Hungary to the GATT, Article 2 of the Agreement on Implementation of Article VI of the General Agreement on Tariffs and Trade 1994, and Section 15 of the Protocol of Accession of China to the WTO, https://ustr.gov/sites/default/files/enforcement/WTO/US.Legal.Interp.Doc.fin.%28public%29.pdf (last accessed 1 October 2018).

[8] Recommendation for a Council Decision authorising the opening of negotiations for a Free Trade Agreement with Australia, COM(2017) 472/F1, http://ec.europa.eu/transparency/regdoc/?fuseaction=list&n=10&adv=0&coteId=1&year=2017&number=472 (last accessed 1 October 2018).

[9] See https://eeas.europa.eu/sites/eeas/files/eu_new_zealand_partnership_agreement_on_relations_and_cooperation.pdf (last accessed 1 October 2018).

[10] See http://trade.ec.europa.eu/doclib/docs/2017/september/tradoc_156056.pdf (last accessed 1 October 2018).

the upgrading of the FTA with Mexico is underway,[11] and FTAs with other Asia-Pacific Partners are actively explored. The EU was not alone in demonstrating confidence in further liberalisation of markets: despite initial reservations, TPP (now dubbed the Comprehensive and Progressive Agreement for Trans-Pacific Partnership (CPTPP) was concluded between the remaining 11 partners.[12]

Despite these efforts to stabilise the international trading system, the Trump administration is on course to modify profoundly the *status quo*: procedurally, it aims at abolishing or severely curtailing the role of the WTO Appellate Body, in substance, it not only takes measures which are incompatible with its obligation under WTO law (every important actor has done so in the past). What is so destabilising is the manner in which these efforts are being undertaken: it seems as if there was no effort made to even pretend that the behaviour was WTO compatible. And why should it be otherwise: 'The WTO is unfair to US'.[13]

III. The Tragedy of the Commons: There Once was an Appellate Body with Seven Members

A. The Trump/Lighthizer Shock

The US is both midwife and godmother of the General Agreement on Tariffs and Trade (GATT)/WTO System and of its DSM. Nevertheless, already the Obama-appointed United States Trade Representative (USTR) did not join the otherwise certain consensus for the renewal of a sitting (Korean) Appellate Body member. The 2016 Annual Report of the Appellate Body[14] describes the situation as follows:

> [O]n 11 May 2016, the DSB Chairman had been informed by [the US'] delegation that it would be unable to support Mr Chang's reappointment. Shortly thereafter, this delegation publicized its reasons for its opposition to Mr Chang's reappointment. Subsequently, Appellate Body members other than Mr Chang, in a letter signed by the Appellate Body Chair, expressed concerns about the public statement of reasons given for opposition to Mr Chang's reappointment.[15]

In a letter to the Chairman of the Dispute Settlement Body (DSB), Appellate Body Members stated that they were

> concerned about the accuracy of some of those reasons and, in particular, about the risks they may carry for the trust that WTO Members place in the independence and impartiality of Appellate Body members, on which the dispute settlement system depends.[16]

[11] See http://trade.ec.europa.eu/doclib/press/index.cfm?id=1694 (last accessed 1 October 2018).

[12] See www.mfat.govt.nz/en/trade/free-trade-agreements/free-trade-agreements-concluded-but-not-in-force/cptpp/ (last accessed 1 October 2018).

[13] See @realDonaldTrump, 6 April 2018, available at https://twitter.com/realDonaldTrump/status/982264844136017921 (last 1 October 2018).

[14] WTO, Appellate Body Annual Report for 2016, WT/AB/27, 16 May 2017.

[15] ibid, Annex 4.

[16] ibid.

With the inauguration of the 45th President and his new USTR Robert Lighthizer, the relationship between the Appellate Body and its onetime mentor reached a new low: Since 2017, the United States refuses to agree to any appointment to the Appellate Body. Recently, the US has linked this position to the continuing service of former Appellate Body members pursuant to Rule 15 of the Working Procedures for Appellate Review:

> A person who ceases to be a Member of the Appellate Body may, with the authorization of the Appellate Body and upon notification to the DSB, complete the disposition of any appeal to which that person was assigned while a Member, and that person shall, for that purpose only, be deemed to continue to be a Member of the Appellate Body.[17]

Rule 15 entered into force in 1996 as part of the Working Procedures for Appellate Review,[18] adopted on the basis of Article 17.9 of the WTO Dispute Settlement Understanding (DSU). At the time, the Appellate Body had communicated a draft to the DSB Chair and the Director-General. As the proposed Rule 15 was not contentious, it entered into force and has been applied in 16 instances since 1996. In two cases,[19] two of the three Appellate Body members completed the disposition of the appeal pursuant to that Rule. During the 22 years of its application, no discontent or grievance was voiced in the DSB or elsewhere.

Due to three vacancies that could not be replaced due to the blocking of the appointment process, the Appellate Body decided to allocate several major cases (DS316/RW, DS353/RW, DS486, DS490/496, DS472/497) to the outgoing member Van den Bossche, 'to deal with the unprecedented workload of appeals, and to preserve the rights of participants and third participants in pending appeals'.[20]

The US now refuses any appointments on the basis of what it perceives as illegal overstaying of former Appellate Body members.[21] It has, in addition, expressed in strong language criticism of the Appellate Body's performance during the last decade: it alleges that the Appellate Body has usurped powers not attributed to it. The implication is that the Appellate Body is operating without proper mandate. The alleged points include, but are not limited to, 'disregard of the 90-day deadline for appeals', 'continued service by persons who are no longer AB members', 'issuing advisory opinions on issues not necessary to resolve a dispute', 'Appellate

[17] See www.wto.org/english/tratop_e/dispu_e/ab_e.htm (last accessed 1 October 2018).

[18] WTO, Working Procedures for Appellate Review, WT/AB/WP/1, 15 February 1996.

[19] US – *Lead and Bismuth II*; US – *Section 211 Appropriations Act ('Havana Club')*.

[20] Letter of the Appellate Body Chair to the Chair of the DSB, Ref.: usb/ih (AB-2), 24 November 2017.

[21] US Statements at the 22 November 2017 DSB Meeting regarding Appellate Body Appointments: Proposal By Argentina, Brazil, Chile, Colombia, Costa Rica, Ecuador, El Salvador, European Union, Guatemala, Honduras, Hong Kong, China; Mexico, Nicaragua, Norway, Pakistan, Peru, Russian Federation, Singapore, Switzerland, Separate Customs Territory Of Taiwan, Penghu, Kinmen And Matsu;, Turkey, Uruguay and Viet Nam (WT/DSB/W/609), https://geneva.usmission.gov/wp-content/uploads/sites/290/Nov22.DSB_.pdf (last accessed 10 October 2018). '… the United States has continued to convene meetings to discuss this issue informally with a number of delegations … we have heard a general recognition that the DSB has the authority to set the term of an AB member under DSU Article 17.2; it follows that the DSB has a responsibility to decide whether a person should continue serving beyond that term … Rule 15 raises difficult legal questions that the DSB should address.'

Body review of fact and review of a Member's law *de novo*' and 'the Appellate Body claims its reports are entitled to be treated as precedent'.[22] Particularly harsh criticism is reserved for the Appellate Body's jurisprudence regarding Trade remedy measures. The USTR voices

> systemic concerns with what it sees as an overly judicially activist Appellate Body that seeks to fill gaps in WTO agreements, which in turn creates new obligations for members and reinterprets what has already been agreed to … the Appellate Body opines on issues not raised in the appeal and creates jurisprudence with no input from members – largely abandoning deference to members in the context of trade remedy investigations.[23]

It would not seem a far-fetched assumption that the main reason for the US behaviour is indeed the sense that the Appellate Body's interpretation of WTO law and particularly on trade remedies law is flawed.[24]

As a consequence of the US refusal to appoint new Appellate Body members, the Appellate Body currently consists of only four members. One member's term ends this year (2018); by the end of 2019, there will be one Appellate Body member left, the Chinese citizen Hong Zhao.

Despite the US rhetoric and its hostile actions, the US continues to use the WTO DSM actively; the USTR highlights its use in his recent report.[25] China was not alone when it expressed confusion as to the fact that

> on one hand, the US is demanding that the WTO dispute settlement system to continue operating 'as normal' as it did in this dispute [China – Anti-Dumping and Countervailing Duty Measures on Broiler Products from the United States], and on the other hand, (…) is actively working to undermine the system by blocking the selection process for vacancies of the Appellate Body.[26]

[22] All quotes from Office of the United States Trade Representative, 2018 Trade Policy Agenda and 2017 Annual Report of the President of the United States on the Trade Agreements Program Office, March 2018, https://ustr.gov/about-us/policy-offices/press-office/reports-and-publications/2018/2018-trade-policy-agenda-and-2017 (last accessed 1 October 2018) 22–28.

[23] Inside US Trade's World Trade Online, 'Appellate Body, China NME Fights to Dominate WTO Dispute Settlement Debate in 2018' (26 December 2017), https://insidetrade.com/daily-news/appellate-body-china-nme-fights-dominate-wto-dispute-settlement-debate-2018 (last accessed 1 October 2018).

[24] The main frustration with that jurisprudence is rooted in the interpretation of Art 17:6 Anti-Dumping Agreement and the Zeroing. See, eg, WJ Davey, 'The Limits of Judicial Processes' in D Bethlehem, D Mcrae, R Neufeld and I Van Damme (eds), *Oxford Handbook of International Trade Law* (Oxford, Oxford University Press, 2009) 460–80, 469 et seq; IM Matsushita, TJ Schoenbaum, PC Mavroidis and M Hahn, *The World Trade Organization: Law, Practice, and Policy*, 3rd edn (Oxford, Oxford University Press, 2015) 390 et seq.

[25] Office of the United States Trade Representative, 2018 Trade Policy Agenda and 2017 Annual Report of the President of the United States on the Trade Agreements Program Office, March 2018, https://ustr.gov/about-us/policy-offices/press-office/reports-and-publications/2018/2018-trade-policy-agenda-and-2017 (last accessed 1 October 2018) 19 et seq.

[26] See Inside US Trade's World Trade Online, 'China Jabs US for Using WTO Dispute Settlement as it Complies in Poultry Fight' (28 February 2018), https://insidetrade.com/daily-news/china-jabs-us-using-wto-dispute-settlement-it-complies-poultry-fight (last accessed 1 October 2018).

However, the US declined on 28 February 2018 to support a proposal sponsored by 63 WTO members to begin filling three vacancies in the WTO Appellate Body.[27]

IV. The EU Reaction

Despite not agreeing with all of the Appellate Body reports, the EU views the current WTO DSM as 'invaluable':

> It is a global public good, and the EU attaches enormous value to it. And in the coming months, we will do what is necessary to support it if it comes under further pressure.[28]

In light of the imminent fading away of the Appellate Body, several proposals are being discussed in DG Trade and capitals.

The most radical one is probably to activate the option to use the majority voting system already previewed by the WTO-Agreement (WTO-A). This would make the US and any other Member, be they the superpowers or landlocked African least developed countries subject to being outvoted. This would almost certainly lead to the US departure, and it is far from clear that the US would be alone in not wanting to be potentially outvoted.

Even from a technical perspective, though, it is far from clear that the DSU allows reversion to majority voting. Article IX WTO-A reads:

> The WTO shall continue the practice of decision-making by consensus followed under GATT 1947.[29] Except as otherwise provided, where a decision cannot be arrived at by consensus, the matter at issue shall be decided by voting.

However, the matter is 'otherwise provided for' in Article 2.4 DSU, which states: 'Where the rules and procedures of this Understanding provide for the DSB to take a decision, it shall do so by consensus'.[30] One of the most distinguished experts on WTO law suggests, though, that this is not the end of the matter[31]: it is argued

[27] ibid.

[28] See EU Statement at the Heads of Delegations meeting, Buenos Aires, Argentina, 13 December 2017, by European Commissioner for Trade Cecilia Malmström, 11th Ministerial Conference of the World Trade Organisation (WTO), available at http://trade.ec.europa.eu/doclib/docs/2017/december/tradoc_156464.pdf (last accessed 1 October 2018).

[29] [Footnote 1 in the original text] The body concerned shall be deemed to have decided by consensus on a matter submitted for its consideration, if no Member, present at the meeting when the decision is taken, formally objects to the proposed decision.

[30] [Footnote 1 in the original text] The DSB shall be deemed to have decided by consensus on a matter submitted for its consideration, if no Member, present at the meeting of the DSB when the decision is taken, formally objects to the proposed decision.

[31] PJ Kuijper, 'The US Attack on the Appellate Body' (2017) 44 *Amsterdam Law School Legal Research Paper* 2–15.

that pursuant to Article XVI:3 WTO-A, Article 2.4 DSU has to cede to Article IX WTO-A. Article XVI:3 WTO-A states:

> In the event of a conflict between a provision of this Agreement and a provision of any of the Multilateral Trade Agreements, the provision of this Agreement shall prevail to the extent of the conflict.

It is far from clear that this argumentation is tenable: while Article II:2 WTO-A specifically indicates that the DSU is indeed a Multilateral Trade Agreement,[32] it would seem questionable whether 'a conflict' for the purposes of Article XVI:4 exists: if the treaty enjoying supremacy specifically provides for the possibility of divergent solutions ('unless otherwise provided for'), it would not seem far-fetched to dispute the 'conflict' between DSU and WTO-A, which is the *conditio sine qua non* for advocating for a majority vote within the parameters of the WTO Agreement.

An additional argument for reverting to a vote (with simple or 'super'-majority)[33] may be that the US behaviour is so extraordinary that the *clausula rebus sic stantibus* (as enshrined in Article 62 VCLT) may be invoked, thereby rendering emergency measures legally possible that the treaty itself fails to provide.[34] While it is far from clear that the very high threshold of the *clausula* would indeed be met, the very argument that the WTO system is dysfunctional to the point that Article 62 VCLT needs to be used would seem a reinforcement of the US position that the system is broken and in need of a new fundament.

Despite the popularity of this approach in some quarters, it would seem that this approach has not gained traction amongst the College of Commissioners and

[32] Art II:2 WTO-A: '2. The agreements and associated legal instruments included in Annexes 1, 2 and 3 (hereinafter referred to as 'Multilateral Trade Agreements') are integral parts of this Agreement, binding on all Members'.

[33] ibid, 13.

[34] See Article 62 VCLT (Fundamental Change of Circumstances):

1. A fundamental change of circumstances which has occurred with regard to those existing at the time of the conclusion of a treaty, and which was not foreseen by the parties, may not be invoked as a ground for terminating or withdrawing from the treaty unless:
   - *(a)* The existence of those circumstances constituted an essential basis of the consent of the parties to be bound by the treaty; and
   - *(b)* The effect of the change is radically to transform the extent of obligations still to be performed under the treaty.
2. A fundamental change of circumstances may not be invoked as a ground for terminating or withdrawing from a treaty:
   - *(a)* If the treaty establishes a boundary; or
   - *(b)* If the fundamental change is the result of a breach by the party invoking it either of an obligation under the treaty or of any other international obligation owed to any other party to the treaty.
3. If, under the foregoing paragraphs, a party may invoke a fundamental change of circumstances as a ground for terminating or withdrawing from a treaty it may also invoke the change as a ground for suspending the operation of the treaty.

in capitals: nobody wants to be seen (or only perceived) as pushing the US out of the WTO, especially as the current President might appreciate that support to overcome his (Republican) party's traditional position that rules-based free trade was overall good for the country.

A less confrontational way to preserve at least a mirror-image of the Appellate Body (present and past …) would be to use the arbitration clause of Article 25 DSU: a significant subgroup of WTO members should agree on a roster consisting of all living Appellate Body members who would serve in panels of three as arbitrators upon appeal. This much discussed proposal would have the benefit of not altering the consensus ground rule, and thus would not force upon the US a course of action not previewed by the DSU. Rather, only the coalition of the willing participating in that exercise would have the benefit of a replica of a functioning Appellate Body (as it will cease to exist by 2019). Of course, this would only be a worthwhile effort if a critical mass of WTO members would commit to such an exercise. Such a critical mass would, for example, be reached if 'Argentina, Australia, Brazil, Chile, China, Colombia, Costa Rica, Ecuador, El Salvador, the European Union, Guatemala, Honduras, Hong Kong, China; Kazakhstan, Korea, Mexico, New Zealand, Nicaragua, Norway, Pakistan, Panama, Paraguay, Peru, the Russian Federation, Singapore, Switzerland; the Separate Customs Territory of Taiwan, Penghu, Kinmen and Matsu; Turkey, Ukraine, Uruguay and Viet Nam',[35] would conclude a binding agreement to replicate the current Appellate Body proceedings, as defined by the DSU, in particular its Article 17, and the Working Procedures for Appellate Review.

Ideally, that agreement would oblige parties to determine, at the end of the consultation phase, that they will not appeal a Panel report by other means than a recourse to what has been coined by a group of Appellate review actioners, 'appeal-arbitration'. Otherwise recourse to such a procedure 'would risk being driven by the particular result of the panel proceedings, and more specifically, one or the other party's (dis-)satisfaction with that result'.[36]

It seems that the idea of an appeal-arbitration replicating the Appellate Body receives widespread support among senior EU officials, despite the increasingly timid hope that the US will submit at some point an acceptable proposal for ending the stalemate. It would behove the EU to combine its rejection of the US ambush tactics with support for its long-time ally where support may be due: It does not seem unthinkable to reduce the length of Appellate Body reports. If the US Supreme Court, the German Constitutional Court and the European Court of Justice (together with its Advocate-General) can do it, it should be possible for the Appellate Body. A remand procedure would liberate the Appellate Body from its

[35] *cf* WT/DSB/W/609 (n 21).

[36] S Andersen, T Friedbacher, C Lau, N Lockhart, JY Remy and I Sandford, 'Using Arbitration Under Article 25 Of The DSU To Ensure The Availability Of Appeals' (2017) *CTEI Working Papers Geneva* para 16.

not always convincing efforts to 'complete the analysis'; and lastly, WTO partners, including China, will have to address how trade remedies law want to address the probably increasing relevance of state control over national economies. The current jurisprudence, and maybe even the law, do not always seem to fulfil their promises to create security and predictability.

A. US Unilateralism is Back

Contrary to what the heading of this chapter indicates, the US tendency to not fully abide by the rules of the WTO was never completely gone. It is difficult for the only large economy in the world that happens to also control the seven seas with its carrier groups and even outer space to feel the same level of deference towards Geneva, as, say, the WTO's host state, Switzerland. However, despite the solid belief in US exceptionalism, and sometimes aggressive tactics, no one doubted the strong underlying commitment to the multilateral trading system that the US had created. This has changed: The 45th US President is on record with a statement that a conflict with WTO rules 'doesn't matter. Then we're going to renegotiate or we're going to pull out. … The World Trade Organization is a disaster.'[37] In his inauguration speech, the US President stated, inter alia,

> it's going to be America First. Every decision on trade … will be made to benefit American workers and American families … We will follow two simple rules: Buy American and Hire American.[38]

The somewhat disturbing central takeaway is not that the current administration is considering potentially WTO-incompatible measures: many states have done that in the past, and pushing the envelope of legality has a long and distinguished pedigree. What is disturbing is that WTO law compatibility seems to be no longer part of the political calculus. This is a new phenomenon.

Its most visible expression is the reactivation of provisions which, without having been scrapped from the body of US statutes, had been somewhat dormant in the last 20 years.

B. Section 301 is Back

In relevant parts, Section 301 reads:

> Whenever the President determines that a foreign country
>
> (1) maintains unjustifiable or unreasonable … import restrictions which impair the value of trade commitments made to the United States or which burden, restrict, or discriminate against United States commerce,

[37] *Financial Times*, 24 July 2016.
[38] See www.whitehouse.gov/inaugural-address (last accessed 1 October 2018).

(2) engages in discriminatory or other acts or policies which are unjustifiable or unreasonable and which burden or restrict United States commerce,

(3) provides subsidies (or other incentives having the effect of subsidies) on its exports .... to the United States or to other foreign markets which have the effect of substantially reducing sales of the competitive United States product ..., ... the President ......

(A) may suspend, withdraw, or prevent the application of, or may refrain from proclaiming, benefits of trade agreement concessions to carry out a trade agreement with such country or instrumentality; and

(B) may impose duties or other import restrictions on the products of such foreign country or instrumentality, and may impose fees or restrictions on the services of such foreign country or instrumentality, for such time as he deems appropriate.

It will be recalled that the Panel in US – *Section 301 Trade Act* (DS152)[39] came to the conclusion that certain authorisations in the US Trade Act of 1974 for the USTR to act unilaterally were not incompatible with Art 23 DSU, which reads:

Article 23 Strengthening of the Multilateral System

1. When Members seek the redress of a violation of obligations ..., they shall have recourse to, and abide by, the rules and procedures of this Understanding.
2. In such cases, Members shall:
   (a) not make a determination to the effect that a violation has occurred ... or that the attainment of any objective of the covered agreements has been impeded, except through recourse to dispute settlement in accordance with the rules and procedures of this Understanding, and shall make any such determination consistent with the findings contained in the panel or Appellate Body report adopted by the DSB ....;
   (b) follow the procedures set forth in Article 21 to determine the reasonable period of time for the Member concerned to implement the recommendations and rulings; and
   (c) follow the procedures set forth in Article 22 to determine the level of suspension of concessions or other obligations and obtain DSB authorization in accordance with those procedures before suspending concessions ......

Despite the obvious contradiction between the DSU obligations and the internal legal situation defined by the US Trade Act that allows the USTR and the President to act unilaterally, the panel came to the conclusion that due to (1) the 'aggregate effect of the Statement of Administrative Action ("SAA")' not to act inconsistently with its obligations under the WTO-A, *and* (2) the US declaration in the proceedings that it would render determinations under Section 304 in conformity with its WTO obligations.

However, the DSB ruling also contains the passage that if the US would repudiate or remove in any way its undertakings contained in the SAA and confirmed in statements before the Panel, the finding of conformity would no longer be warranted.

[39] *United States – Sections 301–310 of the Trade Act of 1974.*

The current enforcement mechanism in WTO law is a compromise between mainly US positions and the EU considerations. The US was allowed to keep the far-reaching consequences for GATT violations (provided for in section 301), by internalising them into the counter-measures provision of Article 22 DSU (suspension of concession, cross-retaliations). For the EU and others this was acceptable, because these far-reaching trade sanctions (usable, in the real world, only by trade powers such as the US, the EU or China) were conditional upon exhausting the WTO DSM, ie after independent adjudicators had examined the validity of both the original claim and of the proportionality of the counter-measures requested (Article 21, 23 DSU). The quasi-automatic approval mechanism ('reverse consensus') was the US' guarantee that those violating their trade interests were not in a position to block the lawful exercise of US pressure through the withdrawing of concessions.

On 22 March 2018 USTR published a report on allegedly unfair Chinese trade practices.[40] In it, the USTR concludes that China has required US companies to transfer their technology to Chinese competitors and otherwise harmed US intellectual property rights holders and US companies seeking to invest in China. Based on the findings in the Section 301 report, the President directed that USTR propose additional tariffs of 25 per cent (in addition to ordinary customs duties and antidumping and countervailing duties) on imports of aerospace, information communication technology, and machinery products, as these sectors are said to be 'supported by China's unfair industrial policy'. Somewhat surprisingly, the President also directed USTR to initiate DSM proceeding against China's technology licensing practices.[41]

One day later, the Chinese Government published the following statement:[42]

> The United States … announced relevant trade measures, ignoring rational voices, and in disregard of the mutually-beneficial nature of China-US trade relations and the consensus reached by the two countries of managing differences constructively through consultations. It is a typical unilateral trade protectionist action. China is strongly disappointed and firmly opposes such an action.
>
> … China … has made great efforts to address the current trade imbalance between China and the US China does not want a trade war with anyone. But China is not afraid of and will not recoil from a trade war. China is confident and capable of facing any challenge. If a trade war were initiated by the US, China would fight to the end to defend its own legitimate interests with all necessary measures.
>
> The actions undertaken by the US … jeopardize international trade order and world economic stability.

[40] Office of the United States Trade Representative, Findings of the investigation into China's acts, policies, and practices related to technology transfer, intellectual property, and innovation under Section 301 of the Trade Act of 1974, 22 March 2018.

[41] See www.whitehouse.gov/presidential-actions/presidential-memorandum-actions-united-states-related-section-301-investigation/ (last accessed 1 October 2018).

[42] See www.china-embassy.org/eng/zmgxss/t1544748.htm (last accessed 1 October 2018).

China announced similar tariffs on US cars, planes and soy;[43] in parallel, China announced the initiation of a complaint against the US in the WTO DSM.[44]

On 5 April the President upped the ante and doubled down on the threat to China:

> On April 3, 2018, the USTR announced approximately $50 billion in proposed tariffs on imports from China as an initial means to obtain the elimination of policies and practices identified in the investigation.
>
> Rather than remedy its misconduct, China has chosen to harm our farmers and manufacturers. In light of China's unfair retaliation, I have instructed the USTR to consider whether $100 billion of additional tariffs would be appropriate under section 301 and, if so, to identify the products upon which to impose such tariffs. I have also instructed the Secretary of Agriculture, with the support of other members of my Cabinet, to use his broad authority to implement a plan to protect our farmers and agricultural interests.
>
> Notwithstanding these actions, the US is still prepared to have discussions in further support of our commitment to achieving free, fair, and reciprocal trade and to protect the technology and intellectual property of American companies and American people. Trade barriers must be taken down to enhance economic growth in America and around the world. I am committed to enabling American companies and workers to compete on a level playing field around the world, and I will never allow unfair trade practices to undermine American interests.[45]

Few in the Western world would not sympathise with some of the points the US is advancing in the Section 301 report. This explains the requests by the EU and Japan to join in the consultations requested by the United States on 26 March 2018 in re *China – Certain Measures Concerning the Protection of Intellectual Property Rights*,[46] which was put forward as follows:

> The EU notes that the request for consultations relates to the apparent discriminatory treatment of foreign entities importing their technology into China, and foreign entities transferring technology as part of their investments in joint ventures within China, with regard to the protection of the intellectual property rights on their technologies.[47]

[43] See www.wsj.com/articles/china-retaliates-against-u-s-with-plans-for-tariffs-on-american-goods-1522829404; World Trade Online, 'As China Unveils its Response to Section 301 Tariffs, Trump Dismisses "Trade War" Claims, 4 April 2018, https://insidetrade.com/trade/china-unveils-its-response-section-301-tariffs-trump-dismisses-trade-war-claims (last accessed 5 April 2018).

[44] 'Statement by Ambassador Zhang Xiangchen on Announcement of Proposed Tariff Actions under Section 301 by the US', available at http://wto2.mofcom.gov.cn/article/chinaviewpoins/201804/20180402728513.shtml (last accessed 2 October 2018).

[45] 'Statement from President Donald J. Trump on Additional Proposed Section 301 Remedies', available at www.whitehouse.gov/briefings-statements/statement-president-donald-j-trump-additional-proposed-section-301-remedies/ (last accessed 2 October 2018).

[46] WT/DS542/1.

[47] See https://docs.wto.org/dol2fe/Pages/FE_Search/FE_S_S009-DP.aspx?language=E&CatalogueIdList=244318,244319,244320,244305,244295,244297,244293,244303,244315,244321&CurrentCatalogueIdIndex=9&FullTextHash=371857150&HasEnglishRecord=True&HasFrenchRecord=True&HasSpanishRecord=True (last accessed 2 October 2018).

In a more detailed fashion, Japan explained its request to join consultations:

> First, China laws, regulations and other measures relating to technology transfers, which are identified in the request for consultations by the United States, are legal instruments with respect to which Japan has held and expressed its concerns for several years. For example, Japan has expressly raised its concerns with these Chinese licensing regulations on patents and know-how in its annual publication entitled 'Report on Compliance by Major Trading Partners with Trade Agreements -WTO, EPA/FTA and IIA-.' As the latest report states that 'a number of restrictive clauses and mandatory warranties contained in the Administrative Ordinance (ie "TIER") are subject to concern from the point of view of Article 3 of the TRIPS Agreement (national treatment) in relation to Article 28(2) of the same Agreement with respect to the right of patent owners to conclude licensing contracts.' Japan has continuous concern about the legal instruments identified in the request for consultations by the United States, which have a commercial impact on Japanese companies that transfer technologies to Chinese partners.
>
> Second, … Japan is one of the largest stakeholders in technology transfer to China.
>
> Third, Japan is also one of the major foreign countries whose nationals possess patent rights in China. … As such, these patent rights possessed by Japanese nationals in China are subject to China's technology transfer laws, regulations and other measures.
>
> Specifically, the Japanese companies which transfer technologies to Chinese companies by contracts are directly affected by the *Regulations of the People's Republic of China on the Administration of the Import and Export of Technologies*, one of the measures identified by the United States, because this measure mandates contractual terms in technology transfer agreements between foreign and Chinese partners, which are disadvantageous to foreign partners, including Japanese companies. With respect to the regulations of China relating to joint ventures, the *Regulations for the Implementation of the Law of the People's Republic of China on Chinese-Foreign Equity Joint Ventures*, for example, denies foreign patent holders the ability to enforce their intellectual property rights against Chinese joint-venture parties after a technology transfer contract is expired. Thus, Japanese companies that have stakes in a joint-venture company with Chinese shareholders are directly affected, particularly when they have their technologies transferred to the joint-venture company.[48]

As the Japanese explanation demonstrates, in particular, the US is far from alone in being dissatisfied with the Chinese compliance with obligations under the WTO-A. Nevertheless, the use of Section 301 is of great concern to America's allies. It will be recalled that it was the EU that requested a panel to evaluate whether Sections 301–310 of the US Trade Act of 1974 authorising certain actions by the US executive branch, the suspension or withdrawal of concessions or the imposition of duties or other import restrictions, in response to trade barriers imposed by other countries. In a somewhat benevolent take on the US justification,

[48] See https://docs.wto.org/dol2fe/Pages/FE_Search/FE_S_S009-DP.aspx?Language=E&CatalogueIdList=244318,244319,244320,244305,244295,244297,244293,244303,244315,244321&CurrentCatalogueIdIndex=8&FullTextHash=371857150 (last accessed 2 October 2018).

the Panel accepted in its report of 376 pages the EU's view that the statutory language in itself constituted a serious threat that unilateral determinations contrary to Article 23.2(a) DSU might be taken.[49] However, it accepted the US argument that the US had removed this threat by the 'aggregate effect of the Statement of Administrative Action ("SAA")' and a statement it had submitted during the proceedings (!) that the US Government would only trigger the possibilities pursuant to Articles 301 et seq (*in casu* Section 304) in conformity with its WTO obligations.

For both the systemic reason of weakening the WTO DSM and for commercial reasons (where will Chinese products flow to if being priced out of the US market?), these are worrying developments.

C. National Security

This may be even more so with regard to the current US administration's rather cavalier use of national security arguments: On 8 March 2018, the US President issued two *Presidential Proclamations*, one *Adjusting Imports of Steel into the United States*[50] and one *Adjusting Imports of Aluminum into the United States*; the latter reads in relevant parts:

> 4. I concur in the Secretary [of Commerce]'s finding that aluminum articles are being imported into the United States in such quantities and under such circumstances as to threaten to impair the national security of the United States …
>
> 5. Section 232 of the Trade Expansion Act of 1962, as amended, authorizes the President to adjust the imports of an article and its derivatives that are being imported into the United States in such quantities or under such circumstances as to threaten to impair the national security …
>
> 7. In the exercise of these authorities, I have decided to adjust the imports of aluminum articles by imposing a 10 percent ad valorem tariff on aluminum articles, as defined below, imported from all countries except Canada and Mexico. In my judgment, this tariff is necessary and appropriate in light of the many factors I have considered, including the Secretary's report, updated import and production numbers for 2017, the failure of countries to agree on measures to reduce global excess capacity, the continued high level of imports since the beginning of the year, and special circumstances that exist with respect to Canada and Mexico. This relief will help our domestic aluminum industry to revive idled facilities, open closed smelters and mills, preserve necessary skills by hiring new aluminum workers, and maintain or increase production, which will reduce our Nation's need to rely on foreign producers for aluminum and ensure that domestic

[49] Panel, *United States – Sections 301–310 of the Trade Act of 1974* (DS 152), in particular para 7.95 et seq.

[50] See www.whitehouse.gov/presidential-actions/presidential-proclamation-adjusting-imports-steel-united-states/; see the modified version of 22 March 2018 www.whitehouse.gov/presidential-actions/presidential-proclamation-adjusting-imports-steel-united-states-2/ (last accessed 2 October 2018).

> producers can continue to supply all the aluminum necessary for critical industries and national defense. Under current circumstances, this tariff is necessary and appropriate to address the threat that imports of aluminum articles pose to the national security.
>
> 8. … Any country with which we have a security relationship is welcome to discuss with the United States alternative ways to address the threatened impairment of the national security caused by imports from that country. Should the United States and any such country arrive at a satisfactory alternative means to address the threat to the national security such that I determine that imports from that country no longer threaten to impair the national security, I may remove or modify the restriction on aluminum articles imports from that country and, if necessary, make any corresponding adjustments to the tariff as it applies to other countries as our national security interests require.[51]

Section 232 of the Trade Expansion Act of 1962 provides the President with broad authority to limit imports for foreign policy reasons. It permits him to 'adjust the imports' of an article if it 'is being imported into the United States in such quantities or under such circumstances as to threaten to impair the national security'. The term 'national security' is not defined in the statute; relevant judicial interpretations of Section 232 are rare. In *Federal Energy Administration v Algonquin SNG, Inc*,[52] the US Supreme Court upheld licence fees imposed under the oil quota systems of Presidents Nixon and Ford. However, the Court did not establish a test for properly invoking the statute nor for defining the term 'national security'.

However, during the last four decades or so, the executive branch has understood Section 232 as granting broad discretion to its actions, beginning with the Carter administration:[53] Despite 'the statutory language and history argu[ing] strongly that the section should be invoked only in the very limited context of restricting imports of critical defence materials', the tendency 'to expand use of the statute' has continued and reached its preliminary climax with the current measures.[54]

The current administration is now applying an interpretation that equals the health of any industry relevant in and for warfare with national security.[55] In light of the famous aside of a former Commandant of the United States Marine Corps that 'amateurs think about tactics, but professionals think about logistics'[56] that

[51] See www.whitehouse.gov/presidential-actions/presidential-proclamation-adjusting-imports-aluminum-united-states/ (emphasis added) (last accessed 2 October 2018).

[52] *Federal Energy Administration v Algonquin SNG, Inc* 426 US 548 (1975).

[53] Efforts by the Carter administration to use Section 232 to render the US less dependent on imported petroleum products were struck down by the courts; *cf* Barry E Carter, 1202 calif.

[54] BE Carter, *International Economic Sanctions: Improving the Haphazard US Legal Regime* (Cambridge, Cambridge University Press, 1988) 99–109.

[55] See, in detail, US Department of Commerce Bureau of Industry and Security Office of Technology Evaluation, 'The Effect of Imports of Aluminum on the National Security – An Investigation Conducted under Section 232 of The Trade Expansion Act of 1962, as Amended' (17 January 2018), www.commerce.gov/sites/commerce.gov/files/the_effect_of_imports_of_aluminum_on_the_national_security_-_with_redactions_-_20180117.pdf (last accessed 2 October 2018).

[56] General Robert H Barrow, USMC, quoted in 'Logistics Quotations, Posted by Naval Supply Systems Command (NAVSUP)', available at www.au.af.mil/au/awc/awcgate/navy/log_quotes_navsup.pdf (last accessed 2 October 2018).

would include most industries: servicemen and women need to be fed, clothed, entertained, they need to drive, shoot, fly, swim, write and store their belongings. It is according to this logic that the Swedish Government, in 1975, wanted to establish quantitative restrictions for foreign shoes.[57] The Swedish Government invoked Article XXI GATT, as it deemed it appropriate to treat 'the planning of Sweden's economic defence in situations of emergency as an integral part of its security policy'. In this light, the preservation 'of a minimum domestic production capacity in vital industries' was deemed necessary.[58] No other GATT contracting party, certainly not the United States, supported the legality of the Swedish measures which ended in July 1977 without the issue gaining much prominence.[59]

The 2018 Section 232 report does, in a nutshell, not take into account that the supply of what is defined as essential goods stems to an overwhelming extent from close allies, in particular the two Western hemisphere countries Canada and Mexico, the EU and other friendly nations.

The US claims that its measures are WTO-compatible due to Article XXI GATT which reads in its relevant parts:

> Nothing in this Agreement shall be construed …
>
> (*b*) to prevent any contracting party from taking any action which it considers necessary for the protection of its essential security interests
>
> (i) relating to fissionable materials or the materials from which they are derived;
> (ii) relating to the traffic in arms, ammunition and implements of war and to such traffic in other goods and materials as is carried on directly or indirectly for the purpose of supplying a military establishment;
> (iii) taken in time of war or other emergency in international relations; …

Pursuant to the US and Russia, the mere invocation is enough to pre-empt any further examination by WTO adjudicative organs. In contrast, most of the literature, while duly taking note of the extraordinary breadth of the invoking state's discretion – after all, it is up to the state taking the action to determine whether it is 'necessary for the protection of its essential security interests' – has spoken out against an unfettered right of the invoking state. Both textual arguments (the fact that bread can be sliced does not make it a *fissionable material*) and the context and purpose of the norm (it is a far reaching exception, but only an exception, not a total exemption of any political question from the scope of application of GATT) would seem to support this view.[60]

[57] Vgl GATT-Doc L/4250, 1.

[58] Vgl GATT Council, Minutes of the Meeting Held October 31, 1975, GATT-Doc C/M/109, 8.

[59] *Sweden – Import Restrictions on Certain Footwear*, GATT-Doc L/4250/Add 1, 1.

[60] M Hahn, 'Vital Interests and the Law of GATT: An Analysis of GATT's Security Exception' (1990–1991) 12 *Michigan Journal of International Law* 558, 582–84; HL Schloemann and S Ohlhoff, '"Constitutionalization" and Dispute. Settlement in the WTO: National Security as an Issue of Competence' (1999) 93 *American Journal of International Law* 424, 433; S Schill and R Briese, 'Self-Judging Clauses in International Dispute Settlement' (2009) 13 *Max Planck UNYB* 61–97 ff.

The US sets a potentially dangerous precedent: export and import restrictions on energy and primary materials of any kind,[61] including those essential for the switch to climate compatible energy production ('green energy'), machinery, high tech products and the like, but also services such as transport, telecommunication, financial services transport taken for commercial reasons will be able to use the US security argument as precedent. Indeed, according to the largely identical positions of the US and Russia presented in *Russia – Measures Concerning Traffic in Transit* (DS 512), the invocation of Article XXI GATT pre-empts the Panel and ultimately the Appellate Body of the right to examine whether the invocation was lawful.

It should be noted that the damage is not just occurring at the grand systemic level. Only weeks after the pertinent presidential proclamations, their effect already nullifies and impairs the promise of the WTO system to create a stable and predictable trading environment: Using the threat of Section 232 measures, the US has pressured South Korea into partial submission;[62] similar offers are actively pursued by the US from other states, including the EU: it seems that the USTR expects 'voluntary' export restraint commitments from states in return from being exempted from Section 232 measures. The following hypothetical case may serve as an illustration of how the US measure already now corrodes and diminishes the effective functioning of WTO law: Assume a Swiss producer of specialty steel (needed, for example, for windmill rotors or other demanding applications) whose only relevant competitors are located in Korea. Given that both products are high-quality and expensive, 25 per cent tariffs (this is the rate currently applied by the US on steel products) will put the hypothetical Swiss producer out of business.

There can be little doubt that the 'compromise' entered into by Korea, a country relying on the US not just for its trade interests, will be followed by others. In fact export oriented smaller WTO members (think, for example, Australia, New Zealand, Singapore, the EFTA countries, Chile, Peru) which command less push-back possibilities than, say China, India, or the EU, will find that the world has changed considerably.

[61] It will be recalled that the attack on Pearl Harbour was interrelated with the Japanese concern of exclusion from access to petroleum products. *cf* N Hill, Was There an Ultimatum Before Pearl Harbor? (1948) 42 *American Journal of International Law* 355–67; see also the documents at www.jacar.go.jp/english/nichibei/popup/pop_26.html (last accessed 2 October 2018).

[62] *cf* https://insidetrade.com/inside-us-trade/korus-currency-deal-will-be-non-binding-lays-ground work-nafta (last accessed 2 Octoberl 2018): '…To avoid being hit by the steel tariff, Korea agreed to a product-specific quota equivalent to 70 percent of its average annual steel export volume to the US from 2015 through 2017. One administration official said that quota should reduce Korea's steel exports to the US by 30 percent in both volume and value. The quota, "will have a giant impact on reducing their exports to us," the official said. Korea decided to accept the 10 percent tariff on aluminum, officials said. One official said the deal with Korea "makes clear" that a quota or other restrictions to prevent transshipment would be required from countries that intend to avoid the Section 232 tariffs. Administration officials said the quota formula it arrived at with Korea would not necessarily be used in other instances. "This is not a one-size-fits-all type thing," one official said. "Does leverage change depending on the size of the economy? Sure. That's why we feel we have a strong hand when dealing with any other country"'.

President Trump has announced that the measures with regard to steel and aluminium are the 'first of many'.[63] If the Trump administration implements that announcement it will be the end of the liberal trading system and will cause enormous economic hardship.

D. The European Reaction

After the EU's efforts to convince the US President that it should be exempted from US measures, being one of its closest allies (at that time, such preferential treatment had already been awarded to Australia), the EU prepared for immediate countermeasures.

It chose, as an internal legal basis for its measures, Article 207 TFEU (not Article 215 TFEU), and Regulation 654/2014 concerning the exercise of the Union's rights for the application and enforcement of international trade rules.[64] Regulation 654/2014 provides the necessary fundament for executive measures by the Commission, which is empowered, pursuant to Article 3, to adopt implementing acts in accordance with Article 291 TFEU that determine the appropriate commercial policy measures. Those implementing acts are adopted by using the 'new' Comitology procedures laid down in Regulation 182/2011.[65]

Pursuant to Article 4(3) of Regulation 654/2014, the Commission may only react to WTO incompatible measures of a third country (EU parlance for a state which is not a Member of the EU), if an adjudication pursuant to the rules of the DSU has taken place; 'their level shall not exceed the level authorized by the WTO Dispute Settlement Body'. Thus, if the EU argument was that the US measures were seen as tariffs in violation of the schedules of commitments which are an integral part of the US' GATT obligations, Article II:6 GATT, and not justified, by either Article XX or XXI GATT, then countermeasures pursuant to Article 22 DSU would only be possible after a DSB decision which under current circumstances may take years. While the timeline prescribed by the DSU would easily buy another two years or so, the blockade of the Appellate Body may render any dispute *permanent*; it would seem imaginable that the US would choose to appeal in case of the success of the complaint. As no functioning Appellate Body may exist by then, such a move would render the dispute, according to the letter of the DSU, certainly not pursuant to its spirit,[66] permanently pending.

[63] See www.forbes.com/sites/stuartanderson/2018/03/23/trump-warns-this-is-the-first-of-many-new-taxes-on-americans/#6bae3f2c3928 (last accessed 2 October 2018).

[64] Regulation (EU) No 654/2014 of the European Parliament and of the Council of 15 May 2014 concerning the exercise of the Union's rights for the application and enforcement of international trade rules and amending Council Regulation (EC) No 3286/94 laying down Community procedures in the field of the common commercial policy in order to ensure the exercise of the Community's rights under international trade rules, in particular those established under the auspices of the World Trade Organization [2014] OJ L189/50–59.

[65] Regulation (EU) No 182/2011 of the European Parliament and of the Council of 16 February 2011 laying down the rules and general principles concerning mechanisms for control by the Member States of the Commission's exercise of implementing powers [2011] OJ L55/13 et seq.

[66] Thus, *abus de pouvoir* and Art 62 Vienna Convention would merit a closer analysis.

However, the EU is of the opinion that the measures are not actions based on security considerations, but rather measures to prevent competitive pressure for the US steel and aluminium industry. For this, the EU can rely on authoritative statements from @realDonaldTrump and by more conventional utterings of the current President: he has stated many times that he wants to insulate American industries and consumers from competition, in order to pursue his idea of what makes America great.

While a detailed analysis of the EU's claim that the US measures are not what they seem to be is beyond the scope of this chapter, the EU position is far from being specious: it is undisputed in both domestic and international law that the entity taking a measure does not get to define the legal quality of the act: sexual assault is sexual assault even though the perpetrator may view it as something less sinister; invoking self-defence does not determine whether indeed reasons for self-defence exist; and a safeguard measure justified with military necessity is still a safeguard measure: Article 11 DSU renders unequivocally clear that a measure must be *objectively assessed*; the acting state does not have the authority to determine the legal nature of its acts.

By now, the EU assessment of the US' actions as a *safeguard* measure is shared by China.[67] The EU line of arguments seems tenable: In the broadest terms, safeguard measures refer to the right of a WTO member to impose temporary tariffs, quotas, tariff rate quotas, or other measures to ensure that its economy or domestic industries do not suffer serious harm from imports and trade concessions. Its legal basis is to be found in the so-called escape clause of Article XIX GATT,[68] which allows WTO members[69] to escape from their WTO obligations by imposing

[67] WTO Doc G/SG/161 of 26 March 2018, *Imposition of a Safeguard Measure by the United States on Imports of Aluminum – Request for Consultations under Article 12.3 of the Agreement on Safeguards by China*: 'On 8 March 2018, the United States of America ("United States") issued a presidential proclamation, indicating that aluminum articles are being imported into the United States in such quantities and under such circumstances as to threaten to impair the national security of the United States, adjust the imports of aluminum articles by imposing a 10 per cent ad valorem tariff on aluminum articles. China takes the view that the above-mentioned measure of the United States is safeguard measure although it's in the name of national security measure … We believe the measures taken by the United States are not consistent with its obligations under the relevant provisions of the GATT 1994 and Safeguards Agreement. In accordance with Article 8.1 of the Safeguards Agreement, China also is exercising its right to trade compensation consultations …'.

[68] The Safeguards Agreement, concluded at the end of the Uruguay Round, was influenced by the experience of the US under Section 201 of the Trade Act of 1974 and reflects the substance of that US law. Pursuant to the Appellate Body, it amplifies and supplements GATT Article XIX, and is thus not in conflict with the latter. In the event of a 'conflict', the provisions of the Safeguards Agreement would prevail. General Interpretive Note to Annex 1A, Multilateral Agreements on Trade in Goods, of the WTO Agreement, reprinted in WTO, *The Legal Texts: The Results of the Uruguay Round of Multilateral Trade Negotiations* (1999) 16. The term 'conflict' is not defined but has been interpreted by the Appellate Body to mean a situation 'where adherence to the one provision will lead to a violation of the other provision': Appellate Body report, *Guatemala – Cement*, para 65.

[69] Art 2.1, n 1 of the Agreement on Safeguards allows a customs union to apply a safeguard measure as a single unit or on behalf of a Member State.

safeguard measures if the following three basic requirements are met:[70] *First*, there must be an increase in imports of the product in question. *Second*, the increase in imports must be caused by developments that were not foreseen and must result from obligations that the country applying the safeguard measure must respect under the GATT. *Finally*, the increase in imports must cause or threaten to cause 'serious injury' to a domestic industry producing a 'like' or 'directly competitive' product.

The EU and China could point to the fact that the current US President has stated many times, both as candidate and in office, that he wants to reduce the US trade deficits and institute policies that lead to consumers buying US products.[71] Increasing the price serves that purpose. The very purpose of the measure is to protect US steel and aluminium producers from competitive pressures. The security argument, the argumentation would continue, presents itself as a sham used to hide the mere protectionist worldview of the Trump administration. This, of course, is only a winning argument, if it can be heard, ie the mere invocation of Article XXI does not have the legal effect of terminating any efforts to 'objectively' assess.

A related, but separate, issue is the question of whether the EU and China have the right to react unilaterally without prior authorisation by the DSB. Pursuant to Article 8.2 of the Safeguards Agreement (SA), the exporting Member States affected 'shall be free', not less than 90 days after the original safeguard measure is applied, to suspend substantially equivalent concessions and other obligations, provided the Council for Trade in Goods has been properly notified and does not disapprove (Article 8.2 SA),[72] unless the state adopting safeguard measures to reach an agreement (within 30 days of consultations) with Member States adversely affected on adequate means of trade compensation (Article 8.1 SA). Pursuant to Article 8.3 SA,[73] this immediate reaction may not be exercised for the

[70] In the first cases under the WTO safeguards regime, the issue of the relationship between GATT Article XIX and the Safeguards Agreement arose in the context of the 'unforeseen developments' requirement; this requirement is included in GATT Article XIX:1(a) but is not repeated in the Safeguards Agreement. See Panel report, *US – Line Pipe*, paras 7.293–7.300, 8.1(6); Appellate Body reports, *US – Lamb*, paras 65–76; *Korea – Dairy*, paras 68–77; *Argentina – Footwear*, paras 76–84. The Appellate Body held that Article XIX:(a) and the Safeguards Agreement should be read together since the Safeguards Agreement defines a safeguard measure under this Agreement as one pursuant to that of Article XIX:1(a).

[71] As examples www.nytimes.com/2018/03/05/us/politics/trade-deficit-tariffs-economists-trump.html (last accessed 10 October 2018); www.washingtonpost.com/news/wonk/wp/2017/01/24/trump-says-making-products-in-the-u-s-is-gonna-be-cheaper-economists-disagree/?utm_term=.426379190797 (last accessed 10 October 2018).

[72] Art 8.2. SA reads: 'If no agreement is reached within 30 days in the consultations under paragraph 3 of Article 12, then the affected exporting Members shall be free, not later than 90 days after the measure is applied, to suspend, upon the expiration of 30 days from the day on which written notice of such suspension is received by the Council for Trade in Goods, the application of substantially equivalent concessions or other obligations under GATT 1994, to the trade of the Member applying the safeguard measure, the suspension of which the Council for Trade in Goods does not disapprove.'

[73] *cf* Art 8.3. SA: 'The right of suspension referred to in paragraph 2 shall not be exercised for the first three years that a safeguard measure is in effect, provided that the safeguard measure has been taken as

first three years that a safeguard measure is in force, provided the safeguard measure in question has been taken as a result of 'an absolute increase in imports' and the measure conforms to the provisions of the Agreement.

Surprisingly, this provision has only been used on two occasions since the WTO came into existence. In 2001, Poland suspended obligations owed to Slovakia on the basis of Article 8.2 SA. It contested the assertion that its compensatory measures were hindered by Article 8.3 SA, arguing that the original safeguard measures adopted by Slovakia were illegal.[74] Articles 8.2 and 8.3 SA again received attention at the beginning of 2002 following the declaration by the EC of its intention to suspend equivalent concessions to compensate for injury suffered as a result of US safeguard measures to protect its steel industry.[75]

In a nutshell, the argument *against* the exercise of the right to adopt compensatory measures to protect the balance of rights and obligations negotiated one's own trade advantages may be summarised as follows:[76] Article 8.2, 8.3 SA will only permit the adoption of unilateral measures during the first three years after the adoption of a safeguard measure,[77] if and to the extent that the WTO's dispute settlement organs have established that the requirements of Article 8.3 SA have been met. This would include the preliminary question of whether or not the original safeguard measure met the requirements of the Safeguards Agreement.[78]

This position does not seem compatible with the clear wording of the Safeguards Agreement: Article 8 SA defines the price to be paid when a Member State wishes to take safeguard measures. In line with the contractual nature of the system of obligations created by the GATT, Member States must first and foremost seek mutual agreement on a new equilibrium between their respective rights and obligations, by defining consensually a 'substantially equivalent level of concessions'. The Agreement allows Member States to deviate from this general rule by way of exception if mutual agreement on the re-balancing of rights and obligations has proved impossible. In this case, WTO law offers the possibility for the Member State affected to re-balance 'autonomously' (ie unilaterally and without

a result of an absolute increase in imports and that such a measure conforms to the provisions of this Agreement.'

[74] See the comprehensive account of the Polish position in WTO Doc G/SG/M/18, para 73, 77 ff; see also *Slovakia – Safeguard Measures on Imports of Sugar,* WTO Doc WT/DS/235/1=G/L/456=G/SG/D18/1, 17 July 2001; *Statement of the Slovak Republic regarding suspension of concessions by Poland on Imports of Margarine and Butter from The Slovak Republic,* WTO Doc G/C/W/312, 5 October 2001; *Statement* by *the Polish Delegation concerning suspension of concessions against Slovakia under Article 8.2 of the Safeguards Agreement,* WTO Doc G/C/W/313, 10 October 2001. The notification of the original safeguard measures by Slovakia is contained in WTO Doc G/SG/N/8/SVK/1.

[75] See WTO Doc G/C/10= G/SG/43.

[76] The following paragraphs are drawing on the author's article *Balancing or Bending – Unilateral Reactions to Safeguard Measures* (2005) 39 *Journal of World Trade* 301–26.

[77] Provided all other requirements are fulfilled; for details, Matsushita, Schoenbaum, Mavroidis and Hahn (n 24) 409–32; P Van Den Bossche and W Zdouc, *The Law and Policy of the World Trade,* 4th rev ed (Cambridge, Cambridge University Press, 2017) 655–68.

[78] See the noteworthy arguments brought forward by the USA, WTO Doc G/SG/M/19, para 131.

prior consent from other Members or WTO organs) its trade relations with the Member taking safeguard measures (thus reducing its set of obligations vis-à-vis that Member) to adopt compensatory measures unilaterally.

In this author's opinion,[79] it would reduce Articles 8.2, 8.3. SA 'to redundancy or inutility',[80] if it was read as referring impliedly to prior authorisation by the DSB. A stronger wording establishing the right to act autonomously and without prior consent of others than the formulation 'shall be free … to suspend' is hard to imagine. Indeed, it would seem to rule out an interpretation of WTO law that would accord the appropriate competence of *ex ante* review of legality to the DSB. The tight schedule provided for in Article 8.2 SA through the establishment of three intertwined deadlines would be rendered a dead letter; indeed, a 90-day deadline (which in turn must accommodate two 30-day deadlines)[81] might (if barely) leave room for an (exceptional) veto raised by the Council for Trade in Goods, but certainly appears incompatible with any reasonable timeframe for a full-blown inter-state dispute settlement procedure: Even under the guidance of the WTO's Secretariat and its tight schedules, the duration of the entire proceedings is closer to three years than to three months.[82]

Like the rules regarding (original) safeguards, anti-dumping measures or countervailing duties, Articles 8.2. and 8.3 SA accord Member States the option to reduce the damaging effects of other Members' behaviour by authorising them to restore the level playing field established in the trade negotiations and disturbed by the unilateral use of safeguard measures.[83]

The Union is obliged, pursuant to Art 4 (2) (b) Regulation 654/2014:

> in the case of rebalancing of concessions or other obligations under provisions on safeguards in international trade agreements, the Union's action shall be substantially equivalent to the level of concessions or other obligations affected by the safeguard measure, in accordance with the conditions of the WTO Agreement on Safeguards …[84]

A week after the US had taken its measures,[85] the Commission sought information and views regarding the EU's economic interests in accordance with Article 9 of Regulation 654/2014 to obtain input to assist it in assessing the necessity and

[79] See Hahn (n 76) 301–26.

[80] According to the Appellate Body in the US – *Standards for Reformulated and Conventional Gasoline*, WTO Doc WT/DS2/AB/R, p 23.

[81] Art 8.2 SA: 'If no agreement is reached within 30 days in the consultations under paragraph 3 of Article 12, then the affected exporting Members shall be free, not later than 90 days after the measure is applied, to suspend, upon the expiration of 30 days from the day on which written notice of such suspension is received by the Council for Trade in Goods, the application of substantially equivalent concessions or other obligations under GATT 1994, to the trade of the Member applying the safeguard measure, the suspension of which the Council for Trade in Goods does not disapprove.'

[82] The 12-month requirement does not take into account the time necessary for implementation.

[83] Hahn (n 76).

[84] Regulation 654/2014 (n 64).

[85] On 16 March 2018, www.reuters.com/article/us-usa-trade-eu-explainer/europes-response-to-u-s-import-tariffs-idUSKCN1GS2CH (last accessed 2 October 2018).

the parameters of possible commercial policy measures.[86] China has now taken the same route. It has announced that it views the US measures as safeguards-in-disguise and has announced that it will unilaterally balance the agreed upon balance of mutual rights and obligations.[87]

V. Conclusion

These are dangerous times for the world trading system: the old order has been under great stress since the success of the last GATT trade round, certainly since China joined. The EU has always been keen to assist its external economic relations with the GATT/WTO system. Together with the US, it was one of the last players using actively bilateral trade negotiations, wanting to keep the WTO as the centre of gravity in its trade policy. When the Union did engage in Deep and Comprehensive FTA (DCFTA) deals, it paid attention in ensuring the compatibility between its DCFTAs and the WTO legal order.

With the benefit of hindsight, one may look back in the years to come and find that the reports of the WTO's imminent death were greatly exaggerated. However, in the meantime, the EU needs to contribute to the WTO staying afloat, including talking with its old ally and friend, but also pushing back when need be, and continue with those willing in Europe, Asia-Pacific and elsewhere to keep markets open. In a world which seems to move to less rules-based approaches, one of the original functions of the Union becomes more evident than ever: to protect the many small and medium-sized European countries from being an afterthought for the world's old and new superpowers: *l'unité fait la force*. It is quite fitting that the Court of Justice has, in its recent Opinion 2/15, strengthened the Union's hand with regard to Europe's external economic relations power, the Common Commercial Policy.

[86] See http://trade.ec.europa.eu/consultations/index.cfm?consul_id=253 (last accessed 2 October 2018).

[87] See WTO Doc G/SG/161 (n 67); World Trade Online, 'China Requests Safeguard Consultations with the US over Steel, Aluminum 232 Tariffs' (26 March 2018), available at https://insidetrade.com/content/china-requests-safeguard-consultations-us-over-steel-aluminum-232-tariffs (last accessed 2 October 2018); Inside US Trade – 04/06/2018, 'At WTO, US Says China has "No Basis" to Retaliate against 232 Tariffs', available at https://insidetrade.com/inside-us-trade/wto-us-says-china-has-no-basis-retaliate-against-232-tariffs (last accessed 2 October 2018).

PART IV

A View from Practice: Comments on Current Developments in the Interface between EU and International Law

12

The Interaction between Public International Law and EU Law: The Role Played by the Court of Justice

RICARDO DA SILVA PASSOS*

Even if the interaction between public international law and EU law has surely been a regular topic explored by the legal doctrine, the fact is that the legal issues involved continue to be of great interest, in particular taking into account the enhanced visibility of the EU as an international actor following the entry into force of the Treaty of Lisbon.

It is also true that this is instigated by the fact that the authors of the EU Treaties never inserted a specific provision on the place of international law in the EU legal system and on the relationship between both, nor on the consequences of the non-respect by the Union of a norm of international law (treaty or customary law). In this regard, the only provision that exists is Article 216, paragraph 2 of the Treaty on the Functioning of the European Union (TFEU), according to which international agreements concluded by the EU, are 'binding upon the institutions of the Union and its Member States'. These agreements are an integral part of the EU legal order as from their entry into force,[1] and have primacy over EU acts.[2] The same applies to customary law[3] and to secondary international law deriving from international agreements such as Association Council decisions.[4]

The European Court of Justice (ECJ) underlined that international law binding the EU ranked between primary law and secondary law.[5] The legal doctrine has been most active and inventive in examining in depth the issues relating to this interaction, but it was, to a large extent, the ECJ's role to lay down the main

* The opinions expressed are personal.
[1] Case 181/73 *Haegeman v Belgian State* ECLI:EU:C:1974:41 para 5.
[2] C-366/10 *Air Transport Association of America and Others* ECLI:EU:C:2011:864 para 50.
[3] C-162/96 *Racke GmbH & Co v Hauptzollamt Mainz* ECLI:EU:C:1998:293.
[4] C-192/89 *Sevinçe v Staatssecretaris van Justitie* [1990] ECR I-3461.
[5] See Racke (n 3); see also C-179/97 *Espagne v Commission* [1999] ECR I-1251.

principles in this matter. The ECJ did so first, because there was a need to affirm the very specific nature and autonomy of the EU legal order *vis-à-vis* international law (and the Member States), and second because it had to establish the conditions for the incorporation of international law in the EU legal order, when it had to control the validity of EU acts. The ECJ acted in this context through different proceedings, namely Opinions delivered in accordance with Article 218(11) TFEU, judgments on the basis of the annulment procedure (Article 263 TFEU) or the preliminary ruling procedure (Article 267 TFEU).

I will limit myself to some general remarks relating to some of the arguments developed in the excellent papers presented by Inge Govaere[6] and by Violeta Moreno-Lax and Paul Gragl.[7]

In these papers the topic of the ECJ case law relating to the autonomy of the EU legal order, its existence and its scope, is critically examined, in particular in the light of Opinion 2/13 concerning the accession of the EU to the European Convention on Human Rights (ECHR).[8] Moreno-Lax and Gragl also revisit the question of the nature of the EU legal order, namely whether the latter is a *sui generis* subject of international law. Lastly, reference will be made to some recent judgments applying international agreements.

I. The EU is Surely a *sui generis* Subject of International Law

Actually, the fact that the EU is a *sui generis* legal order does not seem to be disputed. Nobody can seriously contest that the EU is not an ordinary international organisation, even if it was originally established by international treaties. The case law of the ECJ and the successive modifications of the treaties – which also consolidated this case law, particularly in the treaty of Lisbon – made clear that the treaties are of a constitutional nature.

By 1963, the ECJ had already established that

> the Community constitutes a new legal order of international law for the benefit of which the States have limited their sovereign rights, albeit within limited fields, and the subjects of which comprise not only Member States but also their nationals. Independently of the legislation of the Member States, EU law therefore not only imposes obligations on individuals but is also intended to confer upon them rights that become part of their legal heritage.[9]

[6] In chapter one of this volume entitled, 'Interconnecting Legal Systems and the Autonomous EU Legal Order: A Balloon Dynamic'.

[7] V Moreno-Lax and P Gragl, 'The Quest for a (Fully-fledged) Theoretical Framework: Co-implication, Embeddedness, and Interdependency between Public International Law and EU Law' (2016) 1 35 *Yearbook of European Law*.

[8] Opinion 2/13 of 18 December 2014 *Accession of the EU to the ECHR* ECLI:EU:C:2014 para 157.

[9] Case 26/62 *Van Gend & Loos* ECLI:EU:C:1963:1, judgment of 5 February 1963 at 12.

One year later, in *Costa*, the ECJ modified this sentence and deleted 'of international law',[10] stating that: 'By contrast with ordinary international treaties, the EEC has created its own legal system which became an integral part of the legal systems of the Member States and which their courts are bound to apply'.[11]

This formula has been used ever since. The ECJ clearly distanced itself from international law and established a closer link with the legal orders of the Member States. From the very beginning, the ECJ laid down the principle of direct effect of EU law under certain conditions – which imply that private parties can rely on provisions of international agreements with direct effect conferring rights on them – and the principle of supremacy over the law of the Member States,[12] even if the latter is of a constitutional nature. The ECJ underlined that national courts are obliged not to apply national provisions that conflict with EU law, and must not wait for the national constitutional court to set the national provisions aside.[13]

The primacy of EU law is different from the primacy of international law. Indeed, while the latter leaves contracting parties the choice with form and method – including the choice between a 'monist' and a 'dualist' attitude towards international law – the EU treaties are an integral part of the legal systems of the Member States. When the contracting parties ensure the primacy of international law, they do so in accordance with their own national constitutions. In the EU legal system, by contrast, the treaties created a preliminary ruling procedure with the specific purpose of harmonising the interpretation of EU law and providing the ECJ with exclusive jurisdiction to decide on the validity of EU acts.[14]

Another element that distinguishes the EU legal order from international law is the principle that all EU acts must respect fundamental rights and that this respect constitutes a condition of their lawfulness, which it is for the ECJ to review, in the framework of the complete system of legal remedies established by the Treaty. An international agreement cannot have the effect of prejudicing this principle, which is one of the constitutional principles of the Treaty.[15] With the Treaty of Lisbon, the respect of fundamental rights has been enshrined in the primary law (Article 2

[10] In this regard, Koen Lenaerts underlines that 'cette omission visait ainsi à éloigner l'Union de ses origines puisées dans le droit international, tout en la rapprochant des ordres juridiques des États membres'. K Lenaerts, 'Les fondements constitutionnels de l'Union européenne dans leur rapport avec le droit international' in *La Cour de Justice de l'Union européennes sous la présidence de Vassilios Skouris (2003–2015)* (2015) 368.

[11] *Costa v ENEL* 6/64 ECLI:EU:C:1964:66, judgment of 15 July 1964 at 593.

[12] ibid.

[13] Case 106/77 *Administrazione delle finanze dello Stato v Simmenthal* ECLI:EU:C:1978:49, judgment of 9 March 1978.

[14] See in this regard, G De Baere, 'The Relationship and Interaction between International Law, EU Law and National Law' in J Wouters, C Ryngaert, T Ruys and G De Baere (eds), *International Law: A European Perspective* (Hart Publishing, forthcoming 2018).

[15] C-402/05 P and C-415/05 P *KADI and AI Barakaat International Foundation v Council and Commission* ECLI:EU:C:2008:461 para 285.

of the Treaty on European Union (TEU)) and the Charter of Fundamental Rights now has the same value as the Treaties (Article 6 TEU).

Moreover, an international agreement cannot prejudice two other essential principles of the EU: the principle of conferral of powers and the principle of institutional balance. This has been clearly emphasised by the ECJ, in particular in Opinion 2/13. In the latter, the ECJ has emphasised the specific characteristics of the EU, and its nature of a 'basic constitutional charter'.[16]

II. The Constitutional Autonomy of the EU

According to Moreno-Lax and Gragl

> … by 'elevating' the Union to a legal order which is autonomous from the rest of international law the ECJ has helped the EU legal 'child' to outgrow its international legal 'parent'. It is accordingly unquestionable that, as the distance from international law augmented, the EU legal order became more 'domestic' or 'internal' in nature as a result.[17]

The ECJ played an important role in the determination and identification of the constitutional elements of the EU as an autonomous legal order. That was the result of a case law which developed these principles during the 60 years after *van Gend en Loos*. It is dubious that the ECJ had a 'fully fledged theory of EU law in mind when it developed the concept of an autonomous legal order'.[18] The ECJ has developed its case law on an empirical basis (*de manière 'prétorienne'*) when deciding individual cases. It could not be otherwise, it is in my view not proper for a Court to deliberately build a 'theoretical framework'. I believe, however, that the existing and abundant case law actually provides such a basic 'theoretical framework', which of course will tend to be more concrete and detailed through the judgments delivered. There is though a solid consistency over the years on the main features of the 'constitutional autonomy' of the EU.

Inge Govaere underlined the crucial role of the ECJ in safeguarding a hermetically closed system of EU law for the very survival of the autonomous EU legal order. She refers to structural pressure from within (matters related to the Common Foreign and Security Policy (CFSP)) and externally (incorporation of international agreements, forum shopping, issues related to external dispute settlement mechanisms).

Focusing on this latter pressure, I believe that the ECJ has provided some rather useful responses in its case law, in particular in the *Kadi* judgments and in Opinion 2/13. In *Kadi*, the ECJ affirms the limits of the integration of international

[16] See Opinion 2/13 (n 8) at 2454.
[17] Moreno-Lax and Gragl (n 7) 455–70, 462.
[18] As pointed out by Moreno-Lax and Gragl (n 7) at 465.

law in the EU and stresses the ultimate responsibility of the EU in deciding on the basis of its own interpretation of the protection of fundamental rights. According to Piet Eeckhout,

> where there is a real clash with international law, such as in the case of the UN Security Council's counterterrorism policies, the Court of justice opts for the supremacy of EU law, even in the face of a clear and primordial international conflict norm, such as the primacy of UN Charter obligations.[19]

President Lenaerts wrote a remarkable article about the essential elements of the autonomy of the EU in 2015 in the *Liber Amicorum Vassilios Skouris*.[20] He pointed out that the incorporation of international law can only be accepted if it is certain that the following are respected:

- the principle of conferral,
- the principle of institutional balance, and in particular the exclusive jurisdiction of the ECJ to interpret and review EU law,
- the fundamental rights, as enshrined in the EU Charter.

This does not mean that, as Moreno-Lax and Gragl fear, because of the ECJ case law we would enter into a new era of 'closure and isolationism' in the relationship between the EU legal order and international law.

Such a risk does not exist. Even if the case law of the ECJ, in particular Opinion 2/13, was criticised in some legal doctrine, I believe that the reality is that the EU is acting in a large range of areas of international law, such as: international trade (including international investment law), international environment, law of the sea, human rights law, international security and fight against terrorism and international labour law. The EU is a global actor with legal personality and visibility on the international scene, with a High Representative and an External Action Service.

It is interesting to note in this context that in his speech of 13 September 2017 on the state of the Union before the European Parliament, President Junker mentioned international trade as one of the top priorities of the Commission's Working Program for 2018. He also announced that, beyond the agreements concluded with Canada (CETA) and Japan, the Commission will start negotiations with a view to concluding trade agreements with Mercosur, Mexico, Australia and New Zealand. New challenges are thus to be expected and a more regular use of the advisory opinion procedure, foreseen in Article 218, paragraph 11 TFEU, seems indispensable.

[19] P Eeckhout, 'The Integration of Public International Law in EU Law: Analytical and Normative Questions' in P Eeckhout and M Lopez-Escudero (eds), *The European Union's External Action in Times of Crisis* (Hart, 2016) 196.

[20] See *La Cour de justice de l'Union européenne sous la présidence de Vassilios Skouris (2003–2015)* (n 10).

III. Some Recent Developments Concerning International Agreements

The EU external action shall be guided by the respect of international law, and the EU shall seek to develop relations and build partnerships with third countries and international organisations, and promote multilateral solutions to common problems (Article 21, para 1, TEU). In this respect, recent cases brought before the ECJ demonstrate the existing interaction with international law, in particular the litigation relating to the interpretation of international agreements, like the Morocco Liberalisation Agreement and the Fisheries Agreement, the EU-Turkey statement, and the trade agreements with Singapore (Opinion 1/2015) and the CETA envisaged Agreement (Belgium introduced a request for an advisory opinion on 8 September 2017).

Concerning the very definition of 'international agreement', the General Court, after having examined the overall context, the procedure for its adoption and its content, came to the conclusion that the EU-Turkey statement of 18 March 2016 concerning the irregular migration from Turkey to the EU was not adopted by the European Council but by the Member States. On those grounds, 'even supposing that an international agreement could have been informally concluded during the meeting of 18 March 2016', the General Court considered that it had no jurisdiction to examine an action brought under Article 263 TFEU.[21] This Decision has been challenged before the ECJ. By Order of 12 September 2018, the ECJ dismissed the appeals as manifestly inadmissible. It noted that the appeals were incoherent as they did not indicate with precision the contested elements in the judgment under appeal or the legal arguments specifically advanced, nor did they identify any error of law that the General Court may have committed.[22]

Concerning the EU Agreements with Morocco covering the territory of Western Sahara, a pure subject of international law and of the application also of the Vienna Convention on the Law of the Treaties, the General Court and the Court, followed different approaches.

The case relates to the status of Western Sahara as a Non-Self-Governing-Territory within the meaning of Article 73 of the UN Charter and the consequences as for the agreement between the EU and Morocco concerning liberalisation measures on agricultural and fisheries products. It was brought before the General Court by the *Front Polisario* against the Council.[23] The General Court annulled the Council Decision concluding the agreement. It referred to the legal opinion of the UN Legal Counsel concerning the exploration of resources of non-self governing territories, which stated that:

> Where resource exploitation activities are concluded in Non-Self-Governing-Territories for the benefit of the peoples of those Territories, on their behalf or in

[21] T-257/16 *NM v European Council* ECLI:EU:T:2017:130, Order of the General Court of 28 February 2017.

[22] Joined cases C-208/17 P to C-210/17 P, *NF, NG and NM v European Council* ECLI:EU:C:2018:705.

[23] The Commission intervened in support of the Council, but the European Parliament did not.

consultation with their representatives, they are considered compatible with the United Nations Charter obligations of the administering Power and in conformity of 'permanent sovereignty over national resources' enshrined therein.

The General Court acknowledged that the agreement applies to the territory of Western Sahara. It then considered that the EU enjoys a wide discretion as regards whether it is appropriate to conclude an agreement with a non-Member State which will be applied on a disputed territory (that is to say, Western Sahara). The General Court decided that, taking into account the obligations deriving from international law and the respect of the fundamental rights of the local populations, the Council should have examined all these elements before adopting its Decision, instead of leaving the examination of these considerations only to the Moroccan authorities.[24]

By contrast, the ECJ followed a different approach and set aside the judgment of the General Court.[25] It examined in depth the status of Western Sahara in international law. It considered that the General Court did not draw the consequences of this status as regards the inapplicability of the agreement to the territory of Western Sahara. In view of the separate and distinct status accorded to the territory of Western Sahara by virtue of the principle of self-determination, in relation to that of any State, including the Kingdom of Morocco, the words 'territory of the Kingdom of Morocco' set out in Article 94 of the agreement cannot be interpreted in such a way that Western Sahara is included within the territorial scope of the agreement, as this was tacitly accepted by Morocco and the EU.[26]

In another issue of international law, and as a consequence of the status of Western Sahara, the ECJ pointed out that, in accordance with the principle of the relative effects of treaties, of which the rule contained in Article 34 of the Vienna Convention is an expression, treaties do not impose any obligations, or confer any rights on third States without their consent. The people of Western Sahara must be regarded as a 'third party' within the meaning of this principle of international law, and it has not been showed that they have expressed any such consent to the agreement.[27]

Two recent other cases were also decided by the ECJ and the General Court concerning Western Sahara: Case T-180/14 relating to the Fisheries Partnership Agreement and the 2013 Protocol to this Agreement between Morocco and the EU[28] and Case C-266/16 relating to the request for a preliminary ruling

[24] Case T-512/12 *Front Polisario v Council* ECLI:EU:T:2015:953, judgment of the General Court of 10 December 2015.

[25] Case C-104/16 P *Council v Front Polisario* ECLI:EU:C:2016:973, judgment of the ECJ of 21 December 2016.

[26] ibid para 93.

[27] ibid para 106.

[28] *Fisheries Partnership Agreement between the European Communities and the Kingdom of Morocco* [2006] OJ L141/4; see Case T-180/14 *Front Polisario v Council* EU:T:2018:496, Order of the General Court of 18 July 2018 and Case C-266/16 *The Queen on the application of Western Sahara Campaign UK v. Secretary of State for Environment, Food and Rural Affairs* ECLI:EU:C:2018:118, judgment of 27 February 2018.

submitted by the High Court of Justice and Wales on the interpretation and compatibility with international law of both the Association Agreement, the Fisheries Partnership Agreement and the 2013 Protocol to this Agreement. Here too, the ECJ had to appreciate the territorial scope of the Fisheries Agreement and the Protocol, since the EU vessels fish in the Western Sahara waters. In its judgment of 27 February 2018, the ECJ considered that the waters adjacent to the territory of Western Sahara do not fall within the scope of the Fisheries Partnership Agreement and the 2013 Protocol.[29]

The ECJ referred to its previous judgment of 21 December 2016, concerning the Association Agreement with Morocco, where it held that the concept of 'territory of the Kingdom of Morocco' in Article 94 of that Agreement must be construed as referring to the geographical area over which Morocco exercises the fullness of the powers granted to sovereign entities by international law, to the exclusion of any other territory, such as that of Western Sahara.[30]

The ECJ then examined the relevant provisions of the Fisheries Partnership Agreement concerning its territorial scope, and in particular Article 2(a) of that Agreement, according to which 'Moroccan fishing zone' means the 'waters falling within the sovereignty or jurisdiction of the Kingdom of Morocco'. Under the Convention on the Law of the Sea, the waters over which a coastal State is entitled to exercise sovereignty or jurisdiction are limited exclusively to the waters adjacent to its territory and forming part of its territorial sea or of its exclusive economic zone. On this basis, the ECJ found that since the territory of Western Sahara is not part of the Moroccan fishing zone, the waters adjacent to the territory of Western Sahara are not part of the Moroccan fishing zone. The ECJ added that it would be contrary to the rules of international law, which the Union must observe, if it were agreed that the waters directly adjacent to the waters of Western Sahara were to be included within the scope of that Agreement.[31]

The ECJ went further and added that 'consequently, the European Union could not properly support any intention of the Kingdom of Morocco to include, by such means, the waters in question within the scope of that agreement'.[32] In this context, the ECJ disregarded the argument put forward by the Council and the Commission, according to which the Kingdom of Morocco might be regarded as a 'de facto administrative power or as an occupying power of the territory of Western Sahara'.[33] The ECJ applied the same reasoning to the 2013 Protocol, which contains geographical coordinates of the baselines and its fishing zone.

[29] C-266/16, ibid.
[30] Case C-104/16 (n 25) para 62.
[31] Para 71.
[32] Para 71.
[33] Para 72.

Actually, the ECJ could have given an advisory opinion a long time ago, had the European Parliament not rejected a recommendation in that sense from its Fisheries Committee, on 29 September 2011.[34]

Concerning Case T-180/14, which was suspended until the ECJ gave its judgments in Case C-104/16 P and Case C-266/16, the General Court rejected it by Order of 19 July 2018.[35] It considered that the Front Polisario has no standing to seek annulment of the Council Decisions at stake. The General Court merely followed the ECJ's judgments and noted that, because the agreements (Liberalisation or Fisheries Partnership Agreements) must be interpreted in accordance with the relevant rules of international law as not applying to the territory or the waters adjacent to the territory of Western Sahara, that implies the Front Polisario has no standing to bring the present action.[36]

The consequences of the above ECJ judgment are very important for the future relations between the EU and the Kingdom of Morocco, and of course also for the future of the territory of Western Sahara. Indeed, the ECJ requires that the agreements concluded by the Union shall not apply to the territory or the waters adjacent to the territory of Western Sahara because that would be contrary to the rules of international law. *Quid juris* if, in spite of this requirement, an agreement concluded by the Union is actually applied, with evidence put forward, in the territory or in the waters adjacent to the territory of Western Sahara?

On another subject, on 26 July 2017, the ECJ gave an Opinion[37] concerning the draft agreement between Canada and the EU relating to the transfer of Passenger Name Record (PNR) data from the EU to Canada. The request was introduced by the European Parliament and aimed mainly at having the ECJ's position on the compatibility of the envisaged agreement with the rights of individuals to the protection of their private life and personal data laid down in Article 16 TFEU and Articles 7, 8 and 52(1) of the Charter.

The envisaged agreement was intended to ensure public security by means of a transfer of PNR to Canada and the use of that data within the framework of the fight against terrorist offences and serious transnational crime. That objective is of general interest in the EU and is capable of justifying serious interferences with the rights enshrined in Articles 7 and 8 of the Charter. The ECJ had to assess

[34] The reason why the European Parliament did not wish to request the advisory opinion of the ECJ was probably because it preferred instead to decline to give consent to this Second Protocol to the Fisheries Agreement. Indeed, on 14 December 2011 (three months later), Parliament refused to give consent. The Second Protocol was then renegotiated and the European Parliament eventually gave its consent to the new text on 10 December 2013. See, for further details, R Passos, 'The External Powers of the EP' in P Eeckhout and M Lopez-Escudero (eds), *The European Union's External Action in Times of Crisis* (Hart Publishing, 2016) 92–95.

[35] Case T-180/14 (n 28) at 496.

[36] In the meantime the Front Polisario introduced two other annulment proceedings before the General Court: Case T-275/18 concerning the Euro-Mediterranean Agreement on air services [2006] OJ L386/57 and Case T-376/18, concerning the Council Decision of 16 April 2018 purporting to the conclusion of a new Fisheries Protocol replacing the 2013 Protocol. Both cases are still pending.

[37] Opinion 1/15 of 26 July 2017 *PNR Agreement EU-Canada* ECLI:EU:C:2016.

whether these interferences are limited to what is strictly necessary, and whether the envisaged agreement laid down clear and precise rules governing the scope of the measures provided for.

In substance, the ECJ came to the conclusion that the envisaged agreement:

- was not sufficiently precise as regards the PNR data to be transferred;
- could not foresee the transfer of sensitive data to Canada, because it entailed no precise and solid justification, and because the processing of sensitive data is prohibited by Directive (EU) 2016/681;[38]
- does not ensure that the disclosure of PNR data by the Canadian competent Authority to other Canadian government authorities or to government authorities of third countries will be limited to what is strictly necessary;
- does not guarantee, in a sufficiently clear and precise manner, that the oversight of compliance with the rules laid down in this agreement relating to the protection of individuals with regard to the processing of PNR data will be carried out by an independent authority, within the meaning of Article 8(3) of the Charter.

Following this Opinion, the Commission made it public on 15 September 2017 that Canada agreed to renegotiate the agreement with the EU.[39]

Furthermore, the ECJ had been requested to provide an advisory opinion concerning the trade agreement with Singapore[40] and the trade agreement with Canada.[41] These are two important Opinions. The first clarified the parts of the envisaged agreement on which the Union has exclusive competence and the parts on which the competence is shared with the Member States (mixed competence).

On this latter competence, the ECJ considered that the mechanism foreseen for settling the investment dispute, the Investor-State Dispute Settlement (ISDS) mechanism belonged to the shared competence. In the Advisory Opinion, the ECJ was only requested to examine the question of the competence of the EU to conclude the envisaged agreement.

By contrast, the request for an advisory opinion on CETA, which was referred by the Belgium Government on 6 September 2017, requests the ECJ to examine the compatibility with the Treaties of the arbitration mechanism for investor-state disputes (the Investment Court System – ICS). This mechanism is very different from the one foreseen in the Singapore agreement, which corresponded to the classical arbitration mechanism. The ICS consists of a permanent investment court composed by a Tribunal and an Appeal Tribunal with 15 members.

[38] Directive (EU) 2016/681 of the European Parliament and of the Council of 27 April 2016 on the use of passenger name record (PNR) data for the prevention, detection, investigation and prosecution of terrorist offences and serious crime [2016] OJ L119/ 132–49.

[39] Bulletin Quotidien Europe 11862 of 15 September 2017 at 19.

[40] Opinion 2/15 *EUSFTA* ECLI:EU:C:2017:376.

[41] Opinion 1/17.

In concrete terms, the ECJ shall assess whether the ICS is compatible with:

- the exclusive competence of the ECJ to provide a definitive interpretation of EU law;
- the general principle of equality and the imperative of the '*effet utile*' of EU law;
- the right of access to courts;
- the right to independent and impartial justice.

The ECJ will examine again whether the creation of such a court will have, or not, a negative effect on the autonomy of the EU legal order.

In this regard, in Opinion 2/13 the ECJ established the following five principles:

- the decisions of the international judicial body shall not bind the EU institutions to a particular interpretation of EU law;
- the ECJ has the exclusive competence to interpret EU law in accordance with Article 344 TFEU;
- the international judicial body shall not, in any way, interfere with the division of powers between the EU and its Members States;
- the international judicial body shall not have jurisdiction to interpret EU law in a manner which could affect the monopoly of the ECJ concerning the preliminary rulings procedure;
- it shall not have jurisdiction to appreciate the validity of acts adopted by the EU under the CFSP provisions.

It is a complex issue to ensure the autonomy of the ECJ with the co-existence, and possible interference, of another international judicial body. The ECJ has shown a very rigorous defence of the specific characteristics and of the autonomy of the EU legal order, in particular regarding the conditions of judicial review by another international judicial body. This is a matter of particular interest to Inge Govaere who has recently published a paper on this issue.[42]

[42] I Govaere, 'TTIP and Dispute Settlement: Potential Consequences for the Autonomous EU Legal Order' *College of Europe, Research Paper in Law 01/2016*. See also, F Hoffmeister, 'Of Transferred Competence, Institutional Balance and Judicial Autonomy – Constitutional Developments' in J Czuczai and F Naert (eds), *EU Trade Policy Seven Years after Lisbon, the EU as a Global Actor Bridging Legal Theory and Practice, Liber Amicorum in Honour of Ricardo Gosalbo Bono* (Brill, Nijhoff, 2017) 336. Hoffmeister believes that the conditions laid down by the ECJ in Opinion 2/13 are satisfied. He argues that 'new enforcement chapters on investment matters in EU free trade agreements do not pose a threat to the EU's judicial autonomy'.

13

The *Rosneft* Case as a Good Example of Smooth Interaction between EU Law and International Law in the Most Recent Post-Lisbon Jurisprudence of the Court of Justice

JENÖ CZUCZAI*

I. Introduction

The good and smooth interaction between EU law and international law in the EU legal order is a classical topic, which also has a lot of practical implications. Respect for international law as a principle of Community law had been shown by the Court of Justice very early on, in the late 1980s and 1990s, particularly in the field of Community Fisheries policy.[1] Later on, especially in regards to the emergence of threats caused by international terrorism in the EU, practical necessities called[2] for a more protective jurisprudence from the Court defending the autonomous nature and the rule of law foundation of the EU legal order with special emphasis on the protection of fundamental rights as core constitutional values of the Treaties, even when the EU implemented UN Security

* The views and opinions expressed in this contribution are exclusively personal and those of the author; they do not constitute in any way a formal and official position of the Council nor of the European Council, nor of their Legal Service. The manuscript of this contribution was closed in March 2018.

[1] See in more detail, eg, Case C-286/1990 *Poulsen and Diva Navigation* (1992) ECR I-6019, para 9, or Case C-405/92 *Mondiet* (1993) ECR I-6133, paras 11–13, or in more general terms RR Churchill, *EEC Fisheries Law* (Dordrecht, Nijhoff, 1987) and RA Wessels (ed), *International Law as Law of the EU* (Leiden-Boston, Martinus-Nijhoff, 2012) and A Rosas- L Armati, *EU Constitutional Law – an Introduction*, (Oxford, Hart Publishing, 2018) 57 ff.

[2] See in this respect J Czuczai, 'The Development of a Single Counter-Terrorism Policy in the External Action of the EU – The Role of the Council – Some Legal Aspects after Lisbon' in E Herlin-Karnell and C Matera (eds), *External Dimension of the EU Counter-Terrorism Policy*, CLEER Working Paper, 2014/2, 47–60.

Council resolutions relating to the global fight against international terrorism.[3] This period also raised, indeed, a lot of tensions in the legal practice between EU law and international law, particularly because even today there is no clear-cut rule in EU primary law on where international law should really be placed in the doctrinal hierarchical ranking of norms in the EU constitutional legal order.[4] It is also clear, however, that the EU constitutional acquis is constantly developing,[5] especially after Lisbon, which has led to increasingly richer case law coming out of the Court in relation to the EU Charter of Fundamental Rights ('having the same legal value as the Treaties'). At the same time, today it is also self-evident that when the EU exercises its powers, it can be done in strict observance of international law (Article 3(5) Treaty on European Union (TEU)[6]). After Lisbon, international law has been given a new emphasis; it is now specifically addressed more than ten times in the founding Treaties.[7] Nonetheless, in the last couple of years, some authors have started to opine that the Court jurisprudence has become less 'international law friendly'. They argue that the institutional approach in the EU towards international law is not uniform, whereas the practice of the EU legislature shows an increasingly open and receptive attitude towards international law, the Court of Justice tends to be more restrictive in its attitude with regards to international law underlying the autonomy of the EU legal order.[8]

[3] On the issue of the core constitutional values of the EU, which must be protected at all times in EU external relations after Lisbon, see eg, in a broader context, J Wouters, D Coppens and B de Meester, 'The EU's External Relations after Lisbon' in S Griller and J Willer (eds), *The Lisbon Treaty. European Constitutionalism without a Constitutional Treaty?* (Springer, 2008) 143–203 or specifically focusing on the Court of Justice of the European Union (CJEU) in this respect CA Feinäugle, 'Commission v Kadi. Joined Cases C-584/10 P, C-593/10 P, and C-595/10 P' (October 2013) 107 *The American Journal of International Law* 4, 878–84, etc.

[4] See, for example, Art 216(2) TFEU, which reads as follows: 'Agreements concluded by the Union are binding upon the institutions of the Union and on its Member States', but this provision does not say anything about the hierarchical ranking of international law in the EU legal order, namely whether the EU legal order as such is monist, dualist or some sort of mixed system, if someone wanted to use this categorisation describing the hierarchical link between these two autonomous sets of norms at national level, especially in the context of constitutional protective power-setting.

[5] See on the notion of 'EU constitutional acquis' in more detail J Czuczai, 'Practical Implementation by the Acceding Candidate Countries of the Constitutional Acquis of the EU – Problems and Challenges' in AE Kellermann, JW de Zwaan and J Czuczai (eds), *EU Enlargement – The Constitutional Impact at EU and National Level* (The Hague, TMC Asser Press, 2001) 411–22.

[6] Art 3(5) TEU provides that: 'In its relations with the wider world, the Union shall uphold and promote its values and interests and contribute to the protection of its citizens. It shall contribute to peace, security, the sustainable development of the Earth, solidarity and mutual respect among peoples, free and fair trade, eradication of poverty and the protection of human rights, in particular the rights of the child, as well as to the strict observance and the development of international law, including respect for the principles of the United Nations Charter' (emphasis added).

[7] See in more detail, for example, how the EU contributes to the development of international law, which is now, after Lisbon, specifically required by Art 3(5) TEU in J Wouters and M Hermez, 'The EU's Contribution to the Strict Observance and the Development of International Law at the UNGA 6th Committee' (Working Paper No 177, KU Leuven, Leuven Centre for Global Governance Studies, Institute for International law, 2016) 1–16.

[8] See in more detail, for example, V Moreno-Lax and P Gragl, 'The Quest for a (Fully-Fledged) Theoretical Framework: Co-Implication, Embeddedness, and Interdependency between Public

The very recent *Rosneft* Case[9] was also referred to, in which the Court extended its powers by accepting even the preliminary ruling possibilities, based on Article 275(2) Treaty on the Functioning of the European Union (TFEU), though under strict conditions, in relation to Common Foreign and Security Policy (CFSP)-based restrictive measures targeting individuals and legal entities, etc. A more consistent approach, consisting of a convergence of the attitudes of the different EU actors towards international law is, therefore, called for by them.

As far as I am concerned, personally I don't share this view. First of all, I should note that since I strongly believe in the autonomy of the EU legal order, I wrote a long article in 2012 in defence of the autonomy of the EU legal order *vis-à-vis* the increasingly developing norm-creating activities of international organisations and their possible impact on the integrity of the EU legal system.[10] In this article I welcomed the Court's increasingly protective jurisprudence concerning the autonomous nature of the EU legal order. On the other hand, I also think that respect for international law is, even today, a core value in the constantly evolving and developing jurisprudence of the Court, which personally I also welcome, as a believer in the full respect for and observance of international law.

Since, among the examples, in which, at least according to some authors, the Court went too far in order to defend the autonomy of the EU legal order, the most recent *Rosneft* Case was also mentioned, in this contribution I would like to deal with those two aspects of the *Rosneft* judgment (without, however, writing a fully-fledged case note on it)[11] which, in my view, clearly prove that, even after the

International Law and EU Law' (2016) *Yearbook of European Law* 1–16, as well as Violeta Moreno-Lax's contribution in chapter 2 of this book on 'The Axiological Emancipation of a (Non-) Principle: Autonomy, International Law and the EU Legal Order'. From the most recent relevant jurisprudence (debated in the previously-referred articles) see, for instance, Case C-366/10 *Air Transport Association of America (ATAA)* ECLI:EU:C:2011:864, in particular paras 123 ff; or Case C-308/06 *Intertanko and Others* ECLI:EU:C:2008:312 especially paras 39 ff and paras 51 ff; or Case C-638 /16 PPU *X and X v Belgium* ECLI:EU:C:2017:173 (in which the recalled international law aspects (eg the European Convention on Human Rights (ECHR) or the Geneva Convention) were practically unexamined); or the legality issue of the so-called EU-Turkey joint press statement in Case T-193/16 *NG v European Council* ECLI:EU:T:2017:129 (which the General Court dismissed based on procedural grounds (lack of jurisdiction of the Court), without, however, examining the raised international treaty-making aspects, etc, later on, after appeal, upheld also by an order of the CJEU in Joined Cases C-208/17 to C-210/17 P, *NF, NG, NM v European Council* ECLI:EU:C:2018:705).

[9] See Case C-72/15 *PJSC Rosneft Oil Company v Her Majesty's Treasury et al*, ECLI:EU:C:2017:236, Judgment of the Court (Grand Chamber) of 28 March 2017.

[10] See J Czuczai, 'The Autonomy of the EU Legal Order and the Law-Making Activities of International Organizations – Some Examples Regarding the Council's Most Recent Practice' (2012) *Yearbook of European Law* 452–72.

[11] For a detailed analysis of the *Rosneft* Case see, for example, P Koutrakos, 'Judicial Review in the EU's Common Foreign and Security Policy' (January 2018) *International and Comparative Law Quarterly* 67, 1–35, especially 10, 18–19, 21–23; G Butler, 'The Coming of Age of the Court's Jurisdiction in the Common Foreign and Security Policy' (2017) *European Constitutional Law Review* 13, 673–703, in particular 680, 682–86, 691, 694 and from 699 ff (especially concerning the future of CFSP with special regard to the rule of law); P.Van Elsuwege, *Between Compliance and Particularism: Member State Interests and European Union Law* (Springer, 2018, forthcoming).

Kadi I–II saga[12] or the Court's Opinion No 2/13,[13] first there is still harmony in the Court's constantly developing jurisprudence between the autonomy concept of the EU legal order and the full respect of international law principle and, second, even after the Court's so-called post-Singapore approach concerning the EU autonomous legal order and mixity,[14] the full observance obligation of international law is undisturbedly crucial for the Court and its steadily evolving jurisprudence as signified elegantly, for example, in the *Rosneft* Case itself. This is especially so in terms of how the Court interpreted the EU-Russia Partnership Agreement in so far as its extraterritorial application in the context of the Ukrainian crisis was concerned in order to protect the EU essential security interests, but also, and this is equally important, to maintain international peace and security in accordance with the principles and rules of the UN Charter.

II. The Lisbon Treaty has Given Special Importance to the Full Observance of International Law by the EU

Before I turn to a concrete analysis on the *Rosneft* Case from the above-mentioned two points of view, I think that it is worth recalling very briefly how the Lisbon Treaty has given international law even more emphasis after its entry into force. For example:

- Article 3(5) TEU now makes it clear that: 'In its relations with the wider world, the Union … shall contribute to peace and security … as well as to the strict observance and the development of international law, including respect for the principles of the United Nations Charter' (emphasis added);[15]

[12] Joined Cases C-402/05 P and C-415/05 P *Kadi and Al Barakaat International Foundation v Council and Commission* (2008) ECR I-6351 (*Kadi I*), especially para 282 and Joined Cases C-584/10 P, C-593/10 P, and C-595/10 P *Commission and Others v Yassin Abdullah Kadi* (*Kadi II*) and its case note in (2014) *Common Market Law Review* 1, 24.

[13] Opinion 2/13 *EU Accession to the ECHR* (2014) ECLI:EU:C:2014:2454, especially paras 156 ff, paras 165–67, and paras 174 ff.

[14] See Opinion 2/15 *Singapore FTA* (2017) ECLI:EU:C:2017:376 and the detailed analysis of its impact on the constitutional autonomy of the EU legal order in F Hoffmeister, 'Of Transferred Competence, Institutional Balance and Judicial Autonomy – Constitutional Developments in EU Trade Policy Seven Years after Lisbon' in J Czuczai and F Naert (eds), *The EU as a Global Actor – Bridging Legal Theory and Practice etc.* (Leiden-Boston, Brill-Nijhoff, 2017) 309–36, in particular from 324 ff.

[15] This provision (and in particular the content of the EU's obligation in terms of its 'strict observance' of international law, including the principles of the United Nations Charter) most recently has been explored in more detail by the Court of Justice (Grand Chamber) in Case C-266/16 *The Queen on the application of Western Sahara Campaign UK v Commissioners for Her Majesty's Revenue and Customs, Secretary of State for Environment, Food and Rural Affairs* ECLI:EU:C:2018:118, especially paras 37 ff. It should still be noted that based on settled case law of the Court, reference to international law in the Treaties also includes rules of customary international law. See further, for example, Case C-366/10 *Air Transport Association of America (ATAA)* (2011) ECR I-13755 at para 101.

- Article 21(1) TEU adds that: 'The Union's action on the international scene shall be guided by the principles which have inspired its own creation, development and enlargement, and which it seeks to advance in the wider world: democracy, rule of law, the universality and indivisibility of human rights and fundamental freedoms, ... and respect for the principles of the United Nations Charter and international law' (emphasis added);
- Article 21(2) points b and c TEU further underline that: 'The Union shall define and pursue common policies and actions, and shall work for a high degree of cooperation in all fields of international relations, in order to: ... (b) consolidate and support democracy, the rule of law, human rights and the principles of international law; (c) preserve peace, prevent conflicts and strengthen international security, in accordance with the purposes and principles of the United Nations Charter, with the principles of the Helsinki Final Act and with the aims of the Charter of Paris, including those relating to external borders; ...' (emphasis added);
- Article 214(2) TFEU still specifically points out that: 'Humanitarian aid operations shall be conducted in compliance with the principles of international law ...' (emphasis added);
- Article 216(2) TFEU as a general rule states that: 'Agreements concluded by the Union are binding upon the institutions of the Union and on its Member States' (emphasis added – this is a clear-cut reference to the international law principle of '*pacta sunt servanda*' within the EU legal order);[16]
- Article 347 TFEU requires that: 'Member States shall consult each other with a view to taking together the steps needed to prevent the functioning of the internal market being affected by measures which a Member State may be called upon to take in the event of serious internal disturbances affecting the maintenance of law and order, in the event of war, serious international tension constituting a threat of war, or in order to carry out obligations it has accepted for the purpose of maintaining peace and international security' (emphasis added);
- Article 351 TFEU finally stresses another very special appearance of the international law obligation of '*pacta sunt servanda*' that: '(1) The rights and obligations arising from agreements concluded before 1 January 1958 or, for acceding States, before the date of their accession, between one or more Member States on the one hand, and one or more third countries on the other, shall not be affected by the provisions of the Treaties. (2) To the extent that such agreements are not compatible with the Treaties, the Member State or States concerned shall take all appropriate steps to eliminate the incompatibilities established. Member States shall, where necessary, assist each other to

[16] Explained in more detail by the Court, for example, in Case C-179/13 *Raad van bestuur van de Sociale verzekeringsbank v LF Evans* ECLI:EU:C:2015:12 at paras 35 ff.

> this end and shall, where appropriate, adopt a common attitude. (3) In applying the agreements referred to in the first paragraph, Member States shall take into account the fact that the advantages accorded under the Treaties by each Member State form an integral part of the establishment of the Union and are thereby inseparably linked with the creation of common institutions, the conferring of powers upon them and the granting of the same advantages by all the other Member States' (emphasis added).[17]

Of course, full compliance with international law obligations, when they are being implemented by the EU institutions and by the Member States in the EU legal order, are not always easy and sometimes even raise serious difficulties. Very well-known examples can be found within EU legal practitioners' circles, for instance, the long-standing implementation problems by the EU of Article 9(3)–(4) of the so-called Aarhus Convention on the access to information obligations and the public participation and access to justice requirements in environmental matters.[18] Another difficult area in this context relates to the implementation issues of international norms, adopted by international organisations, of which as a rule the EU and its Member States are also members, for example, in the EU's Common Agricultural and Fisheries Policies.[19] But, more typical are the implementation question-marks surrounding international law obligations (more specifically, UN Security Council resolutions, adopted based on Chapter VII of the UN Charter, or more general obligations, stemming from the UN Charter itself) in the EU legal order, for example, in the context of fighting against international terrorism or in more general terms of maintaining international peace and security, issues which frequently land at the doors of the Court of Justice of the EU in Luxembourg. This is what happened in the below-explored *Rosneft* Case which also concerned the Ukrainian crisis, caused by Russia's destabilising actions against the territorial independence and integrity of Ukraine.

III. The *Rosneft* Case (Its Facts, Main Legal Issues and Court Decision)

The ruling in the so-called *Rosneft* Case was handed down by the Court (Grand Chamber) on 28 March 2017.[20] This case was about a preliminary reference from

[17] An eloquent victory of international law in the application of Art 351 TFEU (ex Art 307 TEC) can be found, for example, in Case C-264/09 *Commission v Slovakia* (2011) ECR I-8065.

[18] See further B Pirker, 'Implementation of the Aarhus Convention by the EU – An Inconvenient Truth from the Compliance Committee' (European Law Blog, 24 April 2017), available at https://europeanlawblog.eu/2017/04/24/implementation-of-the-aarhus-convention-by-the-eu-an-inconvenient-truth-from-the-compliance-committe/ (last accessed 3 October 2018).

[19] See in more detail, Czuczai (n 10) 460 ff.

[20] *Rosneft* (n 9). It should also be noted that there are other related cases, namely direct actions for annulment, initiated either by PJSC Rosneft Oil Company or by other listed legal entities (typically

the UK High Court (England & Wales), Queen's Bench Division (Divisional Court). The questions referred to the European Court of Justice (ECJ) related to the validity and the interpretation of Council Decision 2014/512/CFSP of 31 July 2014 concerning restrictive measures in view of Russia's actions to destabilise Ukraine, including the illegal annexation of Crimae by the Russian Federation (adopted based on Article 29 TEU) as amended, and Council Regulation (EU) No 833/2014 on the same subject matter, also as amended (adopted based on Article 215 TFEU).[21] Without going into the concrete details, the case concerned a set of legal challenges against UK authorities brought by the practically Russian state-owned oil company *Rosneft* partly against the national implementing measures of the mentioned Council's restrictive measures in the UK,[22] but also indirectly against the referred Council legal acts, since PJSC Rosneft Oil Company was specifically listed by these Council restrictive measures and, of course, their implementation in the Member States, and thus also in the UK, impacted upon the listed Russian company in question very negatively.[23]

Rosneft attacked the validity of the subject Council restrictive measures based on several pleas in law, namely (i) incompatibility of the contested Council legal acts with the EU-Russia Partnership and Cooperation Agreement; (ii) violation of the obligations to state reasons and respect for the rights of the defence, the right to effective judicial protection and the right to access to the file; (iii) violation of the principle of equal treatment; (iv) misuse of powers by the Council when adopting the challenged restrictive measures; (v) contradiction between the CFSP restrictive decision and the sanctioning implementing EU Regulation; (vi) violation of the principle of proportionality and Rosneft's fundamental rights, as well as of the principles of legal certainty and of '*nulla poena sine lege certa*'.[24] As known,

Russian banks or the Gazprom Neft against the Council), of course, all typically for the same reasons, and which cases were recently decided, based on the *Rosneft* ruling, which is the subject of this contribution, by the General Court, namely Case T-715/14 *Rosneft v Council*; Joined Cases T-735/14 and T-799/14 *Gazprom Neft v Council*; Case T-732/14 *Sberbank v Council*; Case T-734/14 *VTB Bank v Council*; Case T-798/14 *Denizbank v Council*; Case T-737/14 *Vnesheconombank v Council*; Case T-739/14 *Prominvestbank v Council*, judgments handed down on 13 September 2018, ECLI:EU:T:2018: from 541 to 548.

[21] Council Decision 2014/512/CFSP of 31 July 2014 concerning restrictive measures in view of Russia's actions destabilising the situation in Ukraine [2014] OJ L229/13 as amended and Council Regulation (EU) No 833/2014 of 31 July 2014 concerning restrictive measures in view of Russia's actions destabilising the situation in Ukraine, as amended [2014] OJ L229/ 1 (hereinafter referred to as 'Council restrictive measures').

[22] The Council imposed on all those listed, inter alia, travel restrictions, export bans/prohibitions and other restrictions on trade in goods in the Russian oil sector (including sensitive dual-use items and technologies, in particular in the energy (oil) sector), freezing of assets and other restrictions on access to the capital market by the concerned economic operators (targeted individuals and legal persons) and free exercise of financial and banking services by targeted financial institutions from Russia, etc).

[23] See full description of the related facts of the case in AG Wathelet's Opinion, handed down on 31 May 2016, in ECLI:EU:C:2016:381 at paras 16–29 or in *Rosneft* (n 9) at paras 26–38.

[24] See *Rosneft* (n 9) paras 108–42; 152–70. For the interpretation-related questions, which are not relevant to this article, see paras 171–96.

the Court rejected all the pleas in law, submitted to it by the plaintiff – via the referring UK High Court – concerning the validity of the contested Council legal acts.

For the purposes of this contribution, however, only the first legality-related reasoning is relevant, namely that Rosneft also argued that certain provisions of the restrictive measures adopted by the Union[25] and the validity of which was challenged by it, were in fact in breach of the various provisions of the EU-Russia Partnership and Cooperation Agreement (PCA) (namely with its Articles 10(1) and 12 (trade in goods), Article 36 (cross-border supply of services), Article 52(2), (5) and (9) (free movement of capital)). *Rosneft* also underlined that this Agreement had not been suspended or terminated by the Parties due to the Ukrainian crisis. In response, the Council and the other intervening parties (six Member States and the Commission) questioned whether the invoked provisions of the EU-Russia PCA would have direct effect. They also argued that in any event – and the Court finally accepted this submission, without entering into an examination of the direct applicability of the invoked PCA provisions and the compatibility issue of the contested Council acts with them[26] – the restrictive measures adopted by the Union were correctly based on a special clause, namely on Article 99(1) point (d) of the EU-Russia PCA, which allows any contracting party to take measures which it considers necessary for the protection of 'its national security interests', in the event of 'war' or 'serious international tension constituting a threat of war'.

It should also be mentioned that among the questions referred to the ECJ by the UK High Court there was one which was procedural, and clearly the most important one from an EU law point of view.[27] The UK Court asked the CJEU to pronounce itself on the question of principle about the limits under the Treaties of its own jurisdiction in CFSP matters, taking into account Articles 24–40 TEU and Article 275 (1)–(2) TFEU, in connection with a preliminary reference case relating to the validity and interpretation of a Council Decision, containing individualised restrictive measures (so specifically targeting individuals and legal entities), and which was adopted based on Chapter 2 of Title V of the TEU (which is the special chapter in the Lisbon Treaty for CFSP).

[25] See *Rosneft* (n 9) para 108 and in more detail AG Wathelet's Opinion (n 23), paras 106–52.

[26] See *Rosneft* (n 9) para 110 stipulating that '… there is no need, in this case, to give a ruling on that question, since it suffices to state that, even if the restrictive measures at issue in the main proceedings were not compatible with certain provisions of that agreement, Art 99 of the agreement permits their adoption.' See also Case T-262/15 *Dmitrii Konstantinovich Kiselev v Council* ECLI:EU:T:2017:392, in particular paras 30–35, though it did not make reference to the *Rosneft* ruling of the CJEU, but nonetheless clearly followed it.

[27] One should remember that in Opinion 2/13, the CJEU (full Court) still underlined that '(acts adopted by the EU in the sphere of its CFSP, based on the last sentence of the second subparagraph of Art 24(1) TEU and Art 275 TFEU) … *as EU law now stands … fall outside the ambit of judicial review by the Court of Justice.*' (n 13) para 252.

Although it is not the purpose of this contribution to analyse this part of the judgment, nonetheless, the most relevant message of the *Rosneft* Case has been, beyond doubt, that the Court answered positively to the above-mentioned procedural question and it expanded the preliminary ruling procedure over the restrictive measures, adopted by the Council based on Article 29 TEU, by giving a very wide interpretation to Article 275(2) TFEU and using the rule of law and effective judicial protection requirements, stemming from Article 19(1)–(2) TEU and Article 47 of the EU Charter of Fundamental Rights. By doing so, the Court has further deepened and widened its protective judicial powers, which are based on the notion of the autonomous EU legal order concept and on the closed and widest possible interpretation of the principle of rule of law, based on which the EU is built.[28]

In my view, however, the *Rosneft* Case has equally importantly raised the issue of how to smoothly interconnect EU law and international law whilst safeguarding the distinctive features of the EU legal order, especially its autonomy, by using international law-friendly interpretation techniques of the applicable EU law.

IV. The Special Aspects of the *Rosneft* Case with Regard to the EU-Russia PCA and as Far as Interaction between EU Law and International Law is Concerned

First of all, it should be recalled that the PCA with the Russian Federation was signed – as with almost all the other former members of the ex-Soviet Union – in 1994.[29] It entered into force on 1st December 1997.[30] Pursuant to Article 106 of the EU-Russia PCA, it came into force for an initial period of 10 years with an automatic annual renewal possibility provided that neither Party to the Agreement gives a written notice on its denunciation to the other Party at least six months

[28] However, not everybody is fully happy yet about this 'deepening' and 'widening' judicial practice of the Court in the context of the *Rosneft* judgment, see, eg, S Poli, 'The Common Foreign and Security Policy after *Rosneft*: Still Imperfect but Gradually Subject to Rule of Law' (2017) 54 *Common Market Law Review* 6, 1799–1834.

[29] See Agreement on Partnership and Cooperation between the European Communities and their Member States, of the one part, and the Russian Federation, of the other part [1997] OJ L327/3. See also, for example, for a very deep and comprehensive analysis on this agreement, P van Elsuwege, 'The Four Common Spaces: New Impetus to the EU-Russia Strategic Partnership?' in M Maresceau and A Dashwood (eds), *Law and Practice of EU External Relations Law – Salient Features of a Changing Landscape* (Cambridge, Cambridge University Press, 2008) 334–59.

[30] See Council and Commission Decision No 97/800/ECSC, EC, Euratom of 30 October 1997 on the conclusion of the Partnership and Cooperation Agreement between the European Communities and their Member States, of the one part, and the Russian Federation, of the other part [1997] OJ L327/1.

before it expires.[31] Since this has not happened so far, that is why the EU-Russia PCA is in force even today.

As mentioned above, the key provision for the Court to examine and interpret in the *Rosneft* Case was Article 99(1) point d of the EU-Russia PCA, which provides that

> Nothing in this Agreement shall prevent a Party from taking any measures: 1. which it considers necessary for the protection of its essential security interests: … (d) in the event of serious internal disturbances affecting the maintenance of law and order, in time of war or serious international tension constituting threat of war or in order to carry out obligations it has accepted for the purposes of maintaining peace and international security; … (emphasis added).[32]

The Court established that what happened in Ukraine in 2014 is covered by the just quoted Article 99(1) point d, as the serious tensions between Russia and Ukraine constituted a threat of war, by which the EU and its Member States were also seriously affected. In this respect, the Court stressed

> … at the time when the restrictive measures at issue in the main proceedings were adopted, the Council stated, in the preambles of the contested acts, that the Heads of State or Government of the European Union condemned the unprovoked infringement of Ukrainian sovereignty and territorial integrity by the Russian Federation, that the Council urged the Russian Federation actively to use its influence over the illegally armed groups in order, inter alia, to permit full, immediate, safe and secure access to the site of the downing of the Malaysia Airlines flight MH17 in Donetsk (Ukraine), and that the Union had previously adopted measures in response to the illegal annexation of the Crimea and Sebastopol (Ukraine). In view of those factors, the Council concluded, in recital 8 of Decision 2014/512, that the situation remained grave and that it was appropriate to adopt restrictive measures in response to the Russian Federation's actions destabilising the situation in Ukraine.[33]

In the concrete case a crucial question was – and which was also Rosneft's main defence – how should the EU-Russia PCA be applied in a situation occurring outside the territorial scope of application of that Agreement, namely in Ukraine?

[31] See the precise wording of Article 106 EU-Russia PCA in the OJ reference (n 29) at 30.

[32] It is interesting to draw attention to the fact of how similar the wording of this Article is to the above-quoted last part of Article 347 TFEU!

[33] See *Rosneft* (n 9) paras 114–15 and AG Wathelet's Opinion (n 23), paras 149–50. The main reasoning for both Council restrictive measures, as the Court underlined it, was '… increasing the costs of Russia's actions to undermine Ukraine's territorial integrity, sovereignty and independence and to promoting a peaceful settlement of the crisis. That objective is consistent with the objective of maintaining peace and international security, in accordance with the objectives of the Union's external action, set out in Article 21 TEU.' (See in more detail Recitals (1)–(8) of Council Decision 2014/512 and Recital (2) of Council Regulation No 833/2014). See in this respect the new jurisprudence referred to in n 20 earlier, in particular Case T-715/14 *PAO Rosneft Oil Company et alts v Council* ECLI: EU:T:2018:544, especially paras 165–83, in which the General Court fully followed the *Rosneft* ruling of the CJEU concerning the interpretation of Article 99(1) point d., etc.

This question was also answered by the Court, in my view, in a professional and convincing manner by recalling those specific circumstances, which triggered strong reactions by the international community in relation to Russia's unacceptable actions against Ukraine, and which have had a general scope of implementation obligation in terms of the main objectives of the United Nations' Charter in an EU context by the EU itself as well.[34] In this respect, therefore, it was clear that the full observance obligation of the relevant UN Charter rules, as well as of the related EU law-based principles and values 'could not be blocked by borders'[35] since they have common universal objectives, which led the Court in the *Rosneft* Case to elegantly interconnect EU law with international law, when the Court in a very carefully drawn up conclusion stated the following:

> … the wording of that provision (namely Article 99) does not require that the 'war' or 'serious international tension' constituting a threat of war' refer to <u>a war directly affecting the territory of the European Union</u>. Accordingly, <u>events which take place in a country bordering the EU, such as those, which have occurred in Ukraine and which have given rise to the restrictive measures at issue</u> in the main proceedings, are capable of justifying measures <u>designed to protect essential EU security interests</u> **and** <u>to maintain peace and international security</u> in accordance with the specified objective under the first subparagraph of Article 21(1) and Article 21(2) point c TEU of the Union's external action <u>with due regard to the principles and purposes of the Charter of the United Nations</u>.[36]

With this link, the Court could practically apply Article 99(1) point d of the EU-Russia PCA and consider, therefore, that the challenged Council restrictive measures did not violate the EU-Russia PCA because they were adopted in order to protect the EU's essential national security interests and to maintain peace and security in the region, as required by international law. The measures adopted were clearly justified by the events which had occurred in Ukraine in 2014.[37]

[34] In this respect, AG Wathelet very specifically stressed in his Opinion to the Court that '… it must be emphasised that the Russian Federation has a power of veto within the United Nations Security Council and there is no point in looking for any declaration as to the existence of a threat to peace in the Security Council's resolutions (83) or even in the draft resolutions not adopted by the Security Council, given the (actual or potential) exercise by the Russian Federation of its right of veto (84)', see above n 23 at para 151, including in the accompanying footnotes the concrete references to the relevant UN Security Council resolutions.

[35] See the new tendencies and understandings in terms of broader aspects of the territorial applicability of international law in M Kuijer and W Werner, 'The Changing Nature of Territoriality in International law' (2017) 47 *Netherlands Yearbook of International Law*.

[36] See *Rosneft* (n 9) para 112 (emphasis added); see also paras 113–16.

[37] A similarly good link between EU law and international law was established in a judgment handed down in Case C-310/10 *European Parliament v Council*, see in more detail J Czuczai, 'The Powers of the Council Concerning Emergency of International Terrorism after the Judgment in Case C-130/10 Parliament v. Council' in I Govaere and S Poli (eds), *EU Management of Global Emergencies-Legal Framework for Combating Threats and Crises* (Leiden-Boston, Brill-Nijhoff, 2014) 97–110.

The relevant part of the Court ruling thus concludes that

> In those circumstances, taking into consideration the broad discretion enjoyed by the Council in this area, that institution could take the view that the adoption of the restrictive measures at issue in the main proceedings was necessary for the protection of essential European Union security interests and for the maintenance of peace and international security, within the meaning of Article 99 of the EU-Russia Partnership Agreement. (…) Consequently, an examination of the contested acts in the light of that agreement has disclosed nothing capable of affecting their validity.[38]

V. Conclusions

I think that it can be clearly seen from the above-explored example – in conformity with the increased importance of international law after Lisbon[39] – that the Court pays careful attention to a smooth, well-founded (and even proactive) interaction between EU law and international law in order to protect the EU's essential security interests, in full respect of its duty to maintain international peace and security in accordance with the Charter of the United Nations.[40]

In my view, however, the above-amplified aspects of the *Rosneft* Case, namely the international law-friendly interpretation of the protection of 'essential security interests' in crisis situations standard safeguard clause in the EU-Russia PCA might have, of course, if needed and fully justified by the concrete circumstances, a possible wider relevance for the other PCAs concluded with other ex-Soviet Union countries (which are still in force and contain the same clause). It is also relevant for the so-called association agreements, concluded by the EU and its Member States with third countries in the EU's neighbourhood, in particular with regard to the Stabilisation and Association Agreements (hereinafter: SAA) concluded with the Western Balkan countries and/or what concerns the new type of Framework Association Agreements (including the Deep and Comprehensive

[38] See *Rosneft* (n 9) paras 116–17.

[39] See Czuczai (n 10) especially 454 ff.

[40] It should be remembered that pursuant to Art 103 of the UN Charter, the Charter has superiority over conflicting international agreements, concluded by members of the UN as well as 'maintaining peace and international security' as an overall obligation is a very important founding objective of the UN Charter (see, eg, in this respect Art 1(1), Art 2(3)–(4) and (6), 33(1), 51, 52(1)–(2) of the Charter). The Charter of the UN is available at https://treaties.un.org/doc/publication/ctc/uncharter.pdf (last accessed 4 October 2018).

Free Trade Agreement), concluded with some of the so-called Eastern Partnership countries, namely with Ukraine, Moldova and Georgia in 2014 as well as in principle in terms of Armenia, which partner country recently signed with the EU and its Member States a Comprehensive and Enhanced Partnership Agreement at the end of 2017, etc.[41]

[41] See as examples the very similar or completely identical clauses to Art 99 of the EU-Russia PCA: (i) in the SAA with Albania, Art 124 [2009] OJ L107/166; in the SAA with Montenegro, Art 127 [2010] OJ L108/3; in the SAA with Serbia, Art 127 [2013] OJ L278/14; in the SAA with Bosnia and Hercegovina, Art 123 [2015] OJ L164/2; in the SAA with the former Yugoslav Republic of Macedonia (FYROM), Art 116 [2004] OJ L84/13. It is interesting to note on the other hand that in the SAA, concluded by the EU with Kosovo (without prejudice to its legal status and in line with UNSCR 1244/1999 and with the ICJ Opinion on Kosovo's Declaration on Independence) it does not contain a 'national security interests' protection' safeguard clause as such, just a shortened version of it, under Art 134, exclusively addressing the protection possibility, based on this reason, for not disclosing information linked to national security, see [2016] OJ L71/3. All this shows that the Art 99-type clauses are to be included in full only and exclusively in the so-called mixed agreements, where all the EU Member States are also contracting parties (alongside the EU) to the given agreement, which, for the well-known recognition problems, is not the case with Kosovo (see Art 2 of its SAA and in more detail, P Van Elsuwege, 'Legal Creativity in EU External Relations: The Stabilisation and Association Agreement between the EU and Kosovo' (2017) 22 *European Foreign Affairs Review* 3, 393–410. Kosovo's special example is, therefore, legally logical, since the protection of national security interests in the given context, based on Art 4(2) TEU, falls under the exclusive competence of the Member States (and it should be recalled that the SAA with Kosovo is an EU agreement only). What concerns the new type of Framework Association Agreements (including the Deep and Comprehensive Free Trade Agreement), concluded with some of the Eastern Partnership countries, the same clause like Art 99 in the EU-Russia PCA can also be found, for example, in the Framework Association Agreement, concluded with Ukraine, and its Art 472 [2014] OJ L161, etc.

14

An Incoherent Approach Towards Aarhus and CETA: The Commission and External Oversight Mechanisms

LAURENS ANKERSMIT*

I. Introduction

The Commission's recent approach towards external oversight mechanisms in international agreements is paradoxical. On the one hand, the Commission has objected to the findings of the Aarhus Convention's Compliance Committee (ACCC) on the EU's non-compliance with its obligations under that Treaty on the ground that the ACCC's findings 'do not recognise the EU's special legal order' and 'challenge constitutional principles of EU law that are so fundamental that it is legally impossible for the EU to follow and comply with the findings'.[1] On the other hand, the Commission has been an enthusiastic proponent of creating international tribunals in trade agreements that would have jurisdiction to hear claims by foreign investors against the EU and its Member States, expressing its confidence on multiple occasions on the compatibility of such mechanisms with the Treaties.[2]

This position is puzzling, as the powers of these investment tribunals are far greater than that of a compliance committee such as the ACCC, making them more intrusive on the EU's legal order. Individuals can bring cases before these

* The author would like to thank Professor Ludwig Krämer, Dr Jessica Lawrence, Anne Friel and Anais Berthier for their comments on a previous version of this article. The author worked for ClientEarth in the past, but was not involved in the ClientEarth case before the ACCC, discussed in this article.

[1] Commission, 'Proposal for a Council Decision on the position to be adopted, on behalf of the European Union, at the sixth session of the Meeting of the Parties to the Aarhus Convention regarding compliance case ACCC/C/2008/32' COM(2017) 366 final, 2, 7.

[2] Commission, 'Investment in TTIP and beyond – the path for reform Enhancing the right to regulate and moving from current ad hoc arbitration towards an Investment Court' (Concept Paper, 2015) 9; See also the Commission's interventions at the Greens/European Free Alliance public conference 'Investor-State Dispute Settlement (ISDS) in the EU Law and International Law' held in Brussels on 2 March 2015 and the European Parliament Joint INTA/JURI meeting on 'the compatibility of the Investment Court System in CETA with the Treaties' on 13 October 2016.

investment tribunals and the tribunals would be in the position to deliver binding decisions that may result in significant monetary awards against the EU and its Member States. These awards, in turn, are enforceable throughout the world with only very limited possibilities to review them. The ACCC, by contrast, is a non-judicial body that issues reports on compliance and may issue recommendations. The Aarhus Convention does not provide the complainants with remedies, nor does it prescribe the legal effects of the ACCC's reports in domestic legal orders. One may wonder therefore whether the Commission's position is solely based on sound legal considerations.

The purpose of this contribution is to shed further light on the constitutional limits set by the EU Treaties in relation to external oversight in international agreements concluded by the EU. It will do so by first exploring the legal limits set by the European Court of Justice on the EU's ability to conclude international agreements with external oversight mechanisms, in particular by looking at the relationship between the 'keystone' of the EU's judicial system, the preliminary reference procedure, and powers granted to such mechanisms. It will then make a comparison between the Investment Court System in the Comprehensive Economic and Trade Agreement (CETA) and the ACCC in light of those limits set by the ECJ and their effect on the autonomy of the EU's legal order. The contribution will argue that both the nature of the ACCC as a non-judicial consultative body and its more limited powers pose less of a threat to the autonomy of the EU's legal order than Investment Court System (ICS). Finally, this contribution will discuss the implications of the ECJ's case law and the Commission's positions for the EU's role as a credible actor on the international scene.

II. The EU's Judicial System and International Tribunals

Other contributions in this book have already extensively dealt with the unique features of the EU's legal order and the consequential limitations for the EU to conclude international agreements. The author simply recalls here that in principle, agreements establishing courts that are designed 'in essence, to resolve disputes on the interpretation or application of the actual provisions of the international agreements' are compatible with EU law, provided that the agreement in question safeguards the 'essential character' of the powers of the Union courts and consequently preserves the autonomy of the EU legal order.[3]

[3] Opinion 1/09 *European and Community Patents Court* [2011] ECR I-1137 para 74; Opinion 2/13 *Accession of the European Union to the European Convention for the Protection of Human Rights and Fundamental Freedoms* ECLI:EU:C:2014:2454 para 183; Opinion 1/00 *ECAA* [2002] ECR I-3493 paras 21, 23 and 26. It is thus clear from the EU Treaties that the EU can enter into an international agreement with dispute settlement provisions for disputes between the EU and a third country such as the World Trade Organisation's (WTO) dispute settlement body. Such state-to-state dispute settlement

However, the ECJ has had considerably more difficulty with international courts and tribunals that can hear disputes involving individuals as parties. Such mechanisms may affect the powers of Union courts under the preliminary reference procedure of Article 267 on the Treaty on the Functioning of the European Union (TFEU), a procedure that is fundamental to the EU's legal system. The ECJ rejected the formation of the European and Community Patent Court as it affected the powers of the courts of the Member States to make preliminary references.[4] It also did not accept the draft accession agreement of the EU to the European Convention on Human Rights (ECHR) because, among other things, it would affect the powers of the Court of Justice to give a definitive interpretation of EU law.[5]

The preliminary reference procedure is perhaps the single most important element in the unique construction of the EU legal order. It has allowed the EU to become a legal order of its own by binding the courts of the Member States to the ECJ in resolving disputes that involve questions of EU law. With this procedure, the ECJ was able to ensure that the question of the nature and effect of EU law in national legal orders was not left to domestic courts alone and allowed it to engage with individuals and Member States of the EU for questions of EU law through the courts of the Member States.

This unique judicial set-up empowers the courts of the Member States to hear claims by individuals where questions of EU law are involved and gives effect to any rights these individuals may have on the basis of EU law, while entrusting the ECJ with the task of ensuring that EU law is interpreted and applied uniformly throughout the EU by giving guidance to the courts of the Member States. The preliminary reference procedure therefore ensures that EU law is interpreted uniformly and consistently throughout the Union, that EU law is fully applied, and that individuals' rights are judicially protected.[6]

Indeed, the ECJ has referred to itself and the national courts as the 'guardians of the EU legal order and the judicial system of the EU'.[7] Moreover, the ECJ has referred to the preliminary reference procedure as the 'keystone' of the EU judicial system,

> which, by setting up a dialogue between one court and another, […] has the object of securing uniform interpretation of EU law […], thereby serving to ensure its consistency, its full effect and its autonomy as well as, ultimately, the particular nature of the law established by the Treaties […].[8]

mechanisms do not encroach on any of the powers of the European Court of Justice (ECJ), because the Treaty on the Functioning of the European Union (TFEU) Part Six, title 1, chapter 1, section 5 does not grant the EU courts the power to hear such disputes.

[4] Opinion 1/09 (n 3).

[5] Opinion 2/13 (n 3) paras 236–48.

[6] Opinion 2/13 (n 3) paras 174–175. The autonomy of the EU legal order finds its basis in part in this delicate judicial balance. In Case 26/62 *Van Gend & Loos* [1963] ECR 12, the ECJ concludes *inter alia* from the preliminary reference system that the EEC Treaty created a new legal order.

[7] Opinion 1/09 (n 3) para 66.

[8] Opinion 2/13 (n 3) para 176.

Article 267 is essential for avoiding divergences in the interpretation of EU law and giving EU law its full effect, as well as for ensuring the protection of individual rights.[9]

As a result, any international court system that interferes with the preliminary reference process is particularly dangerous to the autonomy of the EU legal order. It would therefore be essential that any form of international dispute settlement does not negatively affect the relationship and the powers under the Treaties of the courts of the Member States and that of the Union courts.

III. The Investment Court System in CETA and the Aarhus Convention's Compliance Committee

Before assessing the challenges ICS and the ACCC pose to the EU's legal system, it is worth recalling a number of essential features of both mechanisms. This section will also use the *ClientEarth* case before the ACCC as a case study as an illustrative example of such a potential challenge and assess whether a similar case challenging the EU Treaties' standing rules can be brought by a foreign investor under CETA before the ICS.

A. The Investment Court System in CETA

The ICS in CETA is a form of dispute settlement between foreign investors and their host governments. ICS is intended to provide foreign investors with an alternative to domestic courts to resolve disputes between the foreign investor and the government. A foreign investor is entitled to bring a claim for damages on its own behalf or on that of its locally established companies based on an infringement by the host government of several rights contained in CETA.[10] The rights contained in CETA are typical of most investment treaties and include for instance the right to 'fair and equitable treatment' that entitles investors to bring a claim for 'denial of justice in criminal, civil or administrative proceedings'.[11]

ICS is a form of dispute resolution that foreign investors can only use if the dispute cannot be resolved amicably through consultations.[12] However, there is no requirement to exhaust local remedies before making use of ICS.[13] ICS contains an appeal mechanism with the establishment of an Appellate Tribunal.[14]

[9] Opinion 1/09 (n 3) paras 83 and 84.
[10] The rights are listed in Sections C and D of Chapter 8 of CETA. See Article 8.18 (1) CETA.
[11] Article 8.10 CETA.
[12] Article 8.22(1)(b) CETA.
[13] Article 8.22(1)(f–g) CETA.
[14] Article 8.28 CETA.

Tribunals under ICS may issue awards against the host government that grants the foreign investor monetary damages and any applicable interest or alternatively restitution of property.[15] As previous cases under other investment agreements have shown, such claims and awards can be extensive, reaching billions of euros, and allow tribunals to affect vast areas of government decision-making.[16]

Lastly, ICS in CETA contains a strong and detailed system of enforcement of awards. Foreign investors can enforce awards in both the host state and other states and the options of reviewing awards of tribunals are severely limited. This is in line with the rationale of the system as an alternative and independent source of judicial relief, escaping the substantive judicial scrutiny of national courts, and constitutional courts. ICS only has a limited possibility of procedural review in cases of manifest unfairness and exceptionally where the award would violate the forum state's most basic notions of morality and justice.[17]

B. Aarhus Convention's Compliance Committee

The Aarhus Convention is one of the most important international environmental agreements to which the EU is party.[18] It seeks to guarantee the rights of access to information, public participation in decision-making, and access to justice in environmental matters. Like most international environmental agreements, the Aarhus Convention primarily encourages and facilitates compliance through non-judicial means, although the Convention also provides for an opt-in to compulsory state-to-state dispute settlement.[19]

One of the key mechanisms that facilitate compliance in the Convention is the ACCC, a non-judicial consultative body empowered to review compliance *inter alia* based on communications from the public. Article 15 of the Convention requires the Meeting of the Parties to establish arrangements of a non-confrontational, non-judicial and consultative nature for reviewing compliance with the Convention. This compliance mechanism must allow for appropriate public involvement, which may involve 'communications' from the public.[20]

[15] Article 8.39 CETA. In the case of the latter, the award shall provide that the respondent may pay monetary damages representing the fair market value of the property at the time immediately before the expropriation.

[16] G van Harten, *Investment Treaty Arbitration and Public Law* (Oxford, Oxford University Press, 2008). CETA contains a number of provisions that attempt to limit the impact on government decision-making, notably Article 8.9 and Annex 8-A CETA.

[17] Article V of the 1958 New York Convention on the Recognition and Enforcement of Foreign Arbitral Awards 330 UNTS 38; 21 UST 2517; 7 ILM 1046 (1968). The public policy exception is commonly regarded as imposing a very high standard for the state to meet.

[18] Convention on Access to Information, Public Participation in Decision-Making and Access to Justice in Environmental Matters 2161 UNTS 447; 38 ILM 517 (1999).

[19] Article 16 of the Convention.

[20] The Bern Convention has also introduced a so-called 'case-file system' which allows complaints to be filed by non-governmental organisations (NGOs), although this system is based more on passive monitoring than the pro-active role of the ACCC in issuing recommendations.

To that end, the Meeting of the Parties adopted Decision I/7 establishing the ACCC. The Decision sets out the structure and functions of the ACCC, as well as the procedures for submitting complaints. The decision specifies that members of the public may make communications concerning a Party's compliance with the Convention.[21]

The powers of the ACCC underline the consultative and non-judicial nature of the compliance mechanism. While the Committee is required to consider communications from the public, its powers are limited to examining compliance issues and making findings and recommendations.[22] What is more, the Committee does not normally issue those recommendations to the Party concerned but to the Meeting of the Parties, which is responsible for deciding upon appropriate measures to bring about full compliance with the Convention by the Party concerned.[23] The Meeting of the Parties may take several measures, all of which also reflect the consultative, non-confrontational and non-judicial nature of the mechanism.[24] In practice, the Meeting of the Parties generally endorses the findings of the Committee and issues recommendations in line with the Committee's recommendations. Neither the Committee nor the Meeting of the Parties can issue fines, or order cessation or any form of remediation, such as compensation.

There are no provisions in the Aarhus Convention or in the decisions taken by the Meeting of the Parties that explicitly state that Parties are required to abide by any of the recommendations issued by the Committee, whether or not the Meeting of the Parties endorses these findings. Indeed, as the ACCC itself has pointed out, it is entirely for the Parties themselves to implement the obligations under the Convention within their own legal systems.[25] This is in contrast to the awards issued by tribunals under the ICS and, for instance, judgments of the European Court of Human Rights (ECtHR).[26]

[21] United Nations Economic Commission for Europe (UNECE), *Meeting of the Parties to the Convention on Access to Information, Public Participation in Decision-making andAccess to Justice in Environmental Matters, Report of the First Meeting of the Parties, Addendum, Decision I/7, Review of Compliance*, adopted at the first meeting of the Parties held in Lucca, Italy, on 21–23 October 2002, UN Doc ECE/MP.PP/2/Add.8See, section VI. In addition, a Party may make a submission about compliance by another Party or about its own compliance and the secretariat may also make a referral to the Committee.

[22] ibid Rule 13 and 14.

[23] ibid Rule 37. Decision I/1 sets out the rules of procedure of the Meeting of the Parties, see Rule 35 of UNECE, *Meeting of the Parties to the Convention on Access to Information, Public Participation in Decision-making and Access to Justice in Environmental Matters, Report of the First Meeting of the Parties, Addendum, Decision I/1* adopted at the first meeting of the Parties held in Lucca, Italy, on 21–23 October 2002, UN Doc ECE.MP.PP2/Add.2. Generally, every effort shall be made to reach a decision by consensus, but if this is not possible the Meeting of the Parties can decide on substantive issues by a three/fourth majority.

[24] See above n 21, Rule 37.

[25] UNECE, *Findings and recommendations of the Aarhus Convention Compliance Committee with regard to Communication ACCC/C/2008/32 (Part II) concerning compliance by the European Union*, adopted by the Compliance Committee on 17 March 2017, para 39.

[26] Article 46(1) ECHR.

Notwithstanding these limited powers, the ACCC has proven to be a success. It has given citizens and environmental organisations an independent and external means of addressing compliance with the Convention. To date, the ACCC has received 148 communications from the public. One of those communications concerned the EU's compliance with the Aarhus Convention's provisions on administrative and judicial review. As the findings by the ACCC were opposed by the Commission for constitutional reasons relevant for the EU's relationship with international courts and tribunals, this contribution will use this case as a study to assess the compatibility issues identified under section I.

C. Case Study: Denial of Justice by the EU under CETA and Aarhus

Ironically, while the EU's judicial system and the preliminary reference procedure in particular takes such prominence in the EU's ability to subject itself to international courts and tribunals, the system itself has been criticised for not giving effective judicial relief. While the ECJ has maintained that the Treaties offer a 'complete system of judicial remedies' for individuals, Member States, the EU institutions and its agencies and bodies,[27] its jurisprudence on standing for individuals in direct actions before the EU courts are notoriously strict.[28] In defence of this restrictive stance on standing is that individuals can always seek judicial relief in the courts of the Member States and the preliminary reference procedure will ensure that EU rights and obligations will be respected in such procedures.

However, one may question whether Article 267 TFEU is sufficient in providing access to justice.[29] First of all, it is a procedure and not a remedy; a court of a Member State decides on a referral and how to formulate questions and it is not in the hands of the parties to a case. Second, only the highest courts in the Member States are required to make a referral, lower courts are not required to make references. Lastly, the length of the procedure can act as a powerful deterrent for referring by national courts. Therefore, the EU's judicial system itself may be the subject of proceedings before international bodies on grounds of denial of justice. This may be the case both before the ACCC and ICS.

i. ACCC/C/2008/32 European Union

On 1 December 2008 environmental non-governmental organisation (NGO) ClientEarth filed a communication to the ACCC on the EU's compliance with

[27] Opinion 1/09 (n 3) para 70.

[28] L Krämer, 'Acces à la Justice en matière d'environnement: La double mesure de la Cour de Justice de l'Union européenne' (2017) 1 *Revue du Droit de l'Union Européenne* 13.

[29] ibid.

the Aarhus Convention's access to justice provisions.[30] The Aarhus Convention requires parties to provide members of the public access to internal review of decisions with effects on the environment (Article 9(2) of the Convention); access to courts to challenge acts or omissions that contravene environmental law (Article 9(3) of the Convention) and provide adequate and effective remedies (Article 9(4) of the Convention).

In short, ClientEarth alleged that the EU did not comply with those rules because the ECJ's interpretation of the Treaty rules on standing before the EU Courts were too strict and the criteria for access to internal review under the Aarhus Regulation were too limited. In particular, ClientEarth alleged that the ECJ's interpretation of 'individual concern' under Article 263(4) TFEU (the infamous *Plaumann* test) ensured that citizens and NGOs were effectively barred from challenging acts from EU institutions contravening environmental law. Moreover, the Aarhus Regulation did not properly implement Article 9(2) of the Convention because it did not grant individuals other than NGOs access to internal review and its scope was limited to decisions that were of an individual nature.

More than eight years later, on 17 March 2017, the ACCC issued a report containing its findings and recommendations. The ACCC found that the EU had failed to comply with Article 9, paragraphs 3 and 4, of the Convention 'with regard to access to justice by members of the public because neither the Aarhus Regulation, nor the jurisprudence of the CJEU implements or complies with the obligations arising under those paragraphs'.[31]

The ACCC report recommended that the Meeting of the Parties should recommend that all relevant EU institutions 'within their competences take the steps necessary to provide the public concerned with access to justice in environmental matters' in accordance with the Convention. In particular, the ACCC suggested that to the extent that the EU should either amend the Aarhus Regulation or adopt new legislation fully in compliance with the Convention. In relation to the jurisprudence on standing for direct actions, the ACCC recommended an assessment of the legality of the EU's implementing measures in light of the Convention's obligations or interpret EU law in a way, which, to the fullest extent possible, would be consistent with the obligations under the Convention.[32]

The Commission reacted to the ACCC report by proposing that the Council cast a negative vote in the Meeting of the Parties, thus rejecting the report's findings.[33] According to the Commission, 'the Committee findings challenge constitutional principles of EU law that are so fundamental that it is legally impossible for the EU to follow and comply with the findings'.[34] The Commission's main

[30] Communication ACCC/C/2008/32, the Communication can be found at www.unece.org/env/pp/compliance/compliancecommittee/32TableEC.html (last accessed on 4 October 2018).

[31] See above n 25, para 123.

[32] See above n 25, paras 124–26.

[33] See above n 1.

[34] See above n 1, p 7.

contention with the findings was that it did not recognise the EU's special legal order because the findings 'neither acknowledge the central role of national courts as ordinary Court of EU law, nor recognise the system of preliminary rulings under Article 267 TFEU as a valid means of redress'.[35] For the Commission, NGOs and citizens would still have the possibility of finding judicial relief through the courts of the Member States, who would be in the position to make a preliminary reference to the ECJ if necessary. The Commission therefore disagreed with the ACCC's findings because in its view the ACCC did not consider the preliminary reference procedure sufficient as to comply with the Convention.

The majority of the EU's Member States opposed the Commission's proposal, however. As a result, a compromise solution was found in which the EU would accept the draft decision of the secretariat of the Convention subject to several amendments.[36] The findings of the ACCC would no longer be 'endorsed', but the Meeting of the Parties would 'take note of' the findings. Moreover, significant parts of the recommendations were deleted and the EU was only required to 'consider' the recommendations.

The Commission's reaction to the *ClientEarth* case did not go so far as to state that the Aarhus Convention's compliance mechanism was incompatible with EU law. However, its response demonstrates its strong objections to an external body's findings in relation to questions of EU law – particularly when those findings have the potential to interfere with the preliminary reference procedure.

ii. CETA and Denial of Justice

Despite the strong stance it took with respect to the *ClientEarth* case, however, the Commission has raised no such concerns over a potential 'mischaracterisation' of the EU legal system with respect to the ICS system in CETA. This is inconsistent, as ICS raises very similar issues with respect of access to justice in the EU legal order.

Under CETA, foreign investors are entitled to 'fair and equitable treatment' and can therefore bring a claim before the ICS tribunals against the host government for 'denial of justice in criminal, civil or administrative proceedings'.[37] As the Commission pointed out in its submissions before the ACCC in the *ClientEarth* case, 'there have been numerous cases where actions brought by economic operators or associations thereof have been declared inadmissible by the Community judicature'.[38] Therefore, it is certainly conceivable that a foreign investor might

[35] See above n 1, p 5.

[36] Council Decision (EU) 2017/1346 of 17 July 2017 on the position to be adopted, on behalf of the European Union, at the sixth session of the Meeting of the Parties to the Aarhus Convention as regards compliance case ACCC/C/2008/32 [2017] OJ L186/15.

[37] Article 8.10 CETA.

[38] Letter from the Party concerned of 11 June 2009, para 35 and the Appendix. The letter can be found at www.unece.org/env/pp/compliance/compliancecommittee/32TableEC.html (last accessed on 4 October 2018). The Commission provided a non-exhaustive list of 37 cases where economic operators or associations thereof were denied standing before the courts.

be denied standing before the EU courts. While it is undeniable that the Court's standing requirements have a greater negative impact on members of the public and NGOs,[39] the Commission's statements beg the question whether this lack of access to justice before the Union courts could be construed as a breach of CETA's investment provisions by foreign investors.

The Lisbon Treaty has significantly improved the opportunities for economic operators (in contrast to that of members of the public and NGOs) by also allowing challenges of non-legislative acts of general application that are of direct concern and that do not entail implementing measures. However, there may still be instances in which the particularities of the EU legal system may give rise to a claim by a foreign investor based on denial of justice in civil or administrative proceedings. This could happen in a number of different ways.

First of all, there have been several instances since the entry into force of the Lisbon Treaty where the ECJ has denied standing to economic operators for direct actions because of the Court's restrictive interpretation of Article 263(4) TFEU. In *Telefónica v Commission* a multinational telecommunications company was denied standing before the Union courts to challenge a Commission decision addressed to Spain declaring an aid scheme (through tax breaks) partially incompatible with the common market.[40] According to the ECJ, Telefonica could have contested the rejection of an application for grant of the tax advantage in question before the national courts.[41] In *T & L Sugar* a group of sugar cane refiners was denied standing to challenge a series of Commission acts that increased the supply of beet sugar on the internal market and restricted the amount of imports of cane sugar.[42] Here the ECJ found that the applicants did not have standing because they were, first, not directly concerned enough to challenge the measures relating to the production of beet sugar (as they were cane sugar refiners) and, second, because the measures restricting imports of cane sugar entailed implementing measures at national level.[43]

These cases demonstrate that foreign investors might be denied access to justice before EU courts for EU acts that negatively affect their investments, either because they are not directly concerned or because of the ECJ's narrow reading of 'implementing measures'. The first criterion may be relevant when acts might not affect the legal position of the applicant, but its economic position, for instance where the decision benefits a competitor. The latter criterion may still require a foreign investor to breach the law in order to obtain judicial review, a long-standing criticism of the ECJ's case law.[44]

[39] Krämer (n 28).
[40] C-274/12 P *Telefónica SA v Commission* ECLI:EU:C:2013:852.
[41] ibid paras 27–36, 59.
[42] Case C-456/13P *T & L Sugars Ltd and Sidul Açúcares, Unipessoal Lda v Commission* ECLI:EU:C:2015:284.
[43] The alleged mechanical nature of the implementing measures, merely rubber stamping the Commission's acts, was not found to be relevant by the ECJ, see paras 41–50.
[44] Case C-50/00P *Unión de Pequeños Agricultores v Council* [2002] ECR I-6677, Opinion of AG Jacobs, para 43.

In any event, the reliance on Member State courts to bring preliminary references relating to the validity of EU acts implemented by Member State authorities may in itself be seen as inadequate by investment tribunals. Similar to the findings of the ACCC, such tribunals might find that the preliminary reference procedure cannot be a basis for denying direct access to Union courts or be properly considered an appeal mechanism by which investors can have access to the Union courts in order to challenge EU acts.[45]

Moreover, there may be many other aspects of the EU's judicial system that may amount to a denial of justice in civil and administrative proceedings for foreign investors. One obvious example is a situation similar to that of the applicants in the 2008 *FIAMM* case. In *FIAMM*, the undertakings in question suffered economically from retaliatory measures imposed by the United States because of the EU's non-compliance with a ruling of the WTO Appellate Body. The ECJ found that the EU was not liable for these economic losses because the act causing the retaliatory measures was lawful and therefore could not be subject to a claim for damages.[46]

IV. Compatibility with EU Law

The particularities of the EU's judicial system may give rise to successful proceedings before both the ACCC and ICS tribunals, as aspects of the EU system amount to a denial of justice according to both regimes. The question then becomes whether both systems sufficiently safeguard the 'essential character' of the powers of the Union courts and consequently preserves the autonomy of the EU legal order. Several factors suggest that the ICS tribunals in this sense pose a much more significant threat to the autonomy of the EU legal order than the ACCC.[47]

[45] UNECE, *Meeting of the Parties to the [Aarhus Convention], Compliance Committee, Thirty-second meeting, Report of the Compliance Committee Addendum Findings and recommendations with regard to communication ACCC/C/2008/32 (Part I) concerning compliance by the European Union*, UN Doc ECE/MP.PP/C.1/2011/4/Add.1, para 90.

[46] Joined Cases C-120/06P and C-121/06P *FIAMM and others v Council and Commission* ECLI:EU:C:2008:476.

[47] For other academic discussion on the question of compatibility of investment adjudication with EU law see: L Ankersmit, 'The Compatibility of Investment Arbitration in EU Trade Agreements with the EU Judicial System' (2016) 13 *Journal for European Environmental & Planning Law* 46–63; S Gáspár-Szilágyi, 'A Standing Investment Court under TTIP from the Perspective of the CJEU' (2016) 17 *Journal of World Investment and Trade* 701–42; J Kokott and C Sobotta, 'Investment Arbitration and EU Law' (2016) 18 *Cambridge Yearbook of European Legal Studies* 3–19; A Rosas, 'The EU and International Dispute Settlement' (2017) 1 *Europe and the World: A Law Review* 1–29; M Cremona, 'Guest Editorial: Negotiating the Transatlantic Trade and Investment Partnership (TTIP)' (2015) 52 *Common Market Law Review* 351–62 at 360; H Lenk, 'Investor-State Arbitration under TTIP: Resolving Investment Disputes in an (Autonomous) EU Legal Order' (Report for Swedish Institute for European Policy Studies, 2015) 2; A Dimopoulos, 'The Compatibility of Future EU Investment Agreements with EU Law' (2012) 39 *Legal Issues of Economic Integration* 447–71; A Dimopoulos, 'The Involvement of the EU in Investor-State Dispute Settlement: A Question of Responsibilities' (2014) 51 *Common Market Law Review* 1671–1720; A Carta, 'Do Investor-to-State Dispute Settlement Mechanisms Fit in the

A. Adverse Effect on the Powers of Union and Member State Courts

First of all, in contrast to ICS, the ACCC is explicitly not intended to replace domestic legal proceedings and is not to be construed as an alternative to domestic courts. As stated in the Aarhus Convention, the ACCC is of a non-confrontational, *non-judicial* and consultative nature. This is clear from the fact that it does not resolve disputes between Parties to the agreement (this is done by means of dispute settlement under Article 16 of the Convention). It merely reviews compliance (often based on communications from the public), reports, and makes recommendations to the Meeting of the Parties, the main executive body under the Convention. The ACCC therefore does not have powers in itself to resolve disputes and take binding decisions.

Although there is no requirement to exhaust domestic remedies before the public can lodge a communication to the ACCC, the ACCC is required to be and has in practice been deferential towards domestic court proceedings.[48] The ACCC will wait for domestic courts to issue judgments that may ensure compliance with the Convention, before making its findings. In *ClientEarth* the ACCC therefore took great care in awaiting decisions of the EU courts before proceeding with its findings, only issuing its final report more than eight years after the initial complaint by ClientEarth.[49]

By contrast, ICS in CETA is a quasi-judicial body intended to offer investors an alternative form of judicial relief to domestic courts. ICS tribunals have the power to issue binding decisions, compensate investors through monetary awards, and resolve disputes between investors on the one hand and a Party to CETA on the other.

Moreover, under ICS in CETA, foreign investors can bring claims even if domestic courts have not yet had an opportunity to rule upon the legal questions faced by the investment tribunals. In fact, CETA ensures that a foreign investor must choose to bring proceedings either before domestic courts or before an ICS tribunal requiring a foreign investor to discontinue domestic proceedings or

EU Legal System?' (2014) *Environmental Law Network International* 30; J Kleinheisterkamp, 'Investment Protection and EU Law: The Intra- and Extra-EU Dimension of The Energy Charter Treaty' (2012) 15 *Journal of International Economic Law* 85–109; S Hindelang, '4Repellent Forces: The CJEU and Investor-State Dispute Settlement' (2015) 53 *Archiv des Völkerrechts* 68–89; N Lavranos, 'Designing an International Investor-to-State Arbitration System after Opinion 1/09' in M Bungenberg and C Herrmann (eds), *Common Commercial Policy after Lisbon* (Springer, 2013) 199–219.

[48] Decision I/7 (n 21) Rule 21 also provides that 'the Committee should at all relevant stages take into account any available domestic remedy unless the application of the remedy is unreasonably prolonged or obviously does not prove an effective and sufficient means of redress'.

[49] The ACCC decided to wait for ECJ rulings on: 1) a possible new approach towards standing under Article 260(4) TFEU with the entry into force of the Lisbon Treaty; 2) the interpretation of standing rules in light of the EU's accession to the Aarhus Convention; and 3) two cases pending before the ECJ challenging the validity of the Aarhus Regulation.

starting them.[50] This provision thus effectively undermines the powers of domestic courts to hear similar claims and ensures that investment tribunals will be the sole arbitrator for a claim brought by a foreign investor. Indeed, in relation to the investor-state dispute settlement mechanism in the EU-Singapore Free Trade Agreement, the ECJ has observed that such a regime 'removes disputes from the jurisdiction of the courts of the Member States'.[51]

The specific nature of ICS as an alternative to domestic courts of the EU therefore poses a legal problem under the EU Treaties in three distinct ways. First, it may affect the powers of the courts of the Member States to make preliminary rulings. Second, it may inhibit the ECJ's monopoly in giving a definitive interpretation of EU law. Finally, third, it may affect the ECJ's monopoly on deciding on the non-contractual liability of the EU.

i. The Power to Make a Preliminary Reference

As was highlighted above, the importance of Article 267 TFEU in the EU's judicial system can hardly be overstated. The ECJ refers to the provision as the 'keystone' of the Union's judicial system and the courts of the Member States as 'guardians' of the Union's legal order. The courts of the Member States therefore play a vital part in its operation by having the power to make preliminary references to the Court of Justice.[52] As ICS does not require investors to exhaust domestic remedies when bringing a claim before an ICS tribunal and even requires them to discontinue domestic legal proceedings if they want to bring an ICS complaint, foreign investors can and sometimes must[53] avoid going to the courts of the Member States for claims that may involve questions of Union law.

If investors are not required to go to the courts of the Member States first, and will seek judicial relief elsewhere, the powers of those courts of the Member States to make preliminary references and apply EU law are likely to be diminished. This issue has already been pointed out by the Commission in the context of intra-EU Bilateral Investment Treaties.[54] For instance in *Achmea BV v Slovakia* the Commission's legal service argued:

> There are some provisions of the Dutch-Slovak [investment agreement] that raise fundamental questions regarding compatibility with EU law. Most prominent among

[50] Article 8.22(1)(f) and (g) CETA.

[51] Opinion 2/15 *EUSFTA* ECLI:EU:C:2017:376 para 292.

[52] Opinion 1/09 *European and Community Patents Court* ECLI:EU:C:2011:123 para 66; Opinion 2/13 (n 3) para 176.

[53] Although foreign investors can still bring domestic cases, Article 8.22(1)(f)–(g), (2) and (3) makes their claims before an ISDS tribunal inadmissible. So if an investor wants to bring his case before an ICS tribunal the investor is required to not pursue the case domestically.

[54] European Commission, Amicus Curiae submission in *European American Investment Bank AG (EURAM) v Slovak Republic* (13 October 2011); Commission Amicus Curiae submission as quoted by the arbitration tribunal in *Achmea BV v The Slovak Republic*, UNCITRAL, PCA Case No 2008-13 (award on jurisdiction 7 December 2012) para 193.

> these are the provisions of the BIT providing for an **investor-State arbitral mechanism** [...], and the provisions of the BIT providing for an inter-State arbitral mechanism [...]. **These provisions conflict with EU law on the exclusive competence of the EU court for claims which involve EU law, even for claims where EU law would only partially be affected.** The European Commission must therefore [...] express its reservation with respect to the Arbitral Tribunal's competence to arbitrate the claim brought before it [...].[55]

In another *amicus curiae* submission, the legal service of the European Commission pointed out in the context of a Member State investment treaty:

> The arbitral tribunal is not a court or tribunal of an EU Member State but a parallel dispute settlement mechanism entirely outside the institutional and judicial framework of the European Union. Such mechanism deprives courts of the Member States of their powers in relation to the interpretation and application of EU rules imposing obligations on EU Member States, which are presumably relevant in the arbitral proceeding.[56]

The fact that ICS tribunals may only consider EU law as a matter of fact further negatively affects ensuring the full effectiveness of EU law, as EU law may not be fully applied altogether. For instance, where domestic courts may be required to interpret legal acts in light of EU law principles, an investment tribunal might be prevented from doing the same.

Indeed, by negatively affecting the powers of the courts of the Member States to make preliminary references, it is questionable whether ICS safeguards the 'essential character' of the powers of the Union courts and consequently preserves the autonomy of the EU legal order.[57] As Article 267 is essential for avoiding divergences in the interpretation of EU law and giving EU law its full effect, as well as for ensuring the protection of individual rights, it may come as no surprise that the ECJ has had difficulties with international tribunals that may affect those powers.[58] In Opinion 1/09 the Court found that the powers of the national courts to make preliminary references and to interpret EU law may not be affected by introducing a court system in an international agreement that operates entirely outside the EU judicial framework.[59]

Moreover, in contrast to the courts of the Member States, any infringement of EU law by ICS tribunals themselves cannot be corrected via the EU's legal system. ICS in CETA does not foresee the possibility for the EU institutions or individuals negatively affected by such infringement to remedy or discipline them.[60]

[55] As quoted by the arbitration tribunal in *Achmea*, ibid (emphasis added).
[56] *EURAM* (n 54).
[57] See Opinion 2/13 (n 3), para 183.
[58] Opinion 1/09 (n 52) paras 83 and 84.
[59] Opinion 1/09 (n 52) para 77.
[60] Under CETA, the CETA Joint Committee may issue binding interpretations of CETA's investment provisions. This may provide an avenue for the Commission and the Council, if Canada agrees, to correct certain interpretations of the agreement that are contrary to EU law for future cases. It does not however remedy the cases that have already been decided.

In Opinion 1/09 neither the infringement procedure nor the principle of non-contractual liability of Member States for breaches of EU law was a reason for the ECJ to oppose the European and Community Patents Court.[61] Under ICS, it would also neither be possible to claim damages, nor start infringement proceedings for any breach of EU law by ICS tribunals.

ii. *The Power to Give a Definitive Interpretation of EU Law*

ICS may also affect another of the cornerstones of the EU's legal architecture that is inextricably linked to the preliminary reference procedure: the ECJ's monopoly on giving a definitive interpretation of EU law.

The ECJ's exclusive power to give a definitive interpretation of EU law ensures the uniform and consistent interpretation of EU law. It also guarantees that the autonomous nature of EU law and its special characteristics are preserved. As a result, the ECJ has required that international agreements concluded by the Union must not have the effect of binding the EU to a particular interpretation of EU law.[62] In Opinion 2/13, for example, the ECJ held that the draft agreement for the EU's accession to the ECHR was incompatible with the Treaties because it infringed on the ECJ's power to give a definite interpretation of all EU law, including secondary law, and in particular on the power to interpret EU law in light of the rights guaranteed by the ECHR.[63]

ICS faces similar challenges, not least because it operates independently of the ECJ. An ICS tribunal exercises external control over the EU and its institutions the same way as the ECtHR would have: the ECtHR may declare an EU measure in conflict with the ECHR, just as an arbitration body may declare an EU measure in conflict with the investment provisions of EU investment agreements. Similar to the ECtHR, ICS bodies do not have the power to invalidate EU legislation, but merely the power to award damages for a breach of an international agreement.[64] Both systems interpret the respective international agreement, and the EU, as a signatory, and its Court of Justice are bound by these interpretations.[65]

CETA offers a number of safeguards in order to preserve the ECJ's exclusive powers in this regard. First, ICS tribunals must follow the 'prevailing interpretation' of EU law given by domestic courts. Second, ICS tribunals can only assess EU law 'as a matter of fact'.[66] Third, and lastly, CETA stipulates that 'any meaning

[61] Opinion 1/09 (n 52) para 88.

[62] Opinion 2/13 (n 3) para 184.

[63] Opinion 2/13 (n 3) paras 246–47.

[64] Which after conclusion by the EU becomes an integral part of the EU legal order, see Case 181/73 *R & V Haegeman v Belgian State* [1974] ECR 449 para 5.

[65] Opinion 2/13 (n 3) paras 182, 184, 185. Awards of ICS tribunals are binding, see Article 8.41 CETA.

[66] The determination of law as a matter of fact originates from a judgment from the Permanent Court of International Justice in *German Interests in Polish Upper Silesia* from 1925. See German Interests in Polish Upper Silesia (Germ v Pol), 1925 PCIJ (ser A) No 6 (August 25).

given to domestic law by the Tribunal shall not be binding upon the courts or the authorities of that Party'.[67] However, the most obvious way to remedy any incompatibility problems is not included in CETA: there is no provision that requires the prior involvement of the ECJ if a tribunal is faced with a question of EU law. It remains to be seen whether any of the three safeguards that were included are sufficient.

With respect to the first safeguard, following the prevailing interpretation of EU law only partially helps to protect the ECJ's exclusive authority, as this approach begs the question of what the Tribunal has to do if no such prevailing interpretation exists, or if the scope or content of the 'prevailing interpretation' is unclear. The Court of Justice has found that only in exceptional circumstances are the highest courts of the Member States relieved from their duty to make a preliminary reference to the Court of Justice when such courts are faced with questions of Union law.[68] Moreover, the ECJ is also free under EU law to change its opinion and reverse or change its case law.[69] Therefore, the reliance on the 'prevailing interpretation of domestic law' falls short of requiring prior involvement of the ECJ in relation to questions of EU law.[70]

With respect to the second safeguard, it remains to be seen whether the ECJ is willing to accept the distinction between interpretation of EU law as a 'matter of fact' and other ways of interpreting EU law. In addition, the proposed ICS Appeals Tribunal would have the power to review whether an ICS Tribunal has manifestly erred in the appreciation of the facts, including the appreciation of relevant domestic law.[71] This power to review whether the Tribunal has correctly appreciated EU law as a matter of fact would require the involvement of the ECJ as the Appeals Tribunal would be reviewing whether the Tribunal has assessed EU law correctly.[72]

The third safeguard is also problematic. While CETA may provide that the interpretation of EU law is not binding on the ECJ, an award itself is binding on the EU and its institutions.[73] The approach chosen in CETA would thus require the ECJ to endorse the idea that it is merely bound by a decision to transfer funds

[67] Article 8.31(3) CETA.

[68] Case 283/81 *Srl CILFIT and Lanificio di Gavardo SpA v Ministry of Health* ECLI:EU:C:1982:335 para 16.

[69] See for instance Joined cases C-267/91 and C-268/91 *Criminal proceedings against Bernard Keck and Daniel Mithouard* [1993] ECR I-6097; Case C-127/08 *Blaise Baheten Metock and Others v Minister for Justice, Equality and Law Reform* [2008] ECR I-6241.

[70] I am grateful to Professor Krämer for pointing this out.

[71] Article 8.28(2)(b) CETA.

[72] Consider the situation in which one of the Parties appeals because it claims that EU law has been wrongly interpreted by the Tribunal or that the Tribunal did not follow the prevailing interpretation of domestic law.

[73] Article 8.41 CETA states that an 'award issued pursuant to this Section shall be binding between the disputing parties and in respect of that particular case'. In accordance with Article 216(2) TFEU and the Court of Justice's case law therefore, an award which may have been based on a particular interpretation of EU law will be binding on the EU institutions, including the Court of Justice.

and that the reasoning underpinning that decision has no bearing on the EU's judicial system. At the same time, ICS tribunals might very well provide for a specific avenue of judicial relief and set a precedent for future claims. In that sense, there appears to be no possibility to remedy any incorrect assessment made by the ICS tribunals.[74]

iii. Non-Contractual Liability of the EU under Article 340 TFEU

A third adverse effect ICS has on the powers of the EU judiciary is that it may serve as an alternative for damages claims against the EU and thereby affect the ECJ's exclusive powers to rule on the non-contractual liability of the EU.[75] It has been argued that Article 340 TFEU does not preclude the EU from incurring responsibility for violations of an international agreement, and that it therefore does not preclude the EU from concluding an international agreement containing investment protection and ISDS provisions.[76] While it is true that Article 340 TFEU does not preclude the EU from incurring international responsibility *generally*, it is questionable whether the possibility of incurring international responsibility automatically makes a mechanism such as ICS compatible with Article 340 TFEU, not least because the EU institutions cannot circumvent its constitutional framework.[77] The fact remains that the power to decide on damages claims against the EU is exclusive competence of the EU judiciary.

ICS does offer the possibility to claim damages through a judicial mechanism that is an alternative to that of the EU and foreign investors may consider that ICS offers a better opportunity to obtain judicial relief than by going through the EU judicial system. One reason for opting for ICS might be the ECJ's deference towards the legislator in claims for damages. For the ECJ, the 'exercise of the legislative function must not be hindered by the prospect of actions for damages whenever the general interest of the Community requires legislative measures to be adopted which may adversely affect individual interests.'[78] As a result, damages are only awarded if there is 'a sufficiently flagrant violation of a superior rule of law for the protection of the individual'.[79] The sufficiently serious breach entails that

[74] Opinion 1/09 (n 52) paras 86–88.

[75] It is settled case law that 'With regard to the [EU]'s non-contractual liability, such disputes fall within the jurisdiction of the Court of Justice. Article [19 TEU] provides that the Court of Justice has jurisdiction to hear and determine actions seeking compensation for damage brought under the second paragraph of Article [340 TFEU], which covers such non-contractual liability. That jurisdiction of the [EU] Courts is exclusive'. See Case C-377/09 *Hanssens Ensch v European Community* [2010] ECR I-7751 para 16. See also Case C-275/00 *European Community v First NV and Franex NV* [2002] ECR I-10943 para 43; Case C-282/90 *Vreugdenhil v Commission* [1992] ECR I-1937 para 14; Case 281/84 *Zuckerfabrik Bedburg AG and others v Council and Commission* [1987] ECR 49 para 12; Case 101/78 *Granaria BV v Hoofdproduktschap voor Akkerbouwprodukten* [1979] ECR 629 para 14.

[76] Dimopoulos (n 47) 1671–1720 at 1705.

[77] Case 294/83 *Parti écologiste 'Les Verts' v European Parliament* [1986] ECR 1339 para 23.

[78] Joined Cases C-46/93 and C-48/93 *Brasserie du Pêcheur SA v Bundesrepublik Deutschland and The Queen v Secretary of State for Transport, ex parte: Factortame Ltd and others* [1996] ECR I-1029 para 45.

[79] Case 5/71 *Aktien-Zuckerfabrik Schöppenstedt v Council* [1971] ECR 116 para 11.

the EU public authority in question 'manifestly and gravely disregarded the limits on its discretion'.[80] Accordingly, it is very difficult to claim damages for lawful acts of the EU.[81] This strict approach by the ECJ towards damages claims is further exemplified by the obligation of the injured party to 'show reasonable diligence in limiting the extent of the loss or damage, or risk having to bear the loss or damage himself'.[82]

CETA, on the other hand, does not necessarily provide similar safeguards. For example, the remedy under ICS exists irrespective of the legality of the measure under domestic law in contrast to the EU's system of non-contractual liability of the EU. ICS arbitrators are also not part of the system of government of the host state and are not empowered to apply domestic legislation. CETA only offers indirect assurances that arbitrators will consider the impact of their rulings on the legislative function of the host state.[83]

B. The Legally Binding Nature of Decisions and Awards

ICS presents more challenges to the autonomy of the EU legal order than the ACCC because it operates as a form of judicial relief that exists in parallel to the EU judiciary. A significant aspect of this is that in contrast to the ACCC's findings, ICS awards are binding on the EU and its institutions.

That being said, one may wonder whether a decision by the Meeting of the Parties to endorse the ACCC's findings has the same legal effects as an award issued by an ICS tribunal. Even here, a decision of the Meeting of the Parties appears to be less intrusive. The Meeting of the Parties can only take decisions that are in line with the non-confrontational and non-judicial nature of the compliance mechanism, such as issuing recommendations and declarations of non-compliance by endorsing or taking note of the findings.[84] In other words, the Convention does not explicitly contain a provision that makes clear that a Party is bound by a decision of the Meeting of the Parties and therefore functions similarly to an authoritative interpretation of the Convention.[85]

[80] Case C-352/98P *Laboratoires Pharmaceutiques Bergaderm SA and Jean-Jacques Goupin v Commission* [2000] ECR-I 5310 para 43.

[81] Joined Cases C-120 & 121/06P *FIAMM and Fedon v Council and Commission* [2008] ECR I-6513 paras 175–76.

[82] Case C-445/06 *Danske Slagterier v Germany* [2009] ECR I-02119 para 61.

[83] See Article 8.9 CETA.

[84] See Article 10 Convention and Rule 37 Decision I/7 (n 21).

[85] While not legally binding on the Parties from an international law point of view, such an interpretation may produce legal effects and therefore require a Council decision under Article 218(9) TFEU. In fact, the Commission reconsidered its position after initially suggesting that the EU's position in the Meeting of the Parties concerning the ACCC's findings in the *ClientEarth* case did not produce legal effects in the sense of Article 218(9) TFEU. The decision of the Meeting of the Parties can be seen as a formal declaration of non-compliance based on a report issued by the Committee. This is not unlike an authoritative interpretation in the sense of Article 31(3)(a) of the Vienna Convention on the Law of Treaties (VCLT), since the Parties agreed to the compliance procedure and rules of procedure of the Meeting of the Parties by consensus.

By contrast, a decision under the Convention's dispute settlement provisions is legally binding on the parties to the dispute brought before either the International Court of Justice or an arbitration tribunal.[86] Similarly, a decision of a tribunal established under Chapter eight of CETA is binding on the Parties.[87]

C. Remedies Available

A third distinguishing feature between the ACCC's reports and ICS is that the latter provides for remedies. A member of the public that submits a communication to the ACCC has no recourse to any remedy. The ACCC merely reports to the Meeting of the Parties and makes recommendations to it in order to bring about compliance with the Convention by the Party concerned. ICS ensures that a tribunal may award monetary damages to the claimant against the host state. In other words, ICS proceedings have financial consequences, whereas proceedings before the ACCC do not. These financial consequences can be significant and may pose a drain on the public finances of the Party concerned.[88]

D. Enforcement of Decisions and Awards

Lastly, ICS presents a rather unique system of enforcement of awards within the domestic legal orders of the Parties. CETA not only requires a disputing Party to 'recognise and comply with an award without delay', it also ensures that an award is given the status of an award under both the International Centre for Settlement of Investment Disputes (ICSID) and the New York conventions.[89] This means that there is no or limited scope for judicial review of such awards and that execution can also be sought in states other than the Party against which the award was issued.[90]

By contrast, the Aarhus Convention does not contain any explicit provisions about the effects of either the ACCC's findings or the Meeting of the Parties' decisions in the respective legal orders of the Parties. It is therefore up to the Parties to recognise and determine the legal effects such findings and decisions may have in their domestic legal orders.

[86] See Article 16 Aarhus Convention, Articles 59 and 60 of the ICJ statute and point 17 of Annex II of the Aarhus Convention.

[87] Article 8.41 CETA.

[88] To give just one example, in the Rosia Montania gold mine ICSID case, the foreign investor has claimed over 3 billion US dollars plus compound interest, a little less than Romania's annual health care budget. See *Gabriel Resources Ltd and Gabriel Resources (Jersey) v Romania*, ICSID Case No ARB/15/31, Claimant's Memorial, p 416.

[89] Article 8.41(2) CETA.

[90] Article 8.41(4)–(6) CETA.

V. Concluding Remarks on the Commission's Current Approach towards External Oversight in the EU's International Agreements

The European Commission is both the guardian of the Treaties and the EU's default representative in external relations. This dual task may not always be easy. It requires the Commission to be mindful of the EU's constitutional particularities when pursuing its constitutional mandate externally. Yet, the Commission has chosen a remarkable path of vehemently opposing the findings of the ACCC, while at the same time extensively promoting the ICS in its trade agreements.

As this contribution has shown, both external oversight mechanisms may be faced with similar questions of EU law, yet compliance mechanism under the Aarhus Convention is far less intrusive for the EU's legal order than ICS. ICS is explicitly intended as an alternative to judicial relief to domestic courts and may therefore have more significant effects on the powers granted to the EU judiciary in the Treaties. Rulings of ICS tribunals are also binding, may have financial consequences, and can be effectively enforced in domestic legal orders of states, none of which is provided for in the Aarhus Convention.

The Commission's approach is to be regretted. If the Commission is so opposed to endorsing the findings of the ACCC, it should have been even more alarmed by the prospects of the ICS. At the very least, the EU's constitutional particularities could have prompted the Commission to add the question of compatibility of ISDS with the Treaties in its Request for an Opinion in Opinion 2/15. Alternatively, the Commission could have used its very lenient approach towards ICS as an example to endorse the findings of the ACCC. Instead, the Commission has allowed considerable legal uncertainty to persist about ICS while at the same time dealing a substantial blow to international environmental governance under the Aarhus Convention and the EU's global environmental leadership.

INDEX

www.ingramcontent.com/pod-product-compliance
Lightning Source LLC
Chambersburg PA
CBHW071352220926
51613CB00008B/128
9781509923380